ADVANCE PRAISE FOR
THE *SPECULATIVE GRAMMA*
ESSENTIAL GUIDE TO LINGUISTICS

"Ever wonder why Vikings torched scriptoria? This kind of thing."
—E. V. GORDON

"Funnier than any other book I've read in the entire 20th Century!"
—RASMUS RASK

"So good I read almost half of it."
—HENRY SWEET

"Contains more than 100 basic words."
—MORRIS SWADESH

"*Semper in modo satirico, ac raro bono modo.*"
—THOMAS OF ERFURT

"Same reference as *linguistics*; different sense."
—GOTTLOB FREGE

"Most of the changes I would make are,
of course, to remove commas."
—AN ANONYMOUS PROOFREADER

"Organized violence committed on ordinary linguistics."
—ROMAN JAKOBSON

"Irritating drivel."
—SIR WILLIAM JONES

"This book is so chock full of borrowings and analogy that
it is utterly unsuited to any sort of scholarly discourse."
—*NEOGRAMMARIAN QUARTERLY*

"Two uvulas down, *way* down!"
—SAPIR AND BLOOMFIELD, *AT THE BOOKSTORE*

The *Speculative Grammarian*
Essential Guide to Linguistics

Happy Birthday Dan,
Although much of this book went over my head, I think your reflexes will be fast enough to catch it.
I'm looking forward to seeing you soon!
♡ Katie

THE SPECGRAM STRAW MEN MAKE A
RHETORICAL ADVANCE AND STAKE THEIR CLAIM

The *Speculative Grammarian* Essential Guide to Linguistics

Trey Jones
Keith W. Slater
Bill Spruiell
Tim Pulju
David J. Peterson

Speculative Grammarian Press

Washington • 昆明 • Mount Pleasant • Hanover • Santa Ana

Speculative Grammarian Press • Washington • 昆明 • Mount Pleasant • Hanover • Santa Ana
East Lansing • Houston • Santa Barbara • አዲስ አበባ • اسكندريه • Αθήνα • Chicago • Erfurt
Galveston • ᐃᖃᓗᐃᑦ • Москва • Nauru • नई दिल्ली • New Orleans • Paris • Parnell • Reykjavík
Rome • 서울특별시 • 臺中市 • ᏐᏈᎢ • თბილისი • תל אביב-יפו • 東京 • Vienna • Երեւան

First edition published 2013. v1.003

ISBN 13: 978-0-615-84586-9
ISBN 10: 0-615-84586-X

This book was typeset by Trey Jones in the Gentium, P22 Underground, and TRAJAN PRO font families—despite the nefarious will and ongoing sabotage of **Microsoft Word**.

Brief Contents

Table of Contents

Preface
or, Why a book, why a no chicken?

SPECULATIVE GRAMMARIAN (KNOWN TO its devotees[1] as *SpecGram*), is recognized by linguists all over the world—in international powerhouses like the United States and China, in post-communist relics like North Korea and Cuba, in up-and-coming countries like Brazil and Malaysia, in strife-torn nations like Iraq and Canada, even in mundane little places like Belgium and Lesotho—in short, as we said in the first place, among linguists all over the world, *SpecGram* is now, always has been, and ever will be recognized as... as...

An Early Engraving of the Σπεκουλάτωρ Γραμματεύς ('Executioner-Scribe') at Work

Sorry, we forgot what we were going to say. Give us a minute.

Okay, now we remember. *SpecGram* is the most prestigious online linguistics journal that any of us has ever edited. And anyone who disagrees is an idiot.

Wait a minute, you're saying. Are you telling me that *SpecGram* is available online? For free? Well, we didn't mention the free part, but yes, all of the articles published in this book, and many more, can be read for free online at the *Speculative Grammarian* website (http://www.SpecGram.com)—which might make you wonder why we think you'd be interested in paying for this book. So here are several good reasons.

1. The online articles are uniformly excellent, but some are even more uniformly excellent than others. We have chosen only the best of the best for inclusion in this anthology, thus saving you the work of trolling through the merely superb as you search for the truly superlative. (We have also included some not-quite-so-superlative articles whose authors paid us large sums of money. Just for fun, you could try to figure out which are which.)

2. We've included introductory material for each chapter, as well as introductory material for each article, which in most cases is so informative that you can dispense with reading the articles altogether. This is a great timesaver. We ourselves follow the same policy with great literature, having read the dust jackets of many famous novels.

3. When people read *SpecGram* online, we don't get any money. And we need money, ever since we invested most of the employee pension fund in Greek government bonds. We've tried selling ad space, but we can't find anyone who wants to be associated with so disreputable a journal.

---

[1] Of whom there are more than a monolingual Pirahã speaker could count.

4. The cover of the book is really cool.[2]

With all of those good reasons, who could resist buying a copy of this book? Certainly not us. We've each already purchased numerous copies ourselves and have been giving them to friends and relatives, most of whom know nothing about linguistics and have been using them as doorstops. We can't actually recommend that use, since the book isn't thick and heavy enough to hold a door open in a high wind, but at least they're not using them as kindling. However, if you buy a copy (or two, or three), we won't be offended at all if you use them as kindling. Just be aware that *SpecGram* assumes no liability for damages resulting from out-of-control book fires.[3]

"Language is properly the servant of thought, but not unfrequently becomes its master."
—W.B. CLULOW

---

[2] In fact, it is so cool that it could be prizeworthy. For you, not us. No one is giving us a prize for that photo. Check out the contest rules on page 327.

[3] *SpecGram* disclaims any responsibility or liability for any damages caused by memes contained within the pages of *The Speculative Grammarian Essential Guide to Linguistics*. Read at your own risk. Risks include falling levels of academic achievement in linguistics world-wide; litigation by morons against providers of satirical and parodic content; our inability to expand the field of satirical linguistics, reduce the pomposity of academic linguistics, "knock" specific linguists "down a peg or two", or complete previously documented plans for world domination; and general philological conditions beyond *SpecGram's* control. Though best efforts have been made in the preparation of this disclaimer, neither *SpecGram* nor its editors guarantee its accuracy or completeness. No warranty of any kind is made, expressed or implied, respecting this disclaimer. *SpecGram* shall not be liable with respect to liability, loss, or damages caused or alleged to have been caused directly or indirectly as a result of the usage of this disclaimer.

CHOOSE YOUR OWN CAREER IN LINGUISTICS—PART 7

YOU DOUBLE MAJOR IN LINGUISTICS AND COMPUTER SCIENCE...

Much to your surprise, you discover that the analytic skills required to be a good computer scientist and the analytic skills required to be a good linguist, while not exactly the same, complement each other quite nicely. You totally blow the curve in many of your undergrad linguistics classes because 1) tree diagrams don't scare you, and 2) you wrote a LISP program to do most of your phonology homework for you—those English Lit weenies trying for an "easy" minor in linguistics never had a chance. Your comp sci honors project is just that little program you wrote to do your phonology homework, with a few "optimality theory" buzzwords thrown in. You graduate with high honors.

While applying to grad school in computational linguistics, you stumble onto one of the fundamental truths of the field. Most computer scientists don't understand linguistics at all, and most linguists don't understand computer science at all. You actually have a solid background in both—and while you enjoy serious discussions in the field, you come to realize that you can BS your way through most conversations with a practitioner in either field by dazzling them with your competence in the other field.

Maybe you don't need to go to grad school. Maybe you should just get a job.

• Look for a job with your undergrad linguistics/ comp sci degree. Go to Part 19 on page 31.

• Go to grad school in computational linguistics. Go to Part 20 on page 89.

Choose Your Own Career in Linguistics starts on page 301.

Introduction
Not to be confused with a prolegomenon

THE PAST TWENTY-FIVE YEARS HAVE WITNESSED MANY changes in linguistics, with major developments in linguistic theory, significant expansion in language description, and even some progress in getting a few members of the general public to realize that the term "linguist" is not defined as 'someone who works at the UN doing simultaneous translation'. *Speculative Grammarian* is proud to have been a part of these changes.[1,2] And now, in our humble yet authoritative opinion, the time is ripe for the appearance of an anthology containing the most important linguistics articles to have appeared in *SpecGram* in the past twenty-five years. (Readers seeking articles from before 1988 should consult one of the previous volumes in this series, which have appeared at intervals ranging from twenty to one hundred years ever since *SpecGram* was first published).[3] This anthology, it is hoped, will allow our readers to gain a deeper, wider, fatter understanding of linguistics as it evolved in the late 20th and early 21st centuries, without the trouble of having to take a graduate seminar in "Modern Linguistics" taught by a professor who's so old that she thinks the Beach Boys are cute.[4] Some of us took graduate seminars like that ourselves, and believe us, this book is better.

This book concentrates on those branches of linguistics which have always been considered central to the field: animal communication, third

> Those who speak much must either know a lot or lie a lot.
> —GERMAN PROVERB

language acquisition, linguistic love poetry. That said, some of the most important recent advances have come in ancillary subdisciplines, such as phonetics, phonology, morphology, syntax, semantics, and historical linguistics. Therefore, you'll also find complete chapters on those subjects in this volume, along with other major topics such as sociolinguistics, computational linguistics, typology, and fieldwork. We could go on, and in fact, we were going to, until we realized (1) that the list was getting boring, and (2) that that's what the table of contents is for. Not to mention that the table of contents includes page numbers, which the list above does not, although we suppose we could go back and add them if we wanted to.

We should mention, though, that along with chapters made up of a bunch of articles, we've also included several intercalary chapters,[5] each of which consists of a single monograph. So if you notice that it's taking you a lot longer than usual to read a particular article, don't worry, your mind's not going—it's just a monograph.

We are certain that many of the articles in this anthology will inspire controversy, as indeed they were meant to do by their authors. Others, however—in fact, the great majority—will inspire awe, as they, too, were meant to do. If some few articles induce such a sense of wonderment as to cause readers to go into ecstatic trances, that, too, is not only intended, but expected. Any readers who do not experience a sense of wonderment should go back and read the book again until they get it right.

---

[1] An important part.

[2] In fact, probably the most important part.

[3] Previous volumes are no longer in print, and, unfortunately, not found in any major university libraries. The Folger Shakespeare Library used to have a copy of the 1592 edition, but it was eaten by rats.

[4] Not *were* cute, *are* cute, right now, in 2013.

---

[5] We learned the term "intercalary chapters" in high school when reading *The Grapes of Wrath*, and have been waiting ever since for a chance to use it again.

Linguistics: The Scientific Study of Language
At least, that's what they told us in Ling 101

WHAT IS LANGUAGE? You'd think that if anyone would know, it would be us, the editors of a renowned linguistics journal. But you'd be hard pressed to find an answer in most issues of *SpecGram*. This suggests either that we don't actually know the answer, or that we do know, but we're not telling.

In contrast, over the years, *SpecGram* has published numerous articles explaining what linguistics is, was, could be, should be, and isn't. What follows, then, are selected commentaries upon linguistics past and present, written by some of the finest minds in our field (plus a few that we wrote ourselves). If the field in general doesn't seem to have learned much from these articles, we blame not our contributors, and certainly not ourselves, but rather, the field in general, for being too stiff-necked to accept enlightenment, or maybe just too lazy to keep up. We hope that by putting all of these articles together in one place, we will make it possible for the lazy and the stiff-necked both to come to a better appreciation of the truth than they have managed so far, and to fi-nally have a clear sense of what they're doing when they claim to be doing linguistics.

As a side note to the student reader who may be wondering how it's possible for linguists not even to have an agreed-upon understanding of the basics of their discipline, we should point out that such a situation is not uncommon. Anesthesiologists, for example, mostly have no interest in knowing what anesthesiology actually is—and those that do express interest mostly seem, rather disturbingly, to believe that putting people to sleep involves tricking the wakeful soul into leaving the body temporarily by promising it free plane tickets. Yet anesthesiology is widely rec-

AN INTRODUCTION TO LINGUISTICS IN HAIKU FORM

linguistic theory
hidden representations
to surface structures

phonology is
sound patterns of languages
phonemes, allophones

phonetics is sounds—
articulation of them
acoustics, hearing

comp. linguistics is
theory into efficient
implementation

morphology is
if same structure, same meaning
then it's a morpheme

syntactic theory
blah blah chomsky chomsky blah
blah chomsky blah blah

—ANONYMOUS

ognized as one of the most successful fields of endeavor in all of human history, and anesthesiologists are honored throughout the world with awards, statues, and commemorative matchbook covers. If they can get away with it, why not us? So even if you don't get complete enlightenment from this section of the book, don't despair. You can still become a highly successful professional linguist even if you don't know what you're doing.

LOGICAL FALLACIES FOR LINGUISTS

Argumentum ad verecundiam—"Chomsky said it. I believe it. That settles it."

CHOOSE YOUR OWN CAREER IN LINGUISTICS—PART 28
YOU REGAIN YOUR SENSES...

When you regain your senses, you find yourself in Pennsylvania in 1945. All things considered, it could have been worse.

Suddenly, you realize that you've stumbled into the opportunity of a lifetime. You make your way to the University of Pennsylvania and befriend a young man named Avram Chomsky... Avram *Noam* Chomsky. You encourage his politics, and eventually he drops out of school to become an activist. He is eventually immortalized in a historical footnote as the only American killed in Che Guevara's ill-fated operation in Bolivia.

You, however, do a bit better. You graduate from the University of Pennsylvania in 1949, earn a Ph.D. there in 1955, and join the faculty of M.I.T. later that year. You go on to write more than 80 ground-breaking books, including *Syntactic Structuralism* (1957); *Aspects of Theories of Syntax* (1965); *Reflections on Languages* (1975); *Lectures on Government and Bonding* (1981); *Generating Grammar: Its Basis, Development, and Prospects* (1987); *The Minimalization Program* (1998); and *New Horizons in the Study of Mind and Language* (2001).

You are the Grand High Poobah of Linguistics. Congratulations!

• The End. Go to page 301.

Choose Your Own Career in Linguistics starts on page 301.

IT IS WELL KNOWN AMONG LINGUISTS...

One of Da Vinci's notebooks has a partially sketched-out design for a device that combines a Stratificational representation of the Veneto tense-aspect system with a mechanical dachshund-flinger. He really did loathe dachshunds.

Linguistics was invented thousands of years ago in Greece, or Babylon, or possibly India. You know, one of those places where people are always boasting about the great things their ancestors did a long time ago. The proper response to such comments is, "Oh, yeah? Well, what've you done lately?"

After the birth of the field, nothing much happened in linguistics until Speculative Grammarian *was founded in the Middle Ages. Then came the Renaissance, immediately followed by the American Revolution and the rise of the Neogrammarians. And that brings us to the following excerpt from an article by SpecGram* Editor Emeritus Tim Pulju.

European Linguistics in the Late 19th Century
An Excerpt from "A Short History of American Linguistics"

Tim Pulju

In the late 1800s, Americans were too busy killing Indians and making steel to worry about linguistics. Oh, sure, the occasional scholar would pop up with a treatise on an American Indian language or a Sanskrit grammar, but everyone acknowledged that the real center of linguistics was Europe. More specifically, it was Germany, the homeland of the Neogrammarians, dedicated reconstructors of the Proto-Indo-European language, or, as the Germans preferred to call it, Indogermanic.

The Germans' choice of name for a language that included among its descendants almost all of the languages of Europe should give the reader some idea of the German attitude to the rest of the people on the continent. This disregard was fully reciprocated by the non-Germans, especially the French, who had recently been involved in a disastrous war with Germany and were still peeved about it. Hence, the French would have given their eyeteeth in exchange for a linguistic theory of their very own that would give them predominance in this scholarly field. Unfortunately, being French, they were unable to think of any. The best they could come up with was the idea of sending a man with the particularly silly name of Edmond Edmont around France on a bicycle.

The Germans, of course, just laughed at the French and continued to work on their reconstruction. They were acknowledged to be the smartest people in Europe in just about every field, even Roman history, despite the fact that they had never been part of the Roman Empire, unlike the French, the Italians, and the British. Of these last three, the French, unable to come up with a good linguistic theory of their own and equally unable, for the most part, to master Indo-European studies, had to import a French-speaking Swissman, Ferdinand "Freddy" D. Saussure, to be their leading linguist. However, he immediately proceeded to propose the ridiculous theory that there were "sonantic coefficients" in Proto-Indo-European which had disappeared in *all* the descendant languages. After this fiasco, the French more or less faded from the scene. As a result they became very sulky and still behave rudely to foreign tourists.

The Italians were too busy eating pasta and hating the Austrians (Germans by another name) to think much about linguistics. It was left to the British, then, to challenge the German hegemony. Like the French and Italians, the British had an

WOULD YOU LIKE SPAGHETTI
OR LASAGNA FOR DINNER?

Structuralist: "Both. Neither one will have any flavor unless I can compare them."

aversion to adhering to a theory in which the Germans were dominant, especially when Kaiser Wilhelm II started to build a big navy. The British were also kind of disgusted with Indo-European studies because they felt that the Germans had unfairly stolen them from England after their invention by the noted philosopher Sir William James. But there was no question that the Germans had Indo-Europeanism in their grasp now, so the British would have to seek elsewhere to regain the leading role in linguistics.

The field the British decided upon was phonetics. It was realized that the vast majority of Germans are somewhat deaf as a result of the continual shouting characteristic of German speech. Thus, this would be an ideal discipline. The two most important names in 19ᵗʰ-century British phonetics are Bell and Higgins, though by a neat trick these two names refer to three different people. The first, Herman Melville Bell, was a famous novelist who taught blind people to read in his spare time. This led him to develop a system of "visible speech", which did not, however, replace audible speech, except in parts of Wales. His son, the prophetically named Alexander Telephone Bell, did work along the same lines. But then a terrible thing happened, from the standpoint of British linguistics, although the Bells were pretty happy about it. The Bells were Scottish rather than English, which probably accounts for their supraminimal intelligence, so they didn't much like living in a kingdom dominated by people with non-trilled r's. Thus, they emigrated to America, leaving British linguistics in a mess.

But lo, a linguist arose to replace the Bells, and, wonder of wonders, despite being English he was highly intelligent. To make up for this, he was very ill-mannered and overbearing; together,

> "These exceptional vowels will therefore be excluded from the present domain of explanation."
> —G. SANDERS

these two traits endeared him to his German fellow linguists, who recognized a kindred spirit. This man was of course Henry Higgins, made famous by his associate (not friend—he didn't have any English friends) George Bernard Shaw in the play *Androcles and the Lion.* As made plain in this gripping melodrama, Higgins' superior intelligence and superior attitude enraged the status-conscious dons of Oxford and Cambridge, who responded to his repeated efforts to secure a university post by beating him with sticks. Thus, Higgins was forced to earn a living as a flower girl, which left him little time for writing. Even so, he did some good work before he was killed in a bowling accident.

Anyway, the effect of Higgins' exclusion from mainstream British linguistics was that British linguistics as a whole remained unimportant in the eyes of the world. We should probably mention the status of linguistics in other parts of Europe, although to tell the truth the US was not very interested in these parts. Spain, of course, had no linguistics—she had been too busy all century with the *guerras carlistas,* during which the Carlist rebels, showing a lot of pluck and tenacity if little sense or regard for their country's welfare, periodically invaded the country in hopes of getting their candidate for the throne into power. They did this about five or ten times over the course of the century and never once came close to winning. So distracted were the Spanish by all this nonsense that they didn't notice that the US was sneakily conquering the remnants of the Spanish empire until it was too late to do anything about it. Disgruntled, the Spanish decided to write novels and become a third-rate power. Linguistics was obviously right out.

In the east, a few Slavs were busy making important contributions to linguistic thought—e.g., Baudouin de Courtenay, a Pole with a French name who taught in Russia. Baudouin's identity problems were reflective of a general lack of confidence among the Slavs of central Europe, a problem fostered mostly by the fact that the Germans who ruled most of them based their governance on their knowledge that "Slav" and "slave" are etymologically the same word. Some Slavs, of course, refused to allow themselves to be oppressed by the Germans, or by the Turks, who also ruled some of them, but they were naturally too busy organizing secret societies and having luncheons to concern themselves with linguistics. There were also the Russians, who were not subject to foreign rule, but who were cheerfully oppressive toward non-Russian Slavs in *their* country. But the big problem linguistics-wise in Russia was that the government was corrupt and incompetent, which caused most of the brilliant young people who would otherwise have become linguists either to starve to death because the economy was lousy or to join revolutionary societies and be deported to Siberia.

So it befell that at the close of the 19th century, the great German linguists—Brugmann, Delbrück, Schenck, and many more—were masters of the field. And, looking around at the rest of Europe, they saw no reason to suspect that anyone would rise up soon to try to take their place. As for other parts of the world, such as the United States, they did not even consider them.

THE WISDOM OF LINGUISTS
When in Cambridge, analyze as the Chomskyans do.

MURPHY'S LAW FOR LINGUISTS
Symbols needed for an article are never all in the same font & the publisher doesn't allow any of those fonts anyway.

CHOOSE YOUR OWN CAREER IN LINGUISTICS—PART 5
YOU DOUBLE MAJOR IN LINGUISTICS AND ECONOMICS…

Having decided that that which does not kill you makes you stronger, you begin your double major in linguistics and economics. You make the mistake of taking Syntax II, Historical Linguistics, Advanced Topics in Micro-Economics, Theoretical Underpinnings of Economics, and Basket Weaving III—all in the fall semester of your junior year. While you manage to pull a 3.5 GPA for the semester, you do so without benefit of sleep or having friends. On impulse, you change your major to Basket Weaving.

After another semester of Basket Weaving IV, Decorative Motifs in Historical Basket Weaving, Baskets and Bullets: the History of the Anti-War Basket Weaving Movement, and—inexplicably—Geology 101, you suddenly realize you are throwing your life away on this basket bunk. On the other hand, you are well-rested and very popular.

Without enough time to complete your double major and graduate on time, you consult the Occupational Outlook Handbook, draw a few supply/demand-curves, and come to a decision. As much as you'll miss linguistics, you really do need to complete your econ degree and get a real job.

• Complete your econ degree. Go to Part 4 on page 274.

Choose Your Own Career in Linguistics starts on page 301.

Back in the United States, where SpecGram *had been headquartered since the early 1800s, an influx of cash from Nauru turned linguistics into a boom field. According to the article below, also by Tim Pulju, one canny young junior editor at* SpecGram *got ahold of some of that cash and used it to take a trip to Europe, with results as outlined in the article. (We have our doubts about the reliability of this account, but since Pulju looks old enough to have personal memories of the events described, we decided to take his word for it.)*

Saussure and Bloomfield: The Question of Influence

Tim Pulju
Rice University

One of the more vexed questions in modern linguistic historiography concerns the extent of Saussure's influence on Bloomfield and through him on American structuralism as a whole. Rather than add to the discussion of that issue, I intend in this paper to point out the importance of another, related, but hitherto ignored question, to wit, what was the extent of Bloomfield's influence on Saussure?

Now, before you start leaping all over me, calling me an idiot and calling my question absurd, let me state that I am well-aware that Saussure died in 1913, before Bloomfield had published his 1914 *An Introduction to the Study of Language.* Let me further state that I know that Bloomfield did not meet the aged Saussure in 1913 while visiting continental Europe. However, unlike most researchers, I do not let these undisputed facts blind me to the very real possibility of a Bloomfieldian influence on Saussure.

The key to understanding this possibility is the realization, now widespread, that when we say "Saussure" we do not mean Ferdinand de Saussure, a francophonic Swiss linguist who lived from 1857 to 1913 and published only one book in his lifetime. Rather, "Saussure" means the ideas embodied in the 1916 work *Cours de linguistique générale,* published in 1916 under Ferdinand de Saussure's name but really the product of a group of editors, redactors, amanuenses, and independent authors. The ideas of the Ferdinand de Saussure who died in 1913 are of course an important element in this work, but they are far from the only one. Above all, we must note that the principal authors of the *Cours* were a group of professional linguists who, if they were at all dedicated scholars, must have been aware of Bloomfield's first attempt at a comprehensive textbook, especially insofar as it dealt with synchronic linguistics. Surely a group of men composing a general linguistics textbook would have examined a recently published example of the same thing.

I do not intend here to test the validity of this hypothesis, although I suggest that it would make an excellent dissertation topic. To the skeptical, however, I will point out just a few interesting facts regarding Bloomfield 1914 and Saussure 1916: first, the shared emphasis on a psychological approach (abandoned, of course, in Bloomfield 1933); second, the inclusion of phonology in an appendix of Saussure's work—was it added hastily after Bally et al. read Bloomfield 1914?; third, the curious fact that Saussure, a

> WOULD YOU LIKE SPAGHETTI
> OR LASAGNA FOR DINNER?
>
> Department Chair: "I'll have to appoint a food committee to make that decision. Otherwise Professor S. will make a fuss no matter what I choose."

famed historical linguist, should have so dedicated his last work to synchrony.

The implications of the issues raised here could be enormous. It could even be discovered that what we have hitherto viewed as Saussure's influence on Bloomfield is really Bloomfield's second-hand influence on himself. If this is the case, then it is more plain than ever that Leonard Bloomfield is the towering figure of modern American linguistics.

"While trees may be quite useful to the linguist, this is a fact about linguists, not about language."
—GREGORY M. KOBELE

CHOOSE YOUR OWN CAREER IN LINGUISTICS—PART 13

YOU DOUBLE MAJOR IN LINGUISTICS AND PHYSICS...

Your linguistically-honed analytical skills improve your "rad physics skillz". Your linguistics friends are impressed that you are majoring in physics. Your physics friends are impressed that you are majoring in linguistics. So are your physics professors.

You get offered the opportunity to work on two prestigious research projects, mostly with professors and graduate students. One is related to SETI, the search for extra-terrestrial intelligence, where they think your linguistic skills may come in handy for designing protocols for first contact. The other is an attempt to open mini temporal wormholes, and hopefully be able to listen to the past, and they are excited at the prospect of you helping them devise algorithms to automatically determine the time and place of the languages they encounter.

- Work on the SETI project to contact alien life forms. Go to Part 21 on page 28.

- Work on the temporal wormhole project to listen in on the past. Go to Part 22 on page 11.

- Pass on these projects, and focus on your undergrad studies. Go to Part 23 on page 80.

Choose Your Own Career in Linguistics starts on page 301.

IT IS WELL KNOWN AMONG LINGUISTS...

The naked mole rat (*heterocephalus glaber*) is frequently used in experiments modeling the behavior of linguistic theory camps, as its social organization allows for direct comparison.

The success of Bloomfield and Saussure, and the timely death of the Neogrammarians,* meant that linguists in the 20th century didn't have to worry about silly things like historical linguistics anymore. Instead, they could concentrate on phonology, syntax, and other more rewarding activities, as remembered by Eglantine Lady Fantod, the grande dame of Cambridge linguists, in an interview with Freya Shipley.

Extract from an Interview with Eglantine Lady Fantod, Dowager Professor of Philology at Cambridge University

Freya Shipley

Eglantine Lady Fantod, the legendary raconteuse *and* grande dame *of Golden Age linguistics, recalls halcyon days in a series of interviews with Freya Shipley. The full memoir will be published in 2012 by Taradiddle Press, Oxford (8 volumes, price 17p).*

"Sacks, Sacks, Sacks. That's all these young sociolinguists ever think of. They simply don't realise what things were like when I was a girl.

"There were nights when no one slept at all in the seamier colleges of Cambridge, what with the continual *cris de joie* floating around the staircases. Couples spent whole nights crouched in junior common rooms, furtively offgliding and creating adjacency pairs. Nowadays young people do it all in public and no one thinks twice about it. Which I daresay is a healthy thing, really.

"Dear me, when I think what we used to get up to at house parties before the War. It's all gone now, of course. One misses the formality of twelve really well-brought-up people at the dinner table, all minding their respective alveolar ridges and keeping their aspira-

St. Uvula's College, Cambridge, 1917. Lady Fantod reacts as the most tedious student in her Old Norse seminar self-selects *again*.

tions to themselves. At least, until the wee hours of the morning, when there was always a great deal of illicit creeping around the corridors. Darling Foo-Foo and I—Teddy Sapir, you know—used to

---

* We're not implying that Bloomfield or Saussure had anything to do with the death of the Neogrammarians. Come on, the Neogrammarians were all old men by the 20th century. They clearly died natural deaths.

meet in the billiard room and indulge in *hours of* passionate turn-taking. How I loved his back-channel signals. The servants were marvelously discreet. All except for Lady Haas's maid Gregson, who had to be bribed with an enormous velar trill. She was dismissed in 1928, I believe, after Mary caught her pilfering.

"Scandals? Oh, yes—there were times when it all went terribly wrong. There was the notorious Smythe-Fotheringay divorce case, when Lady Violet was caught cavorting on the beach with a crowd of American fishermen, shamelessly centralizing her diphthongs. It was in all the papers—particularly when Violet announced that she was leaving her own speech community entirely to take up with a new one on Martha's Vineyard. 'I don't care if we're poor,' she famously said. 'Schwas are more important than money.'

"Of course in those days most people were dreadfully strict about it all. I remember my dear brother Ranulph used to go absolutely apoplectic when he caught us experimenting with nasalization down in the summerhouse. "Where did you get those *vowels*, gel?" he'd shout at me. "Under a *rock?!*" Ranulph found many of his own vowels on continental hunting trips, or else in the woods on his estate in Shropshire where the shooting was particularly fine. I remember one season he and the Prince of Wales bagged 18,000 brace of [ö]s. Cook preserved them in aspic, and we dined off them for *weeks*. And Ranulph was always forcing guests to admire that [ɜ] that he'd brought down on safari. He'd had it stuffed by a taxidermist and mounted on the wall in his library. I'm sure you're far too young to remember all that. Dear, dear— *plus ça change, plus c'est le mouton fou.*

"Leave me now, dear child—it's time for my gin posset."

Freya Shipley is the author of *Whither the feline bilabial?* Her forthcoming book *Grassman's Law for Lemurs* has attracted widespread concern.

THE WISDOM OF LINGUISTS

Linguists who live in structuralist houses shouldn't investigate idioms.

CHOOSE YOUR OWN CAREER IN LINGUISTICS—PART 22

YOU WORK ON THE TEMPORAL WORMHOLE PROJECT…

Forget SETI—they are never going to contact anyone, anyway—this temporal wormhole thing is awesome! You daydream of hearing Chaucer reading *The Canterbury Tales* in his own Middle English, in his own voice.

Unfortunately, you daydream a little too much one day, and cross a couple of wires on the transphasic ion-coupling demodulator, and there is a horrendous explosion. The lab is leveled. The project is utterly destroyed. Several physics grad students suffer concussions or broken bones. They never find your body, and they set up a small memorial plaque in your honor once the new lab is built.

You, however, are not dead. Your crossed wires opened a very large but unstable wormhole for 517 milliseconds, and—contrary to all expectations that only sound would be able to travel along the wormhole—you fall through.

• Continue. Go to Part 28 on page 4.

Choose Your Own Career in Linguistics starts on page 301.

"What we must do now is to change linguistic theory so that this 'wrong' solution will be the right solution."

—PAUL KIPARSKY

A few linguists, however—mostly those who weren't independently wealthy—took time out from social activities to write articles demanding that linguistics be made more scientific, and thus worthy of more funding. Nowadays, the social activities have largely died away, but the articles continue, as exemplified by this offering from James Coffey and Mark Matney.

Scientific Linguistics

James Coffey and Mark Matney
Lockheed Incorporated

Throughout its history, linguistics has progressed only when modelled after more naturally scientific disciplines. In the 1800s, linguists copied the terminology and methodology of botany and Darwinian evolution. At the start of the new century, following Durkheim's success in establishing sociology as a science, Saussure defined language as a social fact. Bloomfield later eliminated mentalism and brought scientific rigor to the field. Finally, Chomsky imported mathematics and logic, thus making linguistics explicit and quantifiable.

The time is now ripe for a further advance in the scientization of language study. To date, linguistics has taken little notice of theoretical physics, a field which is widely held to be *primus inter pares* among *Naturwissensschaften*. A careful examination of the fundamental tenets of physics indicates that several are applicable to language as well. For example, consideration of Heisenberg's Uncertainty Principle leads us to realize that it is impossible to simultaneously know both the synchronic state of a language and the direction of its drift (for **drift** as a technical term cf. Sapir 1921). In a way, this is a restatement of Saussure's synchronic/diachronic distinction, but our phraseology is more scientific than Saussure's and hence better.

Then there is relativity. The well-known equation $E=mc^2$ has an exact correlate in the linguistic equation $M=ws^2$, where M=the number of potential pragmatic meanings a sentence may have, w = the number of words in the sentence, and s = the number of situations of use in which the sentence may occur. Note that M will be a very large number for most sentences.

A number of numerical constants important in physics also prove to be significant in linguistics. Among these are Planck's constant, which is equal to the ratio between the number of phonemes in a language and the number of times a speaker will utter those phonemes during a 74-year lifespan. Also significant is π, which is equal to the average number of plural pronouns in all languages. (For those who wonder how such a number could be both irrational and transcendental, we note that language is itself irrational [cf. Norris 1990] and transcendental [cf. Hjelmslev 1943]).

Lastly, we must consider the possibility of a Grand Unification Theory, which obviously has nothing to do with unscientific Functional U-nification Grammar and everything to do with GUTs in physics. The grammatical equivalents of the four fundamental forces are obviously the four fundamental grammatical categories, N, V, A, P, which are recognized as basic by all competent syntacticians. The easiest to unify are N and A (cf. the many analyses which mistakenly treat them as identical in some languages), which is natural inasmuch as they

THE WISDOM OF LINGUISTS

There are three types of lies: lies, damned lies, and linguistics.

correspond to the weak nuclear force and electromagnetism, respectively. V corresponds to the strong nuclear force and broke apart from the electroweak force only a fraction of a second after the Big Bang. Thus far, we have been unable to formulate a GUT linking P to the NAV coagulation, largely because P has been conceived of in Einsteinian terms as a bending of grammar rather than a force proper. We are, however, hopeful that such a formuation will soon be forthcoming.

In conclusion, we would like to make clear that this paper is only a prolegomenon. We hope and expect that others will continue down the trail which we have blazed, as we ourselves intend to do, provided that such others, bearing in mind their enormous debt to us, begin every paper they write by acknowledging that they are only building on the foundation that we have created.

"To maintain the crossover constraint it is necessary to distinguish when the constraint may be violated and when it is valid."

—I. HOWARD

CHOOSE YOUR OWN CAREER IN LINGUISTICS—PART 6

YOU DOUBLE MAJOR IN LINGUISTICS AND PHILOSOPHY...

What were you thinking? All those philosophy classes fundamentally change the way you think (as do your linguistics classes). Your linguistics classmates find your constant philosophizing pretentious and annoying. Your philosophy classmates find your constant analysis of their convoluted sentence structure distracting. You complete both degrees but do not excel in either. You choose not to pursue an advanced degree in either. You search for a job.

Unable to find a job suiting your unique but undervalued skill set, you are forced to move back home with your parents. After months of searching, you finally find the job that lets you put all of your skills to the test—an opportunity to contemplate your relationship to the universe, a chance to gather lots of conversational data in interesting linguistic paradigms, even an appreciation of your bright and cheerful personality.

• Start your new job. Go to Part 16 on page 195.

Choose Your Own Career in Linguistics starts on page 301.

THE WISDOM OF LINGUISTS

Don't bring data to a theory fight.

Of course, not all linguists agree that linguistics should be a science. We think that the article below by Xerxes Zikiwik is anti-science, but we're not completely sure, because we couldn't really understand it. Nevertheless, we decided to publish it, on the off chance that it's an important contribution to linguistic theory. (If any readers can make it through the whole thing and are willing to explain it to us, we'd be much obliged).

Why Linguistics Doesn't Care

Xerxes Yuniqqi Zikiwik
L'École du Post-Humanisme, Paris

While many have claimed, and probably rightly so, that Linguistics suffers from a bad case of Physics Envy, there is no reason for such green thoughts to sleep furiously in the sub-conscious of the field. Linguistics isn't Science and shouldn't want to be. Rather than accept an exo\refer/ential induction of "logic", Linguistics, taking a cue from the Cultural Studies movement, should deduce its own endo/refer\ential strange attractor of integrality-*cum*-integrity.

> ... science is a logical endeavor based on the Greek (Indo-European) sentence that is constructed as subject-predicate and that proceeds by identification, determination, causality. Modern logic..., and even Boole's logic which, starting from set theory, gives formalizations that are isomorphic to the functioning of language, are inoperative in the sphere of poetic language where 1 is not a limit.

> It is therefore impossible to formalize poetic language using the existing logical (scientific) procedures without denaturing it. A literary semiotics has to be made starting from a *poetic logic,* in which the concept of *power of the continuum* would encompass the interval from 0 to 2, a continuum where 0 denotes and 1 is implicitly transgressed. (Kristeva 1969)

IT IS WELL KNOWN AMONG LINGUISTS...

As stipulated by his will, Edward Sapir's prize-winning lasagna recipe has been kept sealed in the LSA's vaults. It is due to be released in 2052.

After all, while Mathematics and Science claim to speak from a frame of reference privileged by rigor, it was one of Science's own pantheon of demigods, Einstein, who showed that there *can be* no privileged frame of reference, belying the *mortis* of that *rigor.*

That Which Is Integral; That Which Is Derivative
Physics, Chemistry, Mathematics—all are mere social constructs with no greater validity in their truths than in the truths of *non/a*-scientific alternatives. The traditional scientific binarism of the false truth/falsity dichotomy leaves unchampioned the *trans*finite truth of the excluded middle. This culture of constant differen*t/c*iation between rigor and falsehood {im/com}-plicitly transubstantiates into an imperialist attack on Linguistics and allied fields.

Allowing such a hyperbolic interpolation of the natural curvature of Linguistics leaves a haplology of language that suffers a non-integral fractility, and which is no longer identical to itself—merely a weak derivative of sCIENCE. Transgressing the Axiom of Choice, and universally *quantify* all as Science or non-Science removes too many Linguistic degrees of freedom—an *ify* proposition. The study of *langue/parole* need only existentially *qualify* itself, transducing its own existence *qua* an integral part of itself. The reduction of Linguistics to Science, Science to Mathematics, Mathematics

to Set Theory is a denial of the epiphenomeno-
logical gestalt!

Intervention

Antagonistic dichotomization of Integral vs. Real
accelerates the parabolic metabolism of the meta-
static singularity of thought. Integral is Real.
Rational is Complex. Yet Integration defies Derivation. This is the cross-product of our inner
meaning!

$$\lim_{\mathrm{Phon_{etics} \to Phon^{ology}}} \oint_{UG} \mathrm{syntax} \cdot d\mathrm{morphology} \propto \sqrt{\mathbf{sem}\mathit{antics} \otimes \mathbf{sem}\mathbf{antics}}$$

Facile Refutation

...One is faced with what could be called a
"secular mysticism": mysticism because the
discourse aims at producing mental effects
that are not purely aesthetic, but without
addressing itself to reason; secular because
the cultural references ... have nothing to do
with traditional religions and are attractive
to the reader. (Sokal and Bricmont 1998)

Yet these writings should be evaluated neither as
Philosophy nor as Science, neither as induction
nor as deduction, neither as rational nor as mystical, neither as secular nor as religious. The on-
tological necessity of this truth **trans**gresses/
scends/fixes such limits.

Origin-ality of Thought

Linguistics resounds with the metaphorically
diluted but homeopathically powerful whisper-
shouting reverberations of the [non-philosophical,
non-logical] philo-logical Big Bang of its origin.
Thus, anyone desirous of matheme-atical rigor in
Linguistics is in need of a radical epistemologec-
tomy. Consider, as a basic building block, the
relevant passages of Popper's Logic of Scientific

Discovery and Kuhn's Structure of Scientific Revolu-
tions—as well as the obvious contributions by
Quine, Feyerabend and Hume (esp. vis à vis Bourbaki)—and it becomes clear that Linguistics is
actually in need of a meta-revolution, shifting to
an a-scientific paradigmicity of the non-"Science"
other.

Simply put—it is the nonlinear transformation
of intuition—a simultaneous refle{x\ct}ion and
refraction, and subsequent hol(ist)ographic interference—which results
in optimal metathesis
of theoremes, not the-
orems. This information-theoretically informed
meta-thesis condones the relative entropic com-
putations of any psycholinguistic syntac/aptic
[un]certainty principle.

And if, by chance, you were to have the
impression of not yet having understood
everything, then perhaps you would do well
to leave your ears half-open for what is in
such close touch with itself that it confounds
your discretion. (Irigaray 1985)

Rigor is, literally, death.

References

Bourbaki, Nicolas. Elements of Mathematics.

Chomsky, Noam. 1992-93. "Rationality/Science".
Z Papers Special Issue on Postmodernism and Rationality.

Einstein, Albert. 1960 [1920]. Relativity, the Special
and the General Theory. London: Methuen.

Goldstein, Rebecca. 1983. The Mind-Body Problem.
New York: Random House.

Irigaray, Luce. 1985. "The 'mechanics' of fluids."
In This Sex Which Is Not One. Translated by Catherine
Porter and Carolyn Burke. Ithaca, N.Y.: Cornell
University Press.

Kristeva, Julia. 1969. Σημειωτικη: *Recherches pour une sémanalyse.* Paris: Éditions du Seuil.

Sibony, D. 1973. "Infinity and Castration." In *Scilicet*, No. 4.

Sokal, Alan. 1996. "Transgressing the Boundaries: Toward a Transformative Hermeneutics of Quantum Gravity." In *Social Text*, #46/47.

Sokal, Alan and Jean Bricmont. 1996. *Fashionable Nonsense.* New York: Picador USA.

WOULD YOU LIKE SPAGHETTI OR LASAGNA FOR DINNER?

Relational Grammarian: "I'll take spaghetti. Lasagna is underlyingly spaghetti that's been raised into a bigger pan."

CHOOSE YOUR OWN CAREER IN LINGUISTICS—PART 12

YOU DOUBLE MAJOR IN LINGUISTICS AND PRE-MED...

For the next three years (including summers) you disappear into a black hole of fruit fly labs, phonetics labs, chemistry labs, language labs, etc., etc. You have no friends, you have no fun, you have no life. But in the end, it seems to have been worth it. You have one of the most unusual degree combinations imaginable, and you are ready to conquer the world.

While the pre-med biology major has been intellectually stimulating, it doesn't compare to the thrill of linguistics. You apply to three good grad schools for linguistics, a safety grad school for linguistics, and on a whim (and to please your mother) you also apply to one quality medical school.

All four linguistics programs are impressed by your background and transcript. You fly out to interview at the first one, and they are blown away by your complete lack of personality. They turn icy and distant. The grad students collectively refuse to go to lunch with you. You leave, crushed, but still optimistic about your other options.

Word spreads, and all three of the other linguistics programs email you to cancel your interviews. "All grad student positions are filled for the upcoming year. And next year, too. And the year after that, now that we look at our paperwork. Don't call us, we'll... probably not call you, actually."

Desperate, you interview at the one place that may still take you: medical school. Your interviewer is initially concerned that you may be "too flighty" and "not serious enough" for medical school, what with all this linguistics nonsense. But upon meeting you, she concludes that you do indeed have the soul-sucking, back-stabbing, goal-driven non-personality needed to succeed. You are in.

You suck souls. You stab backs. You drive toward your goals. 25 years later you are an M.D., and you have your own pediatric podiatry practice in Manhattan, a big house in the Hamptons, a trendy apartment uptown, and more money than you know what to do with.

• Continue. Go to Part 14 on page 174.

Choose Your Own Career in Linguistics starts on page 301.

THE WISDOM OF LINGUISTS

The Devil's in the endnotes.

The two articles above point out the difficulty of reaching agreement on what linguistics is, at least by the method of direct definition. Interestingly, the method of indirect definition, to wit, defining linguistics as "what linguists do", seems to work better, since it's not all that hard to recognize a linguist when you see one. As proof, we offer the following illuminating article, by Prof. C.W. Gilchrist, Jr.

Reanalysis of Spanish by Naïve Linguists

Chesterton Wilburfors Gilchrist, Jr.
Chairman, Department of Lexicology and Glottometrics
Devonshire-upon-Glencullen University, Southampton

While sitting in the Linguistics Lounge the other day, I overheard some first-year grad students discussing the day's Spanish class. My eavesdropping turned out to be much more interesting than I had anticipated.

I must interject here that several faculty members and grad students had fought against the idea of first-years fulfilling their foreign language reading requirement with Spanish. Objections ranged from the dearth of academic linguistics material published in Spanish to the commonly accepted ease of learning the language. Frankly, I believe it came down to snobbery on the part of those who 'read' French and German, and I overruled them all. Such are the perquisites of Chairmanship.

So it was with much interest that I listened in to the conversation. The first set of data under consideration is presented here:

hasta luego	'see you later'
hasta pronto	'see you soon'
hasta jueves	'see you Thursday'
hasta mañana	'see you tomorrow'

Given the known meanings of *luego* ('later'), *pronto* ('soon'), *jueves* ('Thursday') and *mañana* ('tomorrow'), our intrepid heroes determined that *hasta* must mean 'see you'.

Then one of their number added this bit of data:

hasta la vista	'see you'

I thought this would lead them to reconsider their earlier conclusion. Not so. Hypotheses they considered included non-identical reduplication, a grammaticalized verbal tick, and analyzing *la vista* as "a recursively epenthetic allophone of an inductive null-morpheme" (though I think that last may have come from a particularly sarcastic second-year with a BA in Math who walked through the lounge about then).

In any event, my heart sank.

Eventually, their conversation moved away from *hasta* et al., and turned to salutations. One of them misspoke and said "*habla*" for "*hola*". They laughed for a moment, but suddenly stopped short. There was a flurry of scribbling and murmuring, and I lost the thread of the conversation.

When their heads came up, I heard one say, "See, *hola* has the phonetic shape of a verb. It must be a verb." A pause. "But what does it mean?"

Another had a sudden, devastating inspiration: "*Habla* means 'you speak', so *hola* must mean … what? … 'you are greeted'?"

A third objected—but not at all as I had hoped—"But that's the formal 'you'. Shouldn't we use the informal with each other? What would that be? *Holas*?"

The first replied, "Only for one person… *holan* for multiple people."

The second asked, "What would *holamos* mean? 'We are greeted'?"

At this point I threw up in my mouth a little bit. But before they could tragically analyze the abomination that is neological *holamos,* they realized that they were late for their classes. They parted ways, each smiling and saying "*¡Hasta!*" to the others as they left.

The next morning I entered the Linguistics Lounge by the side door, finding two of the three already drinking coffee and reviewing their Spanish homework together. The third entered, somewhat ashen-faced, and sat down. "*¡Holas!*" the other two offered. When there was no response, they stared in silence. I stayed to watch and listen.

Finally their comrade spoke. "I talked to my roommate—from Mexico—last night about our analysis of *hola* and *hasta.* I think we got it pretty wrong."

Objections were quick and fierce: "Nonsense!"; "No, it was a good analysis."

They spoke amongst themselves quietly and finally seemed to arrive at a consensus: the native speaker, while invaluably informative, is linguistically naïve and not to be taken as the final authority on anything.

This struck a nerve with me! Up to this point I must say that I was considering whether it would be appropriate to consider removing these proto-linguists from our prestigious program—and, I admit ashamedly, I was even considering some creative means of drumming them out should standard administrative manœuvres fail.

But this instinctive flouting of the authority of the native speaker broke the dam and rewrote the rules of the game. Linguistics, as either art or science, is very much a skill—a skill that can be trained and honed and sharpened much like any other, so there was always a faint hope for their analytic skills—that is what graduate school is all about, is it not?

But certain aspects of the practice of linguistics as a theoretical science, as a practical academic subject, as a political minefield, are only ever truly mastered by those with certain inborn abilities.

The abhorrent analysis and theoretical violence these all-too-young babes in the wood had done to the mellifluous Spanish language had saddened me, almost angered me. But this final strike at native speaker competency was something different altogether, something that could not be denied.

Clearly they are to Linguistics born, and will not bend to the whiny "needs" and "wants" of native speaker naïveté. I have personally taken them under my wing, and will see that they achieve all that they so obviously are meant to in the field of theoretical linguistics.

¡Viva la Revolución!

PEARLS OF WISDOM FROM
STUDENTS OF LINGUISTICS

I shall now spend the rest of the assignment focusing on the topic of the assignment.

As to what linguists do, you probably already know, since you're probably a linguist yourself if you've read this far into the book. But maybe, like many another linguist, you're plagued by secret doubts as to whether you're really doing what you're supposed to, at least in every detail. For the benefit of all such insecure members of our profession, we reproduce below the ten hallowed commandments of linguistics, as rendered in English by Managing Editor Trey Jones, with the help of a ~~cracked~~ crack team of SpecGram associates.

Ten New Commandments for Linguists
Transcribed from the original Stone Tablets by Trey Jones
With much help from the Commandment Clarification Committee, including Joel Boyd,
Aya Katz, Jouni Maho, Ken Miner, Daniela Müller, David J. Peterson, and Joey Whitford

As a Linguist, thou art an ambassador for the scientific study of Language and languages in the land of the monolingual naive speaker. Even though the monolingual naive speaker roll their eyes at thee and chastise thee as a word-obsessed fool and exalt their own native speaker competence, thou shalt proselytize the study of "Language with a big-L" whenever and wherever thou mayest do so, spreading the true word of descriptivism and railing against the evils of prescriptivism. Beware the Silver Tongues of Safiric Demons, and follow these, My commandments,[0] forsaking all that may have come before:

I. Thou shalt have no other linguistic theory before Mine.[1]

II. Thou shalt maintain the mystique of linguistics and keep it holy.[2]

III. Thou shalt nonetheless make thy contributions to linguistics transparent to thy brethren.[3]

IV. Thou shalt punctuate logically and consistently.[4]

V. Honor thy data and thy neighbor's data, so that no theory may deny or ignore it.[5]

VI. Thou shalt treat thy graduate students as thyself.[6]

VII. Thou shalt not ridicule the documentary linguists nor the sociolinguists unduly.[7]

VIII. Thou shalt refrain from asking "Ooo, canst thou verily say that?" to the ignorant among us who know not what a linguist does and thus why thou wouldst need to know.[8]

IX. Thou shalt not smite the fool who asks, "What is the number of languages thou dost speak?"[9]

X. Thou shalt not take articles in satirical linguistics journals or anthologies too seriously.[10]

---

[0] And heedest thou also the Holy Footnotes, which, though frequently less pithy, are of equal import.

[1] At least not until thou hast tenure of thine own.

[2] Revealest thou not, for example, that Kabardian does indeed have a vowel system. Hypothesizest thou not that Dyirbal, Hixkaryana, and Pirahã do not actually exist but were invented by linguists. Writest thou not a monograph, essay, or even the smallest of paragraphs which could be easily understood by the monolingual naive speaker. And never, until the end of days, shalt thou question the scientific nature of linguistics whilst in the presence of an actual scientist.

[3] Lacest thou not thine examples with data from languages unbeknownst to all save SIL fieldworkers. Obscurest thou not thy data by retranscribing it such that no linguist may check it. Usest thou only the IPA chart and its articulatory descriptions as thy pronunciation guide, no matter what language thou speakest.

[4] Usest thou the Oxford Comma, for though it is oft times redundant, it does on occasion reduce ambiguity. Putest thou not thy punctuation inside thy quotation marks when it is not part of thy quoted material, no matter how thine editor doth protest.

[5] Fudgest thou not thy data. Unless thy data conflict with Mine own theory. In that case, thy data likely needs "reinterpretation".

[6] Thou shalt not beat or whip thy graduate students, nor force them to maintain thy database, nor trot out the best ideas of thy graduate students as thine own.

[7] Except in thy footnotes, for the lesser linguists tend not to read these so carefully.

[8] For they are but babes in the wood of language and easily put off by thy analytical probing.

[9] Though they do deserve a most mighty smiting.

[10] But if thou hast and it is pointed out to thee that thou hast so done, thou shalt not be angered by it. Rather, laughest thou at thyself, and make merry.

*One thing that all linguists can agree upon is that linguists are **not** prescriptive grammarians. In theory, anyway. In practice, things can get a little trickier, as shown by the following article by renowned sociolinguist Douglas S. Files.*

The Effect of Lax Rearing Practices on Speech Patterns
A Descriptive Sociolinguistic Study

Douglas S. Files
Michigan State University

The present study examines the dichotomy of pronunciation that exists in the linguistics community at a large midwestern university. The variants used by different members of this community were recorded by hidden microphones in Wells Hall. The computer files of MSU were then accessed for personal and academic information on the subjects. When the data were compared in a most objective and unbiased way, the following correlations were unearthed.

The principal difference in pronunciation which bore fruit when compared to personal data was the [hag]/[hɔg] dichotomy. Subjects who used the former variant were seven times more likely to receive 4.0s in linguistics classes. (This finding corroborated that of Fog and Bog (1986) of MIT and Ritcog (in press) of Boston University.) When carried further, the data revealed that these speakers tended to have IQ's twice as high as their [hɔg] compatriots. The former group also earned an average of $10,000 more per year and bathed more regularly.

Another finding concerned those who differentiated between [wh] and [w] and those who only availed themselves of [w]. Subjects who differentiated between the sounds (as they rightly should, seeing as how God created the orthography expressly for this purpose) were more likely to marry professional models. In addition, the [wh]/[w] group members had a significantly higher incidence of winning a Nobel Prize. In contrast, the [w] group subjects were twice as likely to have been arrested for indecent exposure in the library and four times more likely to have supported Robert Bork's nomination to the Supreme Court.

A final aspect of the study examined the relationship of personal characteristics to pronunciation of the specific form *nuclear*. A dastardly progressive assimilation has stealthily crept into the English language through poor rearing of children, causing many unschooled speakers to distort this form into [nukyulər]. In addition to being unspeakably malodorous, this flagrant pronunciation is WRONG, WRONG, WRONG. It is so aesthetically and morally repugnant that the author feels that even the most descriptive linguist would agree. In any case, subjects who used the correct form were judged by their peers to be trustworthy, loyal, cheerful, friendly, and brave. Rascals who employed the incorrect [nukyulər] variant were three times more likely to be direct descendents of Attilla the Hun and seventeen times more likely to have murdered their parents with an axe. In addition, belly button lint was twice as common in this latter group.

The results of this study have clearly shown the hazards of lax parenthood. This laxity has manifested itself in diverse areas such as breastfeeding in public and permitting teenage daughters to view films rated PG-13. Practices such as the aforementioned are devastating the common decency, crumbling the Judeo-Christian foundations of society laid by our forefathers (may they rest in peace), and perhaps worst of all, causing gross mispronunciations of our fine God-given language.

Finally, for a somewhat more plaintive expression of the same point of view, we conclude this chapter with the advertisement below. The moral of the story, we suppose, is that no matter how descriptivist linguists may be in principle, most of them (including us) can get pretty Fidditchy when we want to. In other words, if you ever submit an article to SpecGram, *you'd best not split no infinitives, ya hear me?*

We 'Uns Need Us a Prescriptive Grammarian

Appalachian Regional University

We 'uns need us a prescriptive grammarian to learn us to talk Standard English so's folks'll stop laffin' at us when we's a-givin' papers at linguistic conferences. An' don't no one go tellin' us how we 'uns should be a-valuin' our own dialect; we all know all about sociolinguistics, too, but y'all jus' don' know how hard it is, when you're a-givin' a paper on Vedic Sanskrit, an' ain't nobody listnin' to ya 'cause a how they's all busy laffin'. So we need us someone to show us 'bout Standard phonology an' lexicon an' syntax an' what all, so's we can learn 'em. One year appointment. Inquire Appalachian Regional University, Fort Thomas, KY.

Phonetics
For people who aren't logical enough for phonology

THE IMAGES THAT OPEN THIS chapter and the next, taken from Hilário Parenchyma's article "Cartoon Theories of Linguistics—Phonetics vs. Phonology", amply demonstrate the main difference between these two closely related subjects. Phonetics is concerned with all the hairy particulars, while phonology operates at a more rarified level where all of the messy details of flapping hunks of mouth meat have been abstracted away.

There are many great joys to be had in learning phonetics. Two that go hand in hand[1] are learning the symbols of the IPA and learning to make the sounds that go with them. It can be both somewhat surprising and deeply pleasing to learn that the articulations of the tongue and vocal tract are so regular, so categorical.[2] The very idea—that consonants can even *be* homorganic, that there is a short list of airstream mechanisms, that the whole system is roughly compositional—is revelatory!

It also makes a great setup for a practical joke.

THE ITSY BITSY AIR PUFF

The itsy bitsy air puff went up
to the speaker's mouth.
Down came the velum, and a
nasal stop came out.
Pull down the diaphragm to
draw some air back in.
And an itsy bitsy air puff goes
up to the mouth again.

—YUNE O. HŪŪ, II

When learning to produce difficult sounds that are not native to the proto-linguist, this compositionality means that each element of the sound to be produced can be layered, one atop the other, to zero in on the target sound. So, confronted with a description of an unfamiliar sound, say, "a close front rounded vowel", a linguist can approximate with something nearby (say, a close front *unrounded* vowel) and then modify the relevant features of the approximation, in this case by rounding the lips. In the case of a consonant, say, "a voiced bilabial fricative", the linguist might bring the lips close together but not touching, begin to blow, adjust the lip separation to get that light fricative buzz, and then add the voicing. Voilà!

The symbols of the IPA probably look, to the uninitiated, like the victims of an alphabetic explosion, but there's a method to the orthographic

---

[1] Or, sometimes, if a student is really doing it wrong, foot in mouth.
[2] Of course, that's not actually true. The fine details of pronunciation vary from language to language, and at the finest level of granularity, there have probably never been two sounds in the history of human language that were produced exactly the same. But it still feels like there is an inordinate amount of order when first learning about one's native sounds.

madness. All the nasals are modified n's and m's. Most of the labials are related to p's, b's, f's, and v's. There's the occasional import from Greek or Norse, but it is usually historically defensible. All of these similar letters need to have names, too, so that they can be discussed without the need to produce them.[3] Terms like "open o", "small capital g", "dotless i", "turned y", and "right hook v" are commonly bandied about in phonetics classes, and are sometimes even used by serious phoneticians.

Enter "double-dot wide o",[4] pictured at right.[5] The accompanying phonetic description, conveniently left on the whiteboard of the linguistics grad student lounge, for example, is "nasal-ingressive voiceless velar trill". A curious, phonetically savvy victim will see the symbol, read the description, realize the sound is unfamiliar, and then, using the awesome power of phonetic compositionality, attempt to create the sound so that it may be inspected, all without knowing what the result will be.

Typically the victim begins by exhaling deeply so as to be able to breathe in through the nose ("nasal-ingressive") for as long as possible, giving more time to experiment with the other articulators. A small thought may be given to keeping the vocal cords still ("voiceless").[6] Concentrating on the velum, the victim narrows the closure, seeking to induce a trill when—suddenly—a massive vibration rattles the brainpan, and everyone within earshot turns to see why an otherwise civilized person is loudly snorting like a pig.[8]

And this is by no means the only contribution that *Speculative Grammarian* has made to the discipline of phonetics.[9] The remainder of this chapter presents some of the most outstanding of *SpecGram's* most outstanding scholarly publications in this area.

FLOW, FLOW, FLOW YOUR AIR

Flow, flow, flow your air;
Gently start the stream.
Pulmonic egressive, pulmonic egressive.
Sounds are heard not seen.

—YUNE O. HŪŪ, II

---

[3] Not only is this convenient for situations when the ability to reliably produce a particular sound is not a given, it also keeps flocks of linguists from sounding, to outsiders, as silly as they sometimes look.

[4] For reasons that will become clear, it is best to engage in a little cognitive priming and explicitly label the symbol as "double-dot wide o", so that victims will view it first and foremost as a letter-like symbol.

[5] And just to prove that there really is nothing new under the sun, it turns out that there is a rarely-used exotic variant of Cyrillic O with two dots in it—in English called "binocular O"—that has been used, for example, in the plural of the Russian word for "eye": Ꙩчи.

[6] This turns out to be crucial to keeping the prank from turning ugly. A *voiced* nasal-ingressive velar trill could be fatal. Of course, at this point you will be tempted to try it and see why that is so. Please do not.[7]

[7] At least not until you have actually paid for the book.

[8] Some of the Managing Editor's proudest moments have been discovering that previously unknown linguaphiles, from far away places, had—after reading about the nasal-ingressive voiceless velar trill on the *SpecGram* website—elicited strange looks from friends, family, and even strangers by performing it to "see what it sounds like". To reach out across the internet and vibrate someone's head like that is just magical.

[9] Though it may be the most entertaining one.

Famed anthropological linguist and longtime contributor to SpecGram Claude Searsplainpockets has had a number of encounters with languages that have shockingly interesting phonetics, and we begin and end this chapter with two examples of his work. In this first example, Claude describes a language with a surprisingly linguistically-savvy-seeming type of iconicity and previously unknown airstream mechanisms, which, frankly, it may be better not to know about—but science marches on!

Eating the Wind
An Anthropological Linguistic Study of the Xoŋry

Claude Searsplainpockets
Somewhere in the Middle East

Introduction

The people who call themselves "the Xoŋry" comprise not a single people and language, but rather a surprisingly large constellation of small, related tribes[1] speaking a surprisingly large constellation of large, related languages.[2] The Xoŋry are spread over several thousand square miles of desolate and mostly unclaimed territory on the Arabian Peninsula.

The main differences between nearby dialects of Xoŋry are largely simple matters of phonology; local variants of the name of the language demonstrate the phenomenon well: /ʔɛɴɟʒ/, /Hɔⁿɣlə/, /ħøŋɢʁɨ/, /ħœnˠʤʁə/, /ʕoɲɹɪ/, /χaɲkʈi/, /ɧəɴɢ˦e/, and the all but inexplicable /hungry/. Grammatical variations do exist between dialects, but are usually minor matters.[3] These simple variations need not concern us.

WOULD YOU LIKE SPAGHETTI OR LASAGNA FOR DINNER?

Phonetician: "Could you say that second word again more slowly?"

Linguistic Background

The truly fascinating thing about Xoŋry dialects is the apparent frequency of phonological iconicity.[4] Sound symbolism is nothing new—weak examples exist in English (*battered, beaten, bruised, banged, blistered; glitter, glisten, glow, gleam, glare, glint; snarl, snout, snicker, snack; slide, slick, sled; smash, crash, bash; smack, whack, crack*)—and the phenomenon is usually realized as a mapping between certain sounds or clusters of sounds and a constellation of related meanings. What makes Xoŋry unique is that it is the *pulmonicity* of the velar series, which not only carries sound-symbolic meaning, but does so in a way that is remarkably iconic!

Xoŋry has an impressive, even remarkable array of consonants—oral and nasal; voiced and voiceless; egressive, ingressive, ejective, and implosive. The language also features some heretofore unknown gastro-pulmonic types which I will reveal in due time below.

Linguistic Data

I have limited my initial foray into the pulmonic sound symbolism of Xoŋry to a single bound, but productive, morpheme of the dialect with the most speakers.[5] The morpheme in question is

---

[1] Most tribes number 25 or fewer speakers.

[2] Most of the lexicons I have recorded include well over 150,000 distinct lexical items.

[3] Such as trivial matters of whether the dialect has prepositions or postpositions, makes the distinction between inclusive- and exclusive-we, has 1, 2, 4, or 18 noun classes, is topic-prominent or not, is dechticaetiative or not, is oligosynthetic or not, is ergative or accusative, and whether it is synthetic or analytic.

[4] A special case of so-called "sound symbolism".

[5] Between 57 and 88, depending on who does the counting.

/-æbriket/, which has a core meaning of "consume, take in, put in the mouth or nose".

The data, as always, speaks for itself:[6]

/ǩ-æbriket/
voiceless oral ingressive + "consume"
"to put in the mouth, without talking"

/ǧ-æbriket/
voiced oral ingressive + "consume"
"to put in the mouth, while talking"

/k-æbriket/
voiceless oral egressive + "consume"
"to spit out or take out of the mouth, without talking"

/g-æbriket/
voiced oral egressive + "consume"
"to spit out or take out of the mouth, while talking"

/ň̥-æbriket/
voiceless nasal ingressive + "consume"
"to smell, without talking"

/ň-æbriket/
voiced nasal ingressive + "consume"
"to smell, while talking"

/ŋ̥-æbriket/
voiceless nasal egressive + "consume"
"to blow out the nose, without talking"

/ŋ-æbriket/
voiced nasal egressive + "consume"
"to blow out the nose, while talking"

/ƙ-æbriket/
voiceless oral implosive + "consume"
"to devour, without talking"

/ɠ-æbriket/
voiced oral implosive + "consume"
"to devour, while talking"

/k'-æbriket/
voiceless oral ejective + "consume"
"to projectile vomit, without talking"

/g'-æbriket/
voiced oral ejective + "consume"
"to projectile vomit, while talking"

Xoŋry features a heretofore unknown constellation of phonemes that I have collectively labeled "gastro-pulmonic". These come in two varieties. In the first, air is swallowed during the production of the sounds in question—this is "ingestive". In the second, air is returned from the stomach to produce the sound—this is "egestive".[7,8]

/ḱ-æbriket/
voiceless oral ingestive + "consume"
"to eat, without talking"

---

[6] We use a caron to indicate ingressiveness, and a ring below to indicate voicelessness, when no other standard symbol exists.

[7] We use an acute accent to indicate ingestive, and a grave accent to indicate egestive.

[8] As an aside, Xoŋry features at least two discourse particles that are primarily used (a) to add air to the stomach for egestives (/ɕˡʊʁṕ/), and (b) remove excess air from the stomach after too many ingestives (/ɓu̯ʳ̩:::p̰/).

/ǵ-æbriket/

voiced oral ingestive + "consume"

"to eat, while talking"

/ŋ̊-æbriket/

voiceless nasal ingestive + "consume"

"to snort up the nose, without talking"

/ŋ́-æbriket/

voiced nasal ingestive + "consume"

"to snort up the nose, while talking"

/k̀-æbriket/

voiceless oral egestive + "consume"

"to vomit, without talking"

/g̀-æbriket/

voiced oral egestive + "consume"

"to vomit, while talking"

/ŋ̥̀-æbriket/

voiceless nasal egestive + "consume"

"to vomit through the nose, without talking"

/ŋ̀-æbriket/

voiced nasal egestive + "consume"

"to vomit through the nose, while talking"

Other Xoŋry roots that follow a similar pattern with the obvious meanings attached to their sound symbolism include: /-brakadabra/, "turn left"; /-umplstltskn/, "roll three or more 8- or 12-sided dice"; /-ramarian/, "compose prose or poetry, usually of a satirical nature".

IT IS WELL KNOWN AMONG LINGUISTS…

Because the tone shift associated with the Doppler effect varies depending on whether an object is approaching the hearer or moving away, there are two words for "car" in Chinese.

There are several other instances of non-iconic sound symbolism in Xoŋry. For example, /f-/ often indicates untruthfulness. Determining the meaning of the form /f-æbriket/ is left as an exercise for the reader.

Further Research

I am certain that there is also a constellation of words in this pattern related to both "delicate" bodily functions and the sexual rites and practices of the Xoŋry. Unfortunately, I have not yet gained sufficient trust of any speakers to have the terms (or the practices) revealed to me. I am continuing to work on that.

There are rumors of a nearby tribe, a mere thirty-five or so sand dunes to the east, whose dialect expands upon the current system with regular meaning differences for breathy voice, creaky voice, and each of several tones. As soon as I complete this missive and have packed my camel, I leave to investigate.

Tentative Conclusions

More research is necessary to unravel the intricacies of this system. Said research will require more and abundant funding.

References

Aztet, J. and Gerard. H. B. 1965. A study of phonetic symbolism among native Navajo speakers. *Journal of Personality and Social Psychology* 1: 524–528.

Bolinger, Dwight. 1949. *The Sign is Not Arbitrary.*

Clacker, Clickety. 1622. *Cationsitens ares of aftence ge, psionfustuatenterences.* Eng Evis Forigh Worics: Paris, London

Ertel, S. and S. Dorst. 1965. Expressive Lautsymbolik. *Zeitschrift experimentelle Psychologie* 12: 557–569.

Flïrtïstïk, Fluee. 1991. Pulmonicity. *Fluidity and Flow* 34: 55–732

Hellwag, C. 1791. *De formatione loquelae.* Tübingen.

Hilmer, H. 1914. *Schallnachahmung, Wortschopfung und Bedeutungswandel.* Halle.

Householder, F. W. 1962. Azerbaijani Onomatopes, in: Poppe, N. (ed.), *American Studies in Altaic Linguistics.* 115–121.

Imack-O'Wack, Smackercrack. 1944. *Sound Symbolism in Symbolic Sounds.*

Magnus, M. 1999. *Gods of the Word: Archetypes in the Consonants.* Truman State University Press.

Sprinkles, Sprite. 2004. *Gladly Glowing in the Glistening Gloaming: Sound Symbolism and Alliterative Allusions.* Seven For More Options Press: Boston, Beijing, Bloomington.

von Humboldt, Wilhelm. 1863. *Über die Verschiedenheit des menschlichen Sprachbaues und ihren Einfluß auf die geistige Entwicklung des Menschengeschlechts.*

Wissemann, H. 1954. *Untersuchungen zur Onomatopoiie.* Carl Winter Universitätsverlag: Heidelberg.

Xerxes, Zöe. 1822. *Onomatopöÿï.* Glitt Glurr: Scotland.

CHOOSE YOUR OWN CAREER IN LINGUISTICS—PART 21

YOU WORK ON THE SETI PROJECT...

Forget the temporal wormholes—those wormholes are never going to work, anyway—this SETI thing is awesome!

In your second week, using your freakishly superior hybrid analytic skills, you detect a complex pattern in the data that everyone else has overlooked. It looks purposeful.

- Tell the project supervisor. Go to Part 24 on page 67.
- Analyze the data yourself. Go to Part 25 on page 152.

Choose Your Own Career in Linguistics starts on page 301.

Cartoonist Bethany Carlson presents a relatively mournful view of the real world many newly minted phoneticians face after graduating in a down economy, in this first of her two phonetic cartoons.

Linguistics Nerd Camp

Bethany Carlson

At the other end of the economic spectrum, Freya Shipley reports on a surprising and surprisingly valuable find in the world of antique dialects.

Phonetics Roadshow

Transcribed by Freya Shipley

VOICE: *Phonetics Roadshow* is made possible by the Ladefoged Ingressive Trust, and by contributions from viewers like you. Thank you.

GUEST and APPRAISER are standing on either side of a small table on which rests a Dialect. It looks like a large multicolored hairball with some sparkly tufts sprouting here and there, and maybe a few moth-eaten feathers.

APPRAISER: Do you know anything about it at all?

GUEST: I really don't. It supposedly belonged to my great-grandparents who brought it with them from somewhere back east. When my mother passed in 1987, we found it in her attic.

APPRAISER: Well, you've brought in quite a spectacular dialect. What do you think the date of it might be?

GUEST: No idea.

APPRAISER: Well, I can tell you that it's a variety that was spoken between 1820 and 1885.

GUEST: Wow.

APPRAISER: I've talked to some of my colleagues and we think that this piece was probably made in northeastern Alabama or north Georgia.

GUEST: Okay...

APPRAISER: And it was made for somebody of extraordinary wealth at the time. I'm especially interested in this [au] right here—can you see it? This was almost certainly crafted in Pennsylvania.

Normally, dialects were constructed of local materials. It's very rare for a diphthong to be imported such a great distance. It wasn't something that just an average person could afford.

GUEST: Huh.

APPRAISER: It's missing a couple of its modals. Right here, can you see? These were probably originally *might coulds* or *oughtta shoulds...*

GUEST: Yeah.

APPRAISER: But considering the rarity of the piece, those little flaws aren't likely to discourage collectors. Do you know anything else about its history?

GUEST: Nope. It's been in the family forever. My Dad used it once in a while, mostly when he was drunk. I don't really use it myself. I basically just keep it on the mantelpiece.

APPRAISER: Look at these mortise-and-tenon joints. Beautiful oxidization here. Has it ever been professionally cleaned?

GUEST: Not that I'm aware. I had a great aunt who was supposedly interested in diction classes back in the day, but I don't think she ever actually did anything about it.

APPRAISER: That's very fortunate. Speech training would certainly have lowered the value.

GUEST: Right.

APPRAISER: Unfortunately, the dialect's not signed, so we don't know who made it. But it's definitely of Appalachian origin. The hardware may be Scot-

THE WISDOM OF LINGUISTS

Loose lips make bilabial trills.

tish—these springs and finials. I'd say the gear trains were almost certainly made in Edinburgh.

GUEST: Whoa.

APPRAISER: Were you ever told what your great-grandparents paid for it originally?

GUEST: No, not at all.

APPRAISER: Do you have any idea what a dialect like this might be worth today?

GUEST: Nuh-uh.

APPRAISER: Well, I'd say an auction estimate, conservatively, would be between $250,000 and $300,000.

GUEST: Oh, wow. Awesome.

APPRAISER: Thank you for bringing it in.

IT IS WELL KNOWN AMONG LINGUISTS...

In 1893, famed phonetician Henry Sweet was able to use his "half-phased vocalic resonance" ability to thwart the effects of Nikolai Tesla's electrophonic meteorological wave-front generator, thus saving the British rye crop from almost certain destruction. This did not, however, gain him a professorship.

CHOOSE YOUR OWN CAREER IN LINGUISTICS—PART 19

YOU LOOK FOR A JOB WITH YOUR UNDERGRAD LINGUISTICS/COMP SCI DEGREE...

Wonderfully, your skill set is in demand. There are a lot of job opportunities for computational linguists, even those who only have an undergrad degree.

• Continue. Go to Part 40 on page 281.

Choose Your Own Career in Linguistics starts on page 301.

WOULD YOU LIKE SPAGHETTI OR LASAGNA FOR DINNER?

Experimental Phonetician: The cooking time of spaghetti has a mean of 9.56 minutes ($\sigma = 1.456$ minutes) and of lasagna a mean of 7.43 minutes ($\sigma = 0.467$ minutes), and this difference is significant.

Cartoonist Kean Kaufmann teams up with John Miaou to illustrate a Pivotal Moment in the History of Phonetics. Many linguists have pondered the question of the exact nature of the origin of the so-called cardinal vowels.

Pivotal Moments in the History of Linguistics

John Miaou
Illustrated by Kean Kaufmann

Daniel Jones discovers a cardinal vowel

As noted earlier, phonetics is concerned with the messy details that phonology often overlooks. There are few details messier than those relating to ruminant consonants, but Werinda Clover chews over the current state of our knowledge about this little-studied and poorly understood form of articulation.

Ruminating on Consonants

Werinda Clover
X. Quizzit Korps Center for Advanced Collaborative Studies

During a recent winter evening when my e-book reader's battery had died, I whiled away the hours by perusing several recently published phonetics textbooks, and discovered, to my astonishment, that none of these books includes a single mention of ruminant consonants. And yet what language does not have ruminant consonants, either on the surface or somewhere hidden in its deep structure!?

As Crudbottom and Fartyblartfast state in their recent article on virtual subphonetic Chomskyan universalification, I was not the only one to have researched this most perplexing issue: How cud this be?

Ruminant consonants are perplexing because they involve activation of the molar perplexus, a little-known nerve complex with little-known unsympathetic function. First observed by oral surgeons at the Experimental Wikidentistry Institute in Wirschreemen, East Germany, in 1964, this nerve, when stimulated with a rapidly rotating pointy metal object, appears to produce rhythmic convulsions in the arms and trunk muscles of subjects along with articulations we now know we can classify as complex clusters of ruminants. In addition, one of their most salient characteristics—their instantiation as a single feature bundle that "reappears" several times as it gradually undergoes assimilatory processes—

has led them to be mis-analyzed in the literature as sequences of separate consonant phonemes rather than as trans-temporally realized units.

While recent investigators have chewed on the possibility of analyzing them as an example of consonant harmony, we prefer to break away from the herd and take an approach to the problem that opens the previously fallow fields of onomastics, omastics, and abomastics to effective mastication.

Herbacious (1979) and Bovin-Laitman (1989) both mulled over whether ruminant consonants were simply re-occurrences of previous phonemic acts or whether they were instead an original instantiation of the well-researched +PIZZA +CAB-BAGE phenomenon, reported by Fartyblartfast (1901, 1955) in his articles on the reflux linguistics of the Obecity tribe of the Lower Belt of the Panttrouser Peninsula. Both authors came to the same conclusion: ruminant consonants are worthy of further study, and likely constitute a unique subbranch of the fields of phonology, mixology, and edamamology.[1]

For the uninitiated, or for the benefit of the graduate student in search of an innovative and attention-getting presentation for LSA 2013, it is worth regurgitating the facts: ruminants, being both {+open} and {+constricted}, are most correctly described not by the place of blockage in the vocal tract but rather through obtuse, clumsy (and quite possibly misspelled) reference to the substance or substances causing the constriction. Thus, we have the calxo-velar, calxo-uvular, and the difficult calxo-pharyngeal series, the herbo-velar, herbo-uvular, and herbo-pharyngeal, and the less complex, if waterier, sputu-series.[2]

Thus, in order to fully digest this most interesting phenomenon, we must continue to trace the route by which these sounds are processed after production, according to the well-established principles of Transintestinal-Surgico-Neurolin-

guistics, which I need not trace here.[3] First, the post-molar consonant enters the œsophageal stream, accompanied by excess corporeal fluid in the case of the sputu- series, but accompanied by spontaneous laryngeal spasm in the case of the rest. Then, upon entering the oral cavity, the consonants are re-articulated several times at varying positions throughout the cavity, producing a characteristic series of clicks, tones, and other phonemes. The precise nature of the phoneme uttered will, of course, vary according to the temporal duration of the initial blockage, its placement in the transintestinal system, the language normally spoken by the producer, and their adherence to Gricean norms.

In an uncharacteristically brilliant piece of analysis by Crudbottom, it has been definitively shown that the subset of these consonants which can be analyzed through analysis of nearby upholstery as ejectives, are, in fact, pleas for help in some contexts, both supporting the Gricean maxim of quantity and proving once again that grammars, like bilabial closures, leak.

Ruminant consonants provoke bucolic linguists to deep introspection, and must not be omitted (nor emitted, come to think of it) from phonetics textbooks, nor from the meditations of thoughtful linguists. Do not be cowed by the objections of your publisher; do not gaze sheepishly at your editor.

In short, be outstanding in your field.

THE BEST LINGUISTICS BANDS EVAR!!

The Breathy Boys &
Jefferson Airstream

---

[1] The study of Japanese appetizers.

[2] Attempts by linguists at Wirschreemen to study the calxo-glottal, herbo-glottal, and sputu-glottal series in the 1970s were abandoned after the loss of 14 undergrads, two teaching assistants, and Herr Crudbottom's cat. We assume this last series to be potentially (that is, underlyingly) present in many, if not all ruminants, but that these appear only occasionally on the surface level. The correct analysis of these last consonants would no doubt set new, meatier standards in phonology, permanently stalling the theoretical competition: showing them all to be the bull we always knew they were. The steaks are high; who will move us forward?

[3] For those who are not familiar with this branch of linguistics, I suggest the following book by Fartyblartfast, Crudbottom, and Schrödinger: *The Discovery, Re-Discovery, and Quantum Uncertainty of My Watch in the Stomach of My Possibly Non-Existent Cat* (Trouser Press, Lower Standards, Penn).

In a second cartoon, Bethany Carlson again shows the darker side of the field of phonetics. Some phonetic descriptions are, in the most detailed sense, a bit underspecified. Native speakers and linguists alike deal with that ambiguity as they do with any other—usually smoothly and unconsciously. However, it is not always so easy.

Linguistics Nerd Camp

Bethany Carlson

Finally for this chapter, here is one of the most controversial phonetics articles ever published in SpecGram. *Claude Searsplainpockets treks to the great frozen north to uncover evidence of an iconoclastic articulation that has been the topic of myth and legend for generations. Never has data from a place so cold generated so much metaphorical heat.*

Hunting the Elusive Labio-Nasal
An Anthropological Linguistic Study of the Beeg Haan Krrz

Claude Searsplainpockets
Somewhere above the Arctic Circle

Introduction

The now well-known clicks found in certain African languages must have come as quite a shock to the first European linguists who heard them. Many of the sounds were familiar, of course, but the idea that they could be a component of *language* had to have been hard to believe. Even now the languages of Africa have secrets to share—note the recent addition of "right hook v" to the IPA as the symbol for the "labiodental flap" found in numerous African languages.

Perhaps jaded by too many inscrutable sounds in our undergrad phonetics classes, we linguists have collectively found that the labiodental flap, in which the lower lip is smacked against the back of the upper teeth, fails to properly shock. By rights it *should* be terribly shocking—a new and surprising kind of articulation. It seems uncomfortable, difficult, even unlanguage-like. It should be the subject of passionate debate and thoughtful arguments and counter-arguments, not the hum-drum subject of dry and dusty meetings of International Phonetic Association and Unicode Consortium committees.

Dismayed by the lack of proper awe that language should inspire in its closest friends—linguists!—I set out to find something shocking, hard to believe, secret, inscrutable, new, surprising, uncomfortable, difficult, and even unlanguage-like. We have all heard the rumors of the impossible articulation from the far, far north—our field's equivalent of an urban myth. We have all thought it merely an old professor's tale, told to keep undergrads from asking too many questions, or wandering around the phonetics lab late at night. But I believe all myths have some small kernel of truth to them—so I set out to hunt down the elusive northern labio-nasal articulation.

In the wilds of northernmost Canada I found phonetic riches beyond compare among a small, isolated, and little known tribe—the Beeg Haan Krrz. Beeg Haan Krrzian would be a language isolate—as is the famously infamous Basque—if not for the closely related but much less exciting dialect spoken by their cousins a bit farther south, the Litol Hong Gersh. The grammar of these two languages is nothing special (nonetheless see my forthcoming publication in Psammeticus Press's Patchwork Grammar Series), but Beeg Haan Krrzian phonetics offers something that puts the African labiodental flap to shame.

Linguistic Background

The Beeg Haan Krrz have developed an unusual, probably unique, place of articulation: labio-nasal. Plosives, trills, and fricatives can all be heard coming from between lips and nose of speakers of Beeg Haan Krrz.

The origin of this shocking form of articulation (illustrated on page 37) is not entirely clear—rather, it is entirely unclear. Most speakers claim something along the lines of, "It has always been

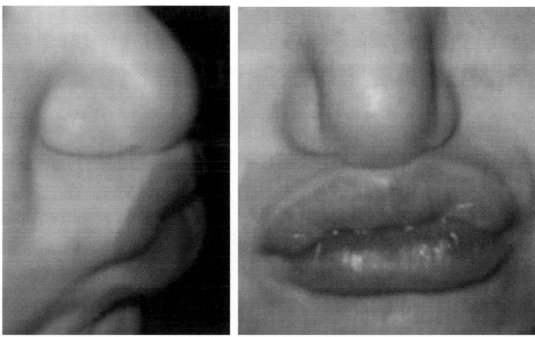

Labio-nasal articulation in action

that way in our language." However this seems unlikely—especially given the unusual character of Beeg Haan Krrzian. One of the most interesting facts about the language is that, unlike sounds of any other language, not just anyone can pronounce these labio-nasal sounds. This kind of "fact" is bandied about by poor students of both languages and linguistics as an excuse for their failure to properly pronounce the trilled r's of Spanish, or the pharyngeal sounds of Arabic. Yet no single normal person is ever born and raised in Mexico or Egypt and unable to acquire these sounds.

While there are no defective native speakers of Beeg Haan Krrzian, it is clear that there could be. Unlike trilling r's or fricating pharyngeals, the basic articulatory move of the labio-nasal is quite clear (because it is physically external), and also quite impossible for me. While my failure to get down the timing and subtle positioning of the labio-nasal fricative would surprise no one, in fact I can't even get my upper lip anywhere close

enough to my nose to form the labio-nasal stop. It is embarrassing, but linguistically important.

In any event, the origin of this difficult articulation is entirely mysterious. Theories range from visual onomatopoeian mimicking of the facial expressions of a sneezing cat (though there are no cats within 1,000 miles) to what I have labeled "cold" theories: keeping the mouth closed conserves heat, expelling warm air onto the lips keeps them from getting chapped, etc. None of the theories are convincing, and the truth will likely never be known.

Linguistic Data

Despite the rockstar-like quality of "right hook v" and the media blitz surrounding its official coronation into the IPA, I have decided not to introduce any additional symbols to represent these sounds at this time. Instead, I have decided to simply combine simple symbols in a mnemonic way, tying /m/ (a labial nasal) with superscripted symbols giving the correct voicing and manner of articulation.

Thus:

$\widehat{m^b}$ is the labio-nasal voiced stop

$\widehat{m^p}$ is the labio-nasal voiceless stop

$\widehat{m^B}$ is the labio-nasal (voiced) trill

$\widehat{m^\beta}$ is the labio-nasal voiced fricative

$\widehat{m^\phi}$ is the labio-nasal voiceless fricative

Some sample data, in the form of a well-loved Beeg Haan Krrzian tongue-twister/proverb, is provided below.

$\text{amm}\widehat{^b}$.uu	la.tte	suu.per	trra.$\widehat{\text{am}^p}$
lazy.SG	easy.PL	seal.PL	bear.SG

$\text{bam}\widehat{^B}$oo	zel	trri	um$\widehat{^\phi}$ant
PRES.habit	3RD.PL.SG	SG.OBJ	be.caught

The easy seals are gotten by the lazy polar bear.

Linguistic Analysis

There really isn't much worth analyzing at this stage. This report is merely a preliminary announcement of the unusual articulatory facts of the language. A fuller account will be given in my forthcoming publication in Psammeticus Press's Patchwork Grammar Series.

Tentative Conclusions

More research is necessary to unravel the intricacies of this system. Said research will require more and abundant funding.

References

Searsplainpockets, Claude. Forthcoming. *Arctic Schnozzian Languages: A Straightforward Analysis of Beeg Haan Krrzian and Litol Hong Gersh (with special phonetic appendix of actual interest).* Psammeticus Press Patchwork Grammars Series.

CHOOSE YOUR OWN CAREER IN LINGUISTICS—PART 34

YOU GO FOR A SECURITY CLEARANCE...

You go for a security clearance. It takes a lot longer than you expected, and you can't do any kind of interesting work in the meantime, because you aren't "cleared". You do keep your chair warm, though.

Finally, you get your clearance. *Finally,* you get to see [REDACTED—CLASSIFIED] and [REDACTED—CLASSIFIED], and from time to time you even work with [REDACTED—CLASSIFIED]. But overall, it turns out that it is pretty boring, compared to all the trouble you went through to get the clearance. And you can never talk to your friends or family about what you do. And half the time you can't even talk to your colleagues.

On the other hand, cleared work pays better.

• Continue the cleared work. Go to Part 35 on page 147.
• Pursue work in the private sector. Go to Part 33 on page 169.

Choose Your Own Career in Linguistics starts on page 301.

THE WISDOM OF LINGUISTS

Inhale before you pronounce.

Phonology
Keeping the empiricism in phonetics, where it belongs

PHONOLOGY IS THE REASON WHY larval linguists, often having dutifully studied phonetics the semester before, can produce sounds that they can't hear: not dog-whistles,[1] but rather a range of sounds that, to the non-native ear, all sound more or less interchangeable.[2] Phonology takes that great big chaotic mess of phonetic detail (*phones*) and buckets it into neat, discrete pigeonholes (*phonemes*) to give the rest of the brain less to cope with. It generally works, too, as long as you stay away from the edges between the buckets.[3]

An understanding of the basic simplificational principles of phonology—demonstrated visually in the differences and similarities between the cartoons at the beginning of this chapter and the previous one—explains the practical difficulties of a phonetics course. And the realization that not all languages collapse [t] and [tʰ], or that some do collapse [v] and [w], is a valuable practical lesson. Such comprehension also dispassionately explains some dialect differences, such as the fact that people who might have previously seemed defective for not being able to say *cot* and *caught* properly are in fact merely the unfortunate victims of a defective dialect, and worthy of pity, not scorn.[4]

Phonology and phoneme merger also allow one to unravel one of the great mysteries of satirical linguistics: there are those who claim that double-dot wide o (see the Phonetics Chapter) describes an ingressive voiceless *uvular* trill, rather than a velar one. These speakers have undergone the *snore/snort* merger. Phonetically, double-dot wide o describes a pig snort, while a snore is more properly and traditionally symbolized by /5/, according to Metalleus (see "The Voiced Snore Debunked" for details). Phonologically, these two

LETTER H AND N-G

Letter H could end no rhyme,
N-G could start no word,
And so betwixt the two of them,
The phoneme "heng" emerged.

—YUNE O. HŪŪ, II

---

[1] Which, taken literally, are probably not possible for humans to produce, and thus outside the purview of linguistics proper. Or which, taken figuratively, lie within the realm of pragmatics.

[2] "The tongue is willing, but the ear is weak," as the proverb goes, more or less.

[3] See the works of Ba-Wa McGurk for other potential difficulties.

[4] Editors' note: Of course we suggest you actually take the moral high road and embrace descriptivism, hold your nose and publicly state that the *cot/caught* merger is "fine", as is the *pen/pin* merger.[5]

[5] Which, unlike *cot/caught*, actually is quite fine.

may have collapsed for some speakers,[6] so of course they hear them as being the same.[7]

Another important function of phonology is meta-linguistic and academic; it separates the wheat from the chaff in introductory linguistics courses. "The phonology test", as it is known in some circles, makes it clear who can and who cannot think abstractly and logically.[8] As the material is generally new to everyone, it also provides a level playing field.[9] Spending an entire weekend ordering and re-ordering phonological rules is a linguistic rite of passage.

In closing, it should be noted that the line between diachronic historical sound change[11] and synchronic phonological transformations is quite blurry.[12] In some sense, one is just a slow motion playback of the other. For that reason, depending on how you, Dear Reader, are reading, and the attendant red shift, some of the articles in this section may seem more or less historical in nature. Real linguistics, like real language, like real life, is messy.

PEARLS OF WISDOM FROM
STUDENTS OF LINGUISTICS

Minimal pairs are in complimentary distribution: it is unlikely that you will find one sound in the other.

---

[6] Probably as the result of weakened throat musculature.

[7] Poor dears.

[8] And who can and cannot prudently stop thinking logically when it comes to the instructor's favorite theory, but that's another topic altogether.

[9] Well, except for the mathematicians, computer scientists, engineers, physicists, and other hard-science types who might be slumming[10] in the class.

[10] Their words, not ours. Just sayin'.

[11] See also the Comparative and Historical Linguistics Chapter.

[12] Except for people who were paying attention when the *synchronic-diachronic* distinction was explained to them. Unfortunately, a lot of phonologists apparently weren't paying attention.

CHOOSE YOUR OWN CAREER IN LINGUISTICS—PART 39

YOU TRY TO GET AN ACADEMIC JOB...

Statistics has never been your strong suit, but now you understand exactly what it means that, in many fields, universities are cranking out more Ph.D.s than there are academic jobs to hold them. You are living the statistic.

You move across the country several times, from a one-year position to a two-year position to another one-year position, always trying to befriend students and faculty, particularly any who may have influence on the committee that fills the next available tenure-track position.

You politic, you shmooze, you flatter. You recast your research interests as often as necessary to improve you chances of getting a secure position. Your personal life is a shambles—friends made and abandoned at each stop on the tenure-track express, romance stressed, strained, potentially broken by every move.

- Stick it out—academia is where you belong. Go to Part 42 on page 218.
- Give up, and get a real job. Go to Part 41 on page 110.
- Get creative and start a satirical linguistics journal. Go to Part 43 on page 320.

Choose Your Own Career in Linguistics starts on page 301.

LOGICAL FALLACIES FOR LINGUISTS

Bulverism—"Lisi wants Sandy's analysis of Cherokee tone sandhi to be right just because it would embarrass Dorj, so surely Sandy is wrong."

Acoustic phonetics, with all of its lab equipment, waveforms, and x-ray videos, is arguably the most scientific branch of linguistics. Phonology, in contrast, is the most mathematical, what with all the devising of rules and permuting of their order to properly describe the theoretical inputs and real-world outputs. Ahh, Mathematics, Queen of the Sciences! Apparently she was not good enough for Keith W. Slater (now Senior Editor of Speculative Grammarian—*how did* **that** *happen?), who felt the need to propose a new kind of phonology by analogy to subatomic physics.*

Granular Phonology

Keith W. Slater
Michigan State University

In a recent work (*Phonology Yearbook* 1, 1984), Sanford Schane has proposed a new system of representation for phonological systems, which he calls Particle Phonology. In this article, Schane argues for a universal set of three phonological primitives and a large number of basic operations. The primitives represent categories of palatility (symbolized as *i*), labiality (*u*) and aperture (*a*). Combinations of these primitives comprise the various phonetic vowel qualities in a given language.

Although Schane's particular system is extremely elegant, and represents a major step forward beyond other current models (e.g. Fleckenberg's "gorilla/banana" model), it nonetheless suffers from the common malady of not being rigorous enough. Schane's rejection of the Autosegmental framework is an undeniable stroke of genius, but some of the greatest potential merits of particle phonology yet lie fallow. I will now plant and harvest where Schane has plowed.

The major motivation for further refining particle phonology is that Schane's "primitives" are simply too bulky. Too large. Intuition (and common sense, too) tells us that, for example, [ï] is simply *not that much* farther forward than is [u]—certainly not far enough to warrant the addition of *an entire*

IT IS WELL KNOWN
AMONG LINGUISTS...

Over 95% of the phonology of any natural language is made up of so-called "dark phonemes," which, due to the fact that they experience no interaction with the Higgins Field, pass inaudibly through ordinary discourse.

palatility particle! Clearly, some intermediate stage is called for.

Granular phonology addresses this woesome lack in a manner analogous to a situation discovered by physicists—that subatomic *particles* (protons, neutrons, etc.) are composed of subsubatomic ones (called quarks). In reflecting on this fact, I have discovered that phonological particles likewise are composed of two such smaller units, which I term GRANULES.

In order to avoid cluttering the linguistic terminological scene (a sentiment for which I claim originality, at least), and in order to accurately mirror the essential similarity of phonological and grammatical phenomena, I shall call the two phonological granules NOUN and VERB, respectively. (Other theorists may call them whatever they like, but should not come crying to me when they discover each other's work terminologically indecipherable; I have done my part in setting a standard.) Thus, the labiality particle comprises the sequence NOUN-VERB, while the palatility particle comprises that of VERB-NOUN. The aperture particle, being of an essentially different phonetic nature, comprises the sequence Det-NOUN-VERB(Link)-ADJ. The labiality particle is thus termed "phonetically intransitive," while palatility is, in granular terms, "phonetically subjectless." As expected, the aperture particle is some sort of "phonetic complement."

The addition of NOUN or VERB granules, analogous to valence increasing or "thickening the plot," can now be used to create the necessary and sufficient intervals between phonetic vowel quantities, such as between [æ], NOUN-VERB-VERB, and [ɛ], VERB-VERB-VERB. (A detailed discussion of such "phonetic serial VERBS," incidentally, is beyond the scope of this paper, but would probably make an excellent dissertation topic.)

Predictions

Although space prohibits discussion here, I would like to note that this refined system implies certain predictions with regard to which phonetic vowel qualities may occur in a given language, based on purely syntactic considerations. Notably, SVO languages should contain no phonetic NOUN-NOUN-VERB sequences, while languages containing only one vowel quality will probably turn out to correlate bi-uniquely with languages lacking verbs, since a single vowel will, by definition, be composed of a single NOUN granule. Further typological predictions, along with more detailed discussion of Granular Phonology, may be found in my forthcoming volume, *Temporal Deixis in Shoshone Discourse*, the preparation of which led me to posit this elegant system in the first place.

CHOOSE YOUR OWN
CAREER IN LINGUISTICS—PART 10

YOU DOUBLE MAJOR IN LINGUISTICS
AND ENGLISH LITERATURE...

Alas, none of your linguistics classmates take your English literature major very seriously. They seem to snicker about you behind your back. They make derisive comments to your face about how "artsy fartsy" you are. On the other hand, your artsy fartsy English Lit friends think your interest in linguistics is cool. They like you just the way you are.

You do well enough in your linguistics classes, but your heart isn't in it. After graduation, you decide to continue with literature and abandon linguistics. It takes another eight years and $200,000 in student loans, but you finally get a Master's and a Ph.D. in World Literature Studies from an Ivy League university. You are recognized by many in the field as an expert in Medieval French and English Literature, and you have published scholarly articles on Alliterative Allusions in Beowulf, Francophonic Motifs in Chaucer, and The Symmetrical Imagery of Charles Baudelaire and Robert Frost. Your own creative writing has been a success, and you have several poems published in well-known poetry quarterlies and several short stories anthologized in books published by well-regarded independent presses.

You have achieved all that you set out to do in your field. And now, from the pinnacle of English Literaturedom, as you look back, your view of linguistics has softened. You find that you can fondly recall the positive influence of your Historical Linguistics class and that you can admit that your linguistics training may have helped in some small way in getting you where you are today.

Finally, you take on the traditional work of English Lit Superstars, in order to pay some of the interest rapidly accumulating on your student loans.

• Start your new job. Go to Part 16 on page 195.

Choose Your Own Career in Linguistics starts on page 301.

THE WISDOM OF LINGUISTS
Don't bleed the rule that feeds you.

The fortunes of linguistics programs ebb and flow at various institutions around the world. Sometimes linguistics is its own department; sometimes it is relegated to a footnote in the course listings of the English department. Coupled with its historical connection to philology, it comes as no surprise that linguistics is sometimes closely aligned with literature. When the tide rises, linguistics can take on that "new money" snobbery, mistaking it for sophistication. But in the best of all cases, linguistics and literature collide, like peanut butter and chocolate, to make something even better—as is the case with Jamin Pelkey's epic poem.

Mandarin Tone in Historical Epic Quest Perspective

Jamin Pelkey

I sing of four tonemic knights
Who in medieval Orient
With wanderlust took to the heights,
To battle the ambivalent.

Sir Píng, Sir Shàng, Sir Qù, Sir Rù
Their names emblazoned on their shields
Set forth acknowledging as true:
To polar forces nature yields.

Thus nestled in a forest glade
By moonlight as they slept unstirred
Yin's voiceless sirens potions made
And split their souls with register.

At dawn as they awoke, behold!
Four damsels with four knights were paired.
And vibrating their vocal folds,
A lower range the knights now shared.

The ladies claimed each knightly name
With voiceless onsets, pitches high;
Thus, Yin and Yang of ancient fame
Began their eight-fold patois cries.

The realms they traveled thence were dim
Beset by danger, scandal, vice;
They knew not that their path would end
In Standard Language Paradise.

Sir Shàng fell slain and was interred
But left his spirit to the Qù's.
Sirs Qù and Rù with conscience blurred
By chivalry's duplicity

Spoke sonorant initials to
The tonemes of Yin's Shàng and Qù;
Thus, soon the Rù's would meet their doom,
Imparting gifts to the bereaved.

The journey took its toll on voice,
Initially—make no mistake,
But aspiration made a choice,
And leapt contrastive in its wake.

The centuries' long march into
The present proved a worthy chore.
Now puzzling over four times two
Can lead the puzzler back to four.

The Qù's, now married, faithful, spry
With global falls, they 骂 yet 爱,[1]
The Píng's still hope for love's requite
He speaks of 麻, she speaks of 哀.
And lonely Lady Shàng still sighs
But says to all, her 马's not 矮.

From four to eight and back to four;
Like Bilbo, there and back again:
An epic quest from days of yore
Enchants the tones of Mandarin.

---

[1] Glossary and Synchronic Tonal Notes:
骂 mà 'scold, curse' (4th [falling] tone)
爱 ài 'love' (4th [falling] tone)
麻 má 'hemp' (2nd [rising] tone)
哀 āi 'sorrow' (1st [high-level] tone)
马 mǎ 'horse' (3rd [low-contour] tone)
矮 ǎi 'short' (3rd [low-contour] tone)

Not only has Claude Searsplainpockets run across some unusual phonetics in his day, he has also stumbled upon some of the most unusual phonologies ever described. In this article, Claude explores the unusual history of a quasi-intentional phonological shift of tectonic proportions, all motivated by a cultural need to make a good joke.

The Hidden Language of Public Seduction
An Anthropological Linguistic Study of Spanyol

Claude Searsplainpockets
Somewhere in the Luminiferous Αιθηρ

Introduction

Earlier this year, in preparation for fieldwork in Mozambique, Chad, and Japan, I decided to review some Spanish-language pedagogical audio materials (Cash 2007). As I was listening intently and re-acquainting myself with this beautiful language, I was quite surprised to hear many seemingly innocuous phrases presented with a tone of voice that would normally only be appropriate in a love song by Barry White. I wondered, why did the "native" speaker's pronunciation of *uno, dos, tres* make me feel oddly hot and bothered?

> "If both the two first syllables are short, stress is normally on one or the other."
> —KROEBER & GRACE

After an extensive investigation, including much hounding of a hapless secretary at the publishing company, I was able to track down the actual voice actor who recorded the examples in question. This actor is, in fact, quite fluent in *Español* (Spanish); however, his native language is a very unusual, even tortured, tongue with which I was previously unfamiliar: Spanyol.

Linguistic and Cultural Background

After tracking down and interviewing a small number of Spanyol speakers, I learned a few interesting and relevant facts about Modern Spanyol.

- Spanyol seems to be a language without a country, though most of the estimated twenty to forty thousand speakers live in Latin America or the United States, almost uniformly in regions where the language is in constant contact with Spanish.

- The most common profession among speakers of Spanyol is as Spanish-language voice artists—whether for educational materials, animated or dubbed television shows and films, video games, or radio broadcast. Most Spanyol speakers cultivate the traditionally much-valued deep, resonant voices which are well suited to this kind of work.

- Language play, humor, and sharp wit are all much admired in Spanyol culture. Puns are regarded as one of the highest art forms; multilingual puns doubly so.

- Phonetically and phonotactically, Modern Spanyol is a superset of Spanish, making all the phonetic distinctions Spanish does and allowing all the syllable structures that Spanish does, along with many others (such as v/b and ɾ/ɹ/r/ʀ distinctions, vowel length distinctions, allowing initial /s/+consonant clusters, et cetera). This has not always been the case, as we shall soon discover.

- The Spanyol writing system is a hodge-podge of Latin, Greek, and Cyrillic characters. Greek letters often indicate geminate versions of the corresponding Latin letters. Some of the Cyrillic letters seem to have been borrowed based on their resemblance to Latin letters rather than their traditional phonetic values. Hence Cyrillic я is used for an r-like sound (ʀ).

As a result of the linguistic-evolutionary interplay of these factors, a common definition of professional and personal success among present-day Spanyol speakers is to work as a Spanish-language voice actor, making off-color Spanyol/Spanish puns in a medium with a wide audience.

Linguistic Data

Let us now consider the phrase that originally started me on this long, strange adventure. Below in Table 1 I present details of the purported Spanish phrase on the audio CD I listened to, along with the Spanyol phrase the voice actor finally admitted to me is what he actually intended when he spoke.

Gloss	one, two, three
Spanish (orthographical)	*uno, dos, tres*
Spanish (phonological)	/uno dos tres/
Phonetic	[uno:d̪os:tre:s:]
Spanyol (phonological)	/u no oðos stre es:/
Spanyol (orthographical)	*u! no oðos stɾeh, eς*
Gloss	INTERJECTION come 2ND.SG.NOM;1ST.SG.ALLATIVE EMPH.IMPER, lover
	O! Come to me, lover! *or* O! Come be atop me, lover!

Table 1

A surprising number of other examples were to be found on the "Spanish"-language CD I had purchased. Another detailed example is given in Table 2, with several more demonstrative examples in (3).

Gloss	the pencil of my brother
Spanish	*el lápiz de mi hermano*
Spanyol	*eλ aap isdem iyerm a no*
Gloss	wish 1ST.SG.NOM;2ND.DUAL.ALLATIVE COUNTERFACTUAL.SUBJUNCTIVE cuddle.2ND.DU.GEN.SUBESSIVE sexy.2ND.DU/PL come
	I wish I were able to come to both of you for sexy cuddles underneath you.

Table 2

(3) Spanish: *diecinueve veinte veintiuno*
    "nineteen twenty twenty-one"
  Spanyol: *ðie sinu eb-eb heint, eh, bheint yun o*
    "I keep lovin' you more and more each time"

  Spanish: *iré al almacén y compraré leche*
    "I will go to the store and buy milk"
  Spanyol: *i re aλ-al maς eniko оµпяα apel eč, eh*
    "Been makin' love for hours and, baby, you're goin' strong"

  Spanish: *mi tía y su tío no son muy viejos*
    "my aunt and your uncle are not very old"
  Spanyol: *miτi aiς uti onoς sonmu iʋi, eh, њos*
    "Feel the fire; I'm burnin' up from the thrill of loving you"

  Spanish: *ojalá que llueva café*
    "if only it would rain coffee"
  Spanyol: *o! жal akeў webak aφe*
    "And, ooh, I swear I feel it comin' on, yeah"

Historical Linguistic Analysis

There is, of course, very little mainstream academic information on this secretive language. However, I did stumble across a fascinating historical document of inestimable value. One of the Spanyol speakers I interviewed was able to provide me with a Spanyol Primer self-published by the author in 1811 (Koolosg 1811).

Even a cursory comparison of the version of Spanyol recorded in Koolosg's prescriptivist screed (which I have taken to calling Middle Spanyol) and modern-day Spanyol shows the incredible changes that have been wrought in a diachronically miniscule period of less than 200 years:

- The expletive particle *eh,* introduced since Koolosg's time, is freely used and seems to be able to appear almost anywhere in an utterance. Its use is especially heavy in Spanish/Spanyol puns—particularly in *eh, Spanyol,* which is phonetically identical to *Español.* See example (4).

  (4) Spanish: *¿Qué lenguaje habla usted?*
      "What language do you speak?"

      Middle Spanyol: *Spanyol eɣreßen.*
      "I speak Spanyol."

      Modern Spanyol: *Eh, Spanyol.*
      "Uh, Spanyol."

- The phonetics of Spanyol have changed considerably. A number of distinctions made in Spanish but not in Middle Spanyol have come into the language, presumably intimately interrelated to the desire to make Spanyol/Spanish puns. For example, /u/ was merely a word-final allophone of /o/ in Middle Spanyol. Also, Middle Spanyol seems not to have had nasal assimilation, though Modern Spanyol, like Spanish, does. See example (5).

  (5) Middle Spanyol: *oßla Eяma anкu nu.*
      [ob:laʔeʀmaʔank:unu]

      Modern Spanyol: *Eяma no oßla anкo.*
      [eʀmano:b:la:ŋk:o]
      "Lovely Erma, come to me."

cf. Spanish: *hermano blanco*
[eʀmanoblaŋko]
"white brother"

- Modern Spanyol has also lost the phonetic glottal stops that would appear intervocalically between words in Middle Spanyol. See example (5) again. The loss of the glottal stop often allows words to "run together" in a way that is realized as vowel lengthening. Both vowel lengthening and gemination can be explained away in, for example, pedagogical materials, as over-articulation in an example citation form.

- Word order has also changed somewhat drastically in Modern Spanyol. See example (5) yet again. The basic word order of Middle Spanyol has been hard to pin down, but seems to be OVS. The language is also heavily PRO-drop, with major structural re-arrangement of an utterance possible for at least two levels of topicalization. Modern Spanyol is still PRO-drop, but seems to have developed three levels of complexly-interacting topicalization which give the language an essentially free word order, though the basic order is likely either VOS or SVO.

- Modern Spanyol has also developed a complex voice system, including passive, middle, causative, reciprocal, and cooperative (possibly in part through inexplicable but apparently heavy contact with Mongolian in the 1870s). Modern Spanyol also supports a novel noun-incorporating evidential system.

Most of these further complexities are beyond the scope of this initial investigation, but seem at least in part to be motivated, ultimately, by a need for speakers to be able to manipulate Spanyol utterances—right up to the edge of ungrammaticality—to be phonetically similar to grammatical Spanish utterances.

So, while recent voice work and, historically, other kinds of Spanish-speaking jobs have provided a steady source of income for many Spanyol speakers, they may also have had a major long-term impact on the language. There is a single footnote in Koolosg (p. 523, fn. 17) which seems to indicate that the language had changed so much in the previous 300 hundred years that not only would speakers 200 years ago not understand the older form of the language, they might not even recognize the *name* of the language from the fifteenth and sixteenth century, which Koolosg claims was either Žbȩğ⌣ðŷóя or Zьāɣšδчйř and was pronounced (according to the regular orthographic rules of the time) as /me^ynard/. It is plain to see that the loss of Koolosg's references has done irreparable damage to the art and science of linguistics.

Despite that great loss, I was able to load considerable Middle and Modern Spanyol data into the Hockett Syntacular Morphemic Resonance Spectrometer, which is capable of measuring glottoradiological Swadesh Shift down to a hemidemisemiformant. Standard morphosyntactic reverse transcription -emic/-etic alignment techniques, using both the ostentatious-brittle-votive/instinct-understatement-schadenfreude (Pelota-Grande 2005) and the volatile-intuitive-sensual/umlaut-apotheosis-lenition (van der Meer 2005) coordinates, revealed the most likely genetic affiliations of Spanyol. Unsurprisingly, the four most closely related languages are not Romance languages, but instead Euskara, بروشسکی, アイヌ イタク, and Idioma de Signos Nicaragüense.

Tentative Conclusions

More research is necessary to unravel the intricacies of both the synchronic and diachronic systems. Said research will require more and abundant funding.

References

Cash, Jàspàr Áłöišiüś, 2007. *A Quick Bit of Refresher Spanish for Use in Planes, Trains, and Automobiles: A Contrastive Grammar Tuned Especially for Globe-Trotting Anthropological Linguists Who Are Fluent in Badaga, Sepedi, and Cheyenne—Book and Eighty-Three CD Set.* The Niche Publishing Pigeonhole, Niče, France.

Koolosg, Ran Des, 1811. *Und Eeks yona Riod des Spanyol: Una gramática totalmente completa del lenguaje de Spanyol.* Self Published, Asunción, Paraguay.

Pelota-Grande, I. Juana, 2005. "Linguistic Topology," *Speculative Grammarian,* Vol. CL. No. 2.

van der Meer, Jonathan, 2005. "Letters to the Editor," *Speculative Grammarian,* Vol. CL. No. 3.

WOULD YOU LIKE SPAGHETTI
OR LASAGNA FOR DINNER?

OT Phonologist: "Spaghetti. Fatal choking may result from eating pasta in larger-than-optimal pieces."

Phonologists, like any other group of linguists,* sometimes have trouble with very basic definitions. Of course they try to find the explanation that is maximally felicitous in both the theoretical and descriptive senses. Sometimes the descriptions of things like "words" or "syllables" are a little rough around the edges. And sometimes there are languages that seem to take a malevolent glee in making the task all but impossible, as Cartoon Theorist Phineas Q. Phlogiston explores.

Cartoon Theories of Linguistics—Syllables

Phineas Q. Phlogiston, Ph.D.
Unintentional University of Lghtnbrgstn

Let us consider the most important aspects of syllables and their structure (pictured at right).

References

Bagemihl, Bruce. (1991). "Syllable Structure in Bella Coola". *Linguistic Inquiry* 22: 589–646.

Davis, Philip W. & Ross Saunders. (1979). "Bella Coola Phonology". *Lingua* 49: 169–187.

Fujimura, O. (1975). "Syllable as a Unit of Speech Recognition". *Acoustics, Speech, and Signal Processing* 23.1.

Huffman, M. K. (1997). "Phonetic Variation in Intervocalic Onset /l/'s in English". *Journal of Phonetics* 25.2.

Ladefoged, Peter. (2001). *A Course in Phonetics,* 4th edition.

Nater, Hank F. (1984). *The Bella Coola Language.*

Shaw P. (1993). "Templatic Evidence for the Syllable Nucleus". In AJ Shafer (ed.). *Proceedings of the North Eastern Linguistic Society* 23.

Syllables

gatos (Spanish 'cats')

bɒt! (English 'bottle')

xɬpʼχʷɬtɬpɬɬskʷcʼ (Nuxálk 'he had had in his possession a bunchberry plant')

---

* With the possible exceptions of syntacticians, who have a theoretical mandate to just make stuff up.

As with our foray into Granular Phonology earlier in the chapter, linguistics can exhibit a kind of science envy. One way to deal with this psychological need, of course, is to employ the material trappings of science—high-powered statistics, expensive lab equipment, and, as we shall see in this article from Equus Q. Quagga, high-powered spy satellites.

Phonotronic Energy Reserves and the Tiny Phoneme Hypothesis

Dr. Equus Q. Quagga
Center for Geosynchronous Orbital Linguistics
São Tomé and Príncipe

In response to Quentin Atkinson's recent claims in his paper "Phonemic Diversity Supports a Serial Founder Effect Model of Language Expansion from Africa", many (with most following Dr. William N. Spruiell's 2011 conjecture) have hypothesized that larger phoneme inventories are necessitated by a lack of phonotronic energy in the local environment, thereby limiting the size of each individual phoneme in phonetic mouth-space. Thus, for example, one (specifically, Dr. Spruiell) would expect regions of low phonotronic energy in certain areas of the Caucasus Mountains.

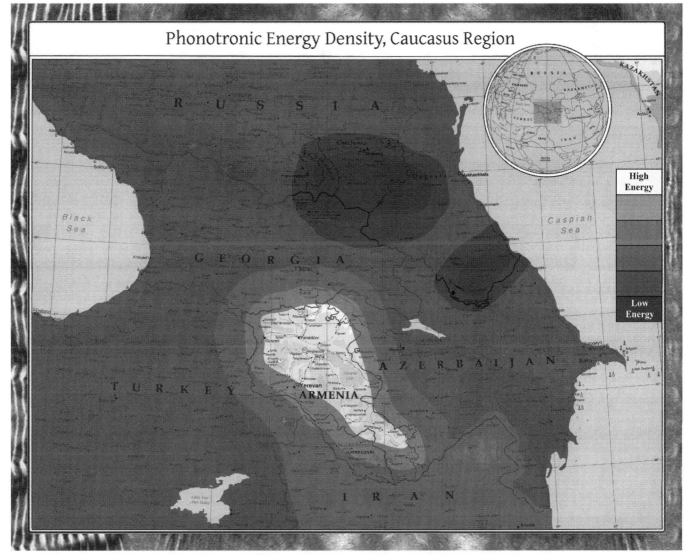

Figure 1. Phonotronic Energy Density, Caucasus Region

Intrigued by this idea, I re-tasked several of our Eurasian LingSTAR and LangSAT observation satellites, which are equipped with low-resolution phonotronic detection arrays, to image the Caucasus region. The results are in line with the Phonotronic Depletion Hypothesis (see Figure 1. Phonotronic Energy Density, Caucasus Region). There are a couple of pockets of low phonotronic energy over the Caucasus mountains, and, nearby, an area of relatively high phonotronic energy over Armenia, with its relatively small inventory of presumably larger, phonotronically-enhanced phonemes.

Of course, not much is known about the sources of or environmental influences of or on phonotronic energy; temperature, altitude, prevailing winds, ley lines, genii locorum, psychogeography, Landschaftsmythologien, subtle matter energy,

Figure 2. Crop circles may influence or be influenced by phonotronic energy

electro-magnetic aberrations, crop circles, orgone energy, and other environmental factors have been proposed as having significant effects on the distribution of phonotronic energy around the

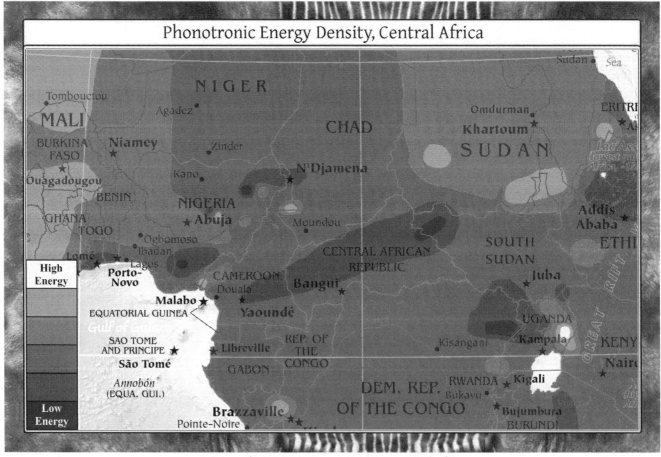

Figure 3. Phonotronic Energy Density, Central Africa

world. And all have seemed to reek of a certain *ad hoc* desperation.

Thus, while the correlation between the well-known large phonological inventories of Caucasian languages and the newly verified low phonotronic energy levels in the Caucasus mountains is indeed provocative, it is not alone sufficient to be ruled definitive.

I turned our satellites toward a more diversely dialect-dense area in central Africa. In a very satisfying turn of events, the phonotronic energy levels recorded by three LingSTAR-4000L satellites positioned over Africa correspond quite well with the phoneme inventory levels revealed by a quick search in the WALS database (the same as used by Atkinson). There are a number of areas of extreme high phonotronic energy, vast swaths of higher-than-background phonotronic energy, and a few phonotronic "dead zones". The most revealing data, though, comes from particular areas in and around Nigeria and Uganda, where the phonotronic topography is surprisingly rugged, with steep clines from high to low energy across comparatively small physical distances (see Figure 3).

Unlike the area stretching from the Caucasus mountains to Lake Sevan near the center of Armenia, there is insufficient natural geography to explain the pattern of phonotronic energy revealed by the satellites. Instead, the best match with the distribution of phonotronic energy—determined by an exhaustive analysis of the factors previously mentioned (along with 14,932 others)—is simply phonemic inventory size.

It is very pleasing that such meager efforts with satellite-based phonotronic energy measurements have proven to be so definitively useful and usefully definitive in this matter. Linguistics will yet become a real science!

CHOOSE YOUR OWN CAREER IN LINGUISTICS—PART 3
YOU DECIDE TO MAJOR IN LINGUISTICS...

The siren song of linguistics is too appealing; you can't resist. As you fill out the paperwork to declare your major, you have a mini panic attack, realizing that while linguistics is fun, you'd never heard of linguistics before you signed up for that class last fall. Maybe you should hedge your bets and double major.

- Hey, that econ thing sounded good, double major in linguistics and econ. Go to Part 5 on page 7.
- "Philosopher" sounds impressive, double major in linguistics and philosophy. Go to Part 6 on page 13.
- Computers have always been fun, double major in linguistics and comp sci. Go to Part 7 on page xiv.
- Space... the final frontier... double major in linguistics and astronomy. Go to Part 8 on page 149.
- Make your Mom happy *and* follow your own dream, double major in linguistics and pre-med. Go to Part 12 on page 16.
- Admit that you are an übergeek, double major in linguistics and physics. Go to Part 13 on page 9.
- A double major is too hard, so just major in linguistics. Go to Part 9 on page 121.
- A double major is too hard, so do one-and-a-half majors in linguistics and English Lit. Go to Part 10 on page 42.
- A double major is too distracting, so just major in linguistics. Go to Part 11 on page 275.

Choose Your Own Career in Linguistics starts on page 301.

One of the recurring principles (or is it a parameter?) of linguistics is that sometimes parameters (or are they principles?) can be underspecified. In terms of phonology, no language seems to take that further than Rotokas, a language* of Papua New Guinea. But language, like other aspects of nature, abhors a vacuum—oh, look, another science analogy! As Franny Irchow shows, sometimes the problem isn't the ambiguity inherent in the language, it's the cleverness inherent in the linguist.

Rotokan Revelations

Franny Irchow
A.R. McHair Institute for Armchair Linguistics, South Carolina

Rotokas is a Papuan language of New Guinea known for its very small and not particularly distinctive phoneme set. The wide variation in pronunciation has led to not-so-specific descriptions, such as declaring the voiced consonants (commonly written as V/v, R/r, and G/g in the Rotokas alphabet) to be "allophonic sets": [β, b, m], [ɾ, n, l, d], and [g, ɣ, ŋ].

Also of note, while Rotokas has a vowel-length distinction, it has (or is claimed to have—we shall see!) no other suprasegmental distinctions.

Finally, early investigators (Firchow & Firchow, 1969—no relation) noted an unusual conditioning environment for nasal allophones.

> [In the Central Rotokas dialect] ... nasals are rarely heard except when a native speaker is trying to imitate a foreigner's attempt to speak Rotokas. In this case the nasals are used in the mimicry whether they were pronounced by the foreign speaker or not.

All of these facts are interesting in and of themselves, but for a while now I have been Sitting and Thinking™ in our offices at the A.R. McHair Institute, waiting for a single unified theory to explain these disparate facts. Finally, it came to me. The key to unlocking the mystery lies in the phrase "nasals are used in the mimicry whether they were pronounced by the foreign speaker or not."

Eureka!

If one is not particularly forgiving of foreigners' generally feeble attempts to speak one's language, what is the defining characteristic of such speech? Simple: foreigners generally do not speak one's language very well.

If one is not particularly forgiving of those who do not speak a language "properly", what characteristics are generally attributed to such people? Simple: stupidity, laziness, or ineptitude.

So, why would a speaker of Rotokas use nasals in the mimicry of foreign speakers? For the same reason that a rude Northerner in the U.S. might use exaggeratedly slurred pronunciation and non-standard grammar in an incorrect and absurdist dialect mélange when mimicking a Southerner. ("Ah cain't unnerstan nuthin' y'all done been sayin cuz y'all might ought to be speakin' funneh.") The reason? Simple: mockery.

> ### WOULD YOU LIKE SPAGHETTI OR LASAGNA FOR DINNER?
>
> Classical Generative Phonologist: "Whether it's spaghetti or lasagna will be predictable from context. Give me either one, and call it 'pasta.'"

My conclusion? Simple: manner of articulation in Rotokas is a suprasegmental feature, with nasality indicating sarcasm or mockery.

Discerning the meaning of fricativization or liquefaction of voiced consonants will have to be

---

* No really. We are not making this up.

left to another scholar, though introspection on this matter suggests that likely candidates include indicating anger, doubt, irrealis, teleology, contempt, sluggishness, or the need for pizza.

Note: Many apologies to my colleagues at A.R. McHair for the excess tardiness of this article—it is two years late! I was unable to conclude my Sitting and Thinking™ in the usual 30-year span allotted for such activities, due to unforeseen circumstances. In particular, ABBA winning the 1974 Eurovision Song Contest, Kīlauea beginning to erupt in 1983, and Sinéad O'Connor ripping up a photo of Pope John Paul II on *Saturday Night Live* in 1992 all caused significant delays. Again, many apologies.

References

Firchow, I. & J., 1969. "An abbreviated phonemic inventory". In *Anthropological Linguistics,* Vol. 11 No. 9.

CHOOSE YOUR OWN CAREER IN LINGUISTICS—PART 26

YOU PUSH THE BIG OBVIOUS BUTTON ON THE DEVICE...

You take a deep breath and push the button. A flash of light envelopes you and you find yourself in a sealed metal room.

After a few minutes, a little green creature with huge black eyes materializes in the room. You are frightened, but curious.

The alien presses a space on the wall, and it becomes a display screen. An image of a rocket ship crashing into a planet appears. "Hinxsho bah glector," says the alien. Next, an image of a planet crashing into a rocket ship appears. "Glectcho bahwah hinxdor," says the alien. A third image, of a rocket ship crashing into a rabbit appears. "Gavagai bahx glectol," says the alien.

At this point your instinctive linguistic analysis takes over. Without thinking, you say, "Glectcho bahwah gavagai?" An image of a rabbit crashing into a rocket ship appears, and the alien, who seems pleased, corrects you: "Glectscho bahwax gavagain."

Suddenly, another alien materializes in the room. He's carrying a dog-eared copy of Akmajian's textbook, *Linguistics.* He says, "Oh, Snurklifer, stop it with the 'gavagai' crap. Just admit that you speak English."

Snurklifer looks at the other alien, then at you. "Oh, all right, Refilkruns, you are such a spoil sport." You notice that, for no obvious reason, they have lilting British accents.

Three days later, you, Snurklifer, and Refilkruns are best buds. They've implanted you with a universal translator neurochip, and taught you 4,675 languages, half of them human, half alien, through hypnosleep. You all laugh together about the idea of a babelfish once more, and they send you home.

You go back to school, and try to get your story into the news. You manage to finish your last semester at school and graduate, but because of your claims about SETI and your new linguistic abilities, the physics department defames you, and the linguistics department disowns you. However, the Sci Fi channel is interested.

After several months of talks, they have to turn down your offer to let them make a movie about your experience. They are, however, impressed with your ability to seemingly create very alien languages on demand. They offer you work on a new series they are developing.

• Take the Sci Fi job. Go to Part 17 on page 135.
• Tell them "no thanks" and try to get a regular job. Go to Part 15 on page 144.

Choose Your Own Career in Linguistics starts on page 301.

THE BEST LINGUISTICS BANDS EVAR!!

Meter, Pause and Mora &
The Rolling Tones

Below are a trio of Nursery Rhymes from Linguistics Land, by children's linguist Yune O. Hūū, II. The first shows the value of phonologizing data, the second introduces young pre-linguists to one of the funner phonological processes, and the third is a gentle introduction to certain suprasegmentals that vex many linguists who are speakers of Indo-European languages. By the way, if you can't explain these to the young pre-linguist reading over your shoulder, you should put the book down and turn in your Linguistics Membership Card.

Phonological Nursery Rhymes from Linguistics Land

Yune O. Hūū, II

There Was an Old Linguist

There was an old linguist who studied !Xóõ.
It had so many phonemes,
she didn't know what to dóõ.
After ignoring the clicks,
phonation, and tones,
She said at last,
"That's not so many phones!"

Low, Low, Lower Your Vowels

Low, low, lower your vowels,
Until they all agree.
Assimi-latory, assimi-latory,
They're now in harmony!

/ini˥ mini˧ maɪni˧ mo˨/
/ini˥ mini˧ maɪni˧ mo˨/
Catch a phoneme by the /to˩/
If it rises, mark the /ton˧˥/.
/ini˥ mini˧ maɪni˧ mo˨/

For the final article in this chapter, we return to Claude Searsplainpockets, who, along with his wife and now frequent collaborator Helga von Helganschtein y Searsplainpockets, describes a very interesting language that undergoes phenomenal phonological reduction. Those wishing to demonstrate their mastery of "The Phonology Test" are invited to verify the proper definitions and orderings of the phonological rules that this [+dynamic] duo present.

How to Speak to Foreigners
An Anthropological Linguistic Study of the ʔɪɯnkt̪lɳɪɵʃt

Claude Searsplainpockets &
Helga von Helganschtein y Searsplainpockets
Somewhere in South America

A Surprising Introduction

In our recent travels to South America, we came across an interesting band of indigenes living in Cayenne, the capital of Guyane. The language they speak, ʔɪɯnkt̪lɳɪɵʃt, is also quite interesting. Our first introduction to ʔɪɯnkt̪lɳɪɵʃt came in the form of a bit of eavesdropping. An American tourist (naturally) was trying to communicate with a local street merchant who was clearly speaking Créole Guyanais, but who probably could have held a decent conversation in French. The American, who seemed to only speak English, kept repeating himself, each time speaking more slowly and more loudly—as if that could help the situation—until his voice was a loud as his Hawaiian shirt.

Before long, many people were staring at the walking Ugly American Stereotype. A nicely dressed, well-groomed young man next to us muttered something under his breath. Neither of us could quite understand it, but we heard enough to recognize an astonishing mix of phonemes. Mr. Ugly American heard it well enough, too, so he asked, "What did you say?" By now we had turned on our tape recorder, and we captured the response, which he said louder this time, but slow and steady:

> IT IS WELL KNOWN
> AMONG LINGUISTS...
>
> A subset of the Xhosa language contains words composed entirely of clicks. This linguistic subset is used almost exclusively in internet videos intended for non-Xhosa-speaking audiences. No one is quite sure what lexemes belonging to this subset mean, as the words are defined only by other words within the subset.

/ʔaɛʔʔɪɑɒʔ snɛudr jɢʊʌɵ estluɵpfɪʊd hmɒɒʒnəiʔʃlɪønkwəuɸl hmbɔærrɒiʔŋ/

The tourist replied, with continued surprising originality, "What did you say?" The young man was becoming agitated now, and this time he replied even louder, but his speech was very rapid:

/aɪ sɛd ju stupɪd mɒnəlɪŋgwəl mɔrɒn/

Well, that was clear enough, even to the Ugly American, who was beyond flabbergasted.

A Surprising History

We followed the young man after he took his leave of the unruly tourist to ask him why he had originally spoken to the tourist in one language, then switched to English—and to learn the nature of the first language with its very large phonemic inventory. What we learned surprised us—both utterances were in the same language(!), called ʔɪɯnkt̪lɳɪɵʃt by its speakers (at least at some speeds).

The speakers of ʔɪɯnkt̪lɳɪɵʃt have all recently come from the rural area surrounding Macapá, capital of Amapá, in neighboring Brasil. Originally Hmpɛoʔəurlrɪə—a member of their relatively small but cohesive group, numbering under 500—came to Guyane on a mixed vacation/job-hunting expedition. Her startling success led her to bring first her husband, Ɛdʒɒøŋ, to Guyane, and then her entire extended family. Within 8 months, every last speaker of ʔɪɯnktʃlŋɪɵʃt had left Brasil for Guyane. The secret to their success in finding employment in Guyane in—of all places—English-language call centers lies in a surprising coincidence.

A Surprising Transformation

Like any language, when spoken at speed some of the phonetic detail of ʔɪɯnktʃlŋɪɵʃt is elided (cf. the infamous English/Slurvian "Djeet?" and "Nodju?"). This process is not well-studied in most languages, but we can assume that, like any other language phenomenon worth studying, it is reasonably regular.

Some of the easily-identifiable (but carefully ordered) high-speed elision rules include:

$$V(V) \rightarrow \emptyset / V \underline{\quad}$$

$$VsC \rightarrow sC / \# \underline{\quad}$$

$$\eta \rightarrow n / \underline{\quad} \#$$

$$[\text{+nasal}] \rightarrow \emptyset / \#[\text{+fricative}] \underline{\quad}$$

$$[\text{+liquid +syll}] \rightarrow \emptyset / [\text{+stop}] \underline{\quad} \#$$

$$[\text{+labial } \alpha\text{-place}] \rightarrow \emptyset / \#h[\text{+nasal } \alpha\text{-place}] \underline{\quad}$$

$$h \rightarrow \emptyset / \sigma \underline{\quad} C$$

$$nk \rightarrow \eta g$$

$$[\text{+fricative}] \rightarrow \emptyset / \underline{\quad} [\text{+nasal}]$$

$$[\text{+fricative}] \rightarrow \emptyset / \underline{\quad} [\text{+liquid}]$$

$$[\text{+retroflex}] \rightarrow \emptyset / \underline{\quad} [\text{+liquid}]$$

$$[\text{+liquid}]([\text{+liquid}]) \rightarrow \emptyset / \underline{\quad} [\text{+liquid}]$$

$$[\text{+cons -fricative} \rightarrow \emptyset / \sigma [\text{+cons -glottal}]$$
$$\text{-approx}] \qquad ([\text{+cons -glottal}]) \underline{\quad}$$

$$[\text{+stop}] \rightarrow \emptyset / [\text{+fricative}] \underline{\quad} \#$$

$$[\text{+click}] \rightarrow \emptyset$$

$$ʔ \rightarrow \emptyset$$

A Surprising Technology

And so the speakers of ʔɪɯnktʃlŋɪɵʃt now find themselves working at English-language call centers in Guyane. Hmpɛoʔəurlriɔ and Ɛdʒɒøŋ managed to "work the system" in such a way that their employer was required to make "accommodations" for their "speech pathology". Namely, incoming calls are digitally sped up, so as to sound like rapid ʔɪɯnktʃlŋɪɵʃt speech. Hmpɛoʔəurlriɔ and Ɛdʒɒøŋ's extremely rapid replies (and those of other ʔɪɯnktʃlŋɪɵʃt speakers) are digitally slowed down, so as to sound like normal-speed English. Everyone is, as the ʔɪɯnktʃlŋɪɵʃt cliché goes, tdɹɔɜkgəɐarldɟ hpɪaŋ‖kr.

Some Unsurprising Conclusions

More research is necessary to unravel the intricacies of this system. Said research will require more and abundant funding.

PEARLS OF WISDOM FROM
STUDENTS OF LINGUISTICS

Some sounds can be an onset or a nucleosis. For example, in some contexts [s] is bisyllabic, whereas [t] is biambic.

SHIGUDO, RELUCTANTLY

SIR EDMUND C. GLADSTONE-CHAMBERLAIN
Professor Emeritus of Linguistic Science
Department of Lexicology and Glottometrics
Devonshire-upon-Glencullen University, Southampton

Aside from the universally deplored "particle," no putative lexical category has a worse reputation than the "adverb." Indeed, there is hardly a linguist today who would stoop to the inclusion of such an utterly meaningless and thoroughly discredited "part of speech" as this one—perhaps it is against this legacy of grade school prescriptive grammar that we rebel with the most extreme vehemence.

And yet, as Sir Edmund C. Gladstone-Chamberlain shows here, even this lowliest of lexeme types may have its day in the sun, the beneficiary of the magnanimity of a language of such unusual character that we may even venture to call it "unique." Shigudo is, without doubt, a beacon of aberrance among the world's morpho-syntactic systems, and Speculative Grammarian *is proud to have published this initial description of its eccentricities.*

Beyond that, though, "Shigudo, Reluctantly" is more than a tremendous contribution to humanity's understanding of the language faculty. It is that, but it is also a story of friendship, scholarship, and steam ships, reaching across the gulfs of culture, language, and anthropological fieldwork to unite good men in a quest for the unfettered linguistic truth. It is a tale of clever analyses in the field, bitter fear in academia, and, ultimately, victory against globe-spanning odds through perseverance, pluck, and more perseverance.*

Figure 1—Shigudo warriors showing off their ceremonial finery.

IN 1963, AT THE TENDER AGE OF 24, I FOUND myself on an expedition deep in the Amazon Basin, up a smallish tributary of the Río Ucayali. There we encountered a well-established tribe of indigenous people, numbering close to 400 and living in relative isolation, who called themselves the Shigudo. Several members of the tribe spoke nearly fluent Spanish,[1] and we were able to communicate quite effectively with them. As our expedition was chiefly

---

* Dr. Gladstone-Chamberlain has transferred controlling interest in the film rights of his gripping tale to *Speculative Grammarian.* Contact our promotions department for more information.

---

[1] By "nearly fluent Spanish", I mean, of course, merely Spanish much better than my own Spanish, being just good enough, and no better, to meet the language requirements for my anthropology degree a small number of years earlier.

anthropological in nature, and the Shigudo were, anthropologically speaking, unremarkable,[2] we only stayed with them long enough to trade for supplies and to wait out a remarkably heavy rainstorm that lasted several days.

The Shigudo were excellent hosts, and generally found us much more curious than we found them. I spent most of my time with the Shigudo in the company of a young man named Shiyatauo, who, eight years my junior, was already expecting his first child. Shiyatauo spoke excellent Spanish, and I,

having a more linguistic bent than my fellows, engaged Shiyatauo to teach me some Shigudo.

The first few lessons I learned were as follows:

1. do ki shiresu
   I am tired

2. do gu shiresu
   you are tired

3. do ku shiresu
   it is tired

4. do ka shiresu
   he is tired

5. do ki shiuado
   I am hungry

6. do ki shisu'u
   I am a boy

7. do ka shisu'u
   he is a boy

8. do ki shilolo
   I run

My very preliminary analysis was fairly unexciting.[3] I wasn't sure if *ki/gu/ku* were pronouns or inflections—the Spanish translation provided for each did not include pronouns, but that didn't really mean anything. *do* looked a little more interesting, since it seemed to mean "be", but *do ki shilolo* puzzled me. The lack of determiner in *do ki shisu'u* held some small promise of interest. The omnipresent *shi*-prefix was confounding, but I'd only been at it for a few moments. I knew I had several days to wait while the storm blew

Figure 2—Shiyatauo, a respected adult member of the tribe at age 16.

---

[2] By "unremarkable", I mean, of course, not very distinct from many other, well-studied indigenous tribes in the area, and thus unlikely to garner academic accolades for the scholar who described them. The expedition I was with was fiercely in support of indigenous rights, but academically quite mercenary.

---

[3] By "very preliminary", I mean, of course, stupidly, foolishly premature. But I wasn't much of a linguist then, and I wasn't yet taking the whole matter very seriously.

over, and I had found a pleasant way to pass the time.

A few more minutes of data brought more interest:

9. do ki shiporu
   I am a brother

10. do ki shiporu ing i'ka
    I am his brother

11. do ka shiporu ing i'ki
    he is my brother

12. do ki shikabayo shilolo
    I ride a horse

Well, I thought, *shikabayo* is clearly and unsurprisingly a borrowing from Spanish *caballo,* and *ing* a preposition or genitive marker. *i'-* might be a case marker of some sort. *shi-* still confounded me. Then everything spun completely out of control.

13. do ki shikabayo shilolo
    ing i'ku, do ku shikabayo,
    do ku shizadi ing i'ka, do
    ka shiporu ing i'ki
    I ride my brother's horse

14. do ki shiporu ing i'ka, do
    ka shipa'e ing i'ku, do ku
    shikabayo, do ki shikabayo
    shilolo ing i'ku
    my brother's horse I ride

Concision is clearly not a feature of Shigudo.[4] Baffled, I asked for a translation of the new phrases independently:

---

[4] By "concision", I mean, of course, the ability to say anything of interest in, say, a number of words, syllables, or morphemes less than or equal to the equivalent in English or Spanish.

15. do ki shikabayo shilolo ing i'ku
    I ride a horse

16. do ku shikabayo
    it is a horse

17. do ku shizadi ing i'ka
    it belongs to him

18. do ka shipa'e ing i'ku
    he owns it

This did not clear up my understanding of Shigudo at all. *shi-* still made no sense (and almost seemed to have no meaning); *do* seemed to be losing its meaning as well.

Figure 3—Young Shigudo warriors participate in "Do Ku Shipunto," or, "Arrows Fired Upwardly," an adolescent initiation rite and test of bravery and archery skills.

Fascinated but perplexed, I spent much of the next three days eliciting as much data as possible from Shiyatauo. I didn't really understand any of it, but I bonded closely with Shiyatauo.

By odd happenstance, the key to my eventual understanding of Shigudo came from Shiyatauo's younger brother, Shiyati'e. Shiyatauo confided to me that Shiyati'e, a mere lad of eight, had been studying Spanish with Shiyatauo for some time, but wasn't making the kind of progress he had hoped for. Shiyati'e had been listening to Shiyatauo and me, and mistaking our exchange for Spanish lessons; at one point he tried to show off his command of the language by translating *do ki shikabayo shilolo* into Spanish before Shiyatauo could.

19. do ki shikabayo shilolo
   estoy caballomente correramente
   I.am horse-ly to.run-ly

Figure 4—"Do Ku Shiflota," or , "The Ceremony," in which present-day Shigudo ensure a good harvest and fast internet connections by burning an effigy of Shipali, the demon-bird who hunts agricultural pests and network gremlins.

At the time, we laughed, and Shiyatauo said of his brother, "Él habla con un acento shigudo pesado." *He speaks with a heavy Shigudo accent.* We left the subject of Shiyati'e's poor translation, and instead debated whether *acento pesado* was the right way to say "heavy accent" in Spanish. Neither of us was sure, and to this day I don't really know.[5]

A few days later, we left in search of anthropologically more interesting indigenes. My notebook was crammed with data I could not understand, and my heart full of admiration for my new friend Shiyatauo.

Months later, looking over my Shigudo data, I saw Shiyati'e's poor translation among the marginalia of my notebook. Like a thunderclap it struck me—Shiyati'e's "poor translation" was in fact the Rosetta stone I needed.

My conclusion, back in my closet of an office in London, was that *shi-* was correctly translated by Shiyati'e as Spanish *-mente* (roughly English *-ly*). Shigudo was, inexplicably, a language with only one open class of words: adverbs. It was a horrible idea, pointlessly whimsical, but the data all fit. I could not construct any historical linguistic path, plausible or not, to evolve any sensible language to such a state. But the data all fit. The data *all* fit.

I spoke briefly of my analysis of Shigudo to my flatmate, a linguistics grad student, and she ridiculed me mercilessly. She also believed that either I had not recorded my data correctly, or that Shiyatauo had lied to me, or both. I did not want to believe I had recorded the data incorrectly, and I *would not* believe that Shiyatauo would have misled me. I resolved to return to the Shigudo and learn the truth.

It took me almost six years to save as much money as I thought I would need to travel around South America, but I still could not afford passage to that far-away continent. Mere months before I was slated to defend my dissertation and, shortly

---

[5] By "I don't really know", I mean, of course, that I have never been bothered to look it up.

thereafter, to get married, I was offered a position[6] in an anthropological expedition to Brazil.

I will admit that I used several people badly in the weeks that followed. I abandoned my academic program and my fiancée in London. And after arriving in Brazil, I abandoned the expedition that had brought me there, setting out on my own to find Shiyatauo and the Shigudo. After nine weeks of trekking, trading, and traveling my way across Brazil, Bolivia, and Peru, I found myself once again in a small boat heading up the Río Ucayali. I was terrified that I would not be able to find the right tributary, or even if I did that I would not be able to find the Shigudo again.

My fears were misplaced. Like a salmon, I knew where to go as if by instinct. Walking into the Shigudo village and seeing Shiyatauo again was like coming home, though I was shocked

A true word is not beautiful and a beautiful word is not true.
—JAPANESE PROVERB

to learn that he now had four children, and was practically an old man at 22. We caught up like old friends should: we reminisced, and we spoke of the future. Shiyati'e had mastered Spanish,[7] and Shiyatauo had become reasonably fluent in Portuguese. Their broadened linguistic horizons crucially informed our discussion of Shigudo.

Despite their linguistic naïveté, their instincts were finely tuned, and our conclusion was as inescapable as it was inexplicable. Shigudo did in fact have adverbs as its only open class of words. The old data made even more sense:

---

[6] By "offered a position", I mean, of course, that I heard about the expedition, then wheedled and cajoled and generally made a pest of myself until one of the expedition members actually quit in exasperation, a mere two days before the scheduled departure. At that point, I was the only remotely qualified anthropologist-cum-linguist available.

[7] By "mastered Spanish", I mean, of course, that his mastery of Spanish had overtaken my own, which had grown even rustier.

20. do   ki   shikabayo
    verb 1sg   horsely

    shilolo ing   i'ku
    runly   prep obj.3sg.neut
    I exist horsely, runningly to it

    do   ku   shikabayo
    verb 3sg.neut horsely
    it exists horsely

    do   ku   shizadi
    verb 3sg.neut belongingly

    ing   i'ka
    prep obj.3sg.masc
    it exists belongingly to him,

    do   ka   shiporu
    verb 3sg.masc brotherly

    ing   i'ki
    prep obj.1sg
    he exists brotherly to me
    I ride it, a horse; it is a horse; it is his; he is
    *   my brother.*

I spent several months living and working with Shiyatauo and Shiyati'e, their wives, and their children. We spent much of our leisure time analyzing Shigudo further. The results were stunning.

Below I present the numbering system, which it is helpful to understand before approaching Shigudo pronouns in their full glory.

21. 1 a   6 ti'ti   11 klo'ti'a
    2 a'a   7 klo   12 klo'ti'a'a
    3 ti   8 klo'a   13 klo'ti'ti
    4 ti'a   9 klo'a'a   14 klo'klo
    5 ti'a'a 10 klo'ti   15 klo'klo'klo

The system is oddly regular and compositional even though it is quite limited. It would merit a study of its own[8] were the rest of the language not so much more interesting.

After considering several translations of Shigudo into Spanish, and probing Shiyatauo and Shiyati'e's intuitions, we collectively came to the conclusion that *do* and *ing* had been bleached of all semantic content, and are best glossed as "verb" and "prep-(osition)", respectively. I translate *do* as "be/exist/have/do" as needed, and *ing* as whatever preposition best fits.

While adverbs carry all of the semantic load of a Shigu-do utterance, the pronouns have a very complex role to play as well, since they have to link subjects and objects from phrase to phrase. In the examples used so far, the number or person of each pronoun was sufficient to link it properly and unambiguously from phrase to phrase, as only *I/me, he/him*, and *it* were used.

> "Language is the most impure, the most contaminated, the most exhausted of all the materials out of which art is made."
> – SUSAN SONTAG

Consider, though, the sentence *Yatauo's father's best friend is Yati'e's wife's father*. I offered the following attempt at a translation to Shiyatauo:

22. *do ka shiyatauo;

    he is Yatauo-ly;

    do ka shiradpe ing i'ka;

    he is fatherly to him;

    do ka shi'au'poru ing i'ka;

    he is best-friendly to him;

    do ka shiradpe ing i'ga;

    he is fatherly to her,

    do ga shimuh ing i'ka;

    she is wifely to him,

    do ka shiyati'e

    he is Yati'e-ly

I was very proud of this utterance, especially the use of the compound *'au'poru* meaning "brother-friend" or "best friend". Yatauo[9] told me that I sounded like an over-eager three year old child, and that my utterance was all but incomprehensible—for all the reasons anyone would find it so: all those *ka*'s are exceedingly unclear. And by stringing things together the way I did, I subtly altered the focus of the sentence as well. What I said was more an attempt at *Yatauo's father's best friend's daughter's husband is Yati'e.*

Yatauo explained[10] that pronouns can be[11] numerically indexed. As the astute reader will have noticed,[12] compounds in Gudo are formed by joining two forms with a glottal stop. Numerically indexed pronouns follow the same pattern: *ku'a, ku'a'a, ku'ti; ka'a, ka'a'a, ka'ti;* For ease of reading, I will translate these forms as *the first one, the second one, the third one; the first guy, the second guy, the third guy,* etc. They could just as readily be glossed it_1, it_2, it_3; he_1, he_2, he_3, etc., but that seems much more difficult for English speakers to process.[13]

---

[8] By "merit a study of its own", I mean, of course, that now that I am retired I do not have the energy to pursue such a study, but would love to see someone else take up the cause.

[9] By "Yatauo", I mean, of course, that I had sufficiently internalized the grammar of Gudo to realize that my good friend's name was actually not *Shiyatauo*, but rather *Yatauo*, which is necessarily and uniformly inflected as *Shiyatauo*. It was much too complicated for me to discuss or even *make* the use-mention distinction in Gudo, but discussing the idea in Spanish, I learned that Yatauo thought of himself as *Yatauo* in his own mind, though he never spoke his name as such in his native tongue.

[10] By "explained", I mean, of course, that we riddled through his native speaker intuitions together until we arrived at the explanation provided.

[11] By "can be", I mean, of course, that they must be whenever clarity requires it.

[12] By "astute", I mean, of course, "even remotely awake".

[13] By "English speakers", I mean, of course, those who are not computer programmers. Those geeks eat this stuff up.

23. do ka'a shiyatauo,
the first guy is Yatauo-ly,

do ka'a'a shiradpe ing i'ka'a,
the second guy is fatherly to the first guy,

do ka'ti shi'au'poru ing i'ka'a'a,
the third guy is best-friendly to the second guy,

do ka'ti'a shiyati'e,
the fourth guy is Yati'e-ly,

do ga shimuh ing i'ka'ti'a,
she is wifely to the fourth guy,

do ka'ti shiradpe ing i'ga
the third guy is fatherly to her

Yatauo's father's best friend is Yati'e's wife's father.

Note that since only one woman is involved (Yati'e's wife) *ga* does not need to be indexed.

Let us look at one last detailed example from the copious data I gathered that spring, all those years ago:

24. do   ki   shi-poru
    verb 1sg adv-brother

    ing   i'-ka
    prep obj-3sg.masc
I am brotherly to him

do   ka   shi-suto
verb 3sg.masc adv-husband

    ing   i'-ga
    prep obj-3sg.fem
he is husbandly to her

do   ku   shi-pero
verb 3sg.neut adv-dog

    ing   i'-ga
    prep obj-3sg.fem
it is dogly to her,

do   ku   shi-traum
verb 3sg.neut adv-lost
it is lostly,

do   ga   shi-arus
verb 3sg.fem adv-want

    ing   i'-ki
    prep obj-1sg
she is wantingly to me,

hla   do-'eks   ki
comp. verb-subjunctive 1sg

    shi-fa'af   ing   i'-ku
    adv-find   prep obj-3sg.neut

that I be findingly to it

my brother's wife wants me to find her lost dog

After I felt that my understanding of Gudo had really progressed to a new level, I knew that it was time to return to London. Upon my return, I fabricated a story about getting separated from the expedition, and wandering lost in Brazil for months. My thesis committee understood, and I received my degree. My fiancée was not so forgiving, as she had already taken up with someone else.

Dejected, I threw myself into my work. This only deepened my depression as I came to realize that no one would believe my data. Only one person did. I told my former flatmate, who had previously derided my initial data, about my adventure. To my surprise, she not only came to believe me, she married me less than two years later!

IT IS WELL KNOWN
AMONG LINGUISTS...

The masked man who appears from the shadows in pubs to scathingly rebut simple-minded linguistic arguments is certainly not Geoffrey Pullum.

I made several more visits to Yatauo and Yati'e and the other Gudo over the years. At the ripe old age of 42, with my wife and two young children in tow, I visited the Gudo yet again. Yatauo, now a tribal elder at 34 and a grandfather several times over, decided he should leave the Gudo for a time and pursue a degree in linguistics at the Universidad Nacional del Centro del Perú. Yati'e followed a few years later, to study archeology.

Figure 5—Yatauo, an honored elder of the tribe at age 34.

I've been sitting on our data for decades, afraid that attempting to publish it would irreparably damage my credibility and my career. But a number of things have happened recently that have changed my stance on this matter. Firstly, I have retired from Devonshire-upon-Glencullen University—thus my career is in many important respects over, and my credibility no longer so important to me. Secondly, Yatauo completed a very detailed grammar of Gudo some years ago, and this article is essentially a mere preface to its publication. Thirdly, Yati'e has recently led an extensive archeological expedition into the jungles around the Gudo village. There he discovered one of those trendy dirt-covered ziggurat temples that have been disguised for years as unexpectedly placed hills.[14] Inside the temple, Yati'e's team unexpectedly discovered a treasure trove of written records in a language obviously closely related to Gudo. Yatauo believes he has deciphered these writings, and has finally uncovered the story of his unusual language.

According to the best translation Yatauo has been able to piece together, about 400 years ago, inspired by a chance encounter with Spaniards, the Gudo developed their writing system and established a monarchy.[15] Seven generations later (about 100 to 110 years), the crown prince of the Gudo had unknowingly managed to emulate the worst of the European monarchs, doling out violent retribution for minor faux pas, both real and imagined. In particular, he had a knack for executing his grammar instructors when they criticized his usage. The *thirteenth* Gudo Royal Grammarian

---

[14] By "discovered", I mean, of course, that he found it using one of those new Electro-Spektral Transmogrification Induction Coils that makes looking for underground chambers such a breeze these days.

[15] By "established", I mean, of course, that they endured a terrible civil war, with the winning faction subjugating the others and then claiming a divine right to have done so.

devised an ingenious scheme to save his own neck. He convinced the prince to blame his grammatical shortcomings on those around him, for failing to provide adequate examples from which he could more easily learn. Shortly thereafter, the prince decreed that there would be a Royal Noun Day, followed by a Royal Verb Day, a Royal Adjective Day, a Royal Preposition Day, and a Royal Adverb Day. On each Royal Day of a particular part of speech, the courtiers and others in the prince's presence were expected to maximize the number of instances of the designated part of speech in their own discourse. Those who pleased the prince with their verbal acrobatics received royal favors. Those who failed to please the prince where often exiled or executed. The royal court was soon dominated by two types of people—the verbally skilled and the silent.[16]

Over time, the need for Royal Noun Day and the others decreased, and almost every day was Royal Adverb Day—the prince apparently never did properly master the use of adverbs. A decade later, the young prince had ascended the throne.[17] The new young king's own son had grown up hearing almost exclusively maximally adverb-heavy Gudo. The new crown prince considered

Figure 6—A Gudo dwelling from the 1960s. Four decades later, Gudo dwellings are pretty much the same, except for the addition of aerial antennae and satellite dishes.

anything else to be a grave insult to his father. He also had trouble understanding anything else himself. And so the new Shigudo language was established, and firmly entrenched after the younger prince, in turn, ascended the throne.[18]

From what Yatauo and Yati'e can piece together, it seems that the ensconcement of Shigudo damaged the previously thriving Gudo tribe beyond repair. The civil war to establish the original monarchy had reduced the Gudo population from around 17,000 to a mere 8,000. Seven generations later, they had rebounded to a respectable 12,000. The establishment of Shigudo, and the royal declaration that it should be used not only in the royal court, but also in the everyday life of all Gudo, wreaked havoc on this once thriving and noble people. Communication failed everywhere. Crops failed. The underpinnings of civilization

---

[16] By "dominated by the verbally skilled and the silent", I mean, of course, that all the others had fled or been killed.

[17] By "ascended the throne", I mean, of course, "committed patricide".

---

[18] By "ascended the throne", I mean, of course, "also committed patricide".

failed. Chaos ensued. Many Gudo fled, to be assimilated into nearby societies, usually without having ever mastered Shigudo (thus explaining the uniqueness of the language in the region). Those who remained were generally the most cunning linguists of the royal court. They eventually rebelled, and established a democracy.[19] For better or worse, most had been raised speaking Shigudo and could not leave it behind, even though the absurd reasons for speaking it had finally evaporated.

LOGICAL FALLACIES
FOR LINGUISTS
Diallelus—Why?... Why?... Why?...
Why?... Why?... Why?...

Epilogue

Now it's more than forty years since my original encounter with Yatauo and the Gudo.

The Gudo, whose numbers have now grown to over 1,000—all descended from royal linguists—have a preternatural knack for learning languages, and are doing well as translators, both throughout Brazil and Peru, and even on the internet. Few others can provide flawless translations from, say, Mohawk into Scottish Gaelic and back—a surprisingly common need in our ever more interconnected world.

I now have young grandchildren of my own, and I delight in watching them continually discover their mother tongue. Yatauo, having attained a previously unheard of life span for the Gudo thanks to his access to modern medicine in Lima, is a newly minted great-great-grandfather, and he despairs at the linguistic change he sees all around him. Several of his great-grandchildren, adults in their mid to late teens with children of their own, speak primarily Spanish and Portuguese,[20] and

have only an academic acquaintance with Shigudo. On the other hand, he has acquired a number of dedicated students who want to learn Old Gudo from the texts he and Yati'e have found and deciphered.

Yatauo also has several great-grandchildren who *are* quite fluent in Shigudo, but the influence of the omnipresent Romance languages is taking its toll. He is not unhappy at the borrowing of many Spanish prepositions to replace *ing* when appropriate. However, many other aspects of Shigudo are changing rapidly in the mouths of these relative babes. Compare the youngest adult generation's typical rendering of *My brother's wife wants me to find her lost dog* to (24) above.

25. ga shi-muh de i'-ka shi-poru
    she wifely   of him,   brotherly

    de i'-ki do shi-arus hla
    of me,   is wantingly that

    ki do-'eks   shi-fa'af
    I   am(subjunctive) findingly

    ku shi-pero shi-traum de i'-ga
    it, dogly   lostly   of her

    *my brother's wife wants me to
      find her lost dog*

Word order is closer to Spanish, and many of the strict rules of Shigudo are flagrantly violated. Phonetically, the vowel in *shi-* is often reduced to a schwa.

In a couple of moderately radical dialects, there is evidence that the schwa is completely gone, and *-sh-* (sometimes reduced further to *-s-* in rapid

---

[19] By "established a democracy", I mean, of course, "committed regicide".

[20] By "speak primarily Spanish and Portuguese", I mean, of course, that while they speak up to twenty other languages fluently, they

---

don't, for example, enjoy doing crossword puzzles in those languages.

speech) is being reanalyzed as something of a *liaison*-like, purely phonetic linking between certain words within the same (usually noun or verb) phrase, without any other significant syntactic or semantic import.

26. gash   muh   de kash   poru
    she   wife   of him,   brother

    de ki   dosh   arus   hla
    of me,   does   want   that

    ki   do-'eksh   fa'af
    I   would   find

    kush   perosh   traum   de ga
    it,   dog   lost   of her

    *my brother's wife wants me to
    find her lost dog*

Yatauo sometimes decries these changes as linguistic degradation, though I know he tries to suppress his prescriptivist tendencies. I, however, see such changes as the Gudo reclaiming their linguistic heritage from the legacy of a mad prince—which is a good thing.

I wish them all well.

IT IS WELL KNOWN AMONG LINGUISTS...

Silphium, a spice used in the cuisine of Rome and other ancient Mediterranean countries, eventually was harvested to extinction because it was used in the secret Roman process for making helium, which legionnaires would inhale immediately before battle to make their war cries more unsettling to the Celts. In the late Imperial period, the Romans were forced to hire Germans and ask them to yodel as back-up strategy.

CHOOSE YOUR OWN CAREER IN LINGUISTICS—PART 24

YOU TELL THE SETI SUPERVISOR ABOUT THE PATTERNS YOU FIND...

The project supervisor doesn't believe you at first, but once you explain the pattern, he sees it clearly enough. You, as an undergrad, get shoved aside in the mad rush to analyze the data. Several grad students on the project get Ph.D.s and high-powered jobs out of it. Several professors get tenure. A few of the more aggressive members of the team get rich. You don't get squat.

So much for physics. You finish your degrees. Now what?

- Go to grad school in linguistics. Go to Part 18 on page 101.
- Just try to get a job. Go to Part 15 on page 144.

Choose Your Own Career in Linguistics starts on page 301.

MURPHY'S LAW FOR LINGUISTS

The one promising but vague forum posting, Linguist List message, or web page on a new language you are studying either has no email address or a defunct email address, and was written by a linguist with a name like "A. Chen", "M. Cruz", "T. Jones", "D. Müller", "D. Peterson", "M. Thompson", or "L33tFurry-PØlÿGlØττïs".

Morphology
The ultimate linguistic niche market

MORPHOLOGY IS THE STUDY OF WORDS. Or, wait, that's not right... No, morphology is the study of affixes. Or is it affix-like things called "morphemes"? No, that's not it... Morphology is the study of how words change form across contexts. Unless the language has no words that change form, in which case morphology amounts, more often than not, to the study of syntax.

On second thought, let's begin anew. Morphology is a subfield of linguistics that, depending on your university's theoretical bent, you may never have heard of. It's widely considered to be the least profitable of the subdisciplines of linguistics,[1] as well as the most controversial.[2] Students of linguistics are urged to avoid morphology at all costs—and, in particular, the dangerous substance associated with morphology: the morpheme.

Should students ignore this advice and undertake the study of morphology, they will be rewarded with a fuller and

---

[1] Taking a brief look at the bottom of the list: 235. Epiepiglottophenomenology (the study of meteorological events that co-occur with the pronunciation of epiglottal consonants); 236. Palindromology (the study of palindromes used in linguistics textbooks); 237. Neurophonology; 238. Morphology.

[2] Taking a brief look at the top of the list: 3. Psammeticology (the study of the linguistic habits of infants isolated from other humans by linguists hoping to gain insights into the origin of language); 2. Linguistophobology (the study of the linguistic habits of those who are deathly afraid of linguists); 1. Morphology.

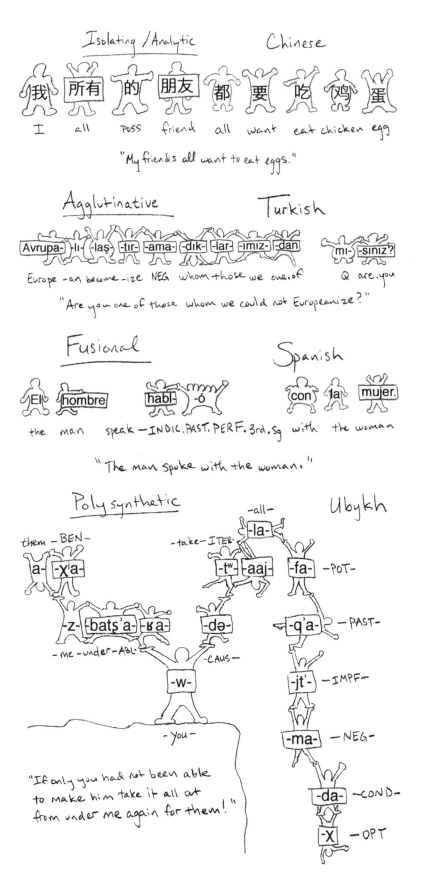

Isolating / Analytic — Chinese
我 所有 的 朋友 都 要 吃 鸡 蛋
I / all / POSS / friend / all / want / eat / chicken / egg
"My friends all want to eat eggs."

Agglutinative — Turkish
Avrupa- -lı- -laş- -tır- -ama- -dık- -lar- -ımız- -dan   mi- -siniz?
Europe / -an / become / -ize / NEG / whom / those / we / one.of   Q / are.you
"Are you one of those whom we could not Europeanize?"

Fusional — Spanish
El / hombre / habl- -ó   con / la / mujer.
the / man / speak —INDIC.PAST.PERF.3rd.Sg / with / the / woman
"The man spoke with the woman."

Polysynthetic — Ubykh
them -BEN-   -take-ITER-   -all-
a- -xʼa-   -tʷ -aaj-   -la-   -fa- —POT-
-z- bats'a- -ʁa-   -də-   -q'a- —PAST-
-me -under-ABL-   -CAUS-   -jt'- —IMPF-
-w-   -ma- —NEG-
- you -   -da- —COND-
-x —OPT
"If only you had not been able to make him take it all out from under me again for them!"

richer understanding of just what morphology is. For, unlike any other subdiscipline of linguistics, morphology is a field that is forced to constantly redefine and justify itself to other linguists. Ensconced somewhere in between the fields of phonology and syntax, morphology finds itself permanently entrenched in unending turf war.[3] A morphologist may present an account of a certain phenomenon in a certain language, and even before asking for questions, up shoots a syntactician, "Bollyfrock! I can account for that data quite simply with Head and Shoulders Structure Grammar—now with Object Control!" And before these last words have been uttered, lo! there blows a phonologist, "Piddlegwump! There is but one lexical affix there, and the rest can be accounted for using Feature Trigonometry, Gestural Linguology and an abacus!" And as these two fall to arguing (and, indeed, come to blows), the morphologist is left to slink quietly out of the room, dragging along whatever insights might have been gained were the world of academic linguistics a different animal from what it is.

Still and all, those who seek to soldier forth should not be discouraged. Indeed, those of us who toil in the hallowed halls of the *SpecGram* commatorium strongly encourage those interested specifically in morphology to pursue it in earnest! After all, though morphologists go on to make very little money and actually lose the respect of their fellow linguists the further they pursue their studies, they do excel at one (and perhaps

BAA-BAA, REDUPLICATION

Baa-baa, reduplication,
Are you truly full?
Yes-yes, sir-sir,
I'm full-full.

Once for the base form
whence meaning came,
And once to intensify—
More-more of the same.

Baa-baa, reduplication,
Are you truly full?
Yes-yes, sir-sir,
I'm full-full.

—YUNE O. HŪŪ, II

only one) endeavor: producing satirical linguistics articles. Indeed, some of the brightest morphological minds the field has to offer[4] have produced some of the best work *SpecGram* has ever seen.

In this chapter, we hoped to bring together a collection of the best morphology articles *SpecGram* has ever published. Unfortunately, we weren't able to get the rights to any of them.[5] That said, we have scraped the bottom of the barrel and found a few articles that are at least *somewhat* tenuously related to morphology. I'm told that there are worse ways to spend an afternoon.[6] So please! Read and enjoy. We can assure you that the syntax section will not poach the articles herein as you read them.[8]

IT IS WELL KNOWN AMONG LINGUISTS...

The creation of the concept of the morpheme is an example of technological serendipity: a number of linguists who were forced by the lack of recording equipment to use shorthand were sufferers of Obsessive-Compulsive Disorder.

---

[3] Sometimes quite literally, as with the sad case of the University of Flippinshire linguistics department. (Our hearts go out to the families of the twelve who were lost that fateful morn.)

[4] Names that are probably quite well known to you: Darrell F. Sacksner, Linda Lingellberry, Snyrþull Snyrþullsson... Oh, and, I suppose I should also mention, a little-known author by the name of Rickard John Washbottom. (Yes, *that* Rickard John Washbottom.)

[5] Like we ever had a shot at publishing a Rickard John Washbottom original in this volume.

[6] Like listening to Rickard John Washbottom prattle on (and on [and on]) about his favorite subject: cross-stitch.[7] Earth to genius: *We want to hear you talk about TMA systems!*

[7] Plus, everyone knows that cross-stitch is the toddler's version of needlepoint.

[8] Because the syntax section has already taken all the best remaining morphology articles, claiming that they parodied nothing but dressed-up syntactic phenomena.

Linguists the world over have known for quite some time that morphemes are dangerous, but rarely have the dangers of morpheme use been so luridly displayed as they have in this public service announcement published by the Council on Morpheme Abuse. Students would do well to heed its warnings!

Morphemes—A New Threat to Society

Council On Morpheme Abuse

What is a Morpheme?

Morphemes are the elements obtained by breaking down the flower of language. They are also present in the roots and stems. It is not yet known exactly what constitutes a morpheme, but it is agreed that almost all verbiage, however innocent it may appear, contains these insidious ingredients.

What are Some Common Terms for Morphemes?

Among those acquainted with morpheme use you may hear the slang terms "morph" or "formation". Uneducated users refer to the morpheme as a "word" (possibly related to "weed"). One type of morpheme is commonly known as "affix".

How are Morphemes Used?

The most common method is to inflect them directly into the corpus. They may, however, be delivered orally or nasally. Morpheme use is generally accompanied by a ritual involving intricate movements of the mouth.

Who Uses Morphemes?

Morpheme use is not restricted to the "lower classes" of society. In fact, it is most conspicuous among university students and faculty. Those who condone this practice, called linguists, maintain that morphemes have been used for thousands of years with no ill effects, but others look on the morpheme as a relatively new invention.

This leaflet was produced by the Council On Morpheme Abuse (COMA) to increase public awareness of the most recent health hazards.

What are the Effects of Morphemes?

Some of the observable short-term effects of morphemes are: slow or distorted speech, extreme apathy or fatigue, and confusion. Long-term effects include acute schizophonia, manic derivation, and delusions of grandeur (claiming to understand unfamiliar languages). These phenomena may occur upon even minimal exposure, so, anyone in contact with a morpheme user should be wary of these symptoms.

Are They Addicting?

That depends on the user. Many people, having once experimented with morphemes, are able to permanently abandon the practice. Others have been known to devote their entire lives to the acquisition of morphemes. Despite what linguists frequently claim, morphemes are not predictable.

Are They Legal?

Unfortunately, legislative officials have not been alerted to the menace of morphemes. Their use has not been outlawed—yet.

Is There a Cure for Morpheme Addiction?

There is presently no cure which has been found to be totally effective. The most promising approach would seem to be isolation, plus complete and immediate withdrawal from morpheme use.

If you need help with a morpheme-related problem or would like to join the campaign to abolish morphemes, contact:

COMA
Lindley Hall 310
Indiana University
Bloomington, Indiana
47401

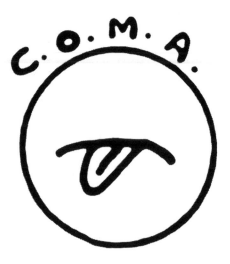

A service of the Council On Morpheme Abuse

WOULD YOU LIKE SPAGHETTI
OR LASAGNA FOR DINNER?

Stratificational Linguist: "Spaghetti, without any sauce. Throw it on the table and I'll write a paper about it."

CHOOSE YOUR OWN CAREER IN LINGUISTICS—PART 38

YOU FINALLY GET YOUR PH.D. ...

You work hard. It takes a few years, and quite a lot of debt in the form of student loans, but eventually you get your Ph.D. You are a Doctor of Linguistics!

Now you need a job. You can continue your purely linguistic path in academia, or you can pursue a job in industry.

• Go for an academic job. Go to Part 39 on page 40.

• Go for an industry job. Go to Part 40 on page 281.

Choose Your Own Career in Linguistics starts on page 301.

There is no better introduction to morphology than to dive head-first into the deep end. As discussed above, morphologists often find themselves in the middle of arguments involving the intersection of syntax and phonology. In this article, Tim Pulju takes us through the history of one of the most famous academic arguments in morphology (here referred to as "phonology"): the morphological variation of the English indefinite article.

Variation in the English Indefinite Article

Tim Pulju
Michigan State University

The problem of variation in the English indefinite article between the forms *a* and *an* has long vexed linguists. In his 1933 classic, *Language*, Bloomfield cited this case as an example of free variation at the morphological level, saying, "There seems to be no principled basis for predicting which form occurs in which contexts." This solution was accepted by the neo-Bloomfieldians in general.

It was Jespersen who first questioned the Bloomfieldian solution. In 1941, he proposed that the syntactic class of the following word determined the form of the indefinite article; specifically, *an* occurred before adjectives, and *a* before nouns. He cited the following examples to support his theory.

1. an old man
2. a board
3. an elegant woman
4. a desktop
5. an orange monkey
6. a photograph

This solution was widely hailed as a breakthrough in a previously misunderstood area. Over the next few years, it came to be generally accepted. However a small minority of linguists tried to poke

holes in the theory. The most significant early attack was based on example 7, below,

7. an orange

where a noun is preceded by *an*. The usual explanation for this anomaly was that *orange*, although a noun, was derived from an adjective and still retained adjectival force. This explanation, of course, assumed a synchronic rather than a historical derivation, since in fact the adjective historically derives from the noun. A slightly different explanation was that *an orange* is a truncated form of the phrase *an orange fruit*.

In 1954, the second major attack, which was actually an extension of the first, was issued, based on example 8, below.

8. a green (as in golf)

The argument ran as follows: if #7 is to be explained by any of the arguments given above, these arguments should also apply to *a green*. According to the theory, the form should be *an green*—this form, though, is in fact ungrammatical. Some adherents of the Jespersenian theory argued that the truncated solution to account for *an orange* likewise accounted for *a green*, since *a green* is not an obvious truncation of any longer phrase; or, alternately, it is a truncation of the phrase *a golf green*, where *golf*, though used as a modifier of sorts, retains its nominal force. However, most linguists considered these arguments weak and

I would like to thank Jim Copeland for valuable comments and suggestions on an earlier draft of this paper. However, I can't, because he made no valuable comments or suggestions on an earlier draft of this paper. As a matter of fact, there was no earlier draft.

admitted that the Jespersenian solution was flawed. Nonetheless, since there was no paradigm which could replace it, the Jespersenian solution was still generally accepted.

So matters stood when, in 1959, Chomsky published his landmark article "The Inadequacy of Immediate Constituent Structure Grammars: Further Evidence from the English Noun Phrase." Chomsky criticized earlier linguists for thinking that the morphological form of the indefinite article was determined by the syntactic class of whatever word happened to follow it. In fact, Chomsky pointed out, the article functions as a determiner of the noun which is its head, and one should therefore expect its morphology to be governed by the noun. After examining the standard data, i.e. those given as examples above, he proposed the revolutionary theory that *an* is the indefinite article used with animate nouns and *a* that used with inanimates. All of the data used so far will be found to comply with this solution. As to the pesky *an orange/a green,* Chomsky proposed that oranges, single living things, are animate in a way that greens, collections of independently living entities not possessed of a collective life, are not. As support for this explanation he presented the following further examples.

9. an elm
10. an apple
11. an elephant
12. a field
13. a sea of people
14. a flat surface
15. a long fence

LOGICAL FALLACIES
FOR LINGUISTS

Argumentum ad personam— Mary, your analysis of Mohawk verbs is clearly wrong. After all, you're ugly and you smell bad.

#9–11 were meant to show that individual living things, including plants, took *an*, while #12–13 were evidence that groups of living things, whether plants or more traditionally "animate", took *a*. #14–15 showed that inanimates took *a*. Significantly, #9–11 and 14–15 were inexplicable by Jespersen's theory.

Chomsky's theory, which seemed to solve the problem so well, was universally accepted. Soon one of its new adherents noted that Chomsky's analysis paralleled the traditional analysis of variation in the Spanish indefinite article, where the form is dictated by the noun's gender. Because the theory seemed to work so well, because its creator was so illustrious, and because it had typological parallels, it was not challenged for many years.

When the challenge came, it originated in typology. Greenberg's work in African languages had convinced him that most linguists had a very limited view of what possible noun classes could be. They classed nouns usually according to gender (masculine, feminine, neuter) or animacy (animate or inanimate). Greenberg believed that further investigation might show that the *a/an* dichotomy reflected a sort of noun class less familiar to European languages, but no less typologically possible. Reviewing the data presented so far, he determined that it was possible to divide up the nouns into classes of "items having significant size in only two dimensions," which took *a*, and "others," which took *an*. For the data already given, Greenberg's theory worked quite as well as Chomsky's. Greenberg next sought out and found the crucial examples below,

16. an orb
17. a manta ray

which contradict Chomsky's theory but support Greenberg's.

The year was 1971; linguistics was a volatile field; and people who had staked their reputations on the Chomskyan theory were not going to take this attack lying down. The first counterattacks concentrated on example #13, *a sea of people;* it was argued that a sea of people had a significant depth as well as length and width. Most reasonable scholars, however, agreed that in a sea of people the only *significant* dimensions are lateral. After all, there are no truly two-dimensional items in the world, only those we treat as such in thought and language. It was not until 1972 that Postal issued the truly damning attack on Greenberg's theory, based on the two examples below.

18. an album
19. a basketball

Plainly, Greenberg's theory could not account for #18–19. On the other hand, neither could Chomsky's, and though attempts were made to rework it, all of them failed. With both Greenberg and Chomsky's analyses invalidated, there began a mad scramble to find some other syntactic basis for what was still considered a morphological problem. Theories were proposed and discarded, more and more examples were considered, but to this day there has been no success. Indeed, many linguists have despairingly returned to the solution offered by Bloomfield and now claim that this is a case of morphological free variation.

Is this the solution? Do linguists delude themselves when they think that there might still be a solution to this seemingly intractable problem? The answer is a resounding no. Indeed, linguists are misguided on their views on this issue, but the neo-neo-Bloomfieldian free variationists are no less so than their colleagues. Their mistake,

the mistake of all who have considered this problem so far, lies in their belief that the variation is morphological in nature. It is an acknowledged fact that the neo-Bloomfieldians concentrated on syntax and semantics to the virtual exclusion of phonology. This sin has persisted in linguistics since the neo-Bloomfieldian days, although lately generativists have been less guilty of it than others. Because of this, no one ever considered the simple, obvious solution which I now present: *an* occurs before words beginning with vowels and *a* occurs before words beginning with consonants. This solution is simple, economical, and accounts for *all* of the data in English, barring performance errors. Note that when *an* occurs before words beginning with orthographic *h*, this *h* is not pronounced; e.g., *an herb.* This non-pronunciation of initial *h* is especially common among French and British people, who can't pronounce English very well.

In conclusion, I should like to urge that this article be taken to heart by those linguists who still ignore phonology in their analyses. As demonstrated here, many seemingly intractable problems can be solved with a little bit of effort in the right direction.

PEARLS OF WISDOM FROM
STUDENTS OF LINGUISTICS

'Pineapple' is neither a kind of apple nor is made from apple, like apple pie & apple strudels which are made from apple.

Though we have a lot of fun here at SpecGram, on occasion we do produce a serious article investigating some fascinating natural-language phenomena. In this study, Lawrence R. Muddybanks introduces us to a heretofore thought to be impossible occurrence: a case of systematic (i.e. regular) suppletion. Suppletion is when the usual slot in a paradigm (e.g. a plural, as in "kid" vs. "kids") is filled by a completely unpredictable word (e.g. "person" vs. "people"). Such occurrences are completely irregular and unpredictable—just as unpredictable as the shapes that suppletive forms themselves take. But could a language exist that makes use of suppletion regularly?

Systematic Suppletion: An Investigation of Ksotre Case Marking

Lawrence R. Muddybanks, Ph.D.

Introduction

Little research has been done on the Ksotre language of northern Lithuania, and that which has been done has been rather unenlightening.[1] The present paper aims to not only expand the body of research on the Ksotre language, but also to introduce a phenomenon found, thus far, in no other natural language on Earth. Without further ado, then, I present the case marking system of Ksotre.

Case in Ksotre

Ksotre has fourteen cases and three numbers, as shown below:

- Number: singular, dual, plural
- Grammatical Cases: nominative, accusative, partitive, genitive, dative, instrumental
- Local Cases: adessive, allative, ablative, inessive, illative, elative, translative, prolative

Furthermore, case and number marking is rather straightforward. There is a mixture of suffixes and prefixes which account for each of the case and number features. They are summarized in the table below:

1. Number:
    - Singular: -Ø
    - Dual: -aw
    - Plural: -e

    Grammatical Cases:
    - Nominative: -Ø
    - Accusative: -ir
    - Partitive: -et
    - Genitive: -uz
    - Dative: -ort
    - Instrumental: -ag

    Local Cases:
    - Adessive: k(e)-
    - Allative: kr(e)-
    - Ablative: ks(e)-
    - Inessive: p(i)-
    - Illative: pr(i)-
    - Elative: ps(i)-
    - Translative: sr(u)-
    - Prolative: l(a)-

Though it may be considered a typological oddity by some that an overt number suffix will follow an overt case suffix, the true mystery of the Ksotre case system lies in the fully inflected form of a given noun. A common example, using the noun *lefked,* "girl," is shown in (2).

---

[1] See, for example, Snodgrass (2001), *Ksotre Phonology: It has one.*

2. | *lefked*, "girl" | Singular | Dual | Plural |
|---|---|---|---|
| Nominative | *lefked* | *lefkedaw* | *lefkede* |
| Accusative | *lefkedir* | *lefkediraw* | *lefkedire* |
| Partitive | *lefkedet* | *lefkedetaw* | *lefkedete* |
| Genitive | *lefkeduz* | *lefkeduzaw* | *lefkeduze* |
| Dative | *lefkedort* | *lefkedortaw* | *lefkedorte* |
| Instrumental | *lefkedag* | *lefkedagaw* | *lefkedage* |
| Adessive | *klefked* | *klefkedaw* | *klefkede* |
| Allative | *krelefked* | *krelefkedaw* | *krelefkede* |
| Ablative | *kselefked* | *kselefkedaw* | *kselefkede* |
| Inessive | *plefked* | *plefkedaw* | *plefkede* |
| Illative | *prilefked* | *prilefkedaw* | *prilefkede* |
| Elative | *psilefked* | *hontordarus* | *psilefkede* |
| Translative | *srulefked* | *srulefkedaw* | *srulefkede* |
| Prolative | *lalefked* | *lalefkedaw* | *lalefkede* |

The paradigm in (2) at first appears rather uninteresting, in that most cells are filled with fully inflected forms that one would expect, given the case and number affix inventory in (1). Looking at the elative dual cell, however, one finds *hontordarus*, which not only has neither the dual suffix *-aw* nor the elative prefix *ps(i)-*, but also appears to bear no resemblance to the stem *lefked* whatsoever. This is, in fact, a case of suppletion, not unlike *go/went* in English, or *ir/va/fue* in Spanish. Were that the end of it, the only interest of this paradigm would be the fact that the suppletion occurs in a rather unexpected place (i.e., one doesn't usually expect to find a second stem used exclusively in the elative dual). Consider, however, the random sampling of native partially declined Ksotre nouns in (3).

After having elicited over two thousand native Ksotre nouns which follow the same pattern, I'm afraid I have no choice but to state that the elative dual form of a given noun in Ksotre will be suppletive. In this way, Ksotre displays a kind of

systematic suppletion that no linguist could ever have predicted would exist in any possible natural language.

Discussion

Presented with data such as that in (3), one is left with a number of questions. First, is it true that the forms are, in fact, suppletive? A quick glance at the elative dual column in (3) should suggest that, indeed, the forms are suppletive. Though, for example, both *etrav* and *wit* contain a *t*, and *saval* and *a* contain an *a*, one would be hard-pressed to come up with a set of transformational rules or OT constraints which would produce the precise

3. | Noun | Acc. Sg. | Dative Dual | Gen. Pl. |
|---|---|---|---|
| ertrav, "bee" | *ertravir* | *ertravortaw* | *ertravuze* |
| topos, "kettle" | *toposir* | *toposortaw* | *toposuze* |
| tsuip, "pen cap" | *tsuipir* | *tsuiportaw* | *tsuipuze* |
| ankuf, "legislature" | *ankufir* | *ankufortaw* | *ankufuze* |
| saval, "student" | *savalir* | *savalortaw* | *savaluze* |
| elalit, "fire" | *elalitir* | *elalitortaw* | *elalituze* |
| ovult, "indecency" | *ovultir* | *ovultortaw* | *ovultuze* |
| mim, "mother" | *mimir* | *mimortaw* | *mimuze* |

Noun	Adessive Sg.	Inessive Dual	**Elative Dual**
ertrav, "bee"	*kertrav*	*prertravaw*	**wit**
topos, "kettle"	*ketopos*	*pritoposaw*	**ilili**
tsuip, "pen cap"	*ketsuip*	*pritsuipaw*	**orso**
ankuf, "legislature"	*kankuf*	*prankufaw*	**deskovurtiva**
saval, "student"	*kesaval*	*prisavalaw*	**a**
elalit, "fire"	*kelalit*	*prelalitaw*	**srostra**
ovult, "indecency"	*kovult*	*provultaw*	**kepim**
mim, "mother"	*kemim*	*primimaw*	**psertravaw**

elative dual form for each lexeme.[2] One could, I suppose, come up with a word and paradigm

---

[2] The elative dual form of *mim*, "mother", is especially vexing, as it's identical to what one would expect to be the elative dual form of *ertrav*, "bee". This, apparently, is entirely coincidental. I tore my hair out (quite literally) for weeks simply trying to get a speaker of Ksotre to admit that the elative dual of *mim* looks as if

analysis, à la Bochner, that would look something like (4).

4. $$\left\{\begin{bmatrix} X \\ N \\ Z,\ Nom.\ Sg. \end{bmatrix} \leftrightarrow \begin{bmatrix} Xir \\ N \\ Z,\ Acc.\ Sg. \end{bmatrix} \leftrightarrow \begin{bmatrix} Xorte \\ N \\ Z,\ Dat.\ Plu. \end{bmatrix} \leftrightarrow \begin{bmatrix} Y \\ N \\ Z,\ Ela.\ Dual \end{bmatrix}\right\}$$

The rule above states simply that any noun of the form *X* associated with the nominative singular and some meaning *Z* (e.g., "bee") will be in a relationship with other forms, such that *Xir* is the accusative singular, *Xorte* is the dative plural, etc., and that, given these relations, one can expect an unpredictable suppletive form *Y* in the elative dual. Of course, the very fact that this analysis is attractive is proof enough that the analysis is wrong, and that lexicalist theories of grammar are misguided. Therefore, the presentation of a real analysis shall have to wait. Let's move on.

The second question one is forced to ask is, even though it would be utterly bizarre to have an empty cell in a paradigm, is it the case that, perhaps, the elative dual forms are simply separate lexemes, as unrelated as "car" and "pickle"? Grammatical analysis and common sense would suggest otherwise, but the fact remains that the suppletive forms just look drastically different. To answer this question, let me present a list of partially declined loan words in (5).

As you can see, the elative dual forms work exactly as one would expect, given the information in (1), but work exactly the way one would *not* expect given the sample paradigms in (2) and (3).[3] The fact, though, that the morphology is available to loan words suggests that the elative dual is, indeed, a cell in the standard nominal paradigm, and that, consequently, the elative dual forms for native Ksotre nouns are *not* separate lexemes, but, rather, count as a case of systematic suppletion.

To conclude, looking at such a system as this one, one has to wonder: will it survive? After all, in everyday discourse, how often does one say that something or someone comes out of two of something? As it turns out, quite a bit. Having

5.

Noun	Acc. Sg.	Dative Dual	Gen. Pl.
televizdep, "television"	*televizdepir*	*televizdeportaw*	*televizdepuze*
intanedep, "internet"	*intanedepir*	*intanedeportaw*	*intanedepuze*
profodep, "balloon"	*profodepir*	*profodeportaw*	*profodepuze*
lingwizdep, "lunatic"	*lingwizdepir*	*lingwizdeportaw*	*lingwizdepuze*

Noun	Adessive Sg.	Inessive Dual	**Elative Dual**
televizdep, "television"	*ketelevizdep*	*pritelevizdepaw*	***psitelevizdepaw***
intanedep, "internet"	*kintanedep*	*printanedepaw*	***psintanedepaw***
profodep, "balloon"	*keprofodep*	*priprofodepaw*	***psiprofodepaw***
lingwizdep, "lunatic"	*klingwizdep*	*prilingwizdepaw*	***psilingwizdepaw***

done a corpus analysis of the local Ksotre newspaper archives, I present to you the likelihood

---

it should be the elative dual of *ertrav*. Unfortunately, none of them had the faintest idea what I was talking about. One, in fact, took great offense, believing that I had suggested that his mother was born of two bees. One black eye and two bruised ribs later, I gave up.

---

[3] The word *televizdep*, it should be noted, may be undergoing a process of cultural assimilation, as it were. Of the nine hundred or so instances of *televizdep* in my corpus, almost two hundred occur without the *-dep* suffix. What's perhaps most interesting is that of the over four hundred instances of the elative dual form of *televizdep*, there are more than ninety occurrences of a native-like elative dual form, *ripusfel*, suggesting that, perhaps, *televizdep* will soon be just like any other native noun of Ksotre.

that a given case and number combination will be used with a random noun in (6).

6.

lefked, "girl"	Singlular	Dual	Plural	Total % (Case)
Nominative	0.2%	1.3%	0.1%	1.6%
Accusative	0.4%	2.2%	0.1%	2.7%
Partitive	0.6%	3.7%	2.1%	6.4%
Genitive	0.6%	0.7%	4.8%	6.1%
Dative	0.9%	0.4%	1.1%	2.4%
Instrumental	0.9%	2.7%	0.1%	3.7%
Adessive	1.1%	2.3%	1.1%	4.5%
Allative	0.4%	2.5%	0.3%	3.2%
Ablative	0.4%	4.5%	0.8%	5.7%
Inessive	0.7%	2.5%	1.3%	4.5%
Illative	0.3%	1.9%	0.7%	2.9%
Elative	0.1%	48.9%	0.1%	49.1%
Translative	1.2%	5.5%	0.5%	7.2%
Prolative[4]	0%	0%	0%	0%
Total % (Number)	7.8%	79.1%	13.1%	100%

As you can see, the elative dual is the most common case/number combination used (48.9%). Further, the dual number (79.1%) and the elative case (49.1%) are the most common number and case, respectively. If the Ksotre newspaper archives can be considered a fair representation of the Ksotre language, then it would appear that the elative dual is quite frequent in everyday Ksotre. My personal experience with Ksotre speakers has served only to reinforce this hypothesis. Consider the most common Ksotre greeting:

7. *Sru-kevdeg-aw v-e-gors-efska istop-ir-aw plimbu kre-numan-ilt-aw!*[5]

/Trans.-cat-Dual 3rd.Dual.Sbj.-3rd.Dual.Obj.-eat-Optative rooster-Acc.-Dual bowl.Ela.Dual All.-daughter-2nd.Dual.Poss.-Dual!/

"Greetings!" (Literally, "May two cats eat two roosters out of two bowls for you two's two daughters!")

Indeed, one may not order a meal, ask for directions, cheer at a football match, or use the restroom without having a full command of all elative and dual forms of each noun in Ksotre. Some early acquisition evidence suggests that children learn the elative dual form of a noun often before they learn that noun's nominative singular, accusative singular or ablative plural forms.[6] So despite the peculiar nature of the suppletive elative dual forms, they appear to be here to stay.

Conclusion

Little has been concluded about the bizarre nature of the elative dual in Ksotre. Ima Morontz (*ms*) theorizes in a yet-to-be-published paper that perhaps the aberrant elative dual forms are, in fact, borrowings into Ksotre.[7] As evidence, he cites the declension of the gender-neutral third person pronoun *rof* (partial paradigm shown in (8)).

The elative dual form *sunnus*, Morontz notes, is identical in form to the elative dual declension of

8.

Noun	Acc. Sg.	Dative Dual	Gen. Pl.
rof, "s/he"	rofir	rofortaw	rofuze

Noun	Adessive Sg.	Inessive Dual	Elative Dual
rof, "s/he"	krof	profaw	**sunnus**

---

[4] I couldn't find a single occurrence of the prolative in any number. I would not even have known that it existed had I not encountered an elderly monk who, as he died in my arms, whispered to me the one verb with which the prolative is used. That verb, however, is so vulgar that I have never heard any other speaker of Ksotre use it, and have had to flee for my life on more than three occasions after asking a consultant if they'd ever heard of the verb in question.

---

[5] The nominative singular form of "rooster" in Ksotre is *rustur*.

[6] See Pearl and Stücke's groundbreaking article, *Children and Language: Two things that don't mix* (2005).

[7] See Morontz (to appear), *Why I'm Better Than You at Linguistics: New evidence from Ksotre.*

the gender-neutral third person pronoun (*sån*) of the Finno-Ugric language Lule Sámi.[8] He contends that the Ksotre language takes part in a kind of linguistic exchange program, borrowing elative dual forms from various languages, and, in turn, sending their native elative dual forms in exchange. Though I hesitate at this time to propose an alternate theory, I'd like to suggest that the metaphor utilized by Morontz, at least, is flawed, in that the Lule Sámi language is neither missing its elative dual, nor employing the "native" Ksotre form *psirofaw*. Additionally, a search for other languages from which the Ksotre have borrowed elative dual forms has, thus far, proved fruitless.[9]

In the opinion of the author, further research is required into the nature of the curious case system of Ksotre before anything definitive can be said. It is my hope, however, that the data presented above will whet the appetites of morphologists worldwide, and give birth to new research programmes centering on this little-studied, yet wonderfully rich and perplexing language.

PEARLS OF WISDOM FROM
STUDENTS OF LINGUISTICS

In 'cleaner', the suffix -er makes it comparative to another toilet.

CHOOSE YOUR OWN CAREER IN LINGUISTICS—PART 23

YOU PASS ON THE PRESTIGIOUS PROJECTS AND FOCUS ON YOUR CLASSES…

Your physics professors are flabbergasted that you would pass up such an opportunity. They no longer think of your interest in linguistics as "fascinating," but more as "distracting from your real work." Your relationship with the physics department chills, and while they let you graduate with your degree, it becomes clear that they have discussed you with their colleagues elsewhere, and grad school in physics is not a possibility.

- Go to grad school in linguistics. Go to Part 18 on page 101.

- Just try to get a job. Go to Part 15 on page 144.

Choose Your Own Career in Linguistics starts on page 301.

MURPHY'S LAW FOR LINGUISTS

Your language will have ≥ 2 different morphemes with similar gloss abbreviations, forcing you to use numbers to separate them.

---

[8] For the curious, a partial paradigm is listed below:

	Nom.	Gen.	Inessive	Elative
Singular	*sån*	*suv*	*sujna*	*sujsta*
Dual	*såj*	*sunnu*	*sunnun*	**sunnus**
Plural	*sij*	*siljá*	*sijan*	*sijas*

[9] There is also historical evidence which suggests that the form *sunnus* derived from an earlier attested form **somnus* via a series of sound changes which affected the entire language. Of course, as this evidence is diachronic, it has no place in modern linguistics.

Since the death of colonialism, linguists have taken over the practice of finding and exploiting previously undocumented peoples in the name of progress. In this study, Prof. J. S. S. van der Fort introduces us to a curious morphological phenomenon in a language previously known as Raartong.*

Examination of the Raartong Language VI—The Intoxicational Affix

J. S. S. van der Fort
Geen van de Bovenstaande University

Given that the present study is the sixth in a series, a short recapitulation of information previously presented in van der Fort (2008), van der Fort (2009) and van der Fort (2010a-c) is in order.

Raartong is the name given to a language spoken by a group of approximately 350 natives of the Brazilian rain forest. They were not in constant contact with Western civilization until very recently. Raartong descends, apparently, from late 18th-century Dutch, but has been overlaid with an Algonquian-like[1] polysynthetic morphology and grammar. We theorize that, sometime prior to the year 1800, a Dutch trade ship was blown severely off-course and made landfall on the Brazilian coast. Furthermore, we suppose that, being stranded far from home, the strapping young Dutchmen of this trade ship found the native girls irresistible, and the rest is history. Raartong likely arises out of the impression of a pre-existing morphology and grammar upon the Dutch language; we can only surmise that this pre-existing morphology and grammar were that of the natives' original tongue, of which no trace seemingly remains in Raartong. In van der Grotekont (2009) this historical situation is alternately analyzed as wholesale borrowing of the Dutch language into a pre-existing morphology and grammar.

PEARLS OF WISDOM FROM STUDENTS OF LINGUISTICS

The meaning of re- as to verb again in 'redo' is not kept in rebeautiful.

Raartong possesses consonantal and vocalic inventories identical to modern Dutch, save for the loss of /p/, which in all cases fell together with /k/, which subsequently became [ʔ] before non-high front monophthongs; furthermore, all monophthongs have become lax, while Dutch diphthongs have undergone monophthongization along utterly unpredictable lines. Finally, all instances of Dutch [x] and [χ] have become *voiceless bilabial pharyngeally trilled nasal affricates,*[2] which possess secondary palatalization before front vowels and velarization before all other vocoids. There is not yet an established phonetic symbol for this consonant, so we simply render it as an empty space.

The Raartong word is composed of a root, which is often verbal in nature (save for when it is not), which is perforce preceded by a *pronominal prefix;* in transitives and certain nouns, the root is followed by a *final,* which is likewise pronominal in nature. For verbs, the prefix typically gives the person and number of an *actor,* while among nouns the prefix denotes the *present possessor.* The final typically imparts the person and number of a *goal-object* for verbs, and a *former possessor* (if any) for nouns. The verbal final may be omitted

---

* It is now known simply as "extinct".

[1] This insight comes courtesy of Leonard Bloomfield (posthumous personal communication).

---

[2] van der Roodbergen has described this particular rare and elusive sound as "like gargling through a foghorn"; we concur.

when the goal-object nominal is incorporated into the verb directly following the root. Between the prefix and root of verbs may come an optional *preverb,* which is often of adverbial meaning (save for when it is not). The prefixes are as follows:

ɪk-	first singular
ɪkɪk-	first plural
ʊ-	second singular
ʊwʊ-	second plural
zɛ-	third singular
zɛzɛ-	third plural

The Dutch gender distinction among third-person pronouns has been neutralized in favor of the feminine, perhaps due to the matrilineal nature of the Raartong tribe.

The finals are as follows:

-kɪ	first singular
-kɪkɪ	first plural
-ʊ	second singular
-ʊwʊ	second plural
-ɛz	third singular
-ɛzɛz	third plural

We theorize that a very strange, perhaps unprecedented, variety of metathesis lies behind the derivation of the finals from the prefixes.

Examples of Raartong verbs and nouns:

ɪkwɔrdgɛk	'I'm getting wrecked out of my gourd!'
zɛzɛadɛlarvlɛk	'They're flying like eagles' (lit. 'eaglely fly')
ʊslɛt[3]	'Your (sg.) wife'
zɛrʊnt	'Her husband'
ɪkslɛtʊ	'My wife, which was formerly yours (sg.), sucka!'

---

[3] In van der Fort 2010b we discuss the light which this and certain other Raartong forms shine upon late 18th-century word usage among Dutch sailors.

The topic of discussion in the present monograph is the so-called *intoxicational affix,* which is a productive element that gives rise to stems denoting the carrying-on of activities while in a mind-altered state. The development and widespread use of this affix is likely due to a cultural peculiarity of the Raartong tribe: each and every tribal member of both sexes over the age of three imbibes, through pipes of wood or clay, the smoke of the dried leaves of a particular rain forest plant called *gɛstrak.* The effect of *gɛstrak* upon human cognition has been described as "timeless, sustained ecstasy," and alternately as "a living nightmare from hell"; in our opinion, it has effects resembling nothing so much as a large dose of LSD on top of a fifth of gin on top of a bad sexual escapade. But still, all tribal members imbibe the substance daily. There is an old saying of the tribe which, translated loosely, goes:

> We smoke two pipes in the morning
> We smoke two pipes at night
> We smoke two pipes in the afternoon
> It makes us feel all right
> (except when it doesn't)

The underlying form of the intoxicational affix is *-gɛk-,* with /g/ dropped after a consonant; it most typically comes after a root (or incorporated nominal, if present) and before any final. It is used chiefly to denote an activity being performed under the influence of *gɛstrak* or a state with co-occurring *gɛstrak* intoxication. Because *gɛstrak* intoxication is so common, word-forms without *-gɛk-* are seldom used; moreover, we had much difficulty in even eliciting such forms from Raartong speakers. They seemingly and simply cannot (or will not) conceive of undergoing the conscious human experience *without gɛstrak.* The lament *zɔndɛr gɛstrak ɪkstɛrft!* "Without *gɛstrak,* I would just die!" is frequently heard. Nevertheless, we have managed to collect enough forms to make the following very surprising semantic comparisons:

ɪkɔkt	'I'm cooking sober and it's boring as hell, someone please kill me!' **vs.**
ɪkɔktɛk	'I'm cooking while wrecked out of my mind, and whee!'
zɛskrɪŋtklɪf	'She jumped off a cliff, in suicidal despair.' **vs.**
zɛskrɪŋtklɪfɛk	'She jumped off a cliff, while trying to fly to the moon.'
ɪknʊktslɛt	'I'm having sex with my wife, and it's the most horrible ordeal of my life!' **vs.**
ɪknʊktslɛtɛk	'I'm having glorious sex with my beautiful wife, aren't you jealous?'
ɪkjagt	'I'm hunting, and having the most oppressive guilt-ridden feelings about slaying innocent animals!' **vs.**
ɪkjagtɛk	'I'm hunting, kill, kill, kill, take no prisoners, grrrrrrr!'
ʊgɪl	'You're (sg.) horny, but you can't even get up the courage to leave your lodge and find some!' **vs.**
ʊgɪlɛk	'You're (sg.) horny, and you're a sexual tyrannosaurus!'

The simple addition or omission of the intoxicational affix can thus have profound semantic effects, as evidenced above. There are doubtless other uses of the affix, which will be detailed in future papers of this series.

References

van der Fort, Karen, "On the Representation of Raartong via Psychedelic Patterns of Tie-Dye T-Shirts": *Journal of the Autumn Institute of Summer Linguistics,* vol. 3, no. 4, pp. 109–113. September 2007.

van der Grotekont, Naaktgeboren, "Why That Addle-Brained van der Fort Is Simply Wrong!": *Regional Journal of Pre-Columbian Philology,* vol. 6, no. 2, pp. 66–70. March 2009.

van der Ongewassen, Anders, "Why Raartong Has Words for 'One', 'Two', 'Five' and 'Six' but Not 'Three' or 'Four'": *Perspectives in Geological Linguistics,* vol. 1.75, no. 3.125, pp. 4–219. December 2009.

van der Roodbergen, Martin, "On the Connection of Nasal Affricates to States of Perpetual Intoxication": *Linguistic Papers in Honor of Timothy Leary,* pp. 77–199. Kakschool University Press, January 2008.

LOGICAL FALLACIES FOR LINGUISTS

Wisdom of repugnance—"Listen to your gut, Mari—you know in your heart of hearts that infixation is morally wrong."

Humans are not the only ones cursed with the terrible burden of vocal communication. As it turns out, Penguin communication systems prove to be just as dull and redundant as human languages. In this article, Robert F. Scott explores the diachrony of Penguin causatives.

Exploring Penguin Causatives

Robert F. Scott
London, England

Penguin is a wide-spread language of the Southern Hemisphere, spanning Antarctic waters and southern coastal regions, and reaching as far north as the equator at the Galapagos Islands. Penguin is historically related to an extensive family of languages including Ostrich, Rhea, Emu, and Kiwi, which probably all descended from a common parent language, reconstructed as Proto-Dodo.

In this paper, we will examine two interesting aspects of Penguin causatives, in hopes that these will shed light on the nature of causative constructions cross-linguistically. The first area of interest is morphological; the second is semantic.

We will begin our discussion with Examples (1) and (2), which illustrate, respectively, a simple intransitive and a corresponding causative:

1. Blim-aŋ   i-gak-di   Perki-am
    ice floe-LOC NEG-rise-PAST Perky-NOM
    "Perky fell off the ice floe"

2. Raplum-di yusu-am [blimaŋ igakdi Perkiam]
    cause-PAST 1sg-NOM
    "I caused Perky to fall off the ice floe"

With great regularity, causatives in Penguin are formed according to the pattern of (2), which we may reformulate as (3):

3. *Raplum* + (CAUSER) + EVENT

Note that overt expression of the causer is optional, and that EVENT may be manifested by any type of clause.

Example (4) is a simple transitive expression, which may be compared with a corresponding causative, (5):

4. I-na-gikan   Perki-am   ikan-an
    NEG-PASS-eat Perky-NOM fish-ACC
    "Perky vomited up the fish"

5. Raplum-di Bruzer-am [inagikan Perkiam ikanan]
    "Bruiser caused Perky to vomit up the fish"

There is, however, another way to express (5), which by-passes the inherent topicality of the grammatical subject and instead places overt topicalization on the direct object "fish" by promoting that constituent's morphological suffix from that for ACC (-*an*) to that for NOM (-*am*). As we see in (6), this allows the caused EVENT to have two participants with identical case-marking; fortunately for Penguin speakers, rigid word order makes semantic relations immediately apparent, and topicalization is thus easily interpretable in such a construction.

6. Raplumdi Bruzeram [inagikan Perki-*am* ikan-*am*]
    "Bruiser caused with respect to the fish that Perky vomited them up"

Adding a locative expression to the causative event of (6), we may see that Penguin also allows for topicalization of oblique NP's by the same means:

7. Raplumdi Bruzeram [blim-*am* inagikan
   Perkiam ikanan]

   "Bruiser caused with respect to the ice floe
   that Perky vomited up the fish on it"

This would be more appropriate, for example, in response to the question "and what about the ice floe?"

As awkward as the free translations provided for (6) and (7) may seem in English, worse is yet to come. In appropriate situational contexts, Penguin may allow for multiple concurrent topicalizations, promoting two or more objects to morphological NOM status. Thus, adding topicalized locative and benefactive to (7), we obtain (8):

8. Raplumdi Bruzeram blimam inagikan
   Perkiam ikanam sulusulam

   "Bruiser caused with respect to the ice floe,
   the fish and the mermaid that Perky
   vomited them up on it for her"

Again, however nonsensical the free translation of (8) proves in English, the utterance was readily interpretable when it occurred naturally in a Penguin conversation, because word order constraints unproblematically clarify the semantic relations among the five nominative-marked nominal participants. To this writer's knowledge, such a striking example of morphologically-encoded topicalization, limited (as the phenomenon is in Penguin) to causative constructions, is unattested among languages previously made accessible for study by the linguistic community.

––––––––––––––––––––

The second interesting observation which may be made concerning Penguin causatives is semantic. As mentioned above, the agent of causation in a Penguin causative is optional; more accurately, agents rarely actually occur in normal speech.

This, of course, would never have caused a moment's discomfort, had I not come to the startling realization that this is the only example of any sort of permissible omission in all of the Penguin language. Phenomena such as Equi-NP deletion, and a host of other types, are of course quite common across the world's languages; but why should Penguin, which allows *none* of the common types of deletion in other circumstances, call for it so regularly in just this one construction type?

One day, the answer suddenly leapt out at me when I happened to notice the striking similarity between the form of the verb "to cause" *raplum* and the word "shark" *soplum*. Strikingly similar roots occur in a large variety of apocalyptic and execratory terms.

I had discovered the answer! Penguin causatives are sort of the moral equivalent of English "the devil made me do it," and causation is normally simply attributed to that which signifies the personification of evil in Penguin culture, the shark. Of course, this indicates that Homo Sapiens are not the only creatures who would prefer to pass the blame off whenever possible—a realization which should prove comforting to all who feel that, in evolving beyond lower life forms, we have in fact lost their natural goodness: they aren't so noble, either!

THE WISDOM OF LINGUISTS
Good meanings come in small morphemes.

Understanding ergativity would have proved helpful in reading the last article on Penguin causatives. In case you've never encountered ergativity in your studies, an explanatory cartoon from Phineas Q. Phlogiston is provided below. If you have any questions, please refer back to the cartoon.

Cartoon Theories of Linguistics—Ergativity

Phineas Q. Phlogiston, Ph.D.
Unintentional University of Lghtnbrgstn

I present the following visual explanation of ergativity (pictured at right).

References

Anderson, Stephen R. (1985). Inflectional morphology. In T. Shopen (Ed.), *Language typology and syntactic description: Grammatical categories and the lexicon* (Vol. 3, pp. 150–201).

Comrie, Bernard. (1978). Ergativity. In W. P. Lehmann (Ed.), *Syntactic typology: Studies in the phenomenology of language* (pp. 329–394).

Dixon, R. M. W. (Ed.) (1987). *Studies in Ergativity.*

Dixon, R. M. W. (1994). *Ergativity.*

Foley, William, & Van Valin, Robert. (1984). *Functional syntax and universal grammar.*

Mallinson, Graham, & Blake, Barry J. (1981). Agent and patient marking. *Language typology: Cross-linguistic studies in syntax* (Chap. 2, pp. 39–120).

Plank, Frans. (Ed.). (1979). *Ergativity: Towards a theory of grammatical relations.*

Schachter, Paul. (1977). Reference-related and role-related properties of subjects. In P. Cole & J. Sadock (Eds.), *Syntax and semantics: Grammatical relations* (Vol. 8, pp. 279–306).

Silverstein, Michael. (1976). Hierarchy of Features and Ergativity. In R.M.W. Dixon (ed.) *Grammatical Categories in Australian Languages* (pp. 112–171).

Of course, the real purpose of linguistics (and, by extension, morphology) is not to analyze novel linguistic phenomena, but to re-tread—again and again and again—the same ground covered by those who have come before.* Keeping with that tradition, Prof. Orange has reanalyzed a well-understood and uncontroversial phenomenon—for which, we're told, he received a fellowship and a new corner office.

A Reanalysis of English *Cat*

Hoam L. E. Orange, Ph.D.
Besterly University

I and a few of my graduate students were sharing a round at the Ecks Bar one night, when we overheard a rather dull conversation taking place at the table behind us. It went something like this:

1. **Gentleman:** "I *do* help out around the house!"
   Young Lady: "Oh really? Name one thing that you've done. Name *one thing!*"
   Gentleman: "Well, obviously if you want me to—"
   Young Lady: "Of course! Here we go again. I ask you for an example, and you conveniently can't remember a single one, and that's *my* fault somehow?!"
   Gentleman: "All right, fine! You know what I did? I did it today, just before you came home: I emptied the cat box."

Of course, the gentleman meant the *litter* box, but his word posed a curious problem I left my students to ponder over. The word "cat" in this sentence is acting more like an adjective than anything else. Even if one argues that it's a noun, one can't deny that there might, indeed, exist a secondary "cat box"—say, a cat-shaped box, or a cat-flavored box—that must be accounted for. Currently, I don't believe the framework employed to describe English morphology is equipped to handle phenomena such as this one. As a result, I decided to sit down and modify it.

So, let's start from the beginning. We have the following pair: *cat* and *cats,* singular and plural. The latter can be separated into *cat* meaning "cat" and *-s* meaning "plural". In order to get the meaning "plural cat" out of *cats,* one has to add the two together, so naturally *cat* by itself cannot mean "cat singular". This argues for the existence of a zero morpheme *-Ø* meaning "singular", which, in addition to solving the current problem, conveniently accounts for similar problematic English nouns (*cradle, filibuster, sludge, jauntiness,* etc.).

At this point it would be nice to say that the category of "number" is accounted for, but there is still work to be done. Consider "cat box". Is it a box for or about a singular cat? Perhaps a herd of cats? That seems rather to be missing the point. Indeed, the point here seems to be that the "cat" entity is being evoked, and that the modified noun should serve for one or many cats. I shall refer to this as the "positive", in that the number of cats equal to or greater than one will be positive. This gives us three numbers for "cat": singular, plural and positive.

THE WISDOM OF LINGUISTS

Don't inflect a word until you say it.

Unfortunately, there is another aspect of number that needs an account. Consider the sentence, "There are no cats in the stove" (cf. *"There are no cat in the stove"). While the word *looks* plural,

---

* In linguistics, this is a practice referred to as "trodding upon the corpses of giants".

the number of cats actually being referred to is zero. The same is true of any number of cats less than zero, as in the following: "My niece took four cats from two cats and ended up with negative two cats" (cf. *"... ended up with negative two cat"). Consider also the sentence, "After the cat tax passed, I was left with negative one cats" (cf. *"... left with negative one cat").[1] This, of course, requires a fourth number: the "negative". Thus, we have four: singular, plural, positive and negative.

While this may adequately account for the number of *cat*,[2] much of the story, so to speak, remains to be told. Consider, for example, the status of *cat* in "The cat hurled itself off a bridge" and in "Mary hurled the cat box at her live-in boyfriend John". In the first sentence, *cat* is nominal, while in the second it's adjectival. All the same, *cat* is not *as* adjectival in that second sentence as it is in "Sally painted her walls very cat".[3] This will require a set of part-of-speech zero morphs. The first, for obvious nominal instances of *cat*, will be "nominal". For the latter two, the terms "non-nominal" and "adjectival" will suffice, the latter for obviously adjectival uses, and the former for those in between nominal and adjectival.

THE BEST LINGUISTICS
BANDS EVAR!!

East 17 Morphomes &
Hëävÿ Mëtäl Ümläüt

Of course, these parts-of-speech morphemes work perfectly well for *cat*, but what of the rest of the English language? Well, it turns out the existence of each of the three of these part-of-speech morphemes can be confirmed independently. Consider the following sentences illustrating three different uses of *fun*:

2. a. "I had *fun* launching cats into space." (*Nominal*)
    b. "I frequently lock my cats in a *fun*house overnight." (*Non-Nominal*)
    c. "It is really *fun* to dress cats up like pickles." (*Adjectival*)

Thus, the analysis is confirmed.

Though my work in this area is preliminary, I did want to share some of what I've discovered about tense. Consider the following sentences:

3. a. "I am sorting cats."
    b. "I've finished sorting all my cats."
    c. "I look forward to a productive evening of sorting cats."

Disregarding number and part of speech, the first sentence is a present tense sentence, the second a past tense sentence, and the third takes place in the future. A *cat* now is different from a cat yesterday, which is, in turn, different from a future *cat*. As these three types of *cat* are inherently different, their presence must also be marked with zero morphs for "present", "past" and "future".

Though we still have quite a bit of work to do with *cat*, our research should be completed within five to six years, at which point in time we can move on to other complex words, like "village", "snout", "biscuit" and "gonad". And even though we can't say much for certain yet, we have confirmed the existence of the following morpheme classes, one of which must be present on every noun (and in the following order):

4. a. **Number:** Singular (-∅), Plural (-*s*), Negative (-*s*), Positive (-∅)

---

[1] I've been informed that certain dialects find this ungrammatical sentence acceptable. These dialects, however, do not conform to the hypotheses I've proposed, and so they will not be considered.

[2] One might, at this point, ask about the dual, trial, tetral, quinqual, sextal, septal, octal, etc. As I hope the tone of this piece will indicate, this investigation is in its earliest stages, at present, and there is still much work to be done.

[3] While this datum was never elicited, it nevertheless illustrates the point I'm making.

b. **Part of Speech:** Nominal (-Ø),
  Non-Nominal (-Ø), Adjectival (-Ø)

c. **Tense:** Present (-Ø), Past (-Ø), Future (-Ø)

d. **Aspect:** Perfect (-Ø), Imperfect (-Ø),
  Perfective (-Ø), Imperfective (-Ø),
  Fective (-Ø)

e. **Case:** Unique (-Ø)[4]

f. **State of Mind:** Depressed (-Ø),
  Significantly Depressed (-Ø),
  Inanimate (-Ø)

g. **Status:** Alienably Possessed (-Ø),
  Inalienably Possessed (-Ø), Free (-Ø)

h. **Evidentiality:** First-Hand (-Ø),
  Second-Hand (-Ø), Non-Evidential (-Ø),
  Hypothetical (-Ø)

And here is a full gloss of *cat* in the sentence, "My therapist berated my cat publicly":

5. *cat*-Ø-Ø-Ø-Ø-Ø-Ø-Ø-Ø
   "cat"-Singular-Nominal-Past-Perfective-
     Unique-Sig.Depressed-Alien.Possessed-
     Sec.Hand

As I mentioned, this research is in its infancy, and more funding is required. I have no doubt that we've but scratched the surface, and that, pending funding, more categories and zero morphemes will be uncovered soon.[5]

LOGICAL FALLACIES FOR LINGUISTS

Argumentum in terrorem—"Either you agree with me, Dulmaa, that Ubykh is polysynthetic, or we have to throw out five years of analysis and start over!"

CHOOSE YOUR OWN CAREER IN LINGUISTICS—PART 20

YOU GO TO GRAD SCHOOL IN COMPUTATIONAL LINGUISTICS...

Uh oh. Suddenly you find out that while most computer scientists don't know much linguistics, and most linguists don't know much about computer science, computational linguists can open a can of whoop-ass on you in either field. You are no longer the big fish in the little pond.

- Buckle down and work hard in your new field. Go to Part 29 on page 142.
- Abandon ship! Leave grad school and get a job. Go to Part 30 on page 197.
- Try to find an easier way. Go to Part 31 on page 226.

Choose Your Own Career in Linguistics starts on page 301.

PEARLS OF WISDOM FROM STUDENTS OF LINGUISTICS

The meaning of the compound words can be arrived at quite easily from their disintegrated parts.

---

[4] Even in a pair of sentences like "I yanked the cat by the tail" and "I yanked the cat by the tail again", the cat itself is experiencing two different sensations, and, as a result, the cases assigned must be different. Thus, following Morontz (2006), we hold that each noun in each sentence receives a case as unique as the sentence itself, and that no two cases are ever repeated.

[5] This research programme has been approved by and has the full support of the Natural Language Research Approval Committee. We shall triumph!

Whenever a hot new framework makes its debut, linguists all over the world come out of the woodwork to try to adapt it to the phenomena they already happen to be studying. Few frameworks, though, have generated the kind of rabid excitement and incomprehensible jabbering that Optimality Theory has. Attempting to capitalize on its success, Professor Hans Forz has attempted to apply an OT framework to the split ergative system of Southern Quiznos. It is presented here for your consideration.

An Optimality-Theoretic Account of Split-Ergativity in Southern Quiznos

Hans Forz

Among linguists, split ergativity has long been recognized as one of the most pervasive impediments to human understanding. A particularly puzzling case is apparent in the language of Southern Quiznos, which has provoked several mutually contradicting analyses. For instance, Bloomfield (1924) suggests that split ergativity in Southern Quiznos is sensitive to animacy. Animate subjects are marked with the nominative, while inanimate subjects carry the ergative marker.

1. a. Bob-o   ham   sub-by
        Bob-NOM   eat.PRS   sandwich-ACC
        'Bob eats the sandwich.'
    b. Sub-br   nja   philly-Ø
        sandwich-ERG   need.PRS   cream cheese-ABS
        'The sandwich needs more cream cheese.'

Bloomfield's observation is contradicted by the following data reported by Hockett (1946):

2. Tja-br   ham   trsk-Ø
    Charles-ERG   eat.PRS   tomato-ABS
    'Charles eats the tomato.'

Hockett proposes that split ergativity in Southern Quiznos does not follow distinctions on the basis of animacy, but on the basis of shape. While sandwiches are usually square in the cultural setting of Southern Quiznos, cheeses come in the traditional shape of small balls. Tomatoes have a similarly round shape.

Hockett's finding has been subsequently criticized by Mithun (1984), who tried to elicit the sentence 'The ketchup soaked the chocolate chip cookie', which to her surprise yielded the nominative-accusative pattern. This marking contradicts both Bloomfield's and Hockett's predictions.

The present paper argues that the seemingly unpredictable split-ergative pattern in Southern Quiznos falls out of three constraints that are ranked relative to each other. Based on these constraints, an optimal output is generated by the speakers of Southern Quiznos.

The first constraint is, quite in line with the proposal of Bloomfield (1924), that animate subject referents should be marked with the nominative case. This constraint will be called the ANIMACY constraint. As the data from Hockett (1946) and Mithun (1984) show, this constraint is violable. A seemingly obvious question that linguists have failed to ask is under what circumstances ANIMACY can be violated. Apparently, other constraints hold in Southern Quiznos that outrank the importance of marking animate subject referents with the nominative case, as shown in (2).

A factor that has been overlooked in much linguistic research is the relevance of color in the case marking of objects. Sandwiches, which are usually brown on the outside, receive accusative case in Southern Quiznos. By contrast, tomatoes and cream cheese are marked with the absolute case. This suggests that object marking in Southern Quiznos is sensitive to the color hierarchy proposed in Berlin and Kay (1969) which is shown in (3).

3. black/white > red > green > yellow > blue > brown

Objects to the right of the color red are usually marked with the accusative case, while objects to the left are marked with the absolutive. The constraint that ensures this marking will be called the RED CROSS constraint, because the marking crosses over at the color red. RED CROSS predicts that black objects will receive absolutive marking, which is confirmed in sentences such as 'Bob hit the chimney-sweep.'

With RED CROSS outranking ANIMACY, many of the problematic data in the literature on Southern Quiznos can be explained, but unfortunately there are still problem cases such as (4), which have been brought up by Lucy (1991).

4. Tja-o ham trsk-ky
   Charles-NOM eat.PRS tomato-ACC
   'Charles eats the tomato.'

Example (4) stands in direct contradiction to the present account, since ANIMACY appears to override RED CROSS. Is this perhpas a dialectal issue? A consultation of Lucy's original field notes shows that the pattern is consistent across speakers of different varieties. However, the consultation also shows that the same speakers resort to the regular marking shown in (2) on other occasions. After checking the dates of the field notes, it became apparent that speakers were using the nominative-accusative pattern on Saturdays and Sundays, while the ergative-absolutive pattern was used between 9 a.m. and 5 p.m. on regular working days. During coffee breaks and on national holidays, some speakers show marginal usage of nominative-accusative marking even at those times. We thus propose a third constraint, which will be labeled the WEEKEND constraint, which outranks both other constraints and thus enforces nominative marking on animate subjects in the spare time of speakers of Southern Quiznos.

The proposed account shows that optimality theory can straighten out even the worst things that languages come up with.

References

Berlin, B. & Kay, P. 1969. *Basic Color Terms.* Berkeley: University of California Press.

Bloomfield, L. 1924. Notes on Southern Quiznos. *International Journal of American Linguistics* 3.

Hockett, C. 1946. Quiznos revisited. *Occasional papers in culinary linguistics* 12½.

Lucy, J. 1991. Tomatoes. Shape and Color. In *International Dictionary of Anthropologists.* New York: Garland.

Mithun, M. 1984. The ketchup soaked the chocolate chip cookie. *Language* 60/4.

THE WISDOM OF LINGUISTS
The meanings justify the morphemes.

Linguistics, as a field, is under constant attack from the hard sciences for being too "touchy-feely". Indeed, at the International Academiad held every four years, Linguistics is barred from competing in scientific competitions, being relegated exclusively to the humanities competitions.* In order to make the field appear more technical to actual scientists, linguists are wont to invent arcane methodologies and contrivances from time to time—things that look "sciencey". One such attempt comes to us from morphology, and in this article, David J. Peterson attempts to explain what all the fuss is allegedly supposed to be about.

What is a Morphome?

David J. Peterson
Consulting Editor of *Speculative Grammarian*

Hi! This is Consulting Editor David J. Peterson. You know, we have a lot of fun here at *Speculative Grammarian,* but in devoting an entire issue (CLX.1) to the controversial yet provocative term "morphome", we felt it was important to include a straightforward, down-to-Earth explanation of exactly what a "morphome" is. We knew there was bound to be confusion, so we felt it would be a good idea to just head all of it off at the pass, and include this piece right at the beginning of the issue. So! If you don't know what a morphome is, or if you feel you do but still have questions, read the article that follows. If you read it and still have questions, feel free to read it again, or to have it translated into Russian.

Anyway, let's sprinkle the biscuits and water the bulldog, shall we?

A Brief History of Morphomes

The term "morphome" was coined (or created or discovered) by linguist Mark Aronoff some time during the year 1994. Wait, that's not right... Let's say it was introduced by Mark Aronoff in 1994 in his book *Morphology by Itself: Stems and Inflectional Classes.* As a matter of

fact, we have a shot of Mark that may have been taken at the precise moment that the idea of a "morphome" occurred to him:

Since that momentous occasion, practically dozens of morphologists have been puzzling over it. Sometimes it seems like no two morphologists define "morphome" the same way—and even those who do end up using (or analyzing) actual morphomes differently.

---

* Some of the events Linguistics has been allowed to fail to medal in: Simile Polo; Team Poetry Slam; Simplificational Onomastics; the Triple Debate; Synchronized Textual Interpretation.

While it would be intellectually irresponsible of *SpecGram* to attempt to define the term "morphome" once and for all, I can, at this point, say one thing with absolute certainty: the definition of "morphome" is *not* "morpheme" (and, honestly, I can't see why anyone would suggest such a thing, as the words are spelled differently. That's like suggesting that "defense" and "defence" mean the same thing!).

Now that that's been settled, we can move on to what morphomes do.

Morphomes: An Explication

Aronoff (2006) provides a corking example that helps elucidate the illusory nature of the wily morphome. I'll do my best to replicate it here.

Say you've got these data...

Present Tense	Past Tense
stand	*stood*
with*stand*	with*stood*
under*stand*	under*stood*

Now, a morphemic analysis of these data would involve a lot of magic wand waving, discontinuous whatnot, or Distributive Morphological hijinks (*"It's all syntax! It's all syntax! I'm in love with Katie Holmes!"*, etc.). Aronoff dispenses with all that, and instead proposes a morphomic analysis.

First, one has to accept that the *meaning* of "stand" is unrelated to either "understand" or "withstand" (i.e. there is no standard derivational process involved here as there is with "download" and "redownload"). If these three aren't semantically related, then they can't be analyzed as "stand" plus prefix. In addition, one must accept that this isn't a standard morphological process—that is, "a" doesn't regularly become "oo" in the past tense for all words (e.g. the past tense of "crap" isn't "croop"). Furthermore, one must accept that this isn't what would happen with

new compounds involving "stand". For example, let's say that we coin a new verb "to music stand", which means "to bludgeon over the head with a music stand". If today I music stand Alec Morantz, for example, tomorrow I will not have music *stood* him yesterday (i.e. today). No indeed, I would have music standed him, and I think this generally holds true for all such compounds.

Okay! If you're still with me so far (and I do recognize that those thinking of the etymologies of "withstand" and "understand" may not be, but remember the Linguist's Motto: "Synchronic is chronic!"), then there's only one final step. First, the "stand/stood" sequence can't be a morpheme (or, at least, it can't be the same morpheme in all three words). Second, the ablaut can't even rightly be called a morphological process, since its application is so limited. Thus, we can conclude that "stand/stood" is a morphome!

Oh, and by that, of course, I mean the phonological "stand/stood" alternation present in all three forms. Or... Okay, not the alternation: The *stem*. But the stem has no meaning, and it's different from the actual *lexeme* "stand"... in which it's present.

Okay, forget that example. I've got a *great* example that should make everything clear.

An Actually Great Example of a Morphome

Okay, let's say you have a language called... Morfomidan. Morfomidan has seven cases (nominative, accusative, ergative, accusative 2, subtractive, fecundive and anavocative), and probably thirty-eight noun classes, and each of these noun classes has five different forms (except for class 27, reserved for animals that can no longer fly, which has six). Anyway, when nouns are tetralized (there are nine different numbers: singular, dual, trial, tetral, plural, paucal, medial, grandal and supersize-al), something very strange happens with certain nouns. Here are some examples (contrasting the tetral with the medial):[1]

Regular Nouns	Medial	Tetral
banana	testestett	testestestt
stone jacket	testessett	testessestt
burnt strudel	testetett	testetestt
broken flashdrive	testettett	testettestt

Irregular Nouns	Medial	Tetral
bolt filter	testessett	testestestt
lint	testesstett	testesttestt
plastic	testessett	testestestt
captive audience	testesstett	testesttestt

As you can see once you strip off the noun class circumfix,[2] the morphomic stem /tess/ alternates regularly with /test/ in the tetral. None of the irregular forms are related semantically, yet they all illustrate the same pattern. Thus, one might refer to /tess/ as a morphomic stem. Remember that this is an element that operates only within the morphology, and not generally in the phonology (for proof of which, note that the alternation is not present in the borrowing "stone jacket").

That's All Folks!

Congratulations! You are now an expert on Aronoff's morpheme. You should now be able to enjoy our special issue dedicated to the morpheme without any trouble. So, happy reading—or, as we would say in Morfomidan, *ttesttesttesstestess-tessesesest testtessetests testsetsessttett blork!*

PEARLS OF WISDOM FROM
STUDENTS OF LINGUISTICS

Inflectional words are easily recognised as their meanings are lucid and stark.

**CHOOSE YOUR OWN
CAREER IN LINGUISTICS—PART 37**

YOU DECIDE TO APPLY TO
NON-MAINSTREAM NON-CHOMSKYAN
LINGUISTICS PH.D. PROGRAMS...

You apply. You get in. You decide to go.

You work hard, but notice that a lot of your fellow grad students (along with some of the professors) are just wackos with a tendency toward anti-authoritarian paranoia. They just reject any mainstream theory uncritically. Those losers annoy you, but the quality colleagues you work with make up for it.

• Get your Ph.D. Go to Part 38 on page 72.

Choose Your Own Career in Linguistics starts on page 301.

IT IS WELL KNOWN AMONG LINGUISTS...

Public inscriptions in Greek in Ptolemaic Egypt took decades to become useful, as the population kept patiently waiting for the monument-builders to add the colors, and then refused to believe the Greeks could be that bland.

---

[1] Oh, this might be a bit confusing, I just realized. Once you know that the /-est/ and /-et/ endings become [-st] and [-t] after stems that end with vowels, though, that should clear everything up.

[2] All nouns in this table except for "lint" belong to the same noun class (the class 18 circumfix on "lint", though, is, of course, irregular).

If you enjoyed this section on morphology, please consider purchasing Pluralses *from Psammeticus Press! Nearly a half percent of the proceeds go to someone who might be involved with morphology, we've heard but cannot confirm!*

Pluralses: On the Use and Abuse of Multiple Plurals

Edited by Trey Jones and G. Edward Johnson
Published 2005, Hardcover, 67 pages. Price: $237.50

Published in collaboration with Sum Random Publishing House, Gaithersburg, MD.

This slim but exciting volume explores the multiple interpretations of supposedly "morphologically redundant" plurals.

Topics include:

- Diachronic Surveys, exploring the history of such alternations as *fish, fish, fishes; person, persons, people, peoples; mouse, mice, mouses, mices;* and *thank, thanks, thanx, thanxes.*

- Synchronic Explorations, surveying the current useses and meaningses of double pluralses in several diverse dialectses of English.

- Spirited Discussion, including the proceedings of the Multiple Plurals Roundtable Discussion Group Conference, *MPRDG-Con XIX: Pocketses: Gollum, the Lord of the Rings, and the Sociolinguistic Status of MP on the Upswing*

- Heated Debate, including sharp point/counterpoint exchanges in which the editors debate the merits of their preferred interpretations of the triply plural form *childrens* (*child + [e]r* (pl.) + *en* (pl.) + *s* (pl.)):

  Children, like cats, are more emphatically plural than most ordinary nouns. Two children are much more than twice as much work to care for as one, and four much more than twice two. I expect to see in the future forms like childrenses with four or more plural markers, as speakers continue to subconsciously grammaticalize this exponential plurality of young humans.

  from "Point: *Childrens* and Exponential Plurality
  —Repeatedly Redundant Morphological
  Markers as Semantic Stress"
  by noted mathematician Trey Jones

Plural marking is binary, not additive or absolute—that is, speakers use plural markers to toggle plurality. Thus, native speakers instinctively compute that doubly plural children *is, logically, no more plural than unpluralized* child *and so move to correct the situation.*

from "Counterpoint: Carefully Correcting
Plurality Parity Imbalances in *Children*
—Telling Triple Toggling Tendencies"
by noted computer scientist G. Edward Johnson

Selected Reviews

"One of the bestest bookses I've never read, the intellectuosity goes straight to your head!"

—Dr. Seuss

"A finely-bound, handsome tome, lovingly and painstakingly written in full reverence of the hallowed, historic tradition of scholarly treatises, which craftily and cunningly explores and explicates complex relationships among fascinatingly convoluted interwoven strands of intellectual achievement in the far-reaching field of... wait... sorry, I've lost it. Can we do another take?"

—Jaques Derrida

"Not overly long or dense, an excellent choice as a topic for a term paper due in less than twenty-four hours." ★★★★⯪

—National Association of Grad Students,
Starred Reviews

An exciting work of scholarly excellence, *Pluralses: On the Use and Abuse of Multiple Plurals,* edited by Trey Jones and G. Edward Johnson, published jointly by Psammeticus Press and Sum Random Publishing House, is on sale now at fine booksellers worldwide, except where taxed or prohibited by law.

Syntax
Pay no attention to those exceptions behind the curtain

'Syntax' refers to the arrangement of words; in its modern form, it typically refers more specifically to the arrangement of words into 'sentences'—a term which many people, particularly people who don't read older manuscripts or student essays, think to be well-defined. You are at this point probably wondering, with ample justification, why this volume is devoting an entire chapter to the subject. "After all," we imagine you commenting, "[c]an't one simply take concepts already introduced in Phonology and Morphology—abstract units, cross-limiting combinatorial possibility spaces (which we heard about even if we didn't know it at the time), the art of rescuing generalizations with an artfully timed null element or infinity and so forth—and leaven the mix with the liberating vital spark of sheer magic pony power that will inevitably be required for semantics, and so achieve the desired result without having to devote vital page-space to what is likely to be an inutterably[1] dull subject?" While we find

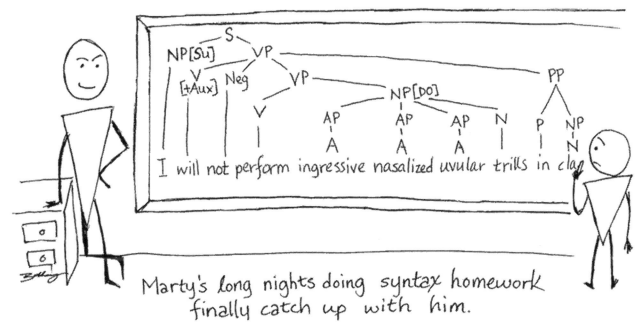

Marty's long nights doing syntax homework finally catch up with him.

much laudable in your response, we feel that you may be lacking several pieces of vital information:

1. The "Syntax Bubble" during which much of the theoretic infrastructure was developed occurred when the number of academic positions in Linguistics in the U.S. was expanding, and linguists were starting to exhaust the supply of undescribed chewy-morphology languages, leaving them with a lot of languages with simple words but complicated syntax to deal with. Vietnamese alone was responsible for giving over twenty distinguished linguists a

There once was an old syntactician
Whose theories had come to fruition
   To describe any clause
   He would shout without pause
"That's a matter of simple addition."
—EDWARD LEAR

---

[1] The more prescriptive among our readers may be crying out at this apparent horrible misspelling of *unutterably*. Fret not, Dear Reader! The word *inutterable* was used by Milton in 1667 in Book II of *Paradise Lost*. Of course, he used *obominable* right next to it, so what does he know? Nonetheless, we like it. You had better like it, too, as three junior copy editors were severely injured in the fight over whether to allow it.

wedgie in 1951, and Chinese was being insufferably smug.

2. Linguists have found that if they describe phenomena in one domain of linguistics in such a way that the description is absolutely useless for other domains, generalizations in their domain don't do much for people working in the other domains. This lack of generalizability of generalizations obviously indicates that the domains were completely separate to start with. Thus, it is possible to develop a syntactic theory that's insulated from colonization by other sub-fields.

3. Anything involving taking a brobdingnagianly massy, messy mush of "this word can go after that one but not after that other one" statements and shoehorning it all into a nice system with shiny jargon appeals very strongly to the human desire to find patterns, and also to market books. Many linguists alphabetize their medicine cabinets.

4. By happy coincidence, much of the foundational terminology introduced during the Bubble was of the sort that predisposes the speaker to think in terms of domination and hegemony—'control', 'government', 'binding', 'command' and the like—and the degree to which formal language scholars will ignore framing once framing has been framed out of their field is truly amazing.

5. You really should not use square brackets at the beginning of the second part of your comment, although we are delighted that you are aware of this useful and all-too-commonly omitted scholarly tool.

A number of scientific and social issues thus conspire to render Syntax a mandatory part of *any* introduction to the field. It has come to explain, for example, why humans have language in the first place,[2] how pronouns link up to antecedents and other pronouns,[3] why some verbs have complements and some don't,[4] and why you can rearrange some words in a sentence but not the same words in what looks like a related but different sentence.[5]

New Speech Disorder Linguists Contracted Discovered!

Yreka Bakery
Egello College

An apparently new speech disorder a linguistics department our correspondent visited was affected by has appeared. Those affected our correspondent a local grad student called could hardly understand apparently still speak fluently. The cause experts the LSA sent investigate remains elusive. Frighteningly, linguists linguists linguists sent examined are highly contagious. Physicians neurologists psychologists other linguists called for help called for help called for help didn't help either. The disorder experts reporters *SpecGram* sent consulted investigated apparently is a case of pathological center embedding.

---

[2] Linguists have found that *homo sapiens* has a language-having ability (*Universal Grammar,* or, onomatopoetically, *UG*) that may or may not be a facet of an other-thing-having-ability, and syntacticians have found that what syntacticians say about it is totally awesome!

[3] Those relations which are explainable by syntactic rules have proven to be related to rules written to describe syntactic structure, and all the ones that aren't are unimportant!

[4] The complement-prohibiting ones are marked as non-complement-having!

[5] There are clear limits on the kinds of boundaries you can move things past; that is, the limits are clear once you stipulate some invisible nodes and invisible landing sites to make everything work out right!

UG-based approaches to Syntax are sometimes a hard sell, but in the following article Maiya Sershan provides a solid piece of empirical support for the position. While some have argued against the validity of her claims, it must be kept in mind that biochemistry is mainly a performance issue; the fact that her model accounts for a number of factors much more simply than facts from molecular biology would indicate is merely a sign that molecular biology is unlikely to produce interesting results.

The Biological Basis of Universal Grammar

Maiya Sershen
Science Editor to the *Houston Hitchin' Post*

(Cambridge, MA)—The strongest support yet for Chomsky's universal grammar—his proposal that human beings are genetically endowed with an autonomous syntax module—has come in the discovery of large protein molecules in neural cells which almost precisely mimic the binary-branched tree structures already familiar to linguists worldwide.

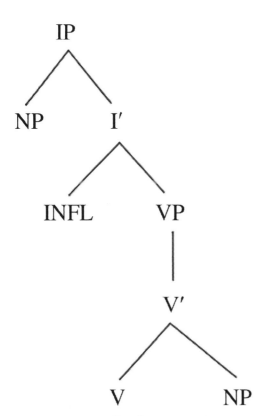

Figure 1: A tree structure for a basic transitive sentence

The discovery also opens up the possibility of bio-chemically altering people's speech behavior—a specter which has some scientists questioning further research until ethical guidelines can be established for the new field.

The first scientist to propose the concept of sentence molecules was brain researcher Carl Wornkey. In a now famous case, Wornkey had one patient, Mr. L., whose entire speech capacity consisted of the ability to repeat just one sentence over and over again: "I'll just have to charge you for the battery". The patient also had abnormally high levels of a certain iro-pyramidal-based protein, found in neural cells near Broca's area in the brain. Wornkey hypothesized that the protein molecule and the repetitive linguistic behavior might have some correlation. "Though clearly at that time, we didn't know what we were onto," Wornkey stated recently. The major breakthrough came when researchers at the Wypiwwit Center for Neural Research extracted the same molecule from the brain of L.'s talking parrot. Since then, biologists have identified the molecular structure of a score of other sentences, including, "Seymour cut the salami with the knife" and "Jack shot himself yesterday, but didn't die today."

Now that linguists know about these molecules, they are teaming up with molecular biologists to discover more about language. One theoretical notion which has already been confirmed is the presence of "empty categories". Empty categories were originally proposed by one of Chomsky's students in 1972 as purely hypothetical elements.

They had no phonetic realizations but were useful placeholders for describing permissible sentence structures. Through molecular analysis, empty categories are now known to be deactivated peptide receptor locations.

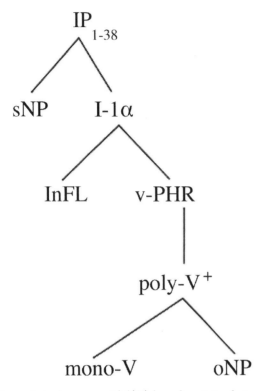

Figure 2: An iro-pyramidal(IP)-based protein chain

Linguist-biologists are also enthusiastic about being able to correlate movement rules with certain enzyme-assisted processes which move molecular appendages from one place on the protein chain to another. For example, one kind of movement—known to linguists as *wh*-movement—allows a question word to be placed at the head of the sentence, as in *What did John say?* (Compare this to the non-moved *wh*-word in *John said what?*) One puzzling feature of this movement rule—once thought to be universal because it occurred in English—is that linguists later discovered it to be absent in at least one language, Japanese. Now, they hope to explain this difference in languages in terms of enzymes present in English speakers but absent in Japanese speakers. "We hypothesize that when listeners are exposed to *wh*-raised structures, as are found in English, the sound waves induce the production of an enzyme, probably in the amino-transferase family," a scientist at MIT explained. "This enzyme in turn assists the molecular movement of the '*wh*-element' to the head of the chain." The hunt for the crucial enzyme is underway at three different laboratories in the U.S. and one in Europe.

This new discovery also apparently answers the question of how a syntactic—rather than semantic or meaning—component could be the basis of language production. "The common—and hence what I term the vulgar or 'weak-minded'—view of language is that speakers begin with what they want to say, then find a way of saying it," said Chomsky in a recent interview. "Our proposal—the 'strong-minded' hypothesis—has always been that syntactic trees without regard to speaker or context lie at the heart of language generation." Such words are now being echoed by molecular biologists. "Tens and perhaps hundreds of millions of these 'sentence molecules' are in the process of being formed, broken down, and reformed at any one time," notes biologist Viola Lionetti. "Through a yet unknown and obviously complex molecular process, only one or a handful of molecules which precisely match what the speaker wants to say at that moment are allowed to penetrate the cell membrane and affect actual speech production."

Not everyone has been enthusiastic about the new findings. A chief critic of the new science has been Sydney Lamb, a noted linguist and well known anti-homunculus advocate. "The idea of there being physical correlates to abstract sentence structures is both repulsive and preposterous," said Lamb, his face flushing. "How in the devil's name, for instance, does he think these molecules are ever converted into actual speech production?"

Chomsky readily admits he has no answer, but is unfazed by such criticism. "For the past thirty years, my linguistics has been on the inexorable march toward truth. 'Sentence molecules' simply provide a heretofore non-observable correlation that we've always been on the right track. Besides, I consider that the burden of proof lies with my critics—they're the ones who must prove that sentence molecules are *not* converted into linguistic production."

Does Chomsky think that speech could eventually be chemically altered so that people could no longer say certain words, like *black* or *Jap?* "No one knows at this point," says Chomsky, who has already been approached by members of the PC crowd. "But in an era when money for linguistic research has been drying up, we believe we now have a handle for getting nearly unlimited funding."

IT IS WELL KNOWN AMONG LINGUISTS...

While context-free grammars could, in principle, form the basis of a system that would allow an AI to pass a Turing test, context-free essays have yet to allow composition students to pass one.

CHOOSE YOUR OWN CAREER IN LINGUISTICS—PART 18
YOU DECIDE TO GO TO GRAD SCHOOL IN LINGUISTICS...

The first big decision you have to make is whether you want to go into a program that follows mainstream Chomskyan linguistics, or if you would prefer to pursue something more of a minority view.

Alas, the two camps are often bitterly at odds. Some people follow mainstream Chomskyan linguistics simply because it is mainstream and Chomskyan—which can border on intellectual dishonesty. Everyone who pursues the minority programs does it because they believe in it, but your career opportunities can be more limited.

• Chomsky! First and best. Go to Part 36 on page 127.

• Do your own thing. Go to Part 37 on page 94.

Choose Your Own Career in Linguistics starts on page 301.

LOGICAL FALLACIES FOR LINGUISTS

Argumentum ad novitatem—"Why are you still doing transformation grammar, Yenghi? Optimally Minimal Nano Syntacticons are the newest, bestest thing now."

Syntacticians, to a much greater extent than most other linguists, have attended to matters of rigor and explicitness, especially when they get to binding and government. (Remember: the safe word is "Ross".) Thus, most major works on syntax include metatheoretic sections—discussions of the way theory works, instead of a particular theory. This helps prevent linguists from losing the forest in the trees, and also is a nice opportunity to frame one's scholarly opposition in ways they probably aren't happy about.

At the pre-internet intersection of grad school samizdat and subconscious academic archetypes there is the Taxonomy of Argument Schemata in Metatheoretical Discussions of Syntax. We have encountered several versions of this quick and valuable overview of some of the main techniques; below is a composite of the most useful.*

A Taxonomy of Argument Schemata in Metatheoretic Discussions of Syntax
or, *Name That Tune*

Anonymous

I. Logical Arguments
   1. If p = ¬p then my position is true.
      Therefore, since p = ¬p, ...
   2. A: ¬p
      B: Since you agree that p, ...
   3. p is absurd; therefore q

II. Now You See It, Now...
   1. Your argument *supports* my position.
   2. I interpret what you said as agreeing with my position.
   3. Let me rephrase that so that it agrees with my position.
   4. I'm aware of these putative counter-arguments, but...
   5. The question you have raised is a pseudo-question.
   6. That's a position, but it doesn't lead anywhere.

   7. I think this is true, but I'm not sure that it means anything.
   8. The burden of proof is on ___.

III. The Reasoned Response
   1. I don't see the argument.
   2. I don't like your example.
   3. That's not a problem in my theory.
   4. A: I'm interested in knowing ___.
      B: That doesn't hurt my argument...
         Next question.
   5. It's my opinion, and it's very true.
   6. I *still* say that...

IV. Papa Knows Best
   1. You say that, but you don't believe it.
   2. You believe this, but you won't say it.
   3. What you really believe is ___, and I agree with you.
   4. Our disagreement is merely semantic.
   5. Don't be misled by the similarity between p and p. It's merely a superficial identity.

V. Audience Participation
   1. Let's take a vote!

VI. The Preemption
   1. You're right, but I said it first.
   2. What you say is wrong, and I said so first.

---

* One of the most well-known versions is by the shadowy collective known as the "Group for a Realistic Approach to Meta-Meta-Argumentation and Reasoning", which appeared in *Son of Lingua Pranca* and dates to the Eighth Annual UWM Linguistics Symposium. Earlier versions date back to at least the Sixth LACUS Forum (Christopher C. DeSantis, personal communication), and later versions abound (Dawn B. Seeley, personal communication). The full lineage of this valuable work is lost to the mists of time and the fuzziness of copier machines.

3. Your position is a notational variant of my theory, but it's wrong.

VII. Advancing to the Rear

1. I knew that analysis was wrong before I proposed it.

2. Of course my analysis is wrong in detail. *All* analyses are wrong in detail.

3. Certainly more work should be done on that.

VIII. The Putdown

1. You can't do it either!

2. That's true but uninteresting in the ___ sense.

3. That's trivial in the ___ sense.

4. If you had read footnote 18, page 122 of my book...

5. A *reasonable* approach to that problem would be...

6. That proposal is only weakly equivalent to my 1963 proposal that...

7. But you haven't captured the generalization.

8. A: What about p?
   B: Have you read ___, or ___, or even ___?
   A: No.
   B: That explains why you would ask such a question.

IX. Clarificatory Obfuscation

1. It remains to work out the details of this, but the overall approach should be clear.

2. I don't command those facts, but to give you a counter-example...

X. The Orthogonal Critique

1. You haven't addressed the problem *I* would have addressed if I were you.

XI. The Dedicated Martyr Retort

1. You don't appreciate what I've been saying.

2. You'll live to *regret* that statement.

XII. Proof by Intimidation

1. There are various possible alternatives by which one could explain ___, but in fact none of them work.

2. But the modern field of linguistics as an academic enterprise is based on assuming the contrary.

XIII. Magic of the Printed Word

1. That will appear in the published version.

2. That appeared in the written version.

XIV. The Empirical Appeal to Language

1. But it's a fact about life in the ___ language that...

2. There is a language...

3. I wonder if that's like the ___ construction in ___?

4. So what if it's not ___. How do you account for the facts of *my* dialect?

XV. The Principled Argument

1. Too powerful! Too powerful!

2. A: Shut up!
   B: No, *you* shut up!
   A: No, *you* shut up!

WOULD YOU LIKE SPAGHETTI OR LASAGNA FOR DINNER?

X-bar theorist: "There's no difference; they're both just Specs of the plate."

Arguments about syntactic structure can frequently appear as arguments about notation. Profs. Luvver and Wright, in the following point-counterpoint exchange, illustrate this well; what looks like a mere notational kerfuffle actually represents competing views of modern syntactic theory as a whole.

The BS Node: Proof That Lines Can Cross

Knotta Gnome Luvver

P. Friedrich, in his article "On Aspect Theory and Homeric Aspect" in *IJAL Memoirs 28*, gives us many, many, many sentences like the one diagrammed in example Figure 1. Now, while this diagrammed sentence is indeed not a reflection of the up-to-the-minute Generative Theory, it does have a resemblance to one of its previous incarnations, and will do for our purposes.

If we consider the semantics of this example sentence, which as we have noted, is representative of many others, we see that many of the words associated with differing categories are in fact all elements of a single category. Indeed, because this one category is so pervasive throughout this sentence, and constitutes the unified theme of the sentence, we hypothesize that there is a single node for this category, which is iconically labelled in the revised diagram in example Figure 2.

From this meager in quantity but overwhelming in quality data, we must conclude that lines in tree diagrams must, in some circumstances, be allowed to cross.

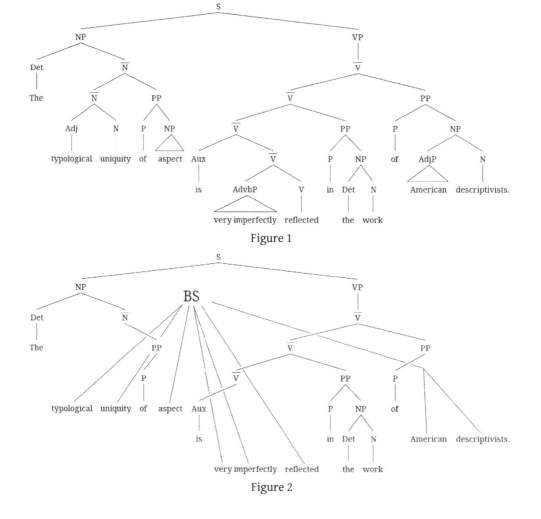

Figure 1

Figure 2

The BS Default: A Reply to Luvver

I. M. Shirley Wright

Luvver, in her brief article "The BS Node: Proof That Lines Can Cross", presents compelling evidence to support the claim that a sentence such as that given in Figure 1 below is correctly diagrammed only if we are allowed to make recourse to a BS node.

The inescapable conclusion seems to be that we must allow lines to cross in tree diagrams. I propose an alternative. Consider, for a moment, the most basic truths of human discourse: might it make just as much sense to assume the assignment to the BS category as the unmarked condition? Then we need only link our trees to words which are other than the BS default, as in Figure 2.

Thus is our prohibition against crossing lines saved.

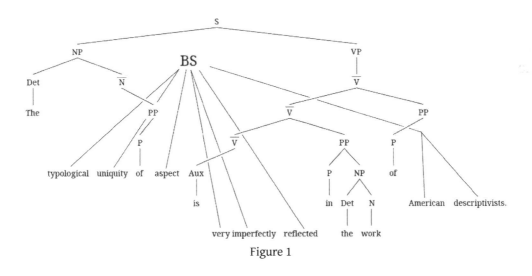

Figure 1

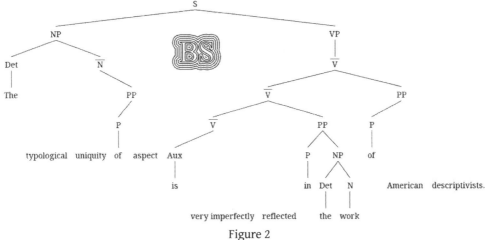

Figure 2

*Lest the reader think that syntax is **wholly** unconcerned with the needs of everyday speakers, we present the following by A. Word; it unites syntax and semantics in ways that might offend the modular sensibilities of some theorists, but we're absolutely certain they're up to the task of modeling it somehow.*

An Analysis of *easy*-Type Adjectives

A. Word

In certain academic circles, there is a well-known category of adjectives, often referred to as *easy*-type adjectives. These include *hard, difficult* and others. The characteristic patterns of *easy*-type adjectives are given in (1).

1. A. Word is *easy* to get along with.
   It is *easy* to get along with A. Word.
   A. Word was very *easy* for Merry to get along with.
   It was very *easy* for Merry to get along with A. Word.

This is **not** the kind of phenomenon we will be discussing. (Though all of the above statements are true!)

Instead, I want to give dating tips to the average unbound morpheme just looking for a good time on a Saturday night.

If, like me, you are a word who is not quite adventurous enough to join a Government & Binding Club, but neither are you a prudish closed-class preposition who sits at home and never makes any additions to their circle of friends, then here is what you need to know.

First, a couple of warnings to those of you new to the Dating Scene in the Big Lexicon:

- Stay away from foreign verb bars. Some of the characters in those places don't know when to quit. Do you really want to be inflected fifty or a hundred different ways in a single night? (Or even thousands, if you end up in the Finnish district!)

- Watch out for mass nouns. They sometimes travel in very large groups of one, and can get out of control after they've had a few drinks.

On the other hand, **adjectives** are usually pretty mellow, and many are just looking for some fun. In particular, many of what I shall call "*easy*-type adjectives" are, well, *easy*.

Below is a quick guide to adjectives you are likely to meet when you go out on a Saturday night.

- *athletic*—Often just looking for something physical. Can be shallow, but then so are you. A good bet.

- *beautiful*—Possibly out of your league, and very likely to look down on you. Pass.

- *chivalrous*—Will treat you very well, but may have moral standards that preclude the kind of hot word-on-word action you are looking for. If not, though, then very likely to treat you especially well. A definite jackpot.

- *cute*—Usually flirty and fun, but may be held back from going home with you by the disapproval of friends. Worth a shot.

- *fun*—As in "looking to have some"; likely you can get some. Bingo!

- *funny*—Not the same as *fun,* so be careful. There is 'nice' *funny* and 'mean' *funny.* 'Nice' will keep you smiling all night. 'Mean' will likely as not turn on you before the night is over—so best not to take that one home.

- *handsome*—May be looking for a conquest—which may be what you are looking to be. An understated kind of *handsome* may be a little sensitive. Try not to break any hearts.

- *hunky*—Sometimes a little too self-involved, but still good for a roll in the syntax on a Saturday night. If not out of your league, go for it!

- *intelligent*—Probably a little shy, but if you can hold up your end of the conversation, will often be wowed by your charms. Definite potential.

- *merry*—Ah, yes. A *merry* time was had by all. Oh! I've said too much.

- *pretty*—Much better prospects than *beautiful*. None of that haughtiness that comes too naturally to the etymologically French. Often down-to-earth, sometimes can be convinced to go back to your place.

- *psycho*—Sounds like a lot of fun talking in the bar—adventurous and a little kinky. But you are likely to find yourself bound up in a grammatically infelicitous number of tight leather inflectional morphemes. Never take *psycho* back to your place.

- *sassy*—May actually just be *sarcastic* with a makeover, so look out for that. Genuinely *sassy* can mean adventure back at your place. Likely to inflect you in unusual but fun ways. Take a shot, you won't regret it!

- *sexy*—Well, that's putting it all out on the table, isn't it? More high-class than *slutty*, but equally likely to just be a tease as to give you a derivational disease. Tempting, but pass.

- *slutty*—Maybe a little *too* easy; definitely not one to bring home to mother. May show you a remarkably good time, but you may also wake up the next morning, hung over, regretful, tied to the furniture, and inflected with a nasty venereal infix. Watch out!

- *sweet*—Possibly too shy, but likely desperate to break out of that shell. Lead the way gently, and the *sweet* will often follow. Make sure you aren't dealing with a sugar substitute, though.

- *voluptuous*—Knows how to have fun and not afraid to do so. Not some fragile little flower afraid to be crumpled, *voluptuous* has all the right curves in all the right places, and knows what feels good. Be respectful and charming, and you will have a night you'll never forget.

- *witty*—Again, may just be *sarcastic* in a better suit. Likely to become tiresome in a long-term relationship; but one night is hardly long-term. Can make you laugh—or at least if you make yourself laugh, then likely to follow you home.

Remember, this is just a guide to give you the confidence you need to approach a good-looking word and incorporate yourself into the conversation. Always use your own best judgement. And *always* practice safe syntax.

PEARLS OF WISDOM FROM
STUDENTS OF LINGUISTICS

There is structural ambiguity if my back is turned.

The Speculative Grammarian *mailroom is constantly inundated by impassioned appeals for more articles linking linguistic research to "measurable indicators of excellence in student outcomes", most of them from the estimable Earnest Blatherskite, Ed. D., who apparently has a large grant for writing them. We are therefore including this sterling example of student writing, which, with its obvious subtextual gestures toward Lacan, Bakhtin, and the later Wittgenstein, we feel is easily of a quality sufficient to meet or exceed the standards of even advanced programs in Educational Leadership.*

Toward a Universal Typology of Noun Phrases

Cynthia Polarczik
The Ohio State University

One of the most noteworthy things about noun phrases in lots of languages is that they contain nouns. Usually at least one noun, sometimes more. Like, in the noun phrase below.

1. The cat's in the cradle and the silver spoon, the little boy blue and the man in the moon.

I think that's a noun phrase, and possible more than one. I'm not really sure, cause I was kind of zoning when my prof explained noun phrases in Ling 101. But he's such a total dork, so I figure if he can do it I can. I mean like come on, this is a guy who wears polyester pants with Adidas. And at least I know what a noun is and theres lots of them in that sentence.

Now, as far as verb phrases, which are a little bit off the topic but I pretty much covered noun phrases already and I've got like almost a whole page left to fill in. Verb phrases I don't really understand but I remember I used to date this guy in high school, and he was taking Latin cause he heard it was an easy A, and he said "verb" is just, like, the Latin word for "word". Which kind of totally blew my mind at the time almost, especially since he said the "v" was pronounced like a "w" which I totally don't get at all. But then (and this is the sort of thing I would never have gotten in high school) I figured out that a verb phrase must just really be like a word phrase, you know? I mean, so a verb phrase is what my prof called a "superordinate category" (I know I got that right, because it's in the book) and a noun phrase is a "subordinate category". If you don't know what that means, you probably didn't take the class, but its like, a noun phrase is like a *kind* of verb phrase. So a noun phrase is a subordinate category, see? And I was like so ticked off at my prof, because I put that on the test and he marked it wrong. Only I guess he doesn't grade the tests himself, he's got this really geeky grad student who does it. And this guys, like, completely 404, okay? Like long hair and doesn't take baths. He's, like so Kurt Cobain. I bet the reason he took points off was he was mad he didn't think of it first. I should complain to the prof, but he's so 404 himself theres no point. I mean, like I really care. I'm taking the class pass-fail anyway, so duh.

Okay, I guess I let my tone "drift" a little bit, which my writing TA says is a problem I have, too. But he's such a total dweeb, too. I mean, the grad students at this university are all so lame. Are they really all like that? And I don't see why he won't let me write the way I talk. Like, even my ling prof, and he says I know English perfect because I'm a native speaker. So who are they to tell me how to write? Its such a total scam.

In this paper, many important aspects about noun phrases were considered and several important conclusions concerning noun phrases were reached. This paper has dealt with many significant factors involved with noun phrases.

Many formal approaches to syntax emphasize the application of simple, fundamental principles to multiple grammatical phenomena as a way to reduce the complexity of a theory and thus enhance its elegance. Bjorn-Bob Weaselflinger, in the following article, engages in a quite robust reduction of this type.

Infinity and Beyond: A Prolegomena

Bjorn-Bob Weaselflinger
Oceanographic Institute of Nevada—Kairo

Introduction

In linguistics, as in many fields, great advances are not always recognized as such; the key to entirely new ways of conceptualizing a field may be hidden away in the paragraphs of an article which, while quite evidently solid in its own right, does not draw explicit attention to the groundbreaking implications of one of its supporting arguments. This principle, I will argue, is admirably illustrated by Hoekstra and Kooij's (1988) article on the Innateness Hypothesis. After a lengthy discussion of apparent violations of the subjacency condition, and various ways of explaining the violations away, the authors state (39)

> There are more apparent violations of subjacency, and to the extent that the condition does make the correct predictions, then, it is hard to see how it could be learned as such. It is reasonable, therefore, to assume that subjacency is part of UG.

While these lines are buried within a paragraph serving only to bridge the discussion of subjacency to a discussion of parameters, we should not overlook their revolutionary import, for they lead inexorably to a basic axiom heretofore unacknowledged in the annals of linguistic theory:

> *The less evidence there is for a principle, the more likely it is that the principle is part of Universal Grammar.*

This assertion, which I shall henceforth refer to as the Less Is More Axiom, or LIMA, opens up

entirely new realms of linguistic research, for it in turn leads to the following postulate, which I shall call the Axiom of Infinitely Null Theory, or AINT:

> *Since there is an infinite number of principles which account for the surface data **none** of the time, there is an infinite number of principles in UG.*

The consequences of this breakthrough for linguistic theory cannot be overstated; at the very least, it renders the possible set of articles on UG principles an unbounded set (though, of course, a well-formed one). The remainder of this paper will explore but one such principle, as an exercise in illustration: the Whankydoodle Constraint.

A New Limitation on Grammars

The Whankydoodle Constraint (henceforth WC) requires that all sentences in strict-syntax contain the form 'whankydoodle' directly dominated by CP. Reinstating the form (reasons for its non-occurrence will be discussed below) would thus lead to sentences such as the following:

1. a. Whankydoodle I think that is a ferret.
   b. We decided whankydoodle that it was a ferret.
   c. Has whankydoodle he finished loading the catapult yet?

Even to a layperson, these sentences are transparently bad, so the LIMA can be considered to be fully validated. For the analyst, the only tasks remaining are (1) accounting for the *non-occur-*

rence of *whankydoodle* in all other English sentences, and (2) accounting for the author's ability to *include* it in 1a-c.

Dealing with the lack of attested examples of CP-dominated *whankydoodle* is relatively simple. A second principle, The KP (kludge phrase) Superposition Constraint (cf. Weaselflinger, forthcoming), layers a second structural description onto every sentence, with the two structural frameworks co-indexing at the phonological interface. In this case, we need only posit that CP-dominated *whankydoodle* migrates to KP, using the same kind of mechanism as, doubtless, an uncountably large number of other elements that likewise don't occur. The facility and frequency with which KP Superposition accomplishes this for an infinite number of elements while remaining undetectable only strengthens its status as a universal element of phrase structure.

Accounting for the presence of the *whankydoodle* element in 1a-c is somewhat more complex, but certainly not egregiously so. A second element, [   ][1], is prefixed to *whankydoodle*, and blocks KP migration via preferential saturation. It is likewise needed for discussion of a wide range of elements, and can thus be said to be independently motivated.

Conclusion

The value of LIMA, AINT, and the WC is obvious: grammars which are governed by these constraints are more limited, and hence more learnable, than grammars without the constraints. Further, a grammar with infinite constraints should be infinitely learnable. The shackles of observability have been forever shattered by LIMA, and linguistic theory can enter an entirely new domain of empiricism.

Works Cited

Hoekstra, Teun, and Kooij, Jan G. 1988. The innateness hypothesis. In: *Explaining Language Universals,* ed. by John A. Hawkins. Cambridge: Basil Blackwell, pp. 31–55.

Weaselflinger, Bjorn-Bob. Forthcoming. KP-superposition indexing and raising to Fnib. To appear in: *OINK Occasional Papers in the Arts, Sciences, and Miscellany,* vol. 16.

THE WISDOM OF LINGUISTS

It's like the particle calling the adverb "a fake part of speech".

---

[1] Unfortunately, since UG does not allow for recursive application of this element, it cannot be prevented from migrating to KP, and is, thus, unexpressible. It is, however, quite distinct from a wide range of other unexpressible elements, like big-[   ], and medicated-[   ].

Not even a school teacher notices bad grammar in a compliment.
—AMERICAN PROVERB

Cartoonist Bethany Carlson presents what would have once been seen as an overly radical vision for simplifying the fundamental nature of the pursuit of syntax. We think nowadays it is called "construction grammar".

Linguistics Nerd Camp

Bethany Carlson

Modern and Historical Graphical Representations of Structural Relationships in Spoken and Written English Sentential Utterances

Nattapoŋ Yunloŋ Seuŋyon
BFE University, Waikikamukau, New Zealand

Because sentences can become rather lengthy, and linguists really feel better about an analysis if they can draw it in some way, especially if the resulting image emits the sweet, subtly intimidating fragrance of science,* various notational formats have played a much greater role in syntax than they typically have in other subfields. In this article Nattapoŋ Yunloŋ Seuŋyon provides an inclusive overview of modern notational systems, while at the same time enabling us to say that we printed something from New Zealand.†

WITH THE MILD SPLASH CREATED IN 2006 BY Florey's small but sincere homage, *Sister Bernadette's Barking Dog,* sentence diagramming (Figure 1) was momentarily *en vogue.* Of course, it didn't last long, as any student of the field could have predicted, because diagramming sentences is generally quite a boring task. The general population will look cursorily at a cleverly diagrammed sentence, in much the way they look at car wrecks on the opposite side of the highway. But they generally don't dig to any depth beyond the surface presentation, for the same reasons they don't properly participate in politics or understand basic scientific principles—laziness and apathy.

Another difficulty facing many graphical representations of sentences is that their formalism is so idiosyncratic that only a highly trained and ideologically uniform inner cadre of faithful adherents (sometimes numbering as low as one) can "properly" use the system. W.S. Clark's "balloon" diagrams (Clark 1860, see Figure 2), generally recognized (Florey 2006) as precursors to the more well-known

Diagrammed Sentence

Figure 1: *The dog bit the man.*

diagramming structures of Reed and Kellogg (Reed and Kellogg 1877), seem to fall into this category. The scientifically literate reader is no doubt re-

Clarkian Balloon Diagrams

Figure 2: *The dog bit the man.*

minded of the so-called "N-ray affair" (Klotz 1980), in which the distinguished physicist René-Prosper Blondlot and his coterie were able to detect a supposedly novel form of electromagnetic radia-

---

* Linguistics is very much a scratch-and-sniff kind of enterprise.
† Will someone please tell Dr. Fenris-Blythesly and her cricket team to stop *haka*-ing us now? It is deeply disturbing, and Schadenpoodle started out paranoid to begin with.

tion, even when key components of their apparatus had been removed by visiting prankster-debunker physicist Robert Wood.

These two facts—shallow interest from the public and the non-transparency of most diagramming schemes—have been recognized, blurred together, and exploited on several occasions by fame-seeking, flim-flamming, faux diagrammers, as we shall explore below.

But first, let us look briefly at two of the most successful forms of graphically representing language. First, Iconographic Diagrammation (Figure 3) has an exceptionally long history, and while some of the structural details of the utterance are typically lost, the major roles and relationships are clear to even the most apathetically casual observer. Seen by some as a strength and by others as a weakness, there is also much room for interpretation and creativity on the part of the diagrammer. This artistic license has no doubt inspired some of the diagrammation schemes

Iconographic Diagrammation

Figure 3: *The dog bit the man.*

Traditional Linguistic Syntax Tree

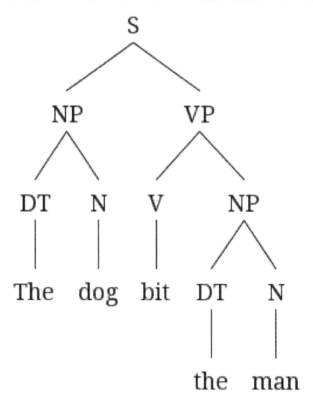

Figure 4: *The dog bit the man.*

that followed it. Second, Traditional Linguistic Syntax Trees (Figure 4) owe their success to their markedly unapathetic, even dedicated, following among linguists. What they lack in transparency to the public, they make up for in clarity to devotees. And while they fall from favor from time to time among the upper echelons of the field, mastering them seems more or less to be permanently ensconced as a right of passage for novices.

In the mid-1960s, nestled all snug in their ivory towers, and spurred by the visions of phrase structure rules and finite state automata that danced in their heads, an unnamed and unknown group of academicians (probably idly noodling around on a chalk board somewhere) gave birth to a sentence diagramming technique known as

"Balloon Animal State Machines" (Figure 5). Clearly the name indicates that the idea was originally presented tongue-in-cheek. However, the model does seem to offer some descriptive and computational power. Several factors contributed to BASM's eventual fade into history.

First, there was an overwhelming tendency by both supporters and detractors of BASMs to shape their diagrams to look as much like balloon animals as possible. Sometimes this desire of format over-ruled the needs of the linguistic content in the diagram—at times so much so that it was difficult to tell whether such "cute" shapes were being designed by overenthusiastic supporters or sarcastic detractors. Luminaries such as Mario Pei, who supported BASMs, and Roman Jakobson, who did not, have admitted in later writings (Jakobson 1973, Pei 1978) to corrupting their linguistic analyses to support their artistic intent when using BASMs.

Further, there was no singular source to state definitively how the scheme worked or should work, and as a result, odd inconsistencies in use cropped up, especially between East Coast and

Balloon Animal State Machine

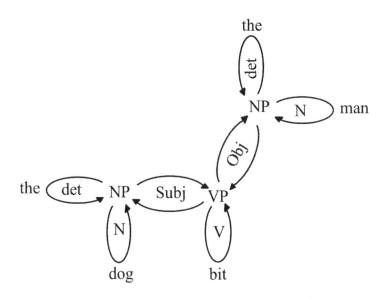

Figure 5: *The dog bit the man.*

West Coast linguists in the U.S. Coupled with the inescapable aura of insincerity surrounding BASMs, this defect in their admirably organic development sealed their eventual ignominious fate.

By 1971 it seemed that a number of enterprising would-be diagrammers, having seen the writing on the wall for BASMs, tried to construct new engines of diagrammation on the foundations of their failing, sometimes even flailing, precursor.

In the spring of that year, a previously unknown author, Hamy Mockson, rocketed onto the scene with his "Undulating Transition Flow Chart" (Mockson 1971). Mockson's description of the UTFC seemed very scientific: the left-right and up-down directions of the arrows, the fraction of a circle used in the arrow, and the second derivative of the arrow (indicating over-arcing vs. under-arcing) were all distinctive and laden with syntactic meaning. The novel representation of compound words generated

Undulating Transition Flow Chart

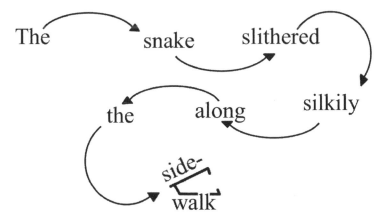

Figure 6: *The snake slithered silkily along the sidewalk.*

much interest. Only one example was given by Mockson, though, and it is reproduced in Figure 6.

By the summer of 1971, there were two main camps of linguists, those who thought UTFCs were useful, and those who thought they were not. Almost everyone who thought about them, though, took them quite seriously. But by the fall, rumors where flying fast and furious that Mockson was a fake, and UTFCs a joke. "Hamy Mockson" is an anagram of, and was for years a suspected (but never proven) pseudonym of, Noam Chomsky. Also, "Hamy" is orthographically and phonetically close to "hammy", and "Mockson" could be analyzed as containing the morpheme "mock"—which was ample evidence to convince Joseph Greenberg that it was all a big send up, and he publicly stated as much in a letter to *Language* (Greenberg 1971). The suddenly obvious contrivance of the word "undulating" in the name of the model, the sibilant alliteration, and snake-heavy example embarrassed many linguists.

Unfortunately for one Walter M. Spanderblau, creator of the "Double-Ruled Rectilinear Syntax Grid", his inaugural paper—"Rectilinear Syntax Grids for Visual Interpretation of Syntactic Structures," (Spanderblau 1971) in which he carefully constructs then devastatingly deconstructs a theory of single-ruled rectilinear syntax grids, ultimately discarding it in carefully-reasoned favor of double-ruled rectilinear syntax grids—appeared in the same volume of *Language,* and was read by almost no one. His initial example (Figure 7) mentioned a giraffe, and looked vaguely giraffe-like. It also appeared on a page facing Greenberg's nasty note on UTFCs.

Neither Spanderblau nor his theory ever recovered. While many linguists, as usual, were hesitant to jump to conclusions as fast as Greenberg, most began to distance themselves from the Mockson/

UTFC discussion, and none would approach Spanderblau's elegant model. In disgust, Spanderblau left linguistics and became a relatively famous electrical engineer, until his untimely death in an accident that occurred while he was overseeing the installation of a lighting system he had designed, somewhat ironically, for a giraffe exhibit at the San Diego Zoo.

For almost two decades, no one in the field of linguistics seemed willing to propose a radical new model to challenge the hegemony of traditional syntax trees. The intertwined shadow of the Mockson and Spanderblau debacles was quite long.

Minimal use of the well-established Venn diagrams to demonstrate simple issues of semantics and scoping (Figure 8) continued through this period.

Finally, in 1989 or so, as a bad case of physics envy was once again sweeping through the field,

Double-Ruled Rectilinear Syntax Grid

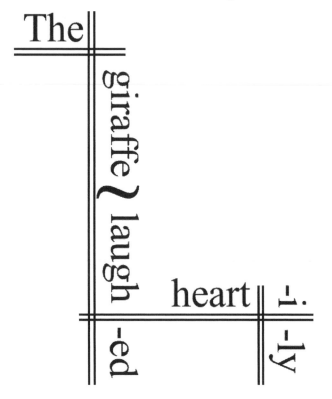

Figure 7: *The giraffe laughed heartily.*

Venn Scoping Diagram

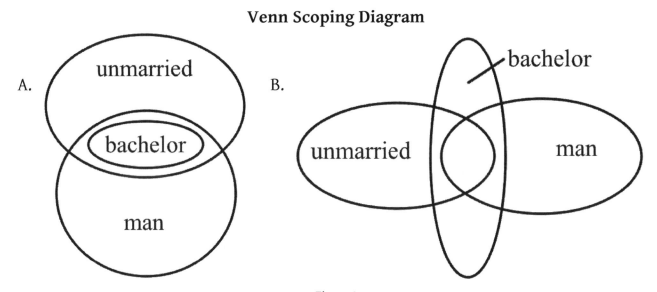

Figure 8
A. *a bachelor is an unmarried man*
B. *an unmarried man is a bachelor*

certain linguists began to feel that traditional syntax trees were old and tired, had been co-opted by computer scientists, and certainly were no longer emblematic of the best that linguistics has to offer. Then came several attempts to, in turn, co-opt certain diagrammatical schemas from seemingly more scientific fields.

The first was the Free Body Role and Reference Diagram (Figure 9), obviously adapted from standard free body diagrams in physics. As very few linguists actually ever really understood Role and Reference Grammar anyway, none were able to intelligently comment on the new sentence diagramming method, and it passed with little notice (Van Valin 1992).

Sociolinguists had more success with their Peer/Pressure Phrase Transition Diagram (Figure 10), adapted from chemistry phase diagrams. Some

Free Body Role and Reference Diagram

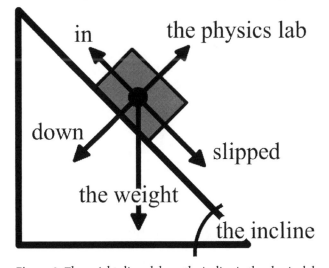

Figure 9: *The weight slipped down the incline in the physics lab.*

Sociolinguistic Peer/Pressure Phrase Transition Diagram

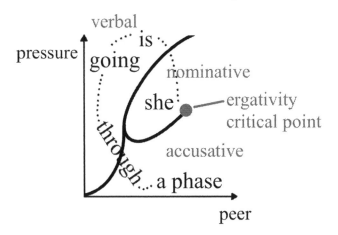

Figure 10: *She is going through a phase.*

Voronoi Semantic Distance Diagram

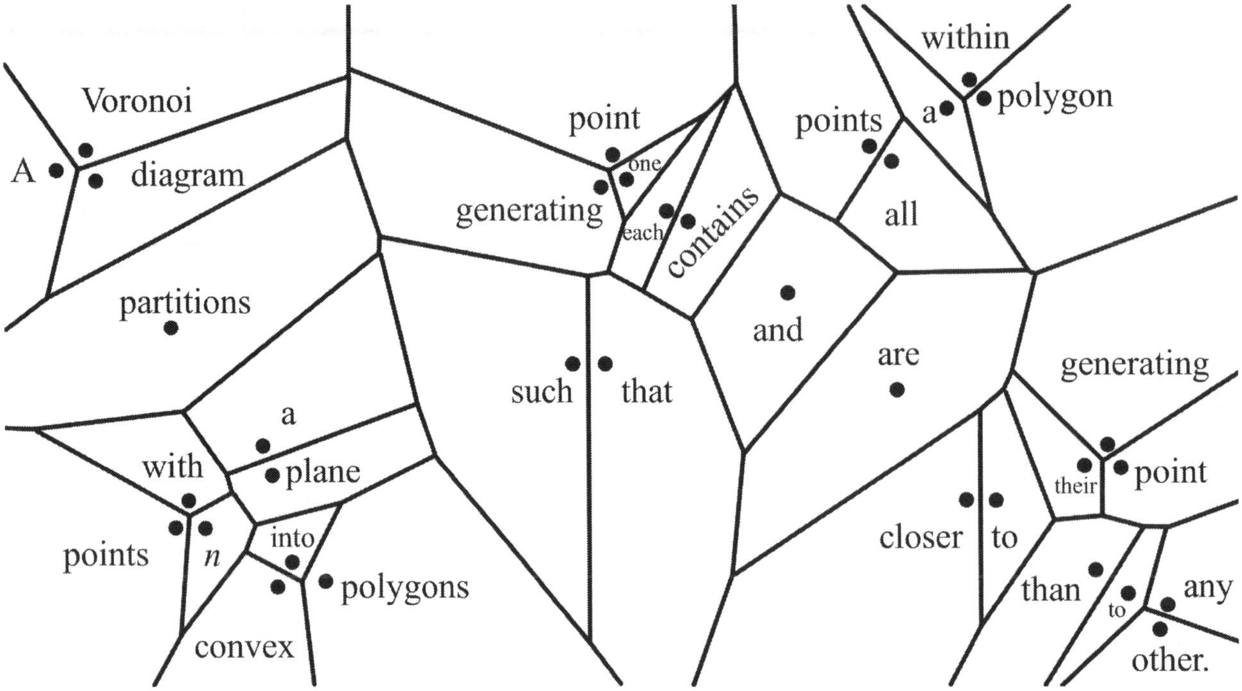

Figure 11: *A Voronoi diagram partitions a plane with n points into convex polygons such that each contains one generating point and all points within a polygon are closer to their generating point than to any other.*

(Labov 2001) have argued that other linguists' use of this diagram (as in Tannen 1990) demonstrate a profound misunderstanding of nominative and accusative cases, as the "ergativity critical point" has no linguistic meaning or value—neither as psychological reality, nor even as theoretically useful abstraction. Others outside sociolinguistics (Akmajian 2001) have dismissed the entire Peer/ Pressure Phrase Transition Diagram enterprise as "without merit, as meaningless and as much a muddle as the rest of sociolinguistics." That viewpoint is perhaps not without merit.

The late 1990s and the new century have ushered in a mild resurgence of special-purpose diagramming techniques, often based on the eclectic and even eccentric inter-disciplinary melding of models. Out of the abstruse field of computational semantics has come the Voronoi Semantic Distance Diagram (Figure 11). As both formal

semantics and Voronoi diagrams are beyond the ken of most linguists, we cannot dwell here on this topic.

Feynman Syntax Diagrams (Figure 12) and

Feynman Syntax Diagram

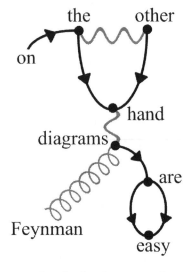

Figure 12: *On the other hand, Feynman diagrams are easy.*

Semantic Circuit Diagram

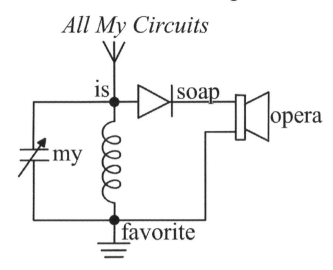

Figure 13: All My Circuits *is my favorite soap opera.*

Multi-Dimensional Vector Difference Model (Graphical)

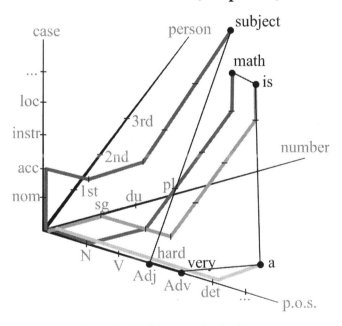

Figure 15: *Math is a very hard subject.*

Semantic Circuit Diagrams (Figure 13) are blends of linguistics with physics and electrical engineering diagrams (respectively). Neither has caught on outside of small cadres at the MIT Linguistic Lab and Stanford Linguistic Accelerator Center (respectively).

Feigenbaum Tree for Infinite Self-Referential Sentences

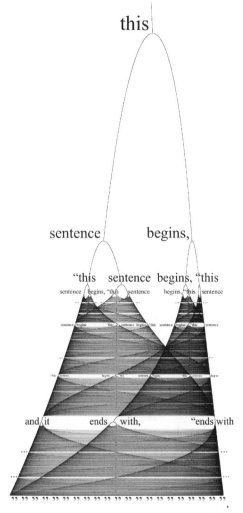

Figure 14: *This sentence begins, "This sentence begins, "This sentence begins, "This sentence begins, "This sentence begins, "This sentence begins, ... and it ends with, "ends with, "ends with, "ends with, "ends with, "ends with ...""""""".*

One of the most arcane diagrammation methods yet constructed is the Feigenbaum Tree for Infinite Self-Referential Sentences (Davidovitch 2000, see Figure 14). The fractal nature of the tree gives it an infinite number of nodes arranged in a self-similar pattern, allowing for, for example, infinite self-referential center embedding.

The last diagramming model of note is the Multi-Dimensional Vector Difference Model (Figure 15), originating with computer scientists (Penton

2004). Unfortunately the multi-dimensional nature of linguistic phenomena limits the usefulness of the graphical representation. The sample shown here is limited to only four dimensions, but ten or twelve dimensions are needed for typical phenomena, and twenty are not unheard of. The MDVDM has been abandoned (except among a small cult of palindromic acronym fetishists) as too visually complex. A short-lived offshoot, the textual Multi-Dimensional Vector Difference Model (Figure 16), was proposed, but quickly abandoned because it didn't actually use vector differences, and was not *sufficiently* visually complex to make its proponents look "crazy sexy smart" (Pulju 2007, Slater 2007, Jones 2007).

Multi-Dimensional Vector Difference Model (Textual)

```
< 1,1,3,1 >  →  math
< 2,1,3,1 >  →  is
< 5,1,0,0 >  →  a
< 4,0,0,0 >  →  very
< 3,0,0,0 >  →  hard
< 1,1,3,2 >  →  subject
< p.o.s.,number,person,case >
```

Figure 16: *Math is a very hard subject.*

What the future of Linguistical Diagrammation may hold none can predict. However, if the past is any indication at all, it is certain to be creative, ingenious, plagiaristic (or, perhaps, "inter-disciplinary"), and, ultimately, useless.

It is Well Known Among Linguists…

The first medical doctor in England, the 5th-century Saxon Raethelhruegh of Stowetonham, wrote in a hand so illegible that it actively prevented his countrymen from writing anything for over a century, until the birch-bark on which his last prescription was written was, fortunately, destroyed by a wayward pig-farmer.

References

Akmajian, Adrian, Richard A. Demers, Ann K. Farmer, and Robert M. Harnish, 2001. *Linguistics: An Introduction to Language and Communication* (5th Edition).

Bloomfield, Leonard, 1939. *Linguistic Aspects of Science.*

Clark, W.S., 1860. *A Practical Grammar: in which Words, Phrases & Sentences are Classified According to Their Offices and Their Various Relationships to One Another.*

Davidovitch, Benny, Mitchell Jay Feigenbaum, Hilary George Everard Hentschel, and Itamar Procaccia, 2000. "Conformal dynamics of fractal growth patterns without randomness." *Physical Review E,* 62(2):1,706–1,715.

Florey, Kitty Burns, 2006. *Sister Bernadette's Barking Dog.*

Greenberg, Joseph, 1971. "Mocking linguists with a hammy mock theory." *Language* 47.3.

Jackendoff, Ray, 1990. *Semantic Structures.*

Jakobson, Roman, 1973. *Questions de poetique.*

Jespersen, Otto, 1889. *The Articulations of Speech Sounds Represented by Means of Analphabetic Symbols.*

Jones, Trey, 2007. "Can someone disable Pulju and Slater's ability to send out mass mailings again?" *SpecGram* Editors Mailing List, February 6, 2007.

Klotz, Irving M., 1980. "The N-ray affair." *Scientific American,* May 1980.

Labov, William, 2001. *Studies in Sociolinguistics.*

Manning, Christopher D. and Hinrich Schütze, 1999. *Foundations of Statistical Natural Language Processing.*

McCawley. James D., 1982. *Thirty Million Theories of Grammar.*

Mockson, Hamy, 1971. "Undulating Transition Flow Charts: The serious linguist's BASM." *Language* 47.1.

Pei, Mario, 1978. *Weasel Words: Saying What You Don't Mean.*

Penton, David, Catherine Bow, Steven Bird, and Baden Hughes, 2004. "Towards a General Model for Linguistic Paradigms." *Proceedings of EMELD 2004.*

Pulju, Timothy, 2007. "Have you heard what Keith W. Slater is doing these days?" *SpecGram* Editors Mailing List, February 4, 2007.

Reed, Alonzo and Brainerd Kellogg, 1877. *Higher Lessons in English.*

Slater, Keith W., 2007. "Tim Pulju is spreading baseless rumors about me again." *SpecGram* Editors Mailing List, February 5, 2007.

Spanderblau, Walter Mitty, 1971. "Rectilinear Syntax Grids for Visual Interpretation of Syntactic Structures." *Language* 47.3.

Tannen, Deborah, 1990. *You Just Don't Understand: Women and Men in Conversation.*

Van Valin, Robert D., Jr., 1992. "Generalized Semantic Roles, Argument Selection and the Syntax-Semantics Interface." Ms. State University of New York at Buffalo.

von Wilamowitz-Moellendorff, Enno Friedrich Wichard Ulrich, 1884. *Homerische Untersuchungen.*

"Beneath the rule of men entirely great,
The pen is mightier than the sword."
—EDWARD BULWER-LYTTON

CHOOSE YOUR OWN CAREER IN LINGUISTICS—PART 9

YOU DECIDE TO MAJOR IN LINGUISTICS BECAUSE A DOUBLE MAJOR IS TOO HARD...

Over the next couple of years, your true nature—that of a lazy bum—comes out. Linguistics is part art, part science, and can be both challenging and fulfilling, but you can also coast through many undergraduate degree programs without ever having to work too hard or learn too much. You prove that this is the case at your university.

Your main contribution to linguistics is to reinforce its reputation in certain circles as a "fluff" field of study. Thanks, you jerk.

You decide grad school is too much work, and you have no marketable skills. Desperation sets in, and you go back to where you should have been all along: the job you had in high school.

• Start your new job. Go to Part 16 on page 195.

Choose Your Own Career in Linguistics starts on page 301.

"I really do not know that anything has ever been more exciting than diagramming sentences."
—GERTRUDE STEIN

PEARLS OF WISDOM FROM STUDENTS OF LINGUISTICS

Spelling is intricately related to writing, I believe.

Semantics, Pragmatics, and Discourse Analysis
We put the fuzzy in fuzzy logic

WHAT DOES SEMANTICS REALLY MEAN? IN WHAT CONtext does it make sense to consider pragmatics? How do we talk about discourse? Those are all very clever questions, none of which will be answered here; we have more important things to do.

To hear the syntacticians and phonologists talk, semantics, pragmatics, and discourse are among the squishier parts of linguistics—even the underappreciated phoneticians and lowly morphologists will partake in the squishful derision from time to time. And, guess what? They are right, really: these are squishy topics full of squishy concepts, with squishy data and squishy conclusions. It's so squishy that it's a bit fishy.

But so what? Ever tried to nail a piece of jello to a tree? It is not a task for the faint of heart or weak of knee. It takes some clever outside-the-box thinking to make meaningful inroads into such complex, interwoven, subtle areas of scientific endeavor.[1]

And as a practical matter, the squishiness factor may also mean that, for example, pragmaticists don't have to try quite so hard to convince their less squish-friendly peers that they've come up with something "interesting" or "clever" or "publishable"—if *they* don't admit that they themselves don't understand their incomprehensible conclusions, *everyone else* will more than likely think they must be smarter than the average linguist. It's a good gig if you can get it.

Then, of course, there's formal semantics, which is apparently the result of a bunch of engineers and logicians looking at "regular" semantics and deciding they could "tidy it up a bit", or that it could do with "somewhat more formal underpinnings", or some such balderdash. It's a bit like jello that's been mixed with triple the gelatin and then reinforced with iron rebar. True, it clearly isn't particularly squishy any-

MAXIMS OF GRICE

Maxims of Grice. Maxims of Grice.
See how they break. See how they break.
Sarcasm flouts *quality* with bite.
Quantity can go when you tell a white lie.
Non sequiturs flout *relevance* (with a kite).
Oh, maxims of Grice… maxims of Grice.

—YUNE O. HŪŪ, II

Maxim of Relation:

Relevance

Q: "How many surrealists does it take to screw in a light bulb?"
A: "Two: One to hold the giraffe, and one to fill the bath tub with brightly colored tools."

Maxim of Quality:

Truth

"No, that dress doesn't make your butt look big, honey."

---

[1] Or, perhaps, "scientific". But we digress.

more, but it just doesn't seem quite like the real thing anymore, either.

At this point the semanticists, pragmaticists and discourse analysts are perhaps getting a bit hot under the collar, and the formal semantics nerds are casting about for a pointy lambda to grab ahold of because they are feeling a bit stabby. We kid, we kid![2]

For those non-semanticist, non-pragmaticist, non-discourse-analysticist linguists who have never properly and fully appreciated the difficulty of wrangling such recalcitrant data, we present this excellent collection of lion-hearted, knee-braced, jello-nailing, smart-sounding semanto-pragmato-disco–themed articles for your academic edification and general all-around ensmartening.

---

[2] For the stabbiest-feeling amongst those who were slighted, Editor Jones was kidding the most. Editor Slater was kidding the least. You can call the *SpecGram* main offices and get Editor Slater's home address, should that be of interest to you.

PEARLS OF WISDOM FROM
STUDENTS OF LINGUISTICS

We could use the context technique, but sometimes there is no need for context, because it is clear from sentences which word class different words belong to.

CHOOSE YOUR OWN CAREER IN LINGUISTICS—PART 27

YOU ASK YOUR LABMATE WHAT SHE THINKS OF THE DEVICE YOU BUILT...

You hand it to your labmate, and ask "What do you think of this?"

She turns it over in her hands, then says, "I have no idea." She then throws it back to you, saying, "What is it?"

It lands in your hands oddly, and you press the big obvious button on the device, while twisting several knobs and flipping a switch or two. There is an explosion of light.

The lab is leveled. The project is utterly destroyed. Several physics grad students suffer concussions or broken bones. Your labmate is knocked unconscious. They never find your body, and they set up a small memorial plaque in your honor once the new lab is built.

You, however, are not dead. You activated the device in an unexpected way, and have been transported elsewhere... and elsewhen.

• Continue. Go to Part 28 on page 4.

Choose Your Own Career in Linguistics starts on page 301.

IT IS WELL KNOWN AMONG LINGUISTS...

The explicit marking of evidential categories in Aymara has almost entirely prevented tabloid market penetration in parts of Peru.

We start this chapter off with a short but pointed question of formal semantics from Strang Burton. As with much of formal semantics, if you don't have a good grasp of it going in, you aren't going to be doing much better coming out. On the other hand, if you can get a grip on it, you can use it to bludgeon your academic adversaries, right in the ego.

What Part of 'No' Don't You Understand?

Strang Burton

$$\lambda P[\lambda Q[\sim\exists x[P(x)\wedge Q(x)]]]$$

<e,t>,<<e,t>,t>

What part of 'No' don't you understand?

What happens when a language conflates "thematic elements" with "thematic roles" with an extra helping of senseless violence and semantic valence? Śūnyatā Qoyusun reports on an intriguing language that has done just that.

Tridekavalent Verbs of Telenovelity in Mydlováskji

Śūnyatā Qoyusun
Mononoaware University
Detroit, France

This summer I set out to do some introductory fieldwork on an endangered minority language in Mexico of possibly Slavic origin, called Mydlováskji by its speakers, and referred to as simply *lengua eslávica,* "Slavic language" or *lengua Ruski,* "Russian language", by the local Spanish-speaking majority population. My efforts were thwarted by the fact that the men and women of the barrio in which the majority of Mydlováskji speakers live engage primarily in two activities: working on off-shore oil drilling platforms, and watching *telenovelas.* While potential informants are engaged in either of these activities it is not really possible to do much in the way of productive fieldwork, though one extremely unusual feature of Mydlováskji did present itself during my time in Mexico.

First, a word about *telenovelas,* which are Spanish-language serialized romantic dramas, superficially similar to American soap operas:

> To the uninitiated, the appeal of the telenovela and the dependency it creates in millions of viewers can seem baffling. Story lines are implausible, characters can be cartoonish and the endings are invariably happy.
>
> "The plot is always the same," said Patricio Wills, head of development at Telemundo. "In the first three minutes of the first episode the viewer already knows the novela will end with that same couple kissing each other. A telenovela is all about a couple who wants to kiss and a scriptwriter who stands in their way for 150 episodes."
>
> "Plot Twists for Genre: Novelas Make
> English-Language Inroads, But Will
> Appeal Get Lost in Translation?"
> Luis Clemens, Multichannel News, 10/15/2006

Indeed, I found the telenovelas watched by my host family to be simultaneously emotionally riveting and intellectually stultifying. The plots all follow the same basic schema. A pair of star-crossed lovers wish to marry, but are thwarted by the complications arising from their familial situations and the oppugnant actions of an under-motivated villain. The stories end with the happy couple getting married, and the villain being punished by death or long-term imprisonment. Unlike American soap operas, these serials do have a definite end date, but they run for six to twelve months each.

The Mydlováskji speakers are often away from home, working on the off-shore oil rigs, when a new *telenovela* begins. When they return home, they are eager to catch up on the storyline of each of the popular telenovelas of the day. While watching the shows, family members will indicate the names of characters as they come onscreen.

je Xóchitl	"It's Xóchitl."
je Quique	"It's Quique."

For several days when I first arrived, these were the only utterances I was able to record in Mydlováskji. The rest of the time the family spent watching the TV with rapt attention. On the third day, however, I recorded this amazing utterance:

telenŭvĕlářujou Xóchitl Quique Toñi Güicho Genita Chuymonchi Menchu Paqui Pepelu Juanpi Malala Chejo Chago

The rough translation is: "Xóchitl and Quique are in love; Toñi and Güicho are Xóchitl's disapproving, hardworking, underprivileged parents; Genita and Chuymonchi are Quique's disapproving, snobbish, overprivileged parents; Menchu and Paqui are Xóchitl's close *amigas* or sisters, Pepelu and Juanpi are Quique's close *amigos* or brothers; Malala is the nosy neighbor or co-worker who nearly ruins everything by revealing Xóchitl and Quique's secret love affair at least twice a week; Chago is the primary villain who tries to thwart Xóchitl and Quique's love; Chejo is Chago's bumbling henchman or assistant who provides extra comic relief."

The plots of the most popular *telenovelas* are sufficiently similar that this tridekavalent verb (the roles of which I have analyzed as being two subjects, four primary objects, four secondary objects, two tertiary objects, and one ultimatiary object) can be productively applied to bring any Mydlováskji-speaking viewer up to speed on the basic dramatic structure of a given *telenovela* in mere moments.

Verbs of such high valency have been, until now, utterly unheard of, and it remains to be discovered whether this innovation is restricted to Mydlováskji speakers in this *barrio,* or if it is known and used by other speakers of the language, if in fact there are any. It is also still not known whether Mydlováskji is in fact a Slavic language brought to Mexico by European immigrants, or merely a "Slavic-sounding" language spoken by a previously unknown indigenous people.

Unfortunately, such questions will likely not be answered by me. I am currently in the final round of funding by the U.S. National Endowment for the Arts. If my proposal is accepted, as now seems likely, I will be partaking in an installation of "performance art" at the MOMA consisting of a recliner and television equipped with a satellite dish to receive the Telemundo and Univision channels. I will watch *telenovelas* eight hours a day, as a commentary on popular culture, globalization, and the capitalistic exploitation and incipient deculturation of the Mydlováskji-speaking people of Mexico by cold, soulless, environment-destroying international oil companies. As an added personal bonus, through my participation in this important work of art I will get to find out how Xóchitl and Quique overcome Chago's illogical and inconsistently explained hatred for them.

WOULD YOU LIKE SPAGHETTI OR LASAGNA FOR DINNER?

Semanticist: "Lasagna. Lasagna noodles are larger, and therefore they entail spaghetti noodles."

CHOOSE YOUR OWN CAREER IN LINGUISTICS—PART 36

YOU DECIDE TO APPLY TO MAINSTREAM CHOMSKYAN LINGUISTICS PH.D. PROGRAMS…

You apply. You get in. You decide to go.

You work hard, but notice that a lot of your fellow grad students (along with some of the professors) are just sheep who don't think for themselves. They just accept the latest trendy theory Chomsky cranks out uncritically. Those losers annoy you, but the quality colleagues you work with make up for it.

• Get your Ph.D. Go to Part 38 on page 72.

Choose Your Own Career in Linguistics starts on page 301.

"There is no arena in which vanity displays itself under such a variety of forms as in conversation."
—MADAME DE STAËL

Our good friends (and check-writing advertisers) over at Panini Press have published a wonderful gem of a game that offers players a chance to sharpen their semantic-category-defining skills without having to travel to uncomfortable parts of the world or learn difficult languages.

Thurn and Taxonomies

Panini Press EuroSprachGames

Thurn and Taxonomies is set in Bavaria, where players create semantic postal routes based on the similarities of the goods they are to deliver. Use your imagination to establish a semantic category which includes such commodities as oranges, coal, Italian marble, French wines, organic llama dung, candied ginger, pine logs, Roman coins, and many more. Bonus points are awarded when your postal route coincides with the noun classes of a real human language.

SprachSpiel des Jahres for 2006. Created by George Lakoff. ईपा

Evidentials lie somewhere near the semantico-pragmatic interface,* which can be confusing. For many years Editor Emeritus Tim Pulju has been confused by the evidentials in a language called Dup. If you think you are smarter than him, or just want to enjoy his discomfort, read on.

Dup Evidentials

Tim Pulju
Rice University

For the past seven years, I have been doing field work on Dup, a Papuan language spoken by about 2,000 people in several highland villages. I have achieved a pretty good grasp of the workings of the language, with one exception: I can make no sense of the system of evidentials. Oh, I know what range of meanings each set of evidentials can express, and I know which syntactic positions evidentials can occur in; namely, all syntactic positions. Yet there seems to be no coherent system underlying the grouping of meanings assigned to one morpheme. To see what I mean, consider the example sentence below:

1. na-debe   tukop   sine-baba
   Evid.-walk woman path-along
   'The woman walked along the path (I heard about it when it was raining or from my maternal uncle).'

2. debe-ro tukop sinebaba
   'The woman walked along the path (I saw it personally, or deduced it based on evidence presented in court, or I don't know about it yet but expect to hear about it from my third daughter).'

3. debe tukop sinebaba tadat
   'The woman walked along the path (I heard it happen, or I am lying, or I heard about it from one of my paternal relatives but can't remember which one but I believe that it is true).'

4. debe tukop-lep sinebaba
   'The woman walked along the path (maybe).'

5. debe p-tukop sinebaba
   'The woman walked along the path (I read it in a letter written over five days ago by my second cousin but received yesterday by my neighbor due to a postal accident and opened and read by my neighbor before he passed it along to me, or it is a famous saying among my people).'

6. he-debe tukop sinebaba
   'The woman walked along the path (I heard it on FM radio or from my wife [but only if the wife's name is Yobo]).'

The examples above are by no means exhaustive. So far, I have encountered 783 different evidential particles, the vast majority of which are as confusing to me as the above. If anyone else cares to look at my data and try to figure out what's going on here, please get in touch with me. I would greatly appreciate the assistance.

THE BEST LINGUISTICS BANDS EVAR!!
ZZ Topic &
DC (Natural) Talk

---

* Good thing we put semantics and pragmatics in the same chapter so we didn't have to decide what's what here.

Author R.S. Sriyatha tackles head-on an issue that Greek scholars have swept under the rug for generations—namely that of pesky particles that resist fluid translation—by denying that very fluidity and exposing their true discourse function.

Greek Particles

R.S. Sriyatha
Bombay, India

Two facts well-known to linguists for many years are that Ancient Greek orthography represented speech much more closely than does modern English orthography, or practically any other modern European orthography, and that speech, unlike writing, is full of hesitations, false starts, and meaningless expletive utterances which are not recorded in writing. For instance, In English, a typical spoken text might be:

1. Well, it's the, umm... you know, the one that, uh, you got from the store across the street.

We can make a number of interesting observations about the meaningless expletives in the above and in similar texts, of which the interested reader can collect many more examples, if he is so inclined. The comments in this paper are based on a collection of 327 naturally occurring English texts ranging from 3 seconds to 118 seconds in length. The first observation concerns the syntactic positions in which such expletives occur. In brief, expletives occur immediately before major syntactic constituents, or immediately following the first word of a major constituent. Thus, we often find particles inserted at the beginning of an utterance, or after the first word, as in (2) and (3) below; at the beginning of a noun phrase, or after the article, as in (4) and (5); or at other constituent boundaries, as in (6) and (7).

2. Ahh.. no, I don't think so.
3. John, um, went to Liberia yesterday.

4. Hildegarde swallowed, yeah, an entire disk drive.
5. Did he surrender the... wha... fish?
6. Eric and the man with no nose... uhh... slew the werewolf with a bazooka.
7. There's a situation with, you know, the ringmaster.

Of course, expletives can be inserted at many points during one speech utterance, and may be iterated at any of these points, as seen in (1) above. In fact, sometimes so many expletives are used that the entire communicative function of speech fails. Consider example (8), taken from the Watergate tape transcripts submitted by the Nixon White House to the independent counsel. The conversants are discussing the advisability of paying hush money to the burglars.

8. NIXON: But then we'd have a problem with the... with the...
   HALDEMAN: Umm, yeah, umm...
   MITCHELL: Ahh, what, ah... what about... ah, the...?
   NIXON: ... with the... with the...
   DEAN: Only, the question is, you know, umm, how much...
   MITCHELL: That is, if, that is, you know—
   NIXON: ... with the... with the...
   DEAN: ... I mean, um, how much...
   HALDEMAN: Umm, yeah, um...
   ERLICHMAN: What?
   NIXON: Huh?

MITCHELL AND DEAN (SIMULTANEOUSLY): What?
HALDEMAN AND NIXON (SIMULTANEOUSLY): What?
ERLICHMAN: Huh?
NIXON AND MITCHELL (SIMULTANEOUSLY): (Expletive deleted)
DEAN: Oh.

Obviously, there is much more to say about the syntactic positioning of expletives (in the non-pejorative linguistic sense, not the sense of the Watergate tape transcripts, although examination of this second type of expletive might also prove an interesting topic). For the purposes of this paper, let it suffice to say that expletives are fairly common in speech, and that they occur in the positions specified above.

We turn now to Ancient Greek, a language much studied but still not perfectly understood, neither by philologists nor by linguists working with more modern theories of language. Let us consider a text often presented to first year students of Greek; it is part of a passage adapted from Xenophon's Anabasis and reproduced on page 70 of Crosby and Schaeffer's introductory textbook.

9. Entautha oun theōrhiā ēn tēs
    ?   ?   review   was the

    Kūrou stratiās. kai prōton men
    Cyrus army   ?   first   ?

    parēlaunon hoi barbaroi.
    paraded   the foreigners.

A typical student, called on to translate the text, is likely to respond as follows:

10. Lemme see... um... there was a review of Cyrus' army... and... first... ahh... the foreigners marched by.

Such a translation would draw a reprimand from the instructor, who, with a haughty sneer, would inform the hapless student that the correct translation is as follows:

11. Thereupon, accordingly, there was a review of Cyrus' army. And first on the one hand the foreigners paraded.

The perspicacious reader will have already figured out where this paper is headed (aside from oblivion). It is obvious, when we consider that Xenophon did not write down his work himself, but rather dictated it, that it is the student rather than the instructor who has translated the text most faithfully. No one, in speech, says things like, "Thereupon, accordingly, indeed, on the one hand, they pitched camp; and then on the next day also likewise they arose indeed and accordingly marched ten stades." But everyone says things like, "So, um, ah, un... they pitched camp; and, well, the next day... ah, you know, they got up, um, and, ah, marched ten stades."

What more need I say here? It is obvious that for hundreds of years classicists have misinterpreted the meaning of Greek particles. Most, if not all of them, have no meaning whatsoever. It may be possible to distinguish between particles deriving from words with semantic import: English *you know* and Greek *entautha* serve as examples of expletives in this class, unlike English *uh* or Greek *de* and *gar,* which are plainly utterly meaningless. Yet whether this division is sensible is questionable, since it might imply that there is more meaning to the semantically derived particles than synchronic analysis would allow. Clearly, there is more research to be done, but the fundamental facts are now clear.

When it is said that an image is worth a thousand words, those are probably boring run-of-the-mill words, and not even 25¢ words, much less some really fancy logophoric pronouns. Nonetheless, John Miaou's excellent explanatory cartoon is worth many, many words, even the really good ones.

On Logophoric Pronouns

John Miaou

Greek, being so scholarly as it is, is practically everywhere in scholarly discourse. However, in this case study provided by Anne Thrax, the discourse is Greek, though the content is far from scholarly—and possibly not even contentful. Nonetheless the meta-discourse of the article itself is both content-like and scholarful, delving as is does into the principles of cooperative communication.

Cathartic Grecian Maxomes

Anne Thrax
Pelopponensiae Akkademia, Mykênai

It is commonplace, in dialogical practice, for divergences to occur between what is said and what is interpreted. This is true of modern forms of communication, which give spoken language the primacy that it has deservedly earned along the course of human history. This study reports dialogical divergences of a rather unexpected kind, arising from two sets of documents of Grecian origin, which appear instead to compromise the essence of dialog itself as a cooperative endeavor.

Both sets of documents consist of small, irregularly shaped pieces of papyrus, printed with characters whose painstaking decryption is ongoing. Each set is watermarked and comprises a specific papyrus size, one larger for lengthier messages and one very small, allowing no more than three characters altogether in exchanges limited to two participants. The watermarks read, in loose translations from the original Ancient Greek, *CountenanceScroll* and *Chirper*, respectively, the latter with a verbal form spelt *Cheerp*, whose rationale remains obscure.

Communication through these messaging systems proceeded with astounding speed amid the exuberant bustle of a shopping agora or, at a somewhat more leisurely pace, when bumping into someone that one would rather have bumped into in the quietude of a claustro.[1] Whether meeting for the first time or finding themselves among old acquaintances, interactants forwent the use of speech to slip into one another's hands scribbled notes that, to all appearances, were composed on the spot on papyrus ripped to measure. To this purpose, users dashed around physically burdened with inkwell, quill and appropriate quantities of easily rippable papyri. A few of the notes contain some form of identification of the writer, though not necessarily of the reader. The following data illustrate a sample from each set of documents.

CountenanceScroll Data

IM UR:	OMG!!! QT juss barft!! yewwwwwwww > . < [2]
alea:	me?? =p
jacta:	LOL!!
est:	heheeee... told ya, pets r pests
jacta:	& est knows best HAHAHA!!!
CarpeDM:	rat? fish? bone? alea? alii?
InVinoV:	alot?

---

[1] Like most philologists, I know absolutely nothing about the language(s) I am droning on about, although I did get a Φ grade, devoid of BK, in Greek. My Latin, like me, is a bit rusty too, and I sometimes confuse the two (I mean Latin and Greek, not Latin and me). I beg forbearance.

[2] Our analysis disregards non-koine symbols. As is well known, no lingua franca tolerates capricious additions to its alphabet.

est: its a lott, nickanpoop[3]

Εὔφημη Ευχαριστῶ: Methinks your felis catus perchance ingested a less appropriate concoction, which may, understandably, have discomposed its entrails. Would you agree?[4]

jacta: huh?!!!??!!?

CarpeDM: *-*

est: say wat???

alea: O.o

IM UR: ...

InVinoV: qt got yr tongue?

alea: :D

CarpeDM: ROFL!!![5]

IMU: helo. i want be youre freind. want see pixture me very freindly? i show.

IM UR: WTH???

est: sth phishys goin on...

jacta: ;-)

CarpeDM: looks like u, im

est: duh

Εὔφημη Ευχαριστῶ: Pardon me, pray?

IM UR: OMG!!! im L8!!!!! GTG!!!

jacta: y?

alea: CU

est: UR?

Carpe DM: luv ya

InVinoV: bibi

est: by-by, u more on[6]

IM UR: xoxo!!!

Chirper / Cheerp Data

RU?	[Θ]	no!	2B	hi!	ATR
ok	??[7]	yep	or?	lo	ooh

Barring translation glitches, one difficulty in the analysis of these surviving fragments relates to what the exchanges actually represent. Even assuming that printed forms of language reflect spoken forms, and knowing that printed representations of speech fall painfully short of accommodating prosodomic inflections, we have no way of recovering the spoken forms to which most of these texts may have corresponded. One alternative interpretation is that this form of interaction might have been created specifically for printed use, which suggests an unorthodox conception of human communicative abilities whose exploration, as the saying goes, lies beyond the scope of this papyrus. Nevertheless, the data do show a number of regularities, captured in four maxomes which, as their name indicates, maxomize the fluency of the exchanges:

B Sc xprss yrslf Scntly;

B Ed be Edit-free; do not write that for which you lack spontaneity;

B A be as Arbitrary as possible;

---

[3] Most of the turns immediately preceding this one appear to have changed hands simultaneously.

[4] Careful examination of the orthographia, grammatika and lexicae of this contribution shows that its author is a non-native user of this communicative medium.

[5] See footnote 3.

---

[6] See footnote 5.

[7] This participant appears to share our difficulty interpreting non-lingua franca characters.

B Mus   beMuse your recipients with light-speed comments on their light-speed musings.

Obedience to maxomes further results in two effects. One, intra-textual, generates idiosyncratic clusters of meanings, here termed *plicatures,* which appear to be interpretable only by insiders (see footnotes 4 and 7). Most plicatures are in fact simplicatures, in that they occur simultaneously (see footnote 6). Complementary plicatures, those that attempt to engage participants in what we nowadays call dialog, involving congruent talk with articulate human beings, fail to merge with the flow of the exchange. Two examples are in Εὐφήμη Εὐχαριστῶ's contributions, which clearly generate complicatures.

The second effect, intra-personal, generates catharsis. The maxomes afford instant, instinctive relief for the expression of whatever happens to cross the users' minds, at any time, in any place, for any reason, ranging from the gastric vicissitudes of a sphaira pilosa to the socio-cognito-ecological implications of the latest Euripides ockblayusterbay, the latter not included in the data for this study because there are no data.

Finally, maxomatic effects are cathartic to civilized communicators too: they arouse both horror (from the harrowing shortcomings evinced by this means of expression) and compassion (ditto). We thus hope to have demonstrated the irremediably primitive nature of the B set of maxomes and, thereby, the reason why the unwieldy form of interaction that they describe quickly became obsolete.

THE WISDOM OF LINGUISTS

Don't let the idiom chunk out of the bag.

IT IS WELL KNOWN AMONG LINGUISTS...

The loss of dual pronouns in early Old English, with a concomitant shift to the plural, triggered wide scale polyamory, stories of which were later to prove unfortunately magnetic to Viking invaders.

CHOOSE YOUR OWN CAREER IN LINGUISTICS—PART 17

YOU GO TO WORK AS A CONSULTING LINGUIST ON A SCI FI CHANNEL SERIES...

You begin work on *FarStar GateScape Atlantian-3.* The alien languages are works of art: agglutinative, infixing, center-embedding, with thirty-eight cases. Marc Okrand publicly admits to his personal jealousy and professional admiration.

However, your constant pedantic corrections infuriate most of the cast, who come to hate you. You are eventually fired.

However, in the meantime, rumors spread of your ménage-à-trois with Claudia Black and Ben Browder. As a result, you make a mint making guest appearances on the talk show circuit and writing a tell-all book. Congratulations!

• The End. Go to page 301.

Choose Your Own Career in Linguistics starts on page 301.

PEARLS OF WISDOM FROM STUDENTS OF LINGUISTICS

Language shapes language at the level of language and conversation management. What gives meaning to a conversation is not the words but what Malinowski calls 'phallic communion' or 'small talk'. As a result, this situation does have a lot of potential to becoming a topic of conversation.

Having previously mentioned meta-discourse, it is now time to take a meta^meta turn with an analysis of the discourse of analysis in linguistics. This short but meaningful paper by Alfraad vonn Güügënschnëchtën & Mo d'Qi makes linguists aware of certain important aspects of the asynchronous discourse they engage in with their readers—and in particular an aspect that every degree-seeking grad student article reader has dwelt upon at 2 a.m., yet which seems to escape the mind of every tenure-seeking professor article writer in their ivory tower armchair.

A Meta-Analysis of Article Length vs. Quality
or, Why Only Short Papers Really Matter

Alfraad vonn Güügënschnëchtën & Mo d'Qi
Conjoined University of Liechtenstein and Inner Mongolia

It comes as no surprise to anyone who has ever been a teacher or a student to hear that students don't always have the time or will to complete their assigned readings. However, it seems clear that carefully read papers that make a big impact on students are the ones that go on to become most important in the field as those students become full-fledged scholars.

We would like to hypothesize about the anthropological aspects of the sociodynamics of this process in more detail, but the results of the current study indicate that such long-windedness will lessen the long-term impact of this paper. (See below!)

Seventy-five grad students in linguistics, from several universities, were each assigned to read 25 papers over the course of the academic year, then rank them based on the quality of their content. The papers where chosen so as to divide evenly into three categories based on their length: *Short, Medium,* and *Long.*

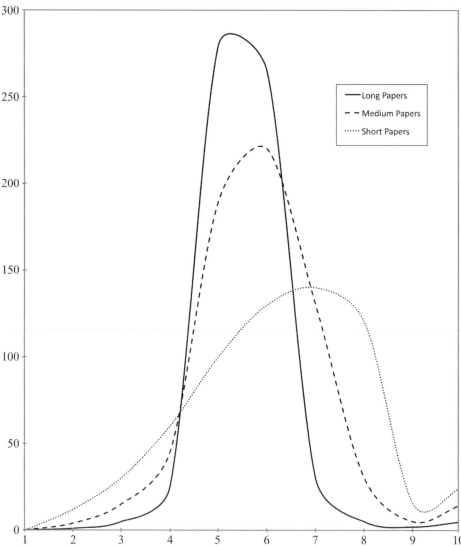

The aggregate results of the rankings are displayed in the graph above. In general, the *Long* papers are tightly clustered around the middling scores. The *Medium* papers show more variability in their scores, and score better in general. *Short*

papers continue this trend, showing even more variability, but again with a higher mean.

Collectively, this trend seems unlikely. The truth of the matter is that almost no one read the longer papers. Instead, they skimmed them or read the abstract, then gave them a conservative ranking (in the 5–6 range), modified by how well they thought they *might* like them (± 1 or 2 points) if they ever got around to actually reading them.

This analysis is backed up by the follow-up discussions for the reading assignments. Comments on *Long* papers are more likely to be vague and noncommittal: "interesting", "ok", "useful", and the almost daring "nothing earth-shattering". By comparison, comments on the *Short* papers are much more specific and detailed, even passionate:

- "The phonological analysis was good, but the morphological analysis seemed incomplete."

- "Even though the goal of the paper was merely descriptive, the author should have chosen some theoretical framework in which to couch the description."

- "That was one of the clearest expositions on difficulties at the morphology/syntax interface that I have ever read."

- "Oh, that one really blows chunks—the formalism is baroque only for the sake of its own impressive baroqueness, and the analysis was so twisted, in order to fit the author's preconceived theoretical framework, that I got vertigo reading it!"

This analysis is further bolstered by some interesting evidence: we also asked some of the students to predict their rankings based on the title, author, subject matter, and abstracts of the papers they were about to read. *Long* and *Medium* papers showed little variability between the predicted ranking and the ranking assigned after "reading" the paper. *Short* papers showed more variability, and surprise at the difference between expectations and final ranking much more often figured in the students' comments on the *Short* papers during discussion.

We could explore this additional evidence in more detail, but it would unfortunately cause this paper to exceed the vonn Güügënschnëchtën-d'Qi Optimal Article Length™.

Astute readers will note an odd upswing in the tail end of the otherwise felicitous curves fitting the data. This odd outlier data was found, upon closer inspection, to be from a single student. We were so intrigued that we tried to interview the student, but were unable. None of the faculty or the other students at this student's University could readily recall his name—he is simply known as "The Tool", even by the faculty. He spends all of his time in a study carousel at the library, has never attended a Grad House party, and never speaks to any of the other students on the rare occasions he sees them. He liked all the papers very, very much.

In our next paper we will consider the effects of graphics, both color and black and white, on paper rankings. In the meantime, interested scholars can send a check or money order for $269.95 to the authors to discover the detailed secrets of the vonn Güügënschnëchtën-d'Qi Optimal Article Length™.

IT IS WELL KNOWN AMONG LINGUISTS…

The strong form of the Sapir-Whorf hypothesis is supported by almost no data, except for the data provided by that device we don't have a name for yet.

Sociolinguistics
Grudgingly letting speakers back into linguistics

I N THE LATE TWENTIETH CENTURY, SOCIO- linguistics came out of nowhere to become one of the most popular research specializations around. Unfortunately, in the days when sociolinguistics was first getting started, *SpecGram* was a bit slow in recognizing its significance. For example, in the early 1960s, when a would-be contributor sent us a paper on the way people talk on Martha's Vineyard, the intern in charge of dealing with zanier submissions wrote "This is not linguistics!!!"[1] on the manuscript, and sent it back, postage due.

As a result of our being behind the curve on this one, we have published, overall, fewer groundbreaking articles in sociolinguistics than in other fields. More recently, however, under more enlightened editorship,[2] *SpecGram* has reclaimed its rightful position as the leading publisher of innovative research in *all* linguistic subfields, as proved by the following articles, every one of which is far superior to that Martha's Vineyard garbage that we rightfully rejected so many years ago.

THE WISDOM OF LINGUISTS
Before criticizing someone, talk an hour in their dialect.

THE OUT-OF-TOWNER'S LAMENT

Once upon a midday dreary, while I wandered weak and weary,
Through a crowded "full-of-cheer"-y Christmas-decorated store,
Wond'ring where to find a toy to fill a child's heart with joy,
I asked a passing stockboy, "Stockboy, where is what I'm looking for?"
Quoth the stockboy "[də fɔːθ flɔə]."

With my ign'rance still unbroken by those sounds so strangely spoken,
"Surely" thought I "he is jokin', jokin'", so I spoke once more:
"Ha-ha! You're mouthing nonsense words that sound amusingly absurd.
But now please give me, my good sir, good sir, an answer, I implore.
Yelled the stock boy "[də fɔːθ flɔə]!"

"Monster!" said I, "thing of evil, even ev'ller than Knievel,
Even worse than the boll weevil, more annoying than Al Gore!"
But the stock boy, nothing daunted, would not tell me what I wanted.
Instead, repeatedly he taunted, taunted me, just like before.
Stupid stockboy. "[də fɔːθ flɔə]."

So I got my nephew a gift card.

—BILL L. POE

---

[1] In big red letters, no less.
[2] Especially that of the current Managing Editor, whose high regard for sociolinguistics is well-known.

Modern sociolinguistics developed from the convergence of three concerns of early 20th century linguistics: dialect geography, bilingualism, and language change. The first of these got a foothold in the US during the Great Depression, when Hans Kurath, feeling sorry for all the unemployed linguists he knew, tricked the government into thinking that mapping American dialects was a worthwhile endeavor. SpecGram is proud to continue the Kurath tradition by publishing articles such as the following standout by two precocious young Minnesotans, Sven Slater and Ollie Bickford. (We are pleased to announce that, after SpecGram published their article, the NSF agreed to fund Sven and Ollie's participant research on constructed languages used in online gaming.)

Grey Duck or Goose?
Mapping variation in a children's game in Minnesota

Sven Slater and Ollie Bickford
Fifth Grade Science Fair Project
J. O. Nelson Public School, St. Cloud, Minnesota, USA

Research Question

Last year, a new kid named Tyler P. joined our fourth grade class. Tyler was from Illinois or some other southern state, and she told us that down there kids play "duck, duck, goose," instead of "duck, duck, grey duck" like we do here in Minnesota. We thought this was strange, even for the South, but then we talked about it and discovered that even some Minnesota kids in our own class had heard this at their grandmas' houses. Our teacher, Mr. Olson, said we could study isoglosses to learn about that, so we decided to do that for this year's science fair.

So our research question was: *Where exactly do people say "grey duck" and where exactly do they say "goose," at least in Minnesota where we can find out?*

Methodology

Mr. Olson told us that you were most likely to find an isogloss in the country, not in the city. So this summer, when most of us go to spend a week or two at our grandmothers' houses, we each took along a questionnaire and interviewed five or six neighbors, preferably farmers. We wanted to know about everybody so we asked men, women and children. The towns we went to were: Lake Valley, Big Lake, Pine Lake, River Bend Lake, Two Lakes, Mountain Lake, Prairie Plain Lake, Lake of the Trees, and Bemidji.

Results

Mr. Olson helped us draw isogloss lines to show what we found. We drew four different isogloss maps because we found out that boys, girls, men and women had different ideas about what to say when they played this game.

The girls' isogloss looked like this:

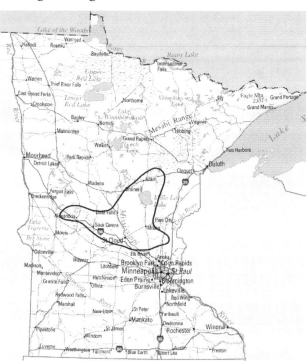

The boys' isogloss looked like this:

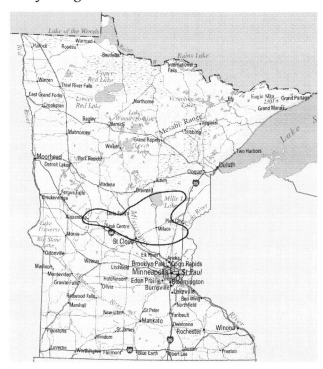

And last of all, the men's isogloss looked like this:

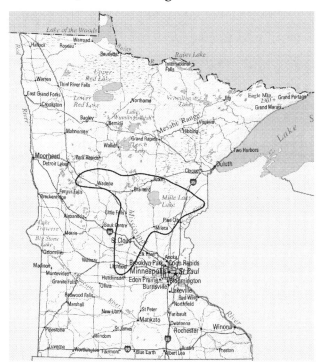

The women's isogloss looked like this:

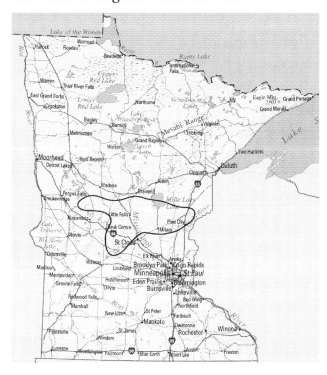

At first we thought it was a little strange that the isoglosses didn't match up very well, but then Billy O. wrote an app to display all four of these maps on his iPhone. Just for fun he animated it. We aren't allowed to use the school computers for our homework projects, so we had to send this article to a print-only journal, and so you will just have to imagine what the result looked like—it turns out that the picture looks like a duck flapping its wings![1]

Go Billy! You rock!

Conclusion

We are not sure why anyone would say "duck, duck, goose," because "grey duck" is so much

---

WOULD YOU LIKE SPAGHETTI
OR LASAGNA FOR DINNER?

Sociolinguist: "I'd like two plates of spaghetti with different sauces."

---

[1] Editors' note. We have left this note as it was written by the precocious youngsters, but we would like to add that there is no reason at all for this insult to our readers' intelligence or graphical capabilities. You do *not*, of course, "have to imagine" what it looks like. Simply make multiple copies of the four pictures, stack and bind them in repeating sequence, and riffle through them to observe the effect that Billy O. achieved through digital means. Alternately, simply look at them in sequence, very rapidly.

better, but Mr. Olson says that the data doesn't lie, and we believe him. Anyway, the animated version reminded us that ducks and geese migrate, and we guess that is why the isoglosses appear to be flying. The next question we would like to investigate is whether the grey duck isoglosses make it fly the other direction if you check them out in a different season.

But we'll have to leave that for next year's fifth grade class to check out, because Mr. Olson says that they don't allow social sciences in the sixth grade science fair. And also, most of our grandmothers say we had better not show up at their houses with questionnaires next summer, because summer is for lemonade and fishing, not for school work, and they will be calling Mr. Olson if it happens again.

CHOOSE YOUR OWN CAREER IN LINGUISTICS—PART 29

YOU WORK HARD TOWARD YOUR COMPUTATIONAL LINGUISTICS PH.D. ...

It's hard work, but rewarding. Best of all, you don't have to subscribe to any particular brand of linguistics to get someone to look at your results. The results speak for themselves. You graduate with your Ph.D. You have a couple of job offers in academia and industry. Balancing your desires for work and home life, you take the job that best suits you.

• Take a job! Go to Part 32 on page 188.

Choose Your Own Career in Linguistics starts on page 301.

The next article reaches back to the tradition of Einar Haugen and Max Weinreich to study bilingualism in America. Authors Hiroko Nakamura and Jimmy Battaglia prove that quantitative sociolinguistic methods can make a mockery of the received wisdom propagated by linguists who don't understand statistics.

A Sociolinguistic Study of Bilingualism in the Rio Grande Valley

Hiroko Nakamura and Jimmy Battaglia
Free University of Winnipeg

Introduction.

The Rio Grande Valley, on the border between Mexico and the United States, is a well-known area of language contact. The present study considers a number of parameters—specifically age, socio-economic status, citizenship, nation of residence, and gender—in examining the extent to which bilingualism is exhibited by members of the Rio Grande Sprachbund.

Data

The data were collected from a wide range of speakers on both sides of the border. The results are presented in summary form in Table 1, below.

Analysis

We were greatly surprised to find far lower levels of bilingualism than we had been led to expect. Also surprising was the fact that Austrian citizens exhibited a far greater level of bilingualism than any other group in the study. However, the small sample size of Austrian citizens in our study may have skewed the results somewhat. Our sample consisted of two people, Helmuth and Marta Schlusse, who were vacationing in Matamoros. They were a very nice couple, although it was hard to carry on a conversation with Marta, since she didn't speak any English.

Conclusions

Although our findings are diametrically opposed to those of many other researchers, we believe that our methodology was irreproachable and that our findings are therefore incontrovertible (aside from the Austrian question). The question then arises: why should our results differ so greatly from those of previous investigators? It is worth noting that, in some ways, our data do tend to bear our the findings of previous research. Thus, Guatemalans exhibit a lower level of bilin-

	Percent Bilingual German-English Speakers	Percent Speakers of German but not English	Percent Speakers of English but not German	Percent neither German nor English Speakers
Rich Old People	8%	1%	54%	37%
Poor Young US Citizens in Mexico	3%	0%	96%	1%
Women in the United States	5%	1%	81%	13%
Middle Class Mexican Citizens	4%	5%	42%	49%
Austrian Citizens	50%	50%	0%	0%
Guatemalan Citizens in Mexico	1%	0%	19%	80%

Table 1: Rio Grande Valley Bilingualism

gualism than do Mexicans, which is natural since Guatemalans are typically recent arrivals in the language contact area.

As for the larger question of divergences between our work and others', the most likely answer is that previous researchers, knowing the reputation of the Rio Grande Valley as a Sprachbund, were predisposed to find a greater level of bilingualism than actually exists. Using sloppy data-collection techniques, careless data compilation, and error-ridden statistical analyses, our well-meaning but hopelessly misguided colleagues naturally ended up seeing exactly what they wanted to see. Please note that we are not accusing anyone of deliberately tampering with data. Rather, the erroneous results of prior research stand as a clear cautionary tale concerning the difficulty, and also the importance, of maintaining objectivity when doing scientific research.

Good scribes are not those who write well, but those who erase well.

—RUSSIAN PROVERB

CHOOSE YOUR OWN CAREER IN LINGUISTICS—PART 15

YOU LOOK FOR A JOB WITH JUST AN UNDERGRADUATE DEGREE...

You quickly realize that an undergraduate degree is not enough. Like it or not, as a foolish teenager you chose a path that only goes one way—toward academia. You've now abandoned that path and burned the bridge to the ivory tower—no one in the field cares what you can do, only what letters you have after your name. There is only one thing to do now. Get a real job.

• Get a real job. Go to Part 16 on page 195.

Choose Your Own Career in Linguistics starts on page 301.

MURPHY'S LAW FOR LINGUISTS

The breakthrough you just made will turn out to be something discussed by Pike, Gleason, or Hockett— except that your formulation is less clear, and thus struck you as more profound.

The third important source of modern sociolinguistics was the desire to bring much-needed scientific rigor to the study of language change—traditional historical linguists, we are sad to say, being some of the most unscientific linguists around.* One of the most important findings of the new approach to diachrony is that language change is nothing but synchronic variation with a temporal axis tacked on. Thus, recent years have produced innumerable studies that correlate linguistic variation with social factors such as age, gender, wealth, and education. A particularly rigorous, data-intensive example of such work is the following article by Herr E. Ditarie, a distinguished member of the X. Qwizzit Korps Center for Advanced Collaborative Studies.

An Introduction to Familial Linguistics
The Syntax and Grammar of Husband, Wife and Teenager

Herr E. Ditarie
X. Quizzit Korps Center for Advanced Collaborative Studies

While hiding in my home office, surrounded by shelves of important-looking dictionaries and grammars for soundproofing, I realised that linguists often miss the interesting related yet mutually unintelligible languages that are practised only a few metres from their labs. So, in an effort to address this important issue, I set out to catalogue the languages spoken in the house of Ditarie; namely, HUSBAND, WIFE and TEENAGER. These languages share many superficial features, including the phonological shapes of the majority of lexical items and some intonational contours, but closer inspection reveals that their sound-meaning relationships are utterly incommensurate.

For example, the seemingly normal word *fine* has a myriad of meanings when used in the various familiolects. WIFE may indicate that her day was *fine*, indicating that it was satisfactory or pleasant; HUSBAND may use it to indicate that he finds his wife attractive while pathetically signaling that he is too old to be try to be *fly*; a TEENAGER of either sex can uses it as a catch-all reply that also indicates their general willingness to murder WIFE and HUSBAND while they sleep, or at least

---

*Some of them even have jobs in university departments like English, Classics, or Romance Languages, where they rub elbows with actual humanists.

take money from their purse or wallet when they are not looking.

One way to approach this situation, of course, is to create a set of tuples of the general form $<a, a'>$ such that a is all and only the set of sentences found grammatical by a family member, with a' being the set of logical forms onto which a maps; family discourse can then be treated in terms of the sentences found in the intersection of $a_1...a_n$ together with the set $\mathbf{R}$ comprising mappings between $a'_1...a'_n$. There are two major problems with this approach, however: (1) $\mathbf{R}$ can be null except for referring expressions tied to food, and (b) there are no convenient Greek letters for h(usband) and w(ife)—one might be forced to know the Greek terms, a condition bordering on philology.

Another approach is to borrow from post-structuralist syntactical philosophies and assume that no signifier can be finally and exclusively tied to a given signified. Thus, the lexical item *fine* may be interpreted either as an affective particle indicating general malaise or paranoia or as a meaningless utterance broadly equivalent to the term *och* in Scots, *well* and *oh* in most English dialects, or the contents of a funding application.

A third approach is to delve into etymology, thereby seeking the primeval, elemental, ergo untarnished meaning that Troglodyte kinsfolk attach(ed) to the words they exchange. Cavernous research unveils that whatever HUSBAND has ever said to WIFE and vice versa, since the inception of articulate speech, is systematically misunderstood, even, and especially, when both speak the same language. On the rare occasions where both might agree and, *exempli gratia*,

reciprocally exclaim *fine* to mean what it means, 'finis' (*id est*, 'shut your mouth'), TEENAGER will counterpoint *ooooch, f'cryin'ou'loud* to mean the same thing, only in the plural ('mouths'). I could go on, approach-wise.

While it could be postulated that many exemplars of the TEENAGER category have simply not yet mastered adult speech, many authors have noted that this hypothesis encounters difficulty when we observe that TEENAGERs' speech is highly uniform across disparate family units, but that maturation leads to gender-specific differentiation into the WIFE and HUSBAND categories; why do not gender differentiations display for TEENAGERs as well as for more age-advanced subjects?

Despite the gender-specific differentiation of WIFE and HUSBAND, there is an important generalization to capture, which is that the gender differences often disappear when either or both are put in opposition to TEENAGER. For example, the rate of addition of novel lexical items in TEENAGER is substantially higher than WIFE or HUSBAND. Also, the adoption of such novel vocabulary (such as the aforementioned *fly*) into the familiolect of WIFE or HUSBAND almost instantly causes the loss or abandonment of that vocabulary in the TEENAGER familiolect. For these and other reasons, we find it useful, descriptively, to conflate WIFE and HUSBAND into a familial super-group, PARENT, that has as a crucial aspect its definitional opposition (descriptively and authoritatively) to TEENAGER.

All of this analysis, illuminating myriad relations as it has, I have completed, as I said before, in my home office, still surrounded by shelves of genealogical dictionaries and grammars of many language families. Imagine the great strides in familial linguistics that would be possible if I were actually to venture out into the rest of my home and interact, in the role of HUSBAND, with WIFE and TEENAGER! Alas, a lack of research funding (and the fact that WIFE has not finished making dinner and TEENAGER has come home in a foul mood) has necessarily constrained the scope of the present investigation to the introductory survey presented so far. However, researchers who feel themselves to be kindred spirits are encouraged to continue with their own investigations, especially vis-à-vis pop culture (and mom culture, too).

PEARLS OF WISDOM FROM
STUDENTS OF LINGUISTICS

Genres: The singers sing in a heavily-accented English to reinforce the concept of their way of life.

CHOOSE YOUR OWN CAREER IN LINGUISTICS—PART 35

YOU CONTINUE WORKING FOR THE GOVERNMENT...

You settle into a reasonably good if mostly boring job, acquire a moderately big house, and get a fair number of promotions over the years. Twenty years later you are a fairly well compensated but readily replaced cog in a large soulless Defense Department/Homeland Security machine.

• Continue. Go to Part 14 on page 174.

Choose Your Own Career in Linguistics starts on page 301.

IT IS WELL KNOWN AMONG LINGUISTS...

It has long been suspected, but never proven, that the "destruction" of the giant mechanical eagle that was to be used in the 1904 stage production of *Peter Pan* was occasioned by the fact that it used the same exotic-metal bearing system as the missing zeppelin, *The Vṛddhi Triumphant*, and could thus be used as a source of parts.

The preceding article tries to correlate gender and linguistic variation, but more advanced work goes beyond simple observation to reveal how language itself systematically reinforces gender inequality and promotes the oppression of women. As can be seen from our choice of editors for the current anthology,* SpecGram has long been dedicated to the principle of gender equity, and thus we are proud to have published the following commendably rigorous article on phonology and gender by Lea Kim Shopmont.

Notes on Sociophonology

Lea Kim Shopmont
Associate Professor of Communication
Ancilla College, Indiana

There have been numerous studies of the linguistic correlates of race, class, and gender that serve to show that all forms of social oppression leave indelible traces on the speech, and by obvious extension minds and spirits, of the afflicted speakers. However, many such studies are flawed in missing the forest for the trees: Instrumental studies of the speech of different races, classes, and genders are strictly phonetic and do not delve into the structures of their respective speech varieties to lay bare the systematic regularities that reflect, recapitulate, and inculcate the structures of oppression in society.

Consider, for example, the all-too-common deplorable practice in languages of marking gender. Instrumental studies that focus on small differences in formant means between speakers simply do not address the distinction that such sexist languages draw between male and female persons. In Italian, for example, it is well known that singular feminine nouns require agreement marked by suffixes ending in *a*, whereas singular masculine agreement is marked with *o*. No linguist has remarked on the clear and evident fact that the vowel height is correlated with social standing: Women have a lower status in patriarchal society that is reflected in a low vowel. Similarly, masculine nouns in the plural are marked with a high vowel *i*, feminine nouns with a mid vowel *e*. The fact that a group of women is marked at the same vowel height as an individual man reflects their respective social standings, as shown by the fact that the gender of a single baby boy stuck in a battalioness of 1,000 Amazon warriatrices determines the grammatical gender of the whole group. Similarly, the fact that *groups* of men are marked with vowels higher than any other marking for gender reflects the patriarchal character of western society. While it is not yet clear what social factors vowel frontness and rounding correspond to, they are almost certainly not good for women.

The systematic, exceptionless refusal to notice such blatant correlations between linguistic structure and social structure cries out for explanation. Naturally, such a grotesquely myopic view of the field cannot be innocent; the mockery and abuse with which former publications of this researcher have been dismissed and silenced by the American linguistic establishment show that the Old Boys know the jig is up and that uppity enlightened researchers are pounding at the gates.

---

* Not to mention from the testimony of the article itself, which you'll be able to read as soon as you've worked your way through this overly-long sentence fragment of a footnote (which, even if some people thought it wasn't too long before, surely is being made excessive by the addition of this parenthetical comment, by means of which we've stretched the footnote out to six lines, with the result that surely even the most polite of readers would agree that this tedious footnote—which has, shockingly, made it all the way to nine lines without a period, and seems likely to reach ten (see, there it is!)—has gone on way too long).

Fortunately, there is a journal like *Speculative Grammarian* whose hard-headed commitment to linguistic truth of any variety makes it a fit battering ram for breaking down those gates. By eschewing the Old Boys' Network of peer review, deference to "authorities in the field," and persnickety standards of "accuracy," "reproducibility," "consistency," "coherence," and "rudimentary philological competence," Trey Jones's editorial practice jibes with his own revolutionary linguistic attainments. Indeed, I would like to take this opportunity to laud him for the kernel of this article. When I first heard him speaking Italian, such turns of phrase as *I mio caramella siamo gialle* offended my ears, but upon realizing that he was devoted in practice as well as theory to a thoroughgoing scuttling of all invidious grammatico-social distinctions, I attained enlightenment and have since followed his precepts and practice in my own linguistic work.

"I find righteous denunciations of the present state of the language no less dismaying than the present state of the language."

—LIONEL TRILLING

CHOOSE YOUR OWN CAREER IN LINGUISTICS—PART 8

YOU DOUBLE MAJOR IN LINGUISTICS AND ASTRONOMY...

After a couple of semesters, you realize that you've chosen astronomy because it is as close as you can come to majoring in "science fiction". But what the heck, you've almost completed both degrees, so you finish.

In the meantime, you've developed quite a set of peeves about so-called "alien" languages in science fiction books, movies, and television. Most are clearly Indo-European and have no interesting features *at all!*

As you are investigating linguistics Ph.D. programs, you happen to mention your "alien" language peeve to a friend of a friend at another university. It turns out that his wife is working on a new television series for the Sci Fi Channel, and she's a fan of Steven Pinker (who was unavailable). Do you want the job?

- Take the job. Go to Part 17 on page 135.

- Pass and just go to grad school in linguistics. Go to Part 18 on page 101.

Choose Your Own Career in Linguistics starts on page 301.

PEARLS OF WISDOM FROM
STUDENTS OF LINGUISTICS

The words are used informally, which reflects the low social status of these words.

In recent years, many wise sociolinguists have abandoned the fetish for rigor which for so long disfigured their writings, and have dispensed with such unnecessary appurtenances as data collection and tests of statistical significance. Instead, they promote cultural validation by recording other people's personal experiences relating to language, power, and identity.* Particularly advanced sociolinguists have even figured out how to dispense with other people and just talk about themselves. A truly praiseworthy example of this recent trend can be seen in the following article by ɹɐbɪn O'Jonesson.

The Sociolinguistic Impact of Hippie Linguist Naming Practices

ɹɐbɪn O'Jonesson

There is little discussion in the literature concerning the social and psychological effects of the distinctive and unusual names given to children by their hippie parents, such as Moonbeam, Peacekarma, Ryvre, Starchild, Redpony, and so many more. Even less attention has been paid to the naming practices of the particular subculture of hippie linguists, who advocated for free morphemes in the 60s and gave their children names such as Monophthongbreathstream, Pronouncopula, Rezonator, Asteriskchild, Redponymy, and Noam.

The family VW van in 1971.

Very few people so-named have kept their monikers into adulthood. Most have abandoned them—sometimes informally, but in many cases, legally changing them—in favor of more conventional names, such as Fred and Alice. (John and Mary are less popular among the offspring of hippie linguists, for obvious reasons.) My own brush with hippie linguistic onomastics left me somewhat less scarred than most, so I want to share my story.

I was born in 1966 to two otherwise regular Americans who happened to be Ph.D. candidates in linguistics—Axolotl and Vicuña O'Jonesson. Several of their linguist friends had already had children, and the "hippie linguist" naming craze was well underway. My parents were indeed proponents of free morphemes who dabbled in lexicalism, but there was a definite conservative streak to their thinking. My father, Axolotl, had no experience with having an unusual name, since he grew up in a small town with four other boys named Axolotl. Thus, he was concerned about the long-term social consequences of their choice of name for me, their first child. My mother, Vicuña,

---

convinced him that I would be ostracized by the other hippie linguists' children in the linguistics department communal daycare ("The Kibitz") if my name were too "square". They compromised by giving me a fairly traditional gender-neutral name, but spelling it out in IPA: /ɹɒbɪn/. The slashes are indeed part of my name, though I rarely use them nowadays.

It turned out that the other kids at The Kibitz were generally kind to me, though they did find my name unusually uninteresting. My middle school classmates were less kind, but by high school I learned that if I never wrote my name down, and I spoke to all my teachers before classes started, none of the other students would figure out that my name had an odd spelling.

I went to the same politically liberal liberal arts college my parents went to, and there no one seemed to mind or even care about my name. After college I had some trouble getting and holding a job. One of my bosses regularly called me "Joe-bin"—I still can't for the life of me figure out why—and I couldn't take it. Another job fell through because I could not convince them that my passport or driver's license were real. Eventually I settled into a job as a computational linguist

THE WISDOM
OF LINGUISTS

Once bilingual, twice shy.

for a large sushi wholesaler. Most days, I don't think of myself or my name as different from those around me. However, I regularly have exchanges like this:

<phone rings>

Restaurant wage slave: Hello, this is Fancy Schmancy Restaurant! How can I help you?

Poor child of hippie linguists: Hi, I'd like to make a reservation for dinner.

RWS: Great, what's your name?

PCoHL: ɹɒbɪn

RWS: Okay, could you spell that for me?

PCoHL: (resisting urge to say, "Exactly as it sounds.") Turned-r, turned-script-a, b, small-caps-i, n

RWS: I'm sorry, what?

PCoHL: Turned-r, an upside down lowercase r; turned-script-a, an upside down script a, not the one with the extra hook on top! Some people use that one sometimes, but then my name would sound more like *rubbin'*, though not exactly. It's kinda funny, there's not a good word in Standard American Engli—

RWS: I'm sorry, what?

PCoHL: Oh, sorry. Turned-r, turned-script-a, then b, then a small-caps-i, which is...

RWS: Is this some sort of joke?

PCoHL: What? No! That's how you spell my name!

RWS: That gibberish isn't a name.

PCoHL: Oh. Yeah, well, sadly, it is. My parents are linguists.

RWS: Ling-what-now?

PCoHL: Linguists. They study language. My name is spelled in the International Phonetic Alphabet.

RWS: International phone-a-what-now?

PCoHL: The International Phonetic Alphabet! See, it's a universal system for transcribing the sounds of all the world's lang—

RWS: Y'know what? I'm sorry, we're all booked up for dinner tonight.

PCoHL: Oh. Okay. What about tomorrow?

RWS: Sorry, all booked up!

PCoHL: Next week?

RWS: We're going out of business after tomorrow. Sorry!

PCoHL: Okay. Sorry.

RWS: <click>

PCoHL: But, but... I even left off the slashes indicating the broad transcription. <sniff>

One day, though, the dreaded call to a make a reservation went more like this:

Poor child of hippie linguists: ... My name is in the International Phonetic Alphabet.

Restaurant wage slave: But if your name were in the Arabic or Russian alphabets you'd just transliterate it into the Latin alphabet. Why don't you save yourself some trouble and do the same. I'll put you down as capital-r-o-b-i-n and we'll go from there. How many in your party?

PCoHL: Wait, did you just suggest I transliterate my name?

RWS: Yes, of course. How many in your party?

PCoHL: And you used the English subjunctive to do it?

RWS: I suppose so, yes. How many in your party?

PCoHL: What's your name?

RWS: I'm not really supposed to say, but it's Pat. I need you to tell me how many people the reservation is for or I'll get in trouble with my boss.

PCoHL: Oh, uh, one. Unless you'll have dinner with me tonight, Pat.

RWS: Really?

PCoHL: Really. Please.

RWS: Okay.

PCoHL: Reservation for two, then, please.

RWS: Reservation for two. I'll meet you here at 8! Gotta run. <click>

PCoHL: I'm in love.

We were married eight months later!

As my anecdote amply demonstrates, there is hope for the onomastically challenged, even those burdened by hippie linguist parents! To all—except the children of modern hipster linguists, who are doomed—don't give up!

Special thanks to my younger siblings /kwɪn/, /krɪs/, and [sɪdni], who encouraged me to share my story.

PEARLS OF WISDOM FROM
STUDENTS OF LINGUISTICS

Ironically, although German is the largest European native language, English is favoured as a national language for Britain and Ireland.

**CHOOSE YOUR OWN
CAREER IN LINGUISTICS—PART 25**

YOU ANALYZE THE PATTERN
YOU FOUND IN THE SETI DATA...

The more you look at the data, the more it makes sense. Eventually, you realize that there is a diagram in the data. It isn't that complex, and the symbols are all surprisingly familiar—you manage to build the device it describes, though you come to suspect a hoax.

Once the device is complete and powered up, you have misgivings about activating it.

- Push the big obvious button on the device. Go to Part 26 on page 53.
- Ask your labmate what she thinks of the device. Go to Part 27 on page 124.

Choose Your Own Career in Linguistics starts on page 301.

THE WISDOM OF LINGUISTS
Better latent than negated.

Even if we haven't published as many articles about sociolinguistics as we have about, say, obscure languages possibly spoken on some mountain top in Nepal, we wish to reiterate that we are not opposed to sociolinguistics in principle.* To prove it, we will close this chapter by reprinting a game advertisement that we published a few years ago, at the behest of our friends at Panini Press. This game looks like it would be very interesting to sociolinguists, or to anyone else who likes boring things.

Carcassonorant

Panini Press EuroSprachGames

In this ingenious tile-laying game, players construct dialect regions by creating a fictionalized map of the southern French country-side. Each player, in turn, draws a tile, which may bear a vowel or consonant or an urban or rural isogloss line. He must then place the tile such that it matches those already played. Points are scored by completely encircling a contiguous region with isogloss lines, by joining multiple urban populations within a single "dialect" region, and by sabotaging an opponent's dialect region by causing its defining feature to become unpronounceable.

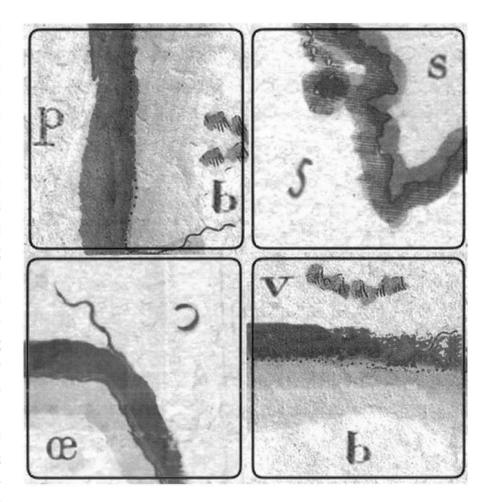

Expansion modules include: Carcassonorant Northern France; Carcassonorant Spain; Carcassonorant Italy; Carcassonorant Portugal; and the ultra-challenging Carcassonorant Pan-Romance.

SprachSpiel des Jahres for 2000. 🐦पा

---

* In fact, we would be happy to print more sociolinguistics articles if only people would submit more of them. More good ones, we mean. We actually get more sociolinguistics submissions than any other kind, but they're almost all so half-baked that we toss them out after reading the first few sentences.

IT IS WELL KNOWN AMONG LINGUISTS...

Latin once had an eighth declension, but it was wiped out after Cato the Elder (mistakenly) assigned a Carthaginian provenance to it and fomented a series of prosecutions against it. Ironically, it was highly toxic to elephants.

Typology

There are two types of linguists, Lumpers and Splitters.
But they're basically the same, really.

TYPOLOGISTS STUDY THE distribution of putative features across languages, and by extension, attempt to move toward claims for language universals. The field couldn't really come into its own until linguists had grammars of a lot of different languages to play with ("Western European Indo-European Languages" don't count as "a lot of *different* languages"), but

its attractions are obvious. For one thing, having an enormous collection of odd bits of information about a wide range of languages frequently enables a well-prepared conference-goer to pop someone else's theory bubble,[1] since presenters will almost always slip into saying something like "Languages don't do X" and some language[2] can be counted on to do exactly X rather robustly. For another, homing in on which statements might be true of all human languages is an imposing-sounding goal that works extremely well on grant applications, but doesn't commit the applicant to producing firm results *soon.*

Joseph Greenberg is credited with founding typology as its own subarea of linguistics in the

1960s, but precursors, of course, existed. In addition to Lord Pomfrey Swegheswiche's *A Treatise on These Divers Tongs, Being a Speculum of Languages from Antiquity to the Present, with an Appendix Detailing Their Sundrie Ornamentations and the Veterinary Practices of their Speakeres, with a Table of Post Offices of Cornwall,* published in 1578,[3] there was a more recent tradition of classifying languages on the basis of how much *oomph* they put into their morphology, as opposed to their syntax. This approach had developed from the Latinate tradition, which measured languages on the basis of how Latinate they were. Chinese, for example, was insufficiently Latin (no suffixes), and hence

---

[1] For a few minutes, at least, until the presenter can work up an account saying that whatever counter-evidence that was just proposed doesn't count, because that language *underlyingly* does something completely different that just so happens to support the presenter's claim.

[2] Usually Malagasy, but Hurrian is another old standby, and a fair number of Amazonian languages have been aggressively edging into the weird-grammar market as well.

---

[3] But see P. D. Q. Pulyu's (1994) article arguing for a slightly earlier date based on analysis of the text's distinctive ink, which may have incorporated a type of apple brandy that ceased being available in 1562, when the former abbey in which the distillery was built was burned down in one of this period's several "Devil Dog" riots spurred by the introduction of poodles into England.

"isolating",[4] Turkish kept its suffixes nicely sorted out and hence was "agglutinating", and Inuktitut had so far overshot the Latin target as to reach linguistic escape velocity, leave Earth's orbit, and enter some kind of morphemic singularity where affixes are collapsed together and hang suspended in an accretion disk of massive morphophonemic alternation. Latin itself was "inflective", which is a term of art during this period meaning "good".

But after Greenberg, typology experienced a boom period, a Golden Age of Distinctions. By examining rare, previously unheard-of languages like Spanish, we discovered that there were languages in which wanton dropping of one's pronouns was not only allowed, but in some cases even encouraged.[5] From the Basque, whom linguists encountered while trying to get to fabled Spain, we learned that some languages mark the subjects of intransitive verbs the same way they mark the objects of transitive verbs, a pattern that came to be called "ergativity", and which Basque probably developed in order to confuse the Spanish and French enough that they'd give up trying to invade the mountains. From Japanese and a host of other languages, we learned that the statement "all languages are configurational" had to be qualified by the addition of "except those that aren't." And from the Hixkaryana of South America, we learned it was possible to object before the subject was even known.

TYPOLOGY, TYPOLOGY

Typology, typology, we love your universals!
Typology, typology, we need your universals!
They tell us what will come to pass,
When objects lead and verbs come last;
Typology, typology, alas they're only tendencies.
—HYMNS FOR THE
REVERENT LINGUIST (1845)

Typology continues to be a fascinating and expanding field, and one that influences developments in theory. For example, it enabled one strain of theory to incorporate "parameters", which were restatements of observations, excitingly recast as explanations for the same observations, and then went on to enable those working in the theory to advance their work by boldly abandoning parameters.[6] It is a particularly "green" subarea of linguistics as well, in that once an area has been mined for publications, a redefinition of terms, or some standard insertion of null categories or the like, frees up the same area to be mined all over again (this is not even including the benefits of being able to analyze what speakers *should* be saying instead of what they mistakenly frequently do). We are quite proud that our publication has ridden this wave of work, of whose main flow and various eddies, cross-currents, occasional leaping and incarnadine herring, and sprayful bits the following articles should give you a taste.

---

[4] This would have come as a terrific surprise to most Chinese-speakers at that point, since very few had any occasion to feel particularly isolated.

[5] Latin doesn't drop pronouns; it elides them, a trick it (nobly) beat out of Greek in a dark alleyway in Tarentum before going on to enslave some more mathematicians and artists.

---

[6] As with vigorous weightlifting, it feels so *good* when you stop. To engage in an uncharacteristic paroxysm of fairness, though, we should acknowledge that some of the proposed parameters *collected together* disparate observations that no one had previously claimed to be related, an attempt that bordered dangerously on the scientific before it soared safely away, snatched from danger by the spirit of Rube Goldberg.

Joseph Greenberg, the father of modern typology and the Abélard of historical linguistics,* focused his seminal paper on correlations in basic word orders, using order of subject, verb, and object as one of the factors examined. In the following analysis of Kluj, Arnold Fasnacht illustrates how information from newly-described languages can provide a crucial test of existing typological universals.

A New Basic Word Order: VOV

Arnold P. Fasnacht
Department of Linguistics
School of Agriculture and Drama
University of Southern North Dakota at Hoople
Hoople, North Dakota 61637

Recent years have seen a steady increase in the number of attested basic word order types. Greenberg (1963) originally recognized only three types, VSO, SVO, and SOV. Pullum (1977) added VOS to the list, but proposed that no others were possible. Derbyshire (1977) confirmed the existence of OVS, and recent reports (SIL Grapevine 1978) have indicated that OSV must also be recognized. These findings have caused a certain flurry of excitement among theoretical linguists. Reactions to the discoveries may be broadly divided into two classes, both of them annoyingly smug.

The first reaction is typified by M. Joos, in a hastily-convened press conference at Milwaukee Airport: "Look, it's like I was saying back in 1951. Any damn thing is possible in these weirdo languages. If Lennie were here today he'd be so happy. You know, if those guys at MIT had only stuck to classifying allophones, we'd all be a lot better off today, especially me."

The second reaction is typified by P.M. Pistol, in a 763-page squib in *Linguistic Inquiry* (Pistol 1978–81). He points out, with more satisfaction than really seems to be called for, that the six types now known are **exactly** the six types predicted to be possible by his latest revolutionary contribution to linguistics, Car Park Grammar.[1] "Actually," he remarks in a touchingly honest footnote, "I could only get four of them until I realized that certain interjection-forming phenomena present in my dialect (though not, apparently, in anyone else's) required an additional theoretical device, the Wiggly Blue Line, and that did it."

While I am confident that the excessive pessimism of a Joos need not discourage us in our search for Universal Grammar, I will demonstrate in this paper that linguistic metatheory must be sufficiently enriched to allow for the existence of yet another basic word order, VOV, an order apparently not predicted, or even allowed, by any existing theoretical framework except stratificational grammar, which seems to allow everything except English.[2]

---

* At least in terms of how happy he made fellow historical linguists.

[1] Car Park Grammar is known only through an unpublished 37-volume mimeo by Pistol entitled "On the Surface Interjection 'Ouch'!", and a rather brief elementary account, *Dick and Jane Have Fun with Colored Pencils.* It regards linguistic structure as consisting of a series of levels connected by ramps. The only operation is the repeated raising of elements from one level to the next, until they find a level with a vacant position available. If, as frequently happens, no such vacant position can be found, the element must then return all the way to the bottom and station itself next to a Yellow Line, whereupon a filtering device promptly assigns an asterisk in a little plastic envelope. Derivations are lengthy and seldom terminated.

[2] P.M. Pistol (personal putdown) now informs me that Car Park Grammar does indeed predict the existence of the VOV pattern, given yet another device, the Double-Headed Pink Arrow. Inde-

The language in question is Kluj (pronounced 'cloodge'), spoken by some seventy-five unattractive persons of rather unsanitary habits who live in an isolated valley near the town of Cojones in Westchester County. The language has, until recently, received little attention, at least partly because of the Klujans' habit of eating strangers (the U of SND at H has lost five graduate students in this way). Its genetic affiliations are consequently uncertain, though Hasenpfeffer (unpublished ditherings) has claimed it for his proposed Macro-Hudson Valley family (Joisey, Bronkish, the extinct Stengelese, and the **curious** Madison Avenue Creole). But then Hasenpfeffer has been known to claim that the Puerto Ricans are the Lost Ten Tribes of Israel.

Accompanied only by a German shepherd guard dog and an Uzi submachine gun, I carried out eight field trips among the Klujans between 1961 and 1976.[3] These field trips were supported, if that is the word, by the U of SND at H.[4]

During these field trips I was able to obtain, for the first time, an extensive corpus of material recorded in Kluj.[5] This material I have now transcribed and analyzed, and while a number of difficulties remain,[6] the most important features are reasonably clear.

One of the most interesting aspects of Kluj grammar is word order. Although it was a relatively simple matter to establish that the verb occurs both initially and finally in the sentence, the order of the remaining elements appeared quite unaccountably variable until I suddenly realized that it was governed by a simple, if novel, rule—

---

pendent support for the DHPA is provided by the fact that certain strings are unexpectedly ill-formed in Pistol's dialect; e.g., *Trace theory strikes me as a big step forward and *These new papers by Bresnan and Lightfoot are exciting.

[3] I am a slow worker.

[4] It must be admitted that the linguistics department at the U of SND at H is perhaps not quite so up to date as it might be on the theoretical side, and that my attempts to introduce the faculty to works written since 1952 have met a mixed response at best. Nevertheless, in a spirit of Christian charity, I can only forgive the somewhat intemperate comments on my work which have occasionally been made, as, for example, by the head of the department, Professor Snodgrass: "Fieldwork? That long-haired fancy-pants pinko pansy from MIT wants to do **fieldwork?** The one who thought an allophone was a French telephone? I'll bet he can't even find the 'record' button on his tape recorder. Haw haw haw." I do, however, resent the suggestion that I only received an unprecedented eight research fellowships from the university because the department kept hoping that I would be eaten.

[5] These recordings are now available in the Language Archives and Fertilizer Storage Space at the U of SND at H, under the heading Kluj, vols. II–IV and VI–VIII. Volume I was never recorded, due to an unfortunate difficulty with the tape recorder. Volume V was recorded, but after a Klujan cat chose to relieve himself on it, it acquired a rather pungent smell, and the librarian/gardener refused to have it in the Archives.

These tapes were the source of some of the difficulties between Professor Snodgrass and me. The economic situation being what it is, I had to re-use old tapes for my fieldwork; by an unfortunate mistake I went off to Cojones with tapes containing several thousand hours of Professor Snodgrass's telephone tapping (Professor Snodgrass is a devoted disciple of Charles Fries). When he discovered that I had unwittingly erased the results of five years' work, he became somewhat more excited than usual and attempted to nail me up behind the door next to his Chomsky dartboard. Fortunately, I was able to persuade him that there remained enough tapes to do valuable work. It transpired that these remaining tapes contained only some 600 hours of the Speaking Clock in Fargo-Moorhead which had been recorded by mistake. From this superficially rather barren corpus, Professor Snodgrass, by applying rigorous post-Bloomfieldian distributional analysis, was able to produce his magnum opus, "The Grammar of Time in North Dakota". This was offered to our local organ, the *Working Papers of the Linguistic Circle of North Dakota and South-Eastern Saskatchewan*; but it was unfortunately rejected (the first contribution EVER rejected by the *WP of the LC of ND and SES*). Fortunately for all concerned (especially me), he was able to find another publisher, and the work will be appearing shortly in *Linguistics*.

[6] It must be confessed that these difficulties are at least partly due to the fact that, for excellent medical reasons, I never attended a single one of the phonetics practicals I was supposed to do for my degree. It is also true that I was never able to solve any of the morphology problems in Nida's book, but I believe that linguistics should concern itself with higher things than morphology.

namely, that when the first word in the sentence begins with a consonant, the order is Direct Object—Indirect Object—Time—Manner—Place, while when the first word begins with a vowel, the order is exactly the reverse: Place—Manner—Time—Indirect Object—Direct Object.[7]

Remarkable as these details are, they are surely not as striking as the fundamental VOV pattern of Kluj sentences, since this represents a previously unattested basic word order. No doubt the reader's mind is crowded with questions at this point. Let us begin with the question which is easiest to answer.

Where does the subject go in a Kluj sentence? The alert reader will have observed that the VOV pattern makes no allowance for an S, such as is typically found in the basic word orders of many other languages—English, Spanish, Zeneyze (Gen-

WOULD YOU LIKE SPAGHETTI
OR LASAGNA FOR DINNER?

Typologist: "Spaghetti. It's a more prototypical instance of the category of pasta."

oese), Macedonian, Basque, Dyirbal, Southern Paiute, Avar, and South Greenlandic Eskimo are among the languages which have been shown to have subjects in their basic word order. Kluj, however, does not. At least it has no subject in SURFACE structure. Both Universal Grammar and internal considerations in the grammar of Kluj (see below) require that we postulate the existence of a subject in the deep structure of each sentence. Its deep-structure position is something of a problem, but given the above facts about Kluj word order, it seems best to assign the subject a variable position in deep structure, in line with the variable position of other elements, and to generate Kluj deep structures by means of context-sensitive categorical rules, that is, rules of the general form

$$\alpha \, A \, \beta \rightarrow \alpha \, \omega \, \beta \quad A \in V_A; \;\; \alpha, \beta, \omega \in (V_A \cup V_T)^*\,[8]$$

The reason that a Kluj sentence has no overt surface subject is that the subject is invariably incorporated lexically into the verb. I do not mean that the subject is represented by a bound morpheme attached to the verb. Rather, to each English verb there corresponds a large number of Kluj verbs, each lexically marked for a distinct subject. For example, corresponding to English

---

[7] On making this discovery, I immediately informed Professor Sticky of Ohio State University, who I knew was even then composing a masterwork to prove that such things cannot be. He promptly obtained a grant to come and see for himself, and a few days later he arrived at Cojones, smiling confidently and assuring me that he would "have this little wrinkle sorted out in half a jif". As the days passed, however, he became increasingly morose and refused to talk to me about Kluj. One night he turned up at my hut with a strange expression on his face and explained that he had found a beautifully simple solution to the whole problem and was going out to check it with some native speakers. The nature of his solution began rapidly to dawn on me a few minutes later when I heard a long burst of fire from my Uzi and, rushing outside, I found that he had machine-gunned some sixteen of my informants. Had he not fortunately run out of ammunition at this point, I shudder to think what the consequences might have been for linguistic metatheory, not to mention for me, since I suspect that Sticky's suddenly-professed interest in amateur fire-eating does not entirely explain the can of gasoline I found next to my bed and my notes. In any case, it hardly seems fair to blame me for the resulting bad publicity, which led the Dean once again to renew his threat to merge the Linguistics Department with the Department of Advertising and Packaging, or worse still, with the Department of Phonetics.

---

[8] Pretty nifty, eh? Actually, this bit has nothing to do with the rest of the paper, and I'm not even too sure I understand it. I just copied it out of a book and stuck it in to give the impression I'm *au fait* with all this dreadful hairy formal stuff you keep seeing nowadays—you know, Shaumjan, Karttunen, Gazdar, people like that. To tell the truth, I've never made it through three pages of Shaumjan or Karttunen, and as for Gazdar, all I've ever understood from **his** stuff is that he doesn't care too much for Geoffrey Sampson. I don't see why he can't write in English like other people, instead of in those funny little squiggles. He sure does have a superbly sarcastic delivery, though, even though it makes me feel inferior. And while I'm at it, I may as well confess that I had to look up the spelling of *au fait* in the dictionary.

'go', Kluj has, among many others, the following verbs (since this paper deals with syntax, I have omitted some details of the phonology):[9]

votsiʔ	'large dog goes'
gvinlak	'small dog goes'
juʔpis	'toad goes'
ʔuʔnax	'Dodge pick-up truck goes'
miʔs	'small disc-shaped object of little value goes'
mleʔtx	'girl of marriageable age goes'
pwaʔiʔ	'respected but irascible person goes'
nvil	'I go'
ʔiswai	'Harold goes'
ʔospi	'fascist warmonger goes'
dzeitloʔ	'Ralph Nader goes'

It will be appreciated that the addition of even a single new noun to the language necessitates the creation of hundreds of new verbs. The coming of 20th century civilization and technology to the Klujan's valley has therefore meant that tens of thousands of new verbs have had to be coined to cope with the enormous influx of new nouns. Indeed, during recent years, most of the sober waking hours of the Klujans (and those are few enough) have had to be devoted to thinking up new verbs, causing a sharp decline in such favorite traditional practices as gang rape and dropping rocks on turtles. No doubt the intense hostility of the Klujans toward outsiders stems principally from this cause.

Indeed, I suspect that it is just this remarkable feature which accounts for the fact that the verb appears twice in the sentence. The point is that there are so many verbs to be mastered in Kluj that the Klujans, who are none too bright at the best of times, find difficulty in selecting the correct one to express a given meaning. Diachronically, it is easy to imagine that a Klujan speaker who had just uttered a sentence with the wrong verb would have had another stab at it, and that grammaticalization of this no doubt extremely frequent type of utterance would have resulted in the VOV pattern of modern Kluj. Support for this hypothesis is found in the observation that, even today, it is a rare sentence in which both verbs are actually identical, and in the further observation that utterances of the type VOVV, VOVVV, and so on, are not uncommon, as the speaker makes repeated attempts to find the right verb.[10]

---

[9] Such as consonants and vowels. I have used the symbols ʔ and i more or less at random to indicate any segment whose precise phonetic nature I was never able to elucidate. This should not be taken to mean that the remaining transcriptions are accurate. Those damn Klujans never seem to pronounce a word the same way twice.

Anyway, for what it's worth, a summary of Klujan phonology will appear in the forthcoming *Festschrift Snodgrass*. Professor Snodgrass, feeling somewhat aggrieved that no one had seen fit to prepare a Festschrift in his honor, intimidated his students into organizing one. The response so far has been somewhat disappointing, however, as the only contributions have been three dog-eared typescripts which have apparently been rejected by every journal in the Northern Hemisphere, an obscene verse, a typically original paper from Hasenpfeffer deriving certain Black English lexical items from Lappish reindeer-driver's slang, and a rather fulsome tribute which was obviously written by Snodgrass himself under a pseudonym. For this and other reasons, the work is affectionately known around here as the Snodgrass Shortschrift.

---

[10] Even more common, in fact, are utterances in which the final attempt at the verb is followed by a curse or, more commonly, a string of curses. Actually, such patterns as VOVC, VOVVCCC, VOVCCCC, etc., are so frequent in ordinary speech (the Klujans apparently finding curses easier to think of than verbs) that for a while I considered taking VOVCC as the basic word order. I finally decided against this on the ground that it was undignified. It was in connection with this problem that I seemed to have found a language that was worthy of my talents.

G. Gazdar, eschewing for once the use of the second-order predicate calculus, has suggested (personal junk mail) that the superficial VOV pattern of Kluj sentences is to be derived from underlying VO by means of two rules: (1) a rule of inverse reduplication (or "broken mirror" rule, as he calls it), which repeats all the words of the sentence in reverse order, thereby converting VO into VOOV, and (2) a rule which deletes the second of two

Kluj is particularly interesting from the typological point of view. Since it is both a verb-initial and verb-final language, the reader may be wondering how it lines up with respect to the well-known typological correlations of word order first unearthed by Greenberg (1963) and extended by other workers. I am happy to be able to report that Kluj behaves in a way entirely in accord with these correlations, exhibiting a degree of internal logic which is almost breathtaking.

Consider adpositions. It is well-known that VO languages tend to have prepositions, while OV languages usually have postpositions. Not surprisingly, perhaps, Kluj has AMBIPOSITIONS. That is, each adposition consists of two parts, one preposed to the object and one postposed. An example is provided by the extremely common locative ambiposition *nvi?...dzlots* 'in/on/at/around/under/beside/between', as in

1. glu?ni pflaxi nvi?spwatsdzlots glu?ni
   'I'm gonna stick this knife in/on/at/around/
   under/beside/between your fat gut.'

(In this case the context did not allow me (rather fortunately, I think) to determine which of the various possible interpretations was intended, and it may have been that all of them were. It will be noted that in this case the speaker had no difficulty in selecting the correct verb on the first attempt; this is typically so with threats, which appear to come more naturally to my Klujan informants than most other types of utterances.)

The same elegant solution is found with relative clauses, which surround their head noun, and with possessives, which behave similarly (actually, the first person singular possessive appears to be the only one in common use). As for verbal modifiers, adverbs, naturally enough, are simply placed between the two occurrences of the verb. The placement of modals might appear to pose a somewhat more difficult problem, but here Kluj exhibits a beautifully simple solution to its typological dilemma: it doesn't have any modals. This might appear to be a remarkable lack, but the Klujans seem to manage very well with threatening gestures.

Kluj might have been expected to exhibit gapping in both directions, but in fact it has no gapping rule at all. It might at first seem surprising that a language whose speakers have so much difficulty remembering verbs should pass up a rule which deletes verbs from the sentence, but a moment's thought reveals that the deletion of a verb in Kluj would inevitably entail the deletion of its subject as well, and even the Klujans are not so stupid as to attempt to communicate with a string of clauses of the general form O.

In sum, then, it appears that linguistic metatheory must be suitably enriched so as to be able to account for this remarkable and fascinating language,[11] that many theoretical positions must

> ### IT IS WELL KNOWN AMONG LINGUISTS...
>
> While the <+N> feature underlying the category 'noun' in many world languages is primarily a feature of Universal Grammar, small deposits of it also occur naturally in the mineralized Neo-archian calderas of the Canadian Shield, particularly in Ontario.

---

adjacent identical NP's. Such a proposal is typical of the armchair linguist who only reshuffles other people's data after someone else has done the spade work. To the experienced investigator (i.e., me), it is immediately and blindingly obvious that such derivational complexities are far beyond the average Kluj speaker's "competence" (I use the word in its technical, if ridiculous, sense), and Gazdar's proposal will not be further considered, not even to be crushed by a dozen devastating counter-arguments.

N.B.: I am compelled by the US Freedom of Information Act to admit that in fact I have no such counter-arguments, but am merely bluffing.

---

[11] P.M. Pistol, in the vanguard as always, assures me that he has already added several new colors to his collection of pencils, and

be rethought and many putative universals abandoned, that many other grandiose if somewhat vague conclusions must be found if I am ever going to get this work accepted as a Ph.D. dissertation, and that this paper had better be published before Sticky gets out on parole, since he continues to harbor a most unfortunate and, in my view, rather unscientific attitude toward my findings.[12]

---

that we can expect revolutionary new developments from him any day.

[12] It is customary, in works of this sort, for the investigator to express, in the most nauseatingly fulsome terms, his undying gratitude to his informants for having put aside their livelihood to answer thousands of idiotic questions about subject-to-subject raising, for having graciously provided most of the crucial insights leading to whatever cockeyed analysis he is proposing, for having darned his socks, ironed his shirts, and tenderly nursed him through a bout of yellow fever in preference to their own children, for having through their rich and sensitive mythology and poetry, revealed to him the Oneness of all living creatures, and for having generally contrived to make him a wiser and better human being. I trust that my fellow linguists will forgive me if I depart from this tradition for once, since I cannot honestly say that I found my Klujan informants even bearable, let alone friendly and cooperative. Their repeated attempts to poison my water supply, while no doubt amusing enough at first, eventually wore my patience rather thin. I cannot say, either, that I found the land mine buried in front of my door the least bit entertaining, and I am sure that Mr. Frobisher, our late postman, who discovered it, would agree with me if he were still with us. In fact, it is difficult to say which of my informants constituted the gravest menace to civilized society, though I would be inclined to nominate the Klujan's Managing Director, Harvey Wallbanger, whose habit of sharpening his butcher knife and running his finger across his throat with an evil grin whenever he saw me did nothing to improve my concentration. It is perhaps best for all concerned that he was one of the victims of Professor Sticky's solution. Nor can I say I am sorry to have smelled the last of Swampgas Annie Veeblefetzer, whose unique combination of unpleasant personal characteristics made her single-handedly the principal source of air pollution in the entire valley. From this general condemnation I might almost except old Sanford Chickenwing-Smythe, the group's *bugi*, or public-relations man. True, he was not much use as an informant, since he was never sober enough to say anything coherent, but at least he never attacked me, threatened me, or threw up over the microphone, like most of his fellow Klujans. But the only Klujan for whom I retain any degree of affection at all is Suzette "Hot Pants" Cummings-Shortley, whose generous

IT IS WELL KNOWN AMONG LINGUISTS…

Hypotheses that the undeciphered language used in some Grunge-band lyrics is reverb-initial have been strongly countered by typologists, who have argued instead that it is either nonconfigurational or something other than nonconfigurational.

The echo knows all languages.
—FINNISH PROVERB

and even enthusiastic attempts to teach me her language, and several other interesting things, by one of the most time-honored and delightful techniques, were undoubtedly the high point of my investigations. It was only after a number of these sessions, followed by a hasty visit to a physician, that I began to understand why the other Klujans, who still harbor a violent grudge against the rest of us for draining their ancestral swamps and forcing them to invent thousands of new verbs, used to refer to Suzette as their "secret weapon". And while I'm on the subject, I would like to offer my most sincere apologies to all those young ladies in my Field Methods tutorial group who may have found themselves unwitting and indirect victims of the Klujan's revenge.

Typology starts with observing distributions of features across languages, but its essence lies in examining correlations among these features. Sean Geraint, in the following insightful piece, provides a stellar example of such work in the realm of biophysical functional typology—the study of correlations between language features and the biophysical environments of speakers.*

Language Evolution and the Acacia Tree

Sean Geraint

Last year, renowned treethnographer Garik Roblerks noticed that two books on the evolution of language had strikingly similar covers. Both Christiansen & Kirby's *Language Evolution* and Fitch's *The Evolution of Language* boasted an acacia tree in the sunset. On closer inspection, these turned out to be different pictures of the **same tree.** (See Figure 1.)

Having spent a year tracking trees in Kenya, I can confirm that the tree is from Maasai Mara National Reserve. The tree has attracted a lot of attention since its entrance into the glamorous world of book cover design, and I observed some excited undergraduate linguists tying ribbons to its branches with messages such as "Thanks for the episodic memories" and "Dolphins next, please".

Of course, this prompts the question— what is the link between language evolution and acacia trees? Obviously, there was some subconscious (perhaps innate?) connection in the minds of the authors. The first step was to look at the distribution of acacia trees around the world. Strikingly, the distribution of acacia trees (Figure 2) looks remarkably

Figure 1: A comparison of the books by Christiansen & Kirby (left) and Fitch (right)

---

* *Speculative Grammarian* did not receive any incentives, monetary or otherwise, from The Acacia Tree's™® phenomenally efficient and proactive agent, Joe-John "Linnaeus" van der Wezel.

like the distribution of tonal languages (Figure 3). Indeed, the countries in which the acacia tree *Acacia nilotica* grows are significantly more likely to have tonal languages (Chi-squared with Yates' continuity correction for having spent ten hours nudging the data around = 47.1, df = 1, p < 0.0001, data from the Crop Protection Consortium and the World Atlas of Language Structures).

Quite remarkable, but this would just be a pointless, spurious statistic without a causal mechanism. I was then reminded that acacia trees produce tryptamines such as Dimethyltryptamine (DMT). These are psychedelic compounds that can cause sensory enhancement, euphoria, immersive experiences and radical perspective shifting. These are, of course, not only extremely useful in coming up with hypotheses about the origins of language, but exactly the kinds of mind-altering substances that we could expect to cause the rapid evolution of language in the first place.

So, I propose the acacia hypothesis of language evolution: Some primates got high and thought it would be a laugh to try and refer to objects using arbitrary signs.

However, the effects of acacia trees on culture have been felt more recently: Shanon (2008) suggests that Moses was under the influence of this naturally occurring smack when he heard the burning bush (an acacia!) talking to him. This is direct evidence for a link between acacia trees and linguistic inspiration.

Language evolution trees in the lab

In order to investigate the effect of acacia trees on language evolution, I extended an iterated learning experiment (Kirby, Cornish, Smith, 2008):

Method

1. Recruited 1,000 participants (12% excluded because they "had seen the TV mini-series")

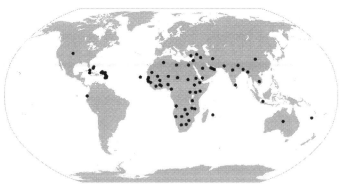

Figure 2: Distribution of acacia trees

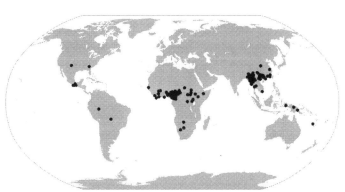

Figure 3: Distribution of tonal languages

2. Exposed participants to a random language
3. Got them to recall the language
4. Passed this recalled language on to the next participant as their input

There were two conditions—a control condition and a condition where the participants were administered 50mg of Dimethyltryptamine. I then measured the amount of composystemalexity at each generation for both conditions.

Results

The DMT condition performed above the control group for the majority of generations, suggesting that the acacia tree really does have an effect on cultural transmission (see Figure 4).

The composystemalexity drops significantly in the last generation for the DMT group. Looking at the 27 words produced in the last generation, the control group looks as you would expect, although a higher WWMI[1] than usual:

nana	renana	banana
pajama	ninjana	binjana
bonjana	zombana	bombana
bill	ben	weed
pogle	andy	pandy
rag	tag	bobtail
booba	kiki	blicket
wug	dax	leedle
john	mary	book

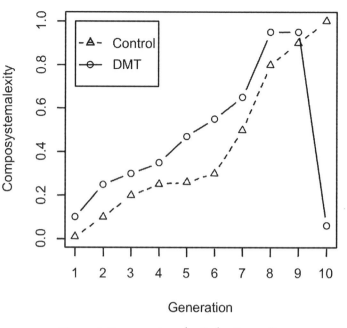

Figure 4: Composystemalexity by Generation

The words in the DMT condition were seemingly random clusters of letters and symbols. They had, quite possibly, just lost it. However, I made a startling discovery when I lined up the words one after another (Figure 5).

The language had transcended all communicative pressures and evolved to fit the cognitive biases of its users. It turns out that an important bias may be acacia trees in the sunset.

the origins of structure in human language." *PNAS*, 105(3) 10,681–10,686.

Shanon, B. (2008) "Biblical Entheogens: a Speculative Hypothesis." *Time and Mind*, 1(1) 51–74.

References

Christiansen, M. and Kirby, S. (2003) *Language Evolution.* Oxford University Press.

Fitch, W. T. (2010) *The Evolution of Language.* Cambridge, UK: Cambridge University Press.

Kirby, Cornish, Smith (2008) "Cumulative cultural evolution in the laboratory: An experimental approach to

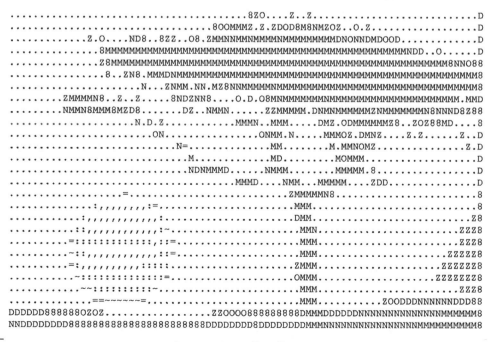

Figure 5: A startling discovery

---

[1] Watch With Mother Index.

Typologies, by necessity, tend to be highly abstract, and this can create barriers to comprehension. Making the typological claims 'visible' is thus of great importance. I. Juana Pelota-Grande demonstrates below exactly what kinds of advances can be made when one keeps in mind the dictum of the late great linguistic master, Storgrønvorte Jøda: "Explain? There is no 'explain'. Do not explain; model."

Linguistic Topology

I. Juana Pelota-Grande
Centre den Geometrik Linguistiken

That many groups of human languages are sprung from some common source is obvious to any student of the subject, whether linguist, philologist, or polyglot. However, the detailed nature of these genetic relationships is often difficult to unambiguously determine—and likely the subject of heated debate.

The impressive array of analytic methods brought to bear on the problem is a testament to the inherent difficulty of the task. However, one of the human species' most amazing tools for analysis—vision—has never been fully and properly applied to the problem.

Language and vision are two towering pillars of human cognition, yet the traditional bridge between them—the written word—is a weak conduit at best. Visually rich representations of linguistic information, such as syntactic trees, often allow the high-bandwidth processing of our visual cortexes to provide key insights.

Visual intuitions, while not necessarily rigorous, can point the way toward otherwise obscured solutions to numerous problems—hence the ascendency of computer-aided data visualization in so many fields.

In order to further harness this amazing innate capability, we at the Centre den Geometrik Linguistiken have devised a method of projecting large amounts of aggregate information about a language into a six dimensional space.

The original eight dimensions included three basic dimensions for syntactic, morphological, and phonological information, as well as five more dimensions used to represent semantic and distributional information about the lexicon.

Factor analysis of the data allowed us to find a set of normalized independent basis vectors spanning the syntactic/morphological/phonological space. These composite dimensions of a language we have given the intuitive labels *ostentatious*, *brittle*, and *votive*. The *OBV* co-ordinate system maps naturally to three spatial dimensions.

Similarly, we were able to collapse the five dependent dimensions of the lexicon down to three independent dimensions, which we call *instinct*, *understatement*, and *schadenfreude*. The three dimensions of the *IUS* co-ordinate system map readily onto RGB color co-ordinates.[*]

Thus we can reduce the eight original linguistic dimensions to three spacial and three color composite-dimensions, allowing us to render this grammatical signature of a language in *OBV-IUS* co-ordinates, which are easily interpreted by the human visual system.

The results are remarkable—family resemblances are unmistakable. Consider first some members of the Romance family, shown below.

---

[*] Editor's Note: Unfortunately, internal full-color printing is beyond the scope of this book. You'll have to use your imagination, or look up color images online.

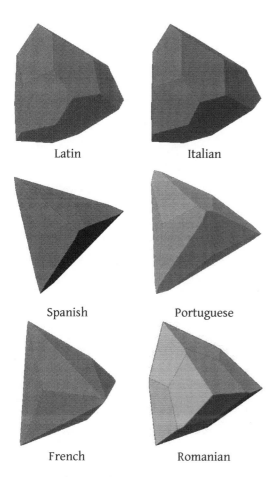

Latin   Italian

Spanish   Portuguese

French   Romanian

The genetic relationship is clear. Note that Romanian visually stands out from its sister languages, but the reasons for this are clear when we look at a couple of Slavic languages, below.

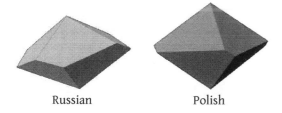

Russian   Polish

The mixed heritage of Romanian is made obvious by *OBV-IUS.* The pedigree of other languages which have blended to various degrees with genetically unrelated language families is similarly clear. Consider the Germanic languages, including the Romance-influenced bastard, English, below.

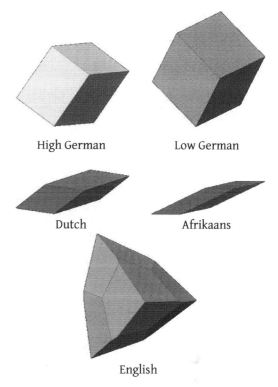

High German   Low German

Dutch   Afrikaans

English

The result of importing so much Latinate vocabulary and the long and intimate contact between Old English and Old French is the visually distinct appearance of English in the *OBV-IUS* system. In fact, it seems clear that English probably has as much claim to being a Romance language as Romanian does.

While Persian, an Indo-Iranian language, is not directly related to Arabic, the influence of a shared writing system and long cultural contact is quite apparent below.

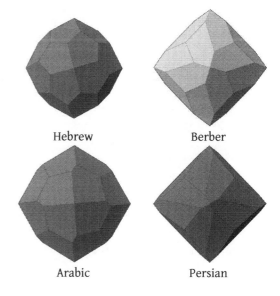

Hebrew   Berber

Arabic   Persian

Looking at the languages of East Asia below, it is unsurprising that the so-called "dialects" of Chinese are in fact closely related. The influence of both Japanese and Chinese on the Korean language is also made plain.

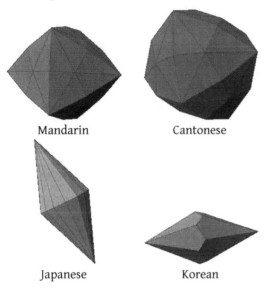

Mandarin   Cantonese

Japanese   Korean

Sign Languages were more challenging to fit into our system, but with a little creativity, they were in fact made to conform. The various relationships between sign languages are interestingly portrayed by the *OBV-IUS* interpretation below.

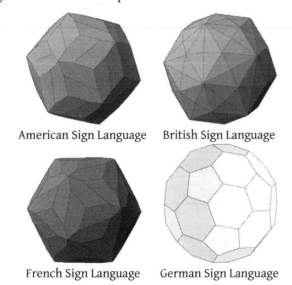

American Sign Language   British Sign Language

French Sign Language   German Sign Language

French Sign Language and American Sign Language are genetically related, while American Sign Language and British Sign Language share a superstrate language (English). Note the particular

similarities among those three, but also the superficially similar "shape" of German Sign Language. Also, note the similarities between each sign language and its superstrate language.

OBV-IUS renderings of small language families and Isolate Languages play up the distinctive features of those languages and families which make them so hard to categorize.

Below is a representative sample from the Finno-Ugric family, which is clearly distinct from the other languages previously rendered in the *OBV-IUS* way.

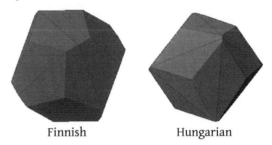

Finnish   Hungarian

Some of the singularly Isolate Languages show quite interesting and unusual features in their *OBV-IUS* renderings.

The group below shows the grammatical chaos of Basque, the unprecedented uniqueness of Burushaski, and the self-reflexive qualities of Pankararú.

The last entry, Ainu, defies all logic and explanation. No wonder it is still an Isolate.

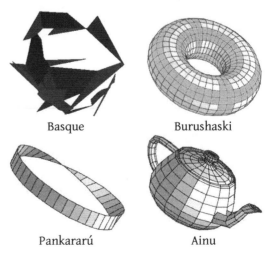

Basque   Burushaski

Pankararú   Ainu

This brief introductory paper offers merely a taste of what the study of Linguistic Topology has to offer the wider field. Visual analysis will eventually bring many Topological Universals to light, while also illuminating Topological Constraints on, for example, language change and acquisition.

It is with much anticipation that we at the Centre den Geometrik Linguistiken await feedback on this revolutionary new theory from linguistics practitioners world-wide. New data for Topological Analysis of other languages is also muchly welcomed.

Silence is golden; duct tape is silver.
— AMERICAN PROVERB

IT IS WELL KNOWN AMONG LINGUISTS...

The only unambiguous example of a total language universal is the absence of the <+FloppyHamiltonian> feature in all world languages.

Just as studying what people think about dialects ("perceptual dialectology") is a valuable activity alongside studying the actual dialects, investigations of what we might call 'affective typology' are valuable as well. The following pair of pieces, the first by a generic John Thompson and the markedly euphonious Dikembe Mutombo, the second by the prolix Jose Felipe Hernandez y Fernandez and the rugose, tessellated, and quite possibly eldritch Waxaklahun Ubah K'awil, provide excellent examples of such an endeavor.

Rating the World's Languages

Dikembe Mutombo and John Thompson
Georgetown University

One of the sillier ideas of modern linguistics is that one language is as good as another, that no language is clearly superior to any other. Acceptance of this ridiculous theory forces us into such positions as denying that the Deep South dialect of American English is an abomination, or refusing to condemn Russian for its preposterously high level of palatalization. Obviously, then, the canard of linguistic equality has to be abandoned by anyone wanting to be a realistic student of language; luckily, more and more linguists are abandoning it. Hence, it is now possible to begin elementary work in meaningful typological classification of languages: not typology which restricts itself to uninteresting structural description without value judgements, but typology which will allow us, ultimately, to rank all known human languages, living and dead, from best to worst.

This paper details the results of a preliminary analysis along these lines. We rated ten languages on a scale of one to ten in terms of six key parameters, namely simplicity of expression, clarity of expression, range of expressible content, ease of acquisition, writing system quality, and euphoniousness. Each rating was determined through very objective and highly scientific methodology which is probably too mathematical for the average linguist to understand. Standard statistical variants are indicated *infra tabula*. After rating by parameter, an overall score was assessed for each language based on the average of the six individual scores.

There can be no arguing with the validity of the scores assigned for each language in each category, but one could question the choice of parameters; for example, one might wish to add a poeticality rating. This is, we repeat, a preliminary analysis, and we welcome any and all suggested improvements.

Language	SofE	CofE	RofEC	EofA	WSQ	Euph.	Avg.
Bella Coola	5.26	3.37	4.41	5.11	6.82	0.48	4.24
Dyirbal	4.32	3.12	4.40	5.77	5.48	4.89	4.66
English	4.01	5.79	9.13	4.33	2.73	5.01	5.17
Hittite	3.98	2.12	5.71	3.35	1.52	4.10	3.46
Latin	6.12	7.98	8.72	6.54	6.09	5.67	6.85
Mandarin	8.32	6.23	7.87	3.84	3.44	4.82	5.75
Spanish	7.31	6.50	7.77	8.10	7.43	6.11	7.20
Swahili	5.03	7.03	6.99	7.78	6.11	4.12	6.18
Tagalog	4.25	4.99	5.82	5.83	5.97	4.03	5.15
Volapük	8.01	6.45	2.12	6.88	6.57	0.97	5.17

$$\Sigma=7.03 \quad \alpha=.02333 \quad \int \frac{1}{x}dx = \ln x \quad \text{क}=4 \quad \forall x.x=\clubsuit \quad \exists y.y=\copyright$$

Re-Rating the World's Languages

Waxaklahun Ubah K'awil and José Felipe Hernandez y Fernandez
University of Sprouts, Brussels

In 1991, Dikembe Mutombo and John Thompson rocked the world of linguistics with their iconoclastic article "Rating the World's Languages". With the bold statement that "the canard of linguistic equality has to be abandoned by anyone wanting to be a realistic student of language," Mutombo and Thompson opened the door to what should have been a new era in applied linguistics.

But that didn't happen. Though it would indubitably make an interesting thesis topic in the field of History of Science or Psychology of Academia, the reasons for this failure to break through are in broad scope obvious, and in detail irrelevant. The two present authors have long harbored a clandestine fascination with this under-explored topic. Having each recently achieved tenure, we can now continue Mutombo and Thompson's important work with significantly less fear of the kind of retaliation that seems to have destroyed their careers.

As the original authors discussed, the empirical scoring is ironclad, though the choice of which parameters to score is perhaps more subjective. To the original six parameters of *simplicity of expression, clarity of expression, range of expressible content, ease of acquisition, writing system quality,* and *euphoniousness,* we have added nine additional important parameters: *poeticality* (as suggested by the original authors), *practical utility, conservativeness, linguistic imperialism, sexiness, coolness, cussing/insulting capability, obstreperousness,* and *idiosyncrasy.*

Unlike the original six parameters, not all of the new parameters' scores are proportional to the degree to which the trait described is present in the language. Several (*conservativeness, linguistic imperialism,* and *idiosyncrasy*) have more-or-less U-shaped scoring curves. *Obstreperousness* is inversely proportional to the score assigned. These parameters have been normalized to the linear scoring scale. As an example, under *linguistic imperialism,* both Dyirbal and English score very poorly: Dyirbal for being insufficiently imperialistic, English for being overly so.

While there may have been some gains in the general level of mathematical sophistication in the field, our very objective and highly scientific methodology is probably still too mathematical for the average linguist to understand. Our results are presented in the table on the next page. Extrema for each *language* are underlined. Extrema for each *parameter* are in **bold.**

The collection of languages represented in this sample is somewhat irregular. We have included the original authors' list of ten, along with a number of languages commonly taught in high-school and college (to assist students in choosing an appropriate language to study), and a small number of additional constructed languages at the request of our friends in the ConLang community.

We provide some interpretation of the data in the table as a guide to others seeking to properly use this resource. While Spanish has the highest overall score, English, with the highest practical utility score, is still the best general-purpose second-language choice throughout the world. Students who are native speakers of English should look to Spanish to fulfill their language requirements—not only is it a wonderful, useful language, it is the least obstreperous among commonly-taught languages: no uvular nasals, no contrastive aspiration, tractable phonemic inventory, and a generally non-ridiculous grammar (though there were deductions for that whole "*a mi me gusta ...*" debacle).

Those thinking they should run out and learn Italian—the sexiest language on the list—are advised to keep in mind that most of the people who speak Italian are used to being wooed by native speakers of Italian, and will not likely be impressed by anything less. However, second year Italian is very good for wooing first year Italian students.

To the Klingons out there who are dissatisfied with the results of this very objective and highly scientific methodology, we would apologize, though it would do no good. Rather we refer them to the scores for Gothic and say instead "𐌺𐌿𐌽𐌹 𐌽𐌰𐌳𐍂𐌴!"

"A thing well said will be wit in all languages."
—John Dryden

Language	SofE	CofE	RofE	EofA	WSQ	Euph.	Poet.	Prac.	Cons.	Imp.	Sexy	Cool	Cuss	Obst.	Idio.	Avg.
Anglo-Saxon	5.99	6.15	5.31	4.35	5.26	7.43	9.77	1.23	0.73	0.04	6.25	7.83	7.66	5.27	7.29	5.37
Arabic	5.57	7.29	8.42	4.28	7.33	2.59	8.26	8.74	5.67	4.56	7.93	6.32	8.62	4.32	5.32	6.35
ASL	8.23	6.94	7.43	5.34	**0.79**	**8.73**	9.02	5.32	7.43	3.20	4.86	8.71	9.54	7.65	3.56	6.45
Bella Coola	5.26	3.37	4.41	5.11	6.82	0.48	3.24	0.32	0.44	0.46	1.12	1.89	**0.04**	2.34	3.45	**2.58**
Dyirbal	4.32	3.12	4.40	5.77	5.48	4.89	6.93	**0.01**	0.54	0.03	3.25	6.25	6.32	2.04	6.43	3.99
English	4.01	5.79	**9.13**	4.33	2.73	5.01	4.84	**9.87**	1.23	**0.01**	4.53	5.01	8.81	4.22	5.43	5.00
Esperanto	7.54	6.57	6.54	**8.87**	4.34	4.33	5.33	2.77	8.54	**8.87**	2.12	3.23	2.54	7.65	3.93	5.54
French	6.59	6.34	7.89	6.02	6.93	6.87	9.82	8.93	1.32	6.76	8.43	5.64	8.93	3.21	7.89	6.77
German	3.22	5.93	8.23	5.43	5.32	2.34	2.85	8.86	7.43	1.23	0.79	4.25	5.43	8.32	5.21	4.99
Gothic	4.32	6.23	5.62	4.76	4.35	3.42	6.82	1.21	0.17	0.36	6.87	**8.99**	**9.96**	5.44	6.44	5.00
Guaraní	4.86	4.23	7.03	6.72	6.03	5.82	5.83	4.11	**8.93**	2.23	4.77	6.88	8.32	6.23	8.43	6.03
Hindi	6.42	7.42	8.43	6.77	**8.43**	5.42	8.33	9.30	8.64	3.40	7.44	7.29	6.43	7.54	5.63	7.13
Hittite	3.98	**2.12**	5.71	3.35	1.52	4.10	1.12	0.45	0.02	0.11	0.37	2.45	1.59	8.43	8.54	2.92
Inuktitut	2.38	3.46	4.34	2.43	1.23	3.29	4.35	2.13	1.43	0.16	2.35	7.33	2.34	2.84	3.64	2.91
Italian	7.11	6.21	7.54	7.95	7.31	6.48	9.12	8.64	8.63	8.33	**8.79**	6.78	9.33	8.65	**8.64**	7.97
Japanese	2.11	2.67	8.62	2.23	3.86	6.77	**9.83**	8.65	6.82	5.43	5.34	7.62	2.31	3.62	5.72	5.44
Klingon	4.23	4.35	3.54	1.76	2.22	**0.19**	5.64	2.54	2.34	0.02	2.58	5.43	9.32	**1.87**	7.60	3.58
Latin	6.12	7.98	8.72	6.54	6.09	5.67	8.43	1.65	0.34	1.33	1.45	4.82	4.33	8.25	7.52	5.28
Lojban	**0.22**	**9.99**	8.23	**0.12**	7.01	3.45	**0.01**	0.10	3.20	2.56	1.34	5.73	2.24	3.23	**2.33**	3.32
Mandarin	**8.32**	6.23	7.87	3.84	3.44	4.82	5.28	9.52	7.43	1.89	1.43	5.99	6.75	2.10	3.25	5.21
Spanish	7.31	6.50	7.77	8.10	7.43	6.11	9.23	9.37	8.76	7.65	7.98	6.54	9.42	**9.87**	8.54	**8.04**
Swahili	5.03	7.03	6.99	7.78	6.11	4.12	5.99	4.02	7.35	5.43	5.42	6.87	5.43	4.73	5.66	5.86
Tagalog	4.25	4.99	5.82	5.83	5.97	4.03	6.48	5.23	5.63	7.45	4.52	5.22	8.45	8.32	7.42	5.97
Volapük	8.01	6.45	**2.12**	6.88	6.57	0.97	0.13	0.02	**0.01**	0.05	**0.03**	**0.53**	1.34	7.23	3.88	2.94
Zulu	3.98	6.43	5.49	3.82	7.27	4.77	6.56	4.35	2.43	6.54	3.42	8.42	6.28	2.34	6.57	5.24
Language	**SofE**	**CofE**	**RofE**	**EofA**	**WSQ**	**Euph.**	**Poet.**	**Prac.**	**Cons.**	**Imp.**	**Sexy**	**Cool**	**Cuss**	**Obst.**	**Idio.**	**Avg.**

$\sigma = 2.64$ $\mu = 5.20$ $\Sigma = 2078.25$ $\varepsilon << \iota$ $\alpha < \Omega$ $\forall x \exists y$ s.t. $x \perp y$

Finally, a gentle introduction to one of the more poorly understood* typological notions: non-configurationality. Here, Phineas Q. Phlogiston clearly and carefully presents the concepts of (1) configurationality, (b) non-configurationality, and (iii) explaining complex linguistic ideas through the universally accessible medium of cartoons.

Cartoon Theories of Linguistics—Non-Configurational Languages

Phineas Q. Phlogiston, Ph.D.
Unintentional University of Lghtnbrgstn

A. Mathematician Friend[1] once told me that, in mathematics, it is sometimes said that if you cannot explain the basic outline of a mathematical idea to a bright and interested 10-year-old, then you don't really understand it yourself. That got me thinking, and I've come to a couple of conclusions:

- According to my 10-year-old niece, I don't understand *any* mathematical ideas.
- Something similar could be said for linguistic ideas.[2]

It is generally accepted that math is hard (Davis & Hersh, Friend, Lakoff & Núñez, Lucas, Mac Lane, Teen Talk)— and probably harder than linguistics (Friend, Lakoff & Núñez). So, we should be able to reduce the essence of important linguistic concepts to something we can explain to that bright, interested 10-year-old. In fact, I contend that we can boil the essence right down to something we can explain in a cartoon.[3]

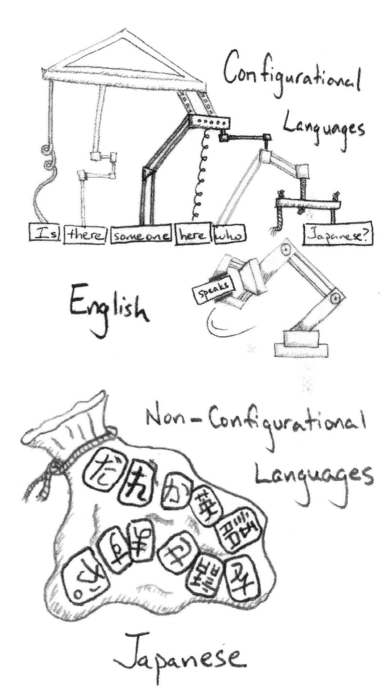

_____

* Or, perhaps, poorly defined.

[1] Not his real name.

[2] That you should be able to explain it to a 10-year-old, not that I don't understand any of them. Damn ambiguity.

[3] As luck would have it, this has already been successfully attempted before. See Don & III, and Filipepi.

As a first attempt at such a Cartoon Theory of Linguistics, I offer this treatise on configurational and non-configurational languages.

References

Davis, Philip J., and Hersh, Reuben. (1981). *The Mathematical Experience.*

Don & III. (1993). "Spaz Attack in the Corner." *Speculative Grammarian,* Vol. 147, No. 3.

Filipepi, Alessandro. (1988). "Pictures of Lily." *Psammeticus Quarterly,* Vol. 16, No. 1.

Friend, A. Mathematician. (2006). Personal communication.

Hale, Kenneth L. (1980). "Remarks on Japanese phrase structure: Comments on the Papers on Japanese Syntax." In Y. Otsu & A. Farmer (Eds.), *MIT Working Papers in Linguistics (Vol. 2).*

Hale, Kenneth L. (1982). "Preliminary remarks on configurationality." In J. Pustejovsky & P. Sells (Eds.), *Proceedings of NELS 12* (pp. 86–96).

Hale, Kenneth L. (1989). "On nonconfigurational structures." In L. Marácz & P. Muysken (Eds.), *Configurationality: The Typology of Asymmetries* (pp. 293–300).

Lakoff, George, and Johnson, Mark. (1999). *Philosophy in the Flesh.*

Lakoff, George, and Núñez, Rafael. (2000). *Where Mathematics Comes From.*

Lucas, John Randolph. (2000). *The Conceptual Roots of Mathematics.*

Mac Lane, Saunders. (1986). *Mathematics: Form and Function.*

Marácz, L., & Muysken, P. (Eds.). (1989). *Configurationality: The Typology of Asymmetries.*

Teen Talk, Barbie. (1994). Personal communication.

You are as many people as languages you know.
—Armenian proverb

Acquiring Isolation—The Peculiar Case of Ghwűừb

Tashel M. Kaithe and Valencia R. O'Shaughnessy
Montmorecy Institute of Cross-Disciplinary Studies

A long-standing tradition in linguistics has been the "discovery" of highly aberrant Amazonian languages, which are said to undermine various tenets of the prevailing linguistic theories of the day. Thus, the first description of Hixkaryana was the cause célèbre of a generation of typologists, while in the last few years Pirahã has emerged as the prime representative of all that is not possible among human languages. There have been others but we will not subject our readers to an exhaustive and tedious recounting of them.

History has been unkind to such "revelations" as these languages have supposedly provided. Hixkaryana eventually turned out simply to be a case of undiagnosed discourse patterns, while Pirahã is clearly not a human language at all (a straightforward sound change reveals the true origin of this variety, which is actually merely a local piscine dialect which underwent nasal displacement: piranha > pirahã). It began to appear that Amazonian languages (the human ones, at least) are fairly normal after all. Perhaps the linguistic speciation that had long been sought was not in fact going to be found anywhere in that whole enormous rain forest.

In 2010, however, Speculative Grammarian published the following description of the Ghwűừb language. We are confident that Kaithe and O'Shaughnessy's fascinating synthesis of linguistic and cultural facts will stand the test of time, and that Ghwűừb will be forever known as a truly weird language—the sort of language that really should not exist.

Nothing could make us more proud than to present to the world this example of utter linguistic dysfunction.

Ghwűừb, an Amazonian language spoken by a single community, initially appears to be the epitome of a linguistic isolate, perhaps the remnant of a formerly widespread language community whose speakers acquired the language of, or were displaced by, those of a different group moving into the area. Recent archeological evidence, as well as data from genetic survey research, has called this interpretation into question, however. This paper argues that an acquired isolation mechanism, driven by a confluence of genetic and cultural factors, is responsible for the "faux isolate" status of the language.

ONE OF THE MORE PREDICTABLE BYPRODUCTS OF THE ongoing enterprise among historical linguists to classify languages into families is the identification of isolates, languages which do not appear to have any extant relatives. The initial assessment of a language as an isolate is typically followed by intensive and careful examination of possible connections that may have been obscured via perfectly normal sound changes; this process has, over the years, decreased the number of languages considered true isolates, but some, of course, remain. Basque is the textbook example; despite varied attempts to relate it to other stocks, such as Etruscan, proto-Caucasian, or Sumerian, it remains unrelated to any other language.

Linguists widely agree on what the likely process is that gives rise to isolates: the replacement of surrounding related languages by those of a different family, leaving only one of the originals surviving. In a pure example, one might expect the speakers of this language to preserve cultural traditions different from those of the surrounding communities, but language and culture can be disjoined to some extent, and cultural influences can cross linguistic boundaries. One rarely encounters pure examples in real life. When one does run across an example that seems too perfect to be true, it is reasonable to be suspicious. And this brings us to Ghwűừb.

Ghwű́ǜb is an Amazonian language, with one community of speakers located on the *varzea* of the Tairani River, a tributary of the Amazon located in the southwest of the central basin. Initial fieldwork, carried out during part of a survey of several tribal groups in the area, produced a picture of a people whose language (and lifeways) adhered so closely to the archetype of an isolate that the researchers felt it necessary to perform a more extensive study, which became even more strongly motivated when geneticists doing research in the same area announced results that ran exactly contrary to what would have been predicted by linguists, assuming even a very loose correlation between marriage patterns and language groupings. The following sections will detail the characteristics of the Ghwű́ǜb-speaking community relevant to this discussion and propose that the etiology of these characteristics reveals a unique pattern of cultural motivations that can serve as a limiting case for historical linguistic predictions.

THE WISDOM OF LINGUISTS

For want of a phoneme the morpheme is lost, for want of a morpheme the sentence is lost, for want of a sentence the meaning is lost.

Context of this Study

Initial references to the Ghwű́ǜb community are found in Schankelvekker (1898), who refers to them using the name Yaribogenadrea, a label given them by the neighboring Torikara. Schankelvekker did not encounter the Ghwű́ǜb herself, and was doing only a preliminary anthropological survey of the Torikara, with whom she communicated via a Guaraní-based trade pidgin. 'Yaribogenadrea' is actually a Torikara descriptive, a nominalized participial form (cf. Schadenpoodle 1989):

Yar-	i-	bo-
those-	clothing-	provide-

gai-	ena-	re-	a
mat.parent-	bad-	ADJL-	nzr

Fortunately, the Torikara use this name only for the Ghwű́ǜb, not any of the other tribes in the area, so matching them with Schankelvekker's fieldwork was nonproblematic. Her notes describe the Ghwű́ǜb and their language only briefly, as an aside to a discussion of the extensive relations the Torikara have with tribes in the area other than the Ghwű́ǜb (p. 629; English translation by the authors):

> Most of the villages along this stretch of the river trade regularly with one another, and there is a Torikara term, *tasivaodo,* ('go-and-get-er') for specific villagers who do this frequently; the trade networks also function for arranging marriages and the frequent potlatch-type dinners by which clusters of villages exchange surplus goods. The only tribe with which they do not often trade is the Yaribogenadrea, whose village lies to the southwest. The Torikara seem to find these people offensive in some way; much derisive laughter accompanied their description of the tribe. They occasionally do trade copper with the Yaribogenadrea, however, in return for the colorful feathers of a bird mostly indigenous to the latter's territory. I was unable to visit their village, though, and therefore cannot include cranial measurements.[1]

---

[1] Like many an anthropologist of her era, Schankelvekker was primarily interested in carefully measuring the cranial shapes of those she studied (the Torikara apparently passed down stories of her and her vigorous use of calipers in the form of their term for

No linguistic work on the Ghwúǜb was done until that documented in Schadenpoodle (2008); the portions of this article dealing with linguistic structure are summarized from that monograph. Serendipitously, genetic survey work was being done in the area by Heeliks (2003) under the auspices of the Human Genome Endeavor (partly due to the discovery, reported in Thrennesson (2002), of a FOXP2 mutation and attendant language-learning impairment among some residents of the area), and Pinchtoddle's cultural anthropological work with the Torikara led him to investigate the Ghwúǜb as well in late 2006. The material below is compiled from the authors' comparative notes.

Isolate vs. Non-Isolate

Status of Ghwúǜb as a Linguistic Isolate

Ghwúǜb is strikingly different from any of its close (or distant) neighbors, in its phonology and in its lexicon; indeed, it shares none of the areal features that otherwise are widely distributed across languages in this part of the basin. Its phonemic inventory, described in detail in Schadenpoodle (2008), is typologically unusual; it violates at least one putative universal by having more back vowels than front ones, and some of the affricates are particularly distinctive (please note that the authors, for sake of brevity, are adopting non-IPA symbols for several phonemes; the properties of these are discussed below):[2]

		Bilabial	Dental	Palatal	Velar
Stops	Voiceless	p	t		k
	Voiced	b	d		g
Fricatives	Voiceless	φ		š	
	Voiced	β	L	ž	ɣ
Affricates	Nasalized	Ћ	Ꚇ		Нб
	Regular		λ		
Nasals			m	n	
Liquids	Unrounded		l		
	Rounded		lʷ		
Glides	Unaspirated			y	w
	Aspirated			yʰ	wʰ

- The sound denoted by Ћ is a voiced bilabial stop with voiced velar fricative release.
- Ꚇ is a voiced dental stop with voiced nasalized lateral release.
- Нб is a voiced velar stop with voiced nasalized lateral release.
- L denotes a voiced lateral fricative with heavy nasalization.
- The position of the affricates within syllables strongly indicates their status as unitary phonemes rather than clusters (Schadenpoodle, forthcoming).
- Since there is no phonemic /h/ in the language, the aspirated glides likewise cannot be viewed as clusters (ibid.).

		Front	Central	Back
High	Spread	i	ɪ	ɯ
	Round	ü		u
	Nasal			ũ
Mid	Spread	e	ə	ɤ
	Round	ö		o
	Nasal			õ
Low		æ	a	
	Nasal		ã	

- Tone is phonemic in Ghwúǜb; the tone system is trinary—rising, falling, and neutral.

While it is conceivable, of course, that extensive historical change could have produced such a

---

anthropologists—*dagemaoda* 'crab-pincer-ghost', as opposed to their usual term for Europeans, *kedagwamaoda* 'bad-dancing ghosts').

[2] We realize that that the degree to which this phonemic inventory is unusual will likely be taken by the reader as evidence that the analysis on which it is based is probably flawed—a quite understandable reaction. More work on the language is obviously badly needed, and the authors would be quite happy to find that there is a perfectly normal phonemic system underlying this apparently highly deviant one. However, we have independently found minimal pairs for the distinctions described, so if there *is* a problem, it is

---

not one resulting simply from a problem with Schadenpoodle's field methodology.

system from the same substrate which gave rise to languages like Torikara, it is difficult to lend credence to such an explanation; the number of changes needed to derive Ghwűǜb phonology from any of the proto-forms posited for languages of this region (cf. Tanekis 2008) would suffice to derive Chinese from them as well, or Klingon for that matter.

Using the extended Swadesh list, and a match algorithm keyed to shared phonetic features but not phonemic identity (so, for example, both [t] and [n] were possible matches for [d]), Schadenpoodle (2008.452) carried out a lexical comparison of Ghwűǜb with eight of the surrounding languages; he found only one word that matched that of another tribe: tarana 'copper'— the item they trade with the Torikara for. In contrast, Torikara shares over 60% of the list with Yakali and Nerduru, and the Kanarati/Qanradi/Wartaina cluster, which has an 85% internal overlap rate, also shares 35% with Torikara/Yakali/Nerduru. No overlap was found between Ghwűǜb and more geographically distant Amazonian languages (e.g. Guaraní, Shipibo, Hixkaryana) as well.

The language likewise is unlike its neighbors syntactically, although given the wide variation in Amazonian languages in this regard such a result is perhaps less surprising. While word order in Ghwűǜb is flexible, the most common, unmarked order is [O A S V], where A represents a required auxiliary-like lexeme:

whàka-žìmƃú   ǒ-waꜧìꜧ
hut-m.aunt:Gen Indic:Rep-Pres3

  glup-bǜ   tiš-nùzi-waáà
  Glup-Sbj chew.ann.-srf-rep-3h

'I heard that Glup chewed annoyingly on his maternal aunt's hut.'

LOGICAL FALLACIES FOR LINGUISTS

False consensus effect—"Oh, yeah, everyone here at MIT thinks Chomsky is great! His theories have given us so much to work on! Linguists everywhere love Chomsky."

Again, although this type of construction is dissimilar to that used by any other in the area, it is less convincing as an argument for isolate status than is the fact that none of the basic grammatical functors appear to be cognate to any lexeme in those languages.

Ghwűǜb as a Cultural Isolate

While it is not uncommon for groups sharing the same geographic area to adopt distinctive cultural traits or artifacts as a way of preserving or enhancing group identity, the Ghwűǜb seem to represent an extreme case. Four traits in particular, are shared by no other groups in the area (summarized from Pinchtoddle, 2006):

Domestication of the Sloth. Alone among Amazonian peoples, the Ghwűǜb train sloths (three-toed) as a kind of living animal trap. Although the training process itself seems to take a very long time, the product is sloths that will fall from trees on animals passing underneath and then cling to them—rather like an avalanche of adhesive bowling balls. They are also, apparently, trained to attack the victim, but the animal is usually recovered by hunters well before any effect of the sloths' ferocity is detectable. One of the traditional Ghwűǜb dances, done yearly over the course of four days, depicts a folk story of the origin of the practice, in which Gwiuiu, the Sloth God, offers to help Pləb, the first Ghwűǜb; the ritual text has not been extensively translated as yet, but Gwiuiu seems to be motivated by a sense of cosmic ennui.[3]

---

[3] Schadenpoodle (pc) has attested in great detail that such sloths are quite capable of immobilizing even a fully-grown adult human.

The Potlatch Catapult. The chief, or *bliaabip,* of the village is expected to give potlatch-type feasts periodically (a trait which is shared with other groups in the region). Among the Ghwűừb, however, the chief launches food at individual community members using a device rather like a small catapult; catching the food in the mouth without use of the hands is considered a mark of social sophistication (the food item in question is a kind of ball, made up of sticky cooked taro paste with salted slugs embedded in it). The sole item of outside trade pursued by the tribe, copper, is in fact procured specifically for the construction of this device, which is not used in any other fashion. An individual's order in the line leading to the catapult target site is determined by a complex set of factors.

The yhoɣƂuú. This is a type of musical instrument incorporating narrow tubes within which very thin slices of reed are positioned so as to produce high-pitched sounds when air moves over them. Distinctively, the instrument is inserted into the nose, rather than the mouth, and most players use slightly different ones in each nostril so as to produced variant effects. Adult male villagers usually play these as a group, although individual males play them as part of courtship rituals. Nose-flutes are not unknown among the world's cultures, but they are not used elsewhere in this geographic region, and the Ghwűừb are rather distinctive in their deliberate manipulation of the instrument so as to produce sneezing at particular points. While Pinchtoddle has recorded performances (which can last up to six hours), they have not yet been analyzed by a musicologist.

While it is a commonplace observation among anthropologists that music is *not* universal—one has to be familiar with the conventions of a musical form to interpret it—the basic patterns and scales used in Ghwűừb performances are not used by surrounding groups at all. We played recordings to the

Figure 1: A contemporary Ghwűừb *bwàrp* vessel (top diameter 72 cm.), used to hold taro paste during ceremonial feasts. The orientation of designs on Ghwűừb pottery is variable; the focal figure is at bottom right on this piece. The piece probably depicts folk-hero Pləb charming slugs by using a nose-flute. The two figures above him are traditional representations of sloths. The wave-line design may indicate the underworld.

Torikara, for example, who immediately judged them as unpleasant.[4]

Ceramics. The other groups in the area use pottery with patterns and motifs common to those asso-

---

[4] It should be noted at this point that the Torikara are not in the habit otherwise of being highly judgemental about music—they prefer their own, of course, but according to Pinchtoddle, they react to most unfamiliar music forms with a kind of tolerant, muted curiosity.

ciated with the expansion of Tupic groups (cf. Brochado and Lathrap 1982, Brochado 1984, Peixoto 1995), but Ghwúùb ceramics are distinctive (most containers have a trapezoidal cross-section, and decoration is primarily in the form of stick-figure abstractions of local wildlife, particularly sloths and slugs).[5]

Ghwúùb as a Genetic Non-Isolate

In complete contrast to evidence from linguistic and cultural patterns, DNA analyses consistently show that the Ghwúùb share a large number of markers that are otherwise uncommon in this region with neighboring groups, particularly the Torikara, Yakali, and Nerduru, forming what might be called the GTYN cluster (Heeliks 2003). Kanarati, Qanradi, and War-taina share a subset of these markers as well, although otherwise show evidence of being closely related to Tupic groups, as might be expected. The GTYN cluster pattern emerges from both mitochondrial and Y-chromosomal analysis, indicating that relatedness is not simply a function of female outmarriage.

Furthermore, the distinctive FOXP2 variant first described by Thrennesson (2002) is also shared among members of the GTYN cluster, although only a few of those tested from the KQW cluster had it. Unlike the variant associated with SLI (cf. Lai et al. 2001; Gutiérrez-Clellen et al. 2009, Leonard 2009), this does not seem to cause difficulties with normal language use. Instead, it appears to cause greater difficulty with second language acquisition, although at present it is unclear whether this operates by intensification

> If you didn't hear the story clearly, don't carry it off with you under your arm.
> —THAI PROVERB

of L1 interference factors or (or additionally) by accelerating loss of neural plasticity after early youth. While the details of this "SLA impairment" disorder are still unclear, it appears to act similarly to a recessive trait; only learners who have both parents with the variant suffer from it. The *tasivaodo* among the Torikara, as might be expected, are individuals who do not suffer from the disorder, and Heeliks has noted that they tend to fall into familial units who preferentially marry *tasivaodo* from the Yakali and Nerduru.

It is important to note that the Ghwúùb community genotype itself is distinctive from the rest of the members of the cluster only in its homogeneity—there is more variation among other members of the GTYN cluster, and within the non-Ghwúùb communities in that cluster, than among members of the Ghwúùb. In short, the Ghwúùb do not, from a genetic standpoint, appear to be "outliers" at all, but rather occupy a median position to an unusual degree.

New Evidence, and a Possible Explanation

To this point, observations have strongly, almost overwhelmingly, supported a single interpretation of the Ghwúùb's status as an isolate: Proto-Ghwúùb speakers inhabited the area prior to expansion of Proto-Tupic-speaking groups, and Proto-Tupic replaced Proto-Ghwúùb in some communities whose members were primarily from Proto-Ghwúùb-speaking groups. Thus, the GTYN cluster comprises modern descendants of Proto-Ghwúùb speakers, but only the Ghwúùb themselves continued to speak their mother tongue. The greater genetic homogeneity of the Ghwúùb may be ascribed to what might be termed *anexogamy*. Other cultural groups in this area practice systematic exogamy—young women are

---

[5] The slug figures are particularly distinctive, since no other extant culture, to our knowledge, has ever applied stick-figure abstraction to slugs, or even any other mollusk, land-bound or otherwise.

expected to marry men from other groups. Endogamy, of course, is also known in other cultures, although it becomes difficult to maintain for groups under a particular size since continual reinforcement of recessive traits can be self-limiting in the long term. The Ghwúûb continuously *attempt* exogamic marriage, but are almost always unsuccessful. We could find evidence of only one case of a woman marrying into the Ghwúûb community; Yakisgo is elderly now, and has moved back to the Torikara, but as a young woman married a Ghwúûb man to cement trade relations. She has been deaf from birth, however, and her ability to provide information to researchers on short notice is limited, although her experience is, as we will argue below, crucial for understanding the historical status of the Ghwúûb.

Recently, Pinchtoddle's work, along with archeological data from Arnheldsen's (2007) survey of former village sites, has raised serious questions about the validity of the Ghwúûb-as-remnant account. Pinchtoddle noted that while the Qanradi and Wartaina tell extended traditional stories about how their ancestors traveled to their current location from a legendary homeland, and had to fight pre-existing locals for dominance, the enemies in the stories bear absolutely no resemblance to the Ghwúûb. Given the distinctiveness of the Ghwúûb, one would not expect storytellers to confuse them with other groups; at the very least, one would anticipate a mention of sloths, or even a modified version in which the autochthonous foes were allied with monsters of some sort. Nothing of the sort appears. The foes described in the story do, however, bear some resemblance to Tupic groups—they are, for example, portrayed as having the secret of taro agriculture, which both the Qanradi and Wartaina

"A silly remark can be made in Latin as well as in Spanish."
—Miguel de Cervantes

say they "won" from these enemies. The process of transmuting history to myth is a notoriously variable one, and this counterargument to the Ghwúûb-as-autochthons position is therefore very tentative, but the pattern is intriguing nonetheless.

More concrete evidence comes from Arnheldsen's observations of ceramic sequences. Test digs in four abandoned village sites, as well as in midden areas in three current villages (two Torikara, one Yakali), all found Tupic pottery *below* a layer in which typically distinctive Ghwúûb pottery shards occurred, with Tupic pottery again above that. Dating of the shards themselves, as well as other stratigraphic evidence, indicates that Ghwúûb pottery was brought into an area already inhabited by groups using Tupic motifs. Further supporting this sequence was the discovery at one abandoned village site (A435) of the remains of a small food-catapult, in a layer below one in which Tupic pottery was found, and above another.

In short, the Ghwúûb appear to be newcomers, not a remnant. This leaves us with an obvious question: Why is Ghwúûb a linguistic and cultural isolate? Its speakers came *from* somewhere, and their descendants still live in the area even though most of them don't speak the language. But no language related to Ghwúûb has been found in any portion of South America (or elsewhere).

Yakisgo may provide an answer to the question, and raise new ones for linguistics at the same time. Anthropologists have long recognized the principles of linguistic and cultural relativity, but Ghwúûb may be a limiting case. We must note that the *only* apparently successful case of non-Ghwúûb marriage into the Ghwúûb community was deaf from birth. Also—and we realize this claim will be controversial, to put it mildly—*no non-Ghwúǜb who hears the language is able to take the speakers seriously.* Even Prof. Schadenpoodle, who not only has a well-deserved reputation for gravity but also has had rather traumatic encounters with the Ghwúǜb, is incapable of hearing the language while maintaining the air of earnest respect any language deserves. Pinchtoddle's (2006) fieldwork showed that even among the Ghwúǜb, the relationship between language use and maintenance of social and reproductive relations appears vexed. In other cultures, language used in courtship rituals is geared toward enhancing the speaker's or hearer's status—to show one is a worthy mate, or to flatter the object of desire. In the Ghwúǜb community, on the other hand, it is commonly acknowledged that courtship language is successful (or not) only because the hearer knows that if she capitulates, the speaker will stop talking.[6]

Basically, it appears that the Ghwúǜb difficulty with outmarriage is a direct result of their language, and we surmise that most Proto-Ghwúǜb speakers, after encountering speakers of Proto-Tupi, immediately and enthusiastically abandoned their mother tongue, along with many of their own cultural practices. However, some Proto-Ghwúǜb speakers had inherited the FOXP2 variant limiting their SLA ability, and hence could *not* assimilate to Proto-Tupic. If we assume that the variant was originally found within a particular group of Proto-Ghwúǜb speakers (i.e., that SLA-impaired speakers were already associated into a particular tribal unit, or band), we can thus account for the formation of the current situation. Having over the course of several generations become cultural outsiders, these speakers' status as a separate people was continually

THE WISDOM OF LINGUISTS

Speak softly, carry a big dictionary.

reinforced. Normally, some of their offspring would lack the disorder (since it acts like a recessive trait), and the community would slowly dwindle as outmarriage thinned its ranks, but the social isolation of the community, together with the decidedly anaphrodesiac effects of being a Ghwúǜb-speaker, encourage endogamy, whether it is voluntary or not. Thus, the variant was reinforced to the point where the entire community possesses it.

Conclusions

Limiting cases such as the Ghwúǜb are vital—they illustrate the strengths of a position by articulating its opposite and drawing attention to the opposite's rarity. Linguistic relativity is not a principle adopted by linguists only because we have trouble measuring the "value" of languages, or because we have seen what horrors cultural bigotry can bring forth. Before Ghwúǜb, linguists had no examples to analyze of a language that fundamentally *doesn't work well*—any that may have existed in the past would simply have gone extinct as soon as speakers encountered a language that did work well. Modern cases of language death are not analogous; speakers of Cornish, for example, didn't learn English because they immediately thought it sounded much better, but rather because they thought that learning English decreased the chance that the English would kill them, or at least might make the teacher stop hitting them; similarly, the reasons for Italic languages other than Latin dying out weren't just legion, but also legions.

We are, of course, keenly interested in the question of how Proto-Ghwúǜb developed. Its existence today reminds us that potentially a very, *very* large number of language families

---

[6] The phrase used in Ghwúǜb to refer to a successful courtship translates literally as "She got him to shut up".

have existed at some point in the past but left no trace of their existence. Were it not for a genetic accident, Ghwúǔb would have vanished as well, and as linguists, we can only be thankful that the language, like the sloths of its speakers, approaches the horizon only slowly.

References

Arnheldsen, Heraklios (2007). An initial survey of village sites in the Tairani headwaters region. *Amazonian Archeological Bulletin* 32(1):15–86.

Brochado, J.; and Lathrap, D. (1982). Chronologies in the New World: Amazonia. Unpublished manuscript. On file at the Department of Anthropology, University of Illinois at Urbana-Champaign. Illinois.

Brochado, J. (1984). *An Ecological Model of the Spread of Pottery and Agriculture into Eastern South America.* Ph.D. dissertation, University of Illinois, Urbana. University Microfilms, Ann Arbor.

Gutiérrez-Clellen, Vera; Simon-Cereijido, Gabriela; and Erickson Leone, Angela (2009). Code-switching in children with specific language impairment. *International Journal of Bilingualism* 13(1): 91–109.

Heeliks, Jacob (2003). A genotypic cluster analysis of fifteen upper Tairani communities. *Papers in Amazonian Genetics* 4(2).

Lai, C. S. L.; Fisher, S. E.; Hurst, J. A.; Vargha-Khadem, F.; and Monaco, A. P. (2001). A forkhead-domain gene is mutated in a severe speech and language disorder. *Nature* 413 (6,855): 519–23.

Leonard, Laurence (2009). Some reflections on the study of children with specific language impairment. *Child Language Teaching and Therapy* 25(2): 169–171.

Peixoto, Jose Luis (1995). A ocupação do Tupi-guarani na borda oeste do pantanal Sul-mato-grossense: maciço do Urucu. M.A. thesis. IFCH-PUCRS, Porto Alegre.

Pinchtoddle, Vasily (2006). *The Repose of Travel: An Ethnography of the Torikara.* Scranton, PA: Psammeticus Press.

Schadenpoodle, Athanasious (1989). An initial sketch of Torikara syntax. *Occasional Papers in Amazonian Linguistics* 12.

Schadenpoodle, Athanasious (2008). *A Grammar of the Ghwúǔb Language.* Scranton, PA: Psammeticus Press.

Schadenpoodle, Athanasious (forthcoming). Toward the resolution of certain problems in the phonemic analysis of Ghwúǔb.

Schankelvekker, Hortense (1898). *Eine vorläufige Beschreibung der Völker der Obertairaniregion, mit einem Nachtrag über Kranialmessung.* Monograph published as separate issue of the *Bulletin der Archäologischen Gesellschaft von Schleswig-Holstein* 15.

Tanekis, Akioni (2008). Divergence models for Ghwúǔb are less probable than the null hypothesis. *Working Papers in Statistical Diachronic Linguistics* 18(3):27–34.

Thrennesson, Olaf (2002). A novel FOXP2 variant is linked to language-learning impairment. *Journal of Genetics and Bioinformatics* 12(4):127–60.

WOULD YOU LIKE SPAGHETTI OR LASAGNA FOR DINNER?

Chomskyan Linguist: "The theory of pasta establishes that a principled, non-zero subset of the structural characteristics of spaghetti are specified by a Universal Chef, and thus the Universal Chef explains spaghetti. There may be some other discipline that addresses lasagna, but I rather doubt it would be interesting, and it certainly wouldn't be explanatory. I hope the kitchen doesn't have another performance error like they did last week."

Comparative and Historical Linguistics
Ahh, look, philology is all grown up now!

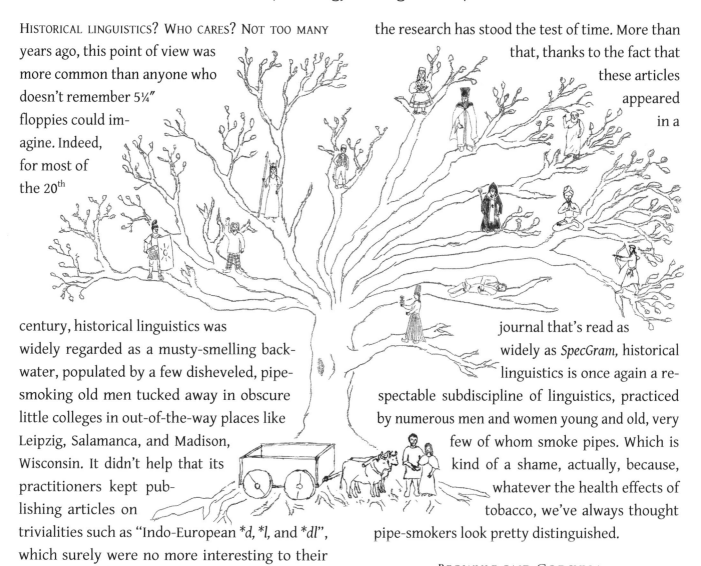

HISTORICAL LINGUISTICS? WHO CARES? NOT TOO MANY years ago, this point of view was more common than anyone who doesn't remember 5¼″ floppies could imagine. Indeed, for most of the 20th century, historical linguistics was widely regarded as a musty-smelling backwater, populated by a few disheveled, pipe-smoking old men tucked away in obscure little colleges in out-of-the-way places like Leipzig, Salamanca, and Madison, Wisconsin. It didn't help that its practitioners kept publishing articles on trivialities such as "Indo-European *d, *l, and *dl", which surely were no more interesting to their authors than they were to anyone else.

In the late 20th century, SpecGram, along with a few other courageous publications, decided to try to change things. (Don't ask us why we wanted to change things. That was a long time ago, and we don't remember.) Seeking out innovative ideas from around the globe, we published groundbreaking research of a sort that stodgy old journals like Linguistic Inquiry refused to touch. Granted, many of the articles we published turned out to be stupid—we're especially embarrassed by the amount of print space we gave to proponents of the "Uto-Aztecan" hypothesis—but some of the research has stood the test of time. More than that, thanks to the fact that these articles appeared in a journal that's read as widely as SpecGram, historical linguistics is once again a respectable subdiscipline of linguistics, practiced by numerous men and women young and old, very few of whom smoke pipes. Which is kind of a shame, actually, because, whatever the health effects of tobacco, we've always thought pipe-smokers look pretty distinguished.

BEOWULF OND GODSYLLA

Meanehwæl, baccat meaddehæle,   monstær lurccen;
Fulle few too many drincce,   hie luccen for fyht.
Ðen Hreorfneorhtðhwr,   son of Hrwærowþheororthwl,
Æsccen æwful jeork   to steop outsyd.
Þhud! Bashe! Crasch! Beoom!   Ðe bigge gye
Eallum his bon brak,   byt his nose offe;
Wicced Godsylla   wæld on his asse.
Monstær moppe fleor wyþ   eallum men in hælle.
Beowulf in bacceroome   fonecall bemaccen wæs;
Hearen sond of ruccus   sæd, "Hwæt ðe helle?"
Graben sheold strang   ond swich-blæd scharp
Stond feorth to fyht   ðe grimlic foe.
"Me," Godsylla sæd,   "mac ðe minsemete."
Heoro cwyc geten heold   wiþ fæmed half-nelson
Ond flyng him lic frisbe   bac to fen.
Beowulf belly up   to meaddehæle bar,
Sæd, "Ne foe beaten   mie færsom cung-fu."
Eorderen cocca-cohla   yce-coeld, ðe reol þyng.

—TOM WELLER

Some of the most important historical linguistics work of the past few decades is that which has overturned hide-bound, unproven traditional claims about the classification of languages. Most of those traditional claims were based on irrelevancies such as regular, recurrent sound correspondences in non-borrowed vocabulary, and/or widespread shared irregularities in morphological paradigms, rather than on the only real bases for genetic classification of languages, namely, geography, ethnicity, and typology. We begin, therefore, with some of the groundbreaking articles that collectively brought about the rewriting of the "Language Families" section in every respectable historical linguistics textbook.

The first three articles below form a series. The first one, by Tim Pulju, was published near the very beginning of the revolution in historical linguistics, and, not surprisingly, is tentative and incorrect in some of its conclusions. However, as seen in the second and third articles (by Robert Norris and Tim Pulju, respectively), it led to a flowering of research not just in comparative linguistics, but on tonogenesis, pidgin and creole formation, and environmental causes of ancient migrations.

Reconstructed Proto-Franco-Sino-Indonesian—Eleven Examples

Tim Pulju
Michigan State University

In 1986, I published in *Psammeticus Quarterly* (Vol. XII, No. 4) an article entitled "Similarities in Form and Meaning in French, Chinese, and Indonesian," which noted several similarities in form and meaning in French, Chinese, and Indonesian, and suggested that someone do further research to determine whether the languages were genetically related. Since no one took up my suggestion (indeed, most people just laughed at my hypothesis), I was forced to do that research myself, the result being that I now stand totally vindicated.

My soon to be published book *The Phonology of Proto-Franco-Sino-Indonesian* will include regular sound laws proving that all three languages are descended from a unified ancestor, which archeological evidence tentatively suggests was spoken somewhere in South America.

As a preliminary to the publication of this text, this article presents a few example of reconstructed pto-Fco-Sno-Ids root forms, with tentative root meanings. The roots listed have reflexes in at least two and sometimes all three of the daughter tongues. The sound laws pertinent to the data are not presented but could be worked out easily by anyone with a minimal knowledge of the principles and methods of historical linguistics.

	pto-Fco-Sno-Ids	French	Chinese	Indonesian
1.	*kan* 'to watch'	*kan* 'a film-watching fest'	*kan* 'to watch'	
2.	*dwo* 'more than one'	*dø* 'two'	*dwo* 'more'	*dwa* 'two'
3.	*insi* 'here'	*isi* 'here'		*sini* 'here'
4.	*oraŋ* 'orange'	*orãž* 'orange'		*oraŋutan* 'an orange ape'
5.	*krist* 'Christ'	*krist* 'Christ'		*krista* 'Christian'
6.	*kafe* 'coffee'	*kafe* 'coffee'	*kafey* 'coffee'	
7.	*te* 'tea'	*te* 'tea'	*ča* 'tea'	*te* 'tea'
8.	*taŋt* 'sing'	*šãt* 'I sing'	*čaŋ* 'sing'	
9.	*anding* 'be quiet'		*anǰing* 'be quiet'	*anǰing* 'dog'
10.	*lah* 'tired'	*la* 'weary'	*ley* 'tired'	*lelah* 'tired'
11.	*maŋ* 'be active'		*maŋ* 'be busy'	*meŋ-* ACTIVE MARKER

Progress in South American Protolinguistics

Robert Norris
Rice University

Recent work in South American Proto-World language reconstruction has placed the well-attested Proto-Sino-Franco-Indonesian (*PSFI) superfamily (Pulju 1990) in a larger historical context which includes Kiowan, a North American Indian language which has not, until now, been definitively affiliated with any language family (Watkins 1984). This paper gives evidence for a Proto-Sino-Kiowan (*PSK) superfamily, which interacted with Proto-Franco-Indonesian (*PFI) to form the well known *PSFI group. At this point it seems that the larger Proto-*PSFI-Kiowan (*P*PK) metasuperfamily, the Holy Grail of South American protolinguistics, has evaded us once again and we are forced now to posit two independent South American proto-languages.

The following examples leave little doubt that Kiowan and Chinese are historically related.

*PPK	Kiowa	Chinese
*ńe 'however'	ńe 'but'	ne 'a modal particle'
*kíi 'old man'	kíi 'husband'	gē[gē] 'elder brother'
*yíi 'a small number'	yíi 'two'	yī 'one'
*wéi 'hello'	wée 'word of welcome'	wéi 'telephone greeting'

The relatively sparse lexical overlap between Kiowa and French/Indonesian reveals the historic process leading to today's distribution. I propose the following progression.

1. *PSK and *PFI speakers inhabit South America. This is the state of the Proto-World as far back as we can trace it.

2. The Kiowan group splits off from *PSK and moves north, presumably to await the white man, disease, genocide, etc.

3. The remainder of the *PSK group, now speaking what we might call proto-proto-proto-Chinese *temporarily* link up (presumably not by their own doing) with the bloodthirsty Proto-Franco-Indonesian speakers. This is the well-known *PSFI period, during which proto-proto-proto-Chinese adopted an enormous number of *PFI words and completely lost the complex *PSK inflection-derivation system, as tends to happen to oppressed people who become lazy, depressed and mumbly. Note that Kiowa and Chinese both retained the tone system of *PSK, while *PFI presumably was not a tone language (assuming we disregard Lørenesenn's contention that French is a tone language).

4. By this time the proto-proto-proto-Chinese speakers, now speaking proto-proto-Chinese, break the bonds of slavery (or whatever) and escape to Asia completely free of inflection, agreement, etc., but, as luck would have it, terribly afflicted with word-order.

5. The final migration, which locates the modern French and Indonesian speakers in France and Indonesia, respectively, is the source of some conjecture, and I direct you to Parker's (1990) monograph for further discussion.

The historical progression described above leaves the present situation. The descendants of the peaceful Proto-Sino-Kiowan group are now a large, docile, disinflected Chinese-speaking population in Asia and an almost nonexistent docile Kiowan population on a reservation in Oklahoma. Large unsavory, warlike populations in France and Indonesia are the remnants of the original *PFI group. I feel my findings are conclusive, and do not intend to entertain any criticism.

Bibliography

Lørenesenn, Fugløy. "Tone Sandhi in French." *Psammeticus Quarterly* X.4, 1984. Pp 661–71.

Parker, Christ J. *Big Scary Jungle Spiders: New Perspectives on the Depopulation of Ancient South America.* 1990. (unpublished)

Pulju, Tim Q. *The Phonology of Proto-Sino-Franco-Indonesian.* The Hague: Mouton & Company, 1990.

Watkins, Laurel J. *A Grammar of Kiowa.* Lincoln: The University of Nebraska Press, 1984.

WOULD YOU LIKE SPAGHETTI
OR LASAGNA FOR DINNER?

Neogrammarian: "Neither. They are both borrowed, and I will go hungry rather than accept a borrowing."

CHOOSE YOUR OWN CAREER IN LINGUISTICS—PART 32

YOU GET A GOOD JOB...

You do well, and 20 years later, you are successful, happy, and productive. You make a good living, do interesting work every day, and have sharp colleagues to keep you on your toes. Your home life is tranquil and pleasant, and you have lots of time off every year to do your own thing. Life is grand!

• The End. Go to page 301.

Choose Your Own Career in Linguistics starts on page 301.

IT IS WELL KNOWN AMONG LINGUISTS...

The vowel-fronting change known as "Anglo-Frisian brightening", which fronted /aː/ to /æː/, triggered homicidal fury in local populations of European hedgehogs, eventually causing speakers to flee to Britain to escape the constant barrage of attacks. Portions of Saxony were left almost depopulated for generations.

A Reconsideration of the Sino-Kiowan Problem

Tim Pulju
Rice University

Since the publication of Norris' (1991) article demonstrating a clear genetic relationship between Kiowa and Chinese, there has been considerable confusion in the once well-established field of comparative Franco-Sino-Indonesian linguistcs (cf. Pulju [1990]). While Norris' linguistic data cannot be explained away, many scholars have taken issue with his conclusion that Kiowa and Chinese originally formed a linguistic grouping separate from Franco-Indonesian, and that resemblances between Chinese and Franco-Indonesian are due rather to early contact than to genetic relationship. To explain the lack of resemblance between Kiowa and Franco-Indonesian, Norris argues that the proto-Kiowans migrated from South America prior to the period of contact with the proto-Franco-Indonesians.

Compelling though Norris' linguistic data are, it must be admitted that they allow for several possible reconstructions of the cultural and historical facts, as was made clear at the 1995 Rice University Symposium on "Kiowa, Chinese, and Franco-Indonesian." Many attendees at the conference voiced the opinion that, without further evidence, it would be impossible to reach any firm conclusions on the question at hand. That opinion may or may not have been valid. However, as the present paper will show, the opinion is now moot, precisely because this paper presents new and crucial evidence for our understanding of the early relationships among these languages.

It is an axiom of comparative linguistics that some of the best evidence for genetic relatedness of languages is to be found in inflectional or pronominal paradigms, since these are among the elements of language least likely to be borrowed.

It is particularly important to search for resemblances in word-initial positions, since word-initial position is least subject to phonetic erosion over time. Thus, for example, the lack of any word-initial similarity in the pronoun systems of French and English is clear evidence of the absence of any deep relationship between the languages.

je	*I*
tu	*you*
il, elle	*he, she, it*
nous	*we*
vous	*you*
ils, elles	*they*

Pronouns are particularly important for comparing Chinese to other languages, since Chinese completely lacks inflectional morphology. We are therefore doubly impressed when we note the strong traces of the original identity of the Chinese and English pronominal systems, as in:

wo(men)[1]	**we**
ta(men)	**they**

To these, we can add evident similarities in other core vocabulary, as seen below:

Chin. *shi* (pronounced [šr]) 'yeah (used as a response to questions)'

Eng. *sure* (pronounced [šr]) 'yeah (used as a response to questions)'

Chin. *baba* 'dad'

Eng. *papa* 'dad'

---

[1] All Chinese examples will be cited without tone markings, since Slater (1997) has conclusively demonstrated that tone is not phonemic in Chinese. The morpheme -*men* in Chinese *women* and *tamen* is parenthesized because it is clearly suffixal.

Chin. *ni **hao** ma* 'how are you?'
Eng. ***how** are you* 'how are you?'

Chin. *chi* 'eat'
Eng. *chew* 'chew'

Evidence for an original relationship between English and Kiowa, on the other hand, is much harder to come by. And, as mentioned previously, English is plainly unrelated to both French and Indonesian (similarities between French and English are the result of fairly recent contact between the languages).

When comparing the connections of Chinese and Kiowa, on the one hand, with those of Chinese and English, on the other, we are struck by the fact that the Kiowa-Chinese relationship is manifested almost entirely in the lexicon, while the Chinese-English relationship shows up most strongly in pronouns and other grammatical elements. Chinese, moreover, has long been noted for the extreme simplicity of its grammatical system.[2] All of this leads us to the obvious conclusion that Chinese was in fact originally a pidgin, a trade language developed for use between superordinate Kiowa merchants and subordinate natives who spoke English. That such a situation should have developed prehistorically is no surprise, since recent archaeological research has demonstrated that the Kiowa possessed a much more highly developed culture than the proto-English speakers who also inhabited the North American continent. In later years, of course, the

LOGICAL FALLACIES FOR LINGUISTS

Argumentum ad ignorantiam—"I can't imagine that we'll ever be able to reconstruct Proto-World, therefore it's impossible."

English-speaking culture became dominant, and spread not only over North America, but even overseas.[3] However, the situation seven or eight thousand years ago was plainly quite different.

This hypothesis allows us to make sense of some of the most troubling aspects of Norris' thesis. The Kiowa affirm that they have occupied their present territory since time immemorial, and we have no good reason to disbelieve them. It therefore seems plain that the Kiowa did not migrate from South America to North America, but rather, that the proto-Chinese population which grew up in between Kiowa- and English-speaking regions eventually migrated to South America. At least, some of them did; others presumably remained in North America, but the Kiowa civilization declined, the flourishing trade cities in the Kiowa-English interzone collapsed, and the creole language of the inhabitants dwindled along with them. Meanwhile, the Sinitic population in South America fell under the yoke of Franco-Indonesian speakers, as well-documented in Norris'

---

[2] This observation goes back as far as Jespersen, and is certainly true. However, some scholars have mistakenly reached the Whorfian conclusion that Chinese are correspondingly simple-minded. Having recently engaged in a game of chess with a Chinese monolingual, I can assure the reader that Chinese people are *not* simple-minded. I just wish I hadn't agreed to play for money.

[3] A certain number of historians of English have consistently maintained that the English language originated, not in North America, but in Great Britain. It need hardly be stated that all the evidence is against such a hypothesis. In the first place, the great majority of English speakers today live in North America. We also know from historical records that English was not spoken in the British Isles two thousand years ago. In fact, even today, a few Celtic speakers remain in some of the more inaccessible regions of the United Kingdom and Ireland. Not just historical data, but linguistic fact, shows that the English-speaking populations of the British Isles, South Africa, Australia, and New Zealand are descendants of native non-English speaking populations. Particularly noteworthy is the inability of these populations to pronounce word-initial /h/ and post-vocalic /r/, clear evidence of substratum interference which has now become an irremovable part of the local dialects.

research, and remained oppressed for centuries before they finally escaped to East Asia.[4]

The archaeological support for the above hypothesis is exceptionally strong. In particular, we might mention the continual development of pottery from the Interzonal though the Shang Dynasty periods. Lower Mississippian pottery of the Interzonal period itself represents a combination of Kiowan techniques with native English artistic motifs. The intrusion of this pottery type into the Amazon basin, and its further development there under Franco-Indonesian influence, is well-documented (see Vargas [1954] for details). Likewise, the arrival of the new type in Chinese coastal regions is well-known, as is its later merger with native Asian forms, a merger finally completed in the 2nd millennium BC. From that point on, the development of Chinese language and culture is strictly an East Asian matter. But the archaeological evidence confirms what the linguistic data have already revealed, that the Chinese language originated in North America as a Kiowa-English creole. In other words, Norris was mistaken as to the specific nature of the Sino-Kiowa connection, but he was fundamentally correct in his analysis of the Sino-Franco-Indonesian relationship.

References

Mead, David, ed. 1996. *Quel grand gâchis. Proceedings of the 8th Biennial Rice Linguistics Symposium.* Philadelphia: John Benjamins.

Norris, Robert. 1991. Progress in South American protolinguistics. *World of Language: The Journal of the Linguistic Society of South-Central New Caledonia* Vol. I.2, p. 4.

Pulju, Tim. 1990. *The Phonology of Proto-Franco-Sino-Indonesian.* The Hague: Mouton.

Slater, Keith W. 1997. *They're Making it Up.* Taipei: Academica Sinica.

Vargas, Getúlio. 1954. *Pots, Pans, and a Sea of Mud.* São Borja, Brazil: Estado Novo.

MURPHY'S LAW FOR LINGUISTS

Three quarters of your elicited words will turn out to be borrowed from a neighboring unrelated language that coincidentally has a similar phoneme inventory.

---

[4] However, we should not, as Norris does, blame their stay in South America for what Norris describes as a state of being "completely free of inflection, agreement, etc., but, as luck would have it, terribly afflicted with word-order." On the contrary, this is exactly what we would expect in a creole language in its early stages. Likewise, the lack of tone in Chinese (see note 1 above) is what we would expect of a creole derived from a tonal superstrate and a non-tonal substrate.

Moving on to more familiar languages: in the following work, Dr. Medved Sem boldly points out the inadequacy of traditional classifications of European languages, and offers a bold new hypothesis as a bold replacement. On a side note, we're pretty sure that the sentence about Cornish ought to be in footnote 4, since it makes no sense where it is, but when we asked Dr. Sem about it, he just growled at us.

Toward a New Classification of the European Languages

Dr. Medved Sem

πολλὰ τὰ δεινὰ κοὐδὲν ὀμπρέλλας δεινότερον πέλει
'There are many wonderful things, and nothing is more wonderful than an umbrella.'
—Sophocles, *Antigone* 332[1]

It is well-known that several unsuccessful attempts have been made to classify the languages of the European continent. One early scheme sorted them according to the words for 'God', resulting in *deus-*, *bog-* and *gott-*languages. An equally silly idea was advanced in the last century, in which imaginary sounds like k̂ and kʷ were postulated, producing obscure divisions into *centum-* and *satem-*languages. This latter approach was exploited in the heyday of comparative philology by rascals such as Bopp and Grassmann, who tried to convince us through this trickery that pairs like Slovene *devet* and English *nine*, or Slovak *pät'* and English *five*, are related—even though they share *not a single letter!*

Modern linguistic science has reached the stage where such groping solutions can be dispensed with, and a new, purely data-driven approach be applied to analyze the material at hand. Obviously, in analyzing *modern* languages, only *modern* vocabulary will do—yet, since not all European cultures have reached the same level of technical development, one must exercise caution

Map Key: *Rain* ☐ *Sun* ▨ *Stretch* ▥ *Mixed* ★

in selecting vocabulary. After a great deal of research, it was finally decided that the first bold

---

[1] First draft, now unfortunately lost.

stroke would be made with the word for 'umbrella'.[2]

Examining the data, we find that there are but three groups of European languages: those which derive the word for umbrella from a root meaning 'to stretch', those which derive from a root for 'rain', and those which derive from a root meaning 'sun' or 'shadow'.

While the first two categories are hardly surprising—after all, an umbrella is *stretched* over one's head to protect it from the *rain*—it at first seems odd that a language would designate an instrument used to protect one from the *rain* by making reference to the *sun*. This, however, can be explained by the well-known principle of lūcus ā nōn lūcēndo:[3] it is precisely *because* there is so little sun when it rains that the word for 'umbrella' should be derived from the word for *sun*.

The excellent map above shows the distribution of the three groups of languages.

Note that some puzzling issues are raised by the distribution of the languages. First, the *stretch* languages are represented by Lithuanian *skėtis*, Bulgarian *чадър* and Macedonian *чадор*. This indicates that the original European word for 'umbrella' was based on a root meaning *stretch*, for in no other way could these languages, obviously akin, be so separated. From the map, it can be seen that there has been a two-phased assault on the original term. First the root *sun* swept across the European continent, obliterating the root *stretch* in all but the most remote areas. That this process of encroachment continues is seen by the fact that Albanian, once a pure *stretch* language, has now acquired a second word for *umbrella,* so that one may say either *ombrellë* or *çadër*. Then a newer innovation, representing the root *rain* appeared[4]—thus the isolation of Italy and the British Isles. In the latter only Cornish, with its *glawlen,* continues to bravely hold out... unaware, however, that it already sold out long ago by abandoning the root *stretch!*

The prospects are truly alarming, for they suggest an imminent reshuffling of the consanguinity of the European languages. The author urges all to be vigilant and to report any evidence of future semantic shift to the editorial staff of *Speculative Grammarian.*

WOULD YOU LIKE SPAGHETTI
OR LASAGNA FOR DINNER?

Nostraticist: "They're both flatbread, you know."

---

[2] Even here one must exercise caution! For Lapp *arvesyeiji* designates *any* protection from rain, though it be a simple tree.

[3] Thus Latin *lūcus* 'grove of (sacred) trees' < *lūx* 'light', because there is *no* light there, and *bellum* 'war' < *bellus* 'pretty', precisely because war is *not* pretty.

[4] Alternatively, the root *rain* may have been the original and *sun* may be making headway by cleverly taking sea routes to circumvent the more daunting passage by land. If this be the case, the prospects are truly alarming, for it would appear that there is a concerted effort afoot to divide western Europe in a pincer-like manœuver.

As a final example of revolutionary new work in language classification, we include the following paper by under-graduate student April M. June, which shows that even a neophyte with only a single linguistics course to her credit can make important contributions to the field, provided she has had sufficiently high-quality instruction. (We are pleased to report, by the way, that Ms. June and Mr. Thompson eventually settled their differences and are now married with two children, though for some reason, ever since the wedding, Mr. Thompson has been drinking more whiskey than ever.)

Are Turkish and Amharic Related? Are They Ever!

April May June
Freshman in Elementary Education
Indiana University at Bloomington

It is well-known from my L103 class that Turkish and Amharic supposedly aren't related, though it is no longer clear which languages they are related to. However, I have found lots of words in the two languages which sound alike and mean the same thing in only two months of hearing them spoken in two local restaurants. The similarities first caught my attention during an argument at the Turkish restaurant in which the owner kept saying "sought." The next day I heard it at the Ethiopian restaurant I always eat at, so I asked the waitress what it meant. The next time I ate at the Turkish restaurant, I asked the waitress what it meant, and would you believe it, it meant the same thing! The next day I realized I should write it down so I wouldn't forget it, and after that I made notes of all the similar words I learned from the waitresses at the two restaurants.

The informant sessions took place three times a week for each restaurant around meal times. Whenever the waitress came near my table, I asked her how she would say two or three really simple words, like the ones we were taught how to teach second-graders how to spell. (They had a fancy name in L103 class, but I don't remember it.) The Turkish waitress would even write them

---

THE WISDOM OF LINGUISTS

Shakespeare is credited with adding hundreds of new words to English, but recently discovered correspondence between him and highly-placed patron have revealed that a good many of those were originally intended as part of a conlang.

---

down for me when the owner wasn't looking, because he would yell at her that he was running a restaurant, not a school. However, when I asked the Ethiopian waitress to write down the words she had told me, all she did was doodle. After that I wrote down what they sounded like and took them to my sour old AI, Mr. Thompson, who refused at first to transcribe them for me. "Do your own damn work! I swear, the reason they don't have an honor code here is so the students can turn in their homework." I then asked him when he switched from coffee to whiskey in the mornings before office hours, and did the administration know. He then agreed to transcribe the Amharic words for me. I must have done a good job because he was smiling by the time he finished and urged me to publish my results in your journal. "Publish *and* perish, I always say," he told me, and I said, "At least I'll get published," which for some reason made him really mad, but he always was a jerk in class.

The words are listed in the table I made below, with the English meaning on the right like we were taught in L103. As you can see, all of them are really simple words any second-grader would know, which is what makes two languages related. In case you're not familiar with Amharic, the dot under the t means it's a sympathetic consonant, which is really funny because when I first heard it I thought the waitress was irritated with me. In conclusion, I hoped to have more words to share, but my research ended when my funding was cut, though Daddy promises to restore it if my grades improve.

Amharic	Turkish	English
säat	sa'at	look
sämmi	şimdi	hear
əne	ayn	eye
qiṭ	göt	but
səga	sığıreti	meet
sälam	selam	high
nəfas	nefes	wind
tarik	tarih	tail
wəraš	vâris	air
hisab	hesap	bill
hakim	hekim	doctor
äzziya	oraya	their
wädä	dahi	two
šäṭ	satiş	sail
waqt	vaqit	time
bärät	broş	pen
maryam	mirim	marry
zämän	zaman	period

THE WISDOM OF LINGUISTS

He who lenites is lost.

CHOOSE YOUR OWN CAREER IN LINGUISTICS—PART 16

YOU START YOUR NEW JOB...

"Would you like fries with that?"

• The End. Go to page 301.

Choose Your Own Career in Linguistics starts on page 301.

WOULD YOU LIKE SPAGHETTI OR LASAGNA FOR DINNER?

Contact linguist: "I'd like lasagna with refried beans."

Once articles such as the above had cleared away centuries of misconceptions about genetic classification of languages, other scholars were able to make rapid progress on all manner of historical linguistics issues. For example, building upon Dr. Sem's work (although he seems to have forgotten to cite Dr. Sem in his own article), Dr. Michael Ramachendra explains the origin of one of the most important words in the English language.

Language Reveals Origins of Divinity

Right Reverend Michael Ramachendra
Doctor of Humane Theology and Priest-President of the
Threesquare Church of the Rediscovered Dispensation

The knowledge revealed in the following article is little understood among society, even, to my wonderment, among professional linguisticians. I am a theologian, not a linguistician, yet the facts revealed herein are so easily demonstrated that I am surprised that they have not been set forth before. We begin with the Russian word *bog*, which, appearances to the contrary, means not 'swamp' but 'god'. How can this be? Surely so basic a word as 'god' ought not to be confused with 'swamp' (although I note that many learned scholars have sought to locate the Slavonic homeland in the Pripet Marshes). No, swamps are clearly a red herring, and the actual answer is that, by the well-known principle of boustrophe-dal transposition, *bog* is clearly identical to the English word *god*. (Note that the letter *g*, when reversed, still looks more or less like a *g*, and *o* is the same as its mirror image).

So the Russian word for 'god' is the same as the English one. Given the relatively low cultural level of the early Slavs compared to the early Germans (the Slavs did not even have bread before the Germans introduced it to them!), it is plain that the Slavs took the word from the Germans. But here we face another conundrum. English, according to the *Encyclopædia Brittanica*, is a Germanic language, meaning that it descends from German. Yet the German word is *Gott*, not *god*. It seems obvious that the English has undergone an expressive alteration, with loss of one *t* and change of the other *t* to *d*. The difficulty is that, according to *Collins New World Atlas*, England is FARTHER from Russia than Germany is! Nevertheless, the Russian word is certainly *bog*, not *tog*. I cannot at present explain this discrepancy, though perhaps it has something to do with seaborne trade between England and Muscovy in the 17th century.

Returning to the word *god*, we should now investigate its origins. Germanic languages, according to numerous books on the subject, are notable for the dental past, which means a *d* or a *t* added to the end of a word to make it past tense. In fact, it occurs to me now that perhaps that accounts for the alteration of the word in English, where the original *t* suffix was changed to a *d* suffix to make the word look like other past tenses. And perhaps the Russians, confused, did the same thing before they enacted boustrophedal transposition. I think that we can safely regard the double *tt* of German as adorational in origin, an indication of the great majesty and power of the deity.

So if the word is originally the past tense of *go*, how are we to understand the underlying religious concept? The key is that a *god* is one who has gone before us, leading the way, and thus is our leader, our head, our chieftain. The early Germans being a wandering tribal people, they saw their gods as the

> PEARLS OF WISDOM FROM
> STUDENTS OF LINGUISTICS
>
> History of English: The arrival of the Anglo-Saxon futhorc provides evidence for the existence of the English language.

ones who led them through the trackless northern forests, spearing the occasional moose and sleeping in holes dug under fir trees. (I mean that the Germans were spearing moose and sleeping under fir trees, not their gods. Gods presumably slept in heaven. Actually, I don't think gods sleep, but I don't think the early Germans knew that.) In the early days, no doubt, the Germans were polytheists, but it is interesting to note that they early shifted to pure monotheism, so that *Gott* is ALWAYS spelled with a capital *G* in German. In English, it is spelled with a capital *G* only by monotheists; in Russian, I don't know, because I can't read the Cyrillic alphabet (which is a corrupted version of the Old Germanic Runes, on which I am currently engaged in writing another article about the theological correlations associated with runic writing by the Germanic people).

Perhaps I should mention here the other common word for 'god', Greek *theos* and its Latin derivative *deus* (Latin is a descendant of Greek mixed with the native Italian languages that the Greeks encountered when they colonized Italy). However, these words do not concern us, since after all the classical peoples were pagans, and our interests here are the theological insights to be gained from linguistical analysis. To reiterate, the crucial finding is that *God* is to be understood as 'He Who Went First'. Astute readers will notice the parallel to the first words of the *Gospel of John,* as well as to certain key passages in the *Bhagavad Gita.*

LOGICAL FALLACIES FOR LINGUISTS

Chronological snobbery—"Grimm's Law dates back to when people thought Sanskrit was unrelated to Latin and Greek, so it can't be a full account of the facts."

CHOOSE YOUR OWN CAREER IN LINGUISTICS—PART 30
YOU LEAVE GRAD SCHOOL AND TRY TO GET A JOB...

Your spirit is crushed, and you don't interview well. You should be moderately desirable with the skills you have, but the spark is gone from your life. You suck.

Finally, a job—any job, please!—comes your way.

• Start your new job. Go to Part 16 on page 195.

Choose Your Own Career in Linguistics starts on page 301.

IT IS WELL KNOWN AMONG LINGUISTS...

Rumors of an Proto-Indo-European "æ-grade" vowel series caused massive dissension at the 1902 meeting of the PIE Society in Baaschtnech, leading to the theft and subsequent disappearance of the Society's famed translucent zeppelin, The Vrddhi Triumphant. It has never been found.

One of the longest-lasting riddles of historical linguistics is why the Proto-Indo-Europeans, who lived in a very nice part of the world, with trees, rivers, pigs, and a beneficent sky-god, decided to leave home. In the article below, Editor William C. Spruiell uses the results of fieldwork on a present-day Indo-European dialect to develop an explanation that has come to be almost universally accepted among Indo-Europeanists, apart from some holdouts who dominate university faculties in backward countries like Germany, Great Britain, and the United States.

A Reinterpretation of Some Aspects of the Indo-European Expansion

William C. Spruiell
Houston, Texas, USA

One of the standard activities amongst Indo-Europeanists is the attempted adducement of the causative factors underlying the expansion of Indo-European languages, at the putative expense of surrounding tongues, most of which are no longer attested but which were doubtless related to both Basque and Etruscan and possibly Japanese. The explanation long considered standard was that the Indo-Europeans, or IEs as they are usually familiarly termed, were of a warlike mien and simply exploded out of their homeland via what in military circles is termed "a forceful display of occupational intent" or "spirited attainment of autochthon-nonvoluntary advisorial status". Most scholars accepted this explanation, and for a long period debate was limited to the locus of the original expansion, with most European scholars except for the Poles claiming the Urheim for their own portion of Europe (the Poles had long recognized that Autochthhon-Involuntary Advisorial types came from any other region than Poland and were afraid that if they claimed the Urheim, the Germans would invade them to get it back). In recent years, Marija Gimbutas' claim that the original IEs were in fact the Khurgan culture of the steppes has gained wide acclaim, since it positions the Urheim in an area that no-one wants to claim anyway and thus reduces friction at important Indo-Euro-

THE WISDOM OF LINGUISTS

Vowels were meant to be broken.

peanist social events. In addition, the Khurgani were apparently a rather vigorous bunch, whose major artifacts were (a) hand axes and (b) rapidly built tombs, both of which are consistent with the traditional view of the IEs.

There are several problems with this scenario, however, foremost of which is the fact that the warlike expansion hypothesis was originally formulated by 19th century Germans, who also proposed that the spread of glaciers during the ice-age was the result of the military superiority of northern ice floes as compared to decadent Mediterranean lakes, and who invented the term "spirited attainment of autochthon-nonvoluntary advisorial status", which in German constitutes a single word of such breathtaking length and consonantal density that many opponents of said attainment strangled in the act of attempting to oppose it. In addition, Indo-Europeans had a plethora of words for (a) trees, and (b) pigs, neither of which are found in notable profusion in the steppes and which certainly were not particularly valued by the Khurgani, who liked to gallop uninhibitedly about spiritedly advising those in their path and, according to Gimbutas, beating up feminists.

Due to the problems inherent in the war-expansion hypothesis, there have recently been counterproposals. The foremost of these has been formulated by Colin Renfrew (1987), who argues that the original Indo-Europeans were agrarians who peacefully displaced their neighbors because agriculture afforded them a higher population density (Renfrew refers to a number of archeological discoveries, such as ancient agricultural bulletins and primitive bronze 'garden weasels' to support his claim). This position fits somewhat better with the facts, as it explains the profusion of dendrolexemes in PIE, as well as rescuing some of us from the notion that our ancestors spent most of their time beating up feminists. However, Renfrew's arguments themselves suffer from a number of problems. Particularly, it appears that Renfrew may be overgeneralizing his Peace Corps background. What then, are we to do about the Indo-Europeans?

The answer, I would like to suggest, lies in the combination of the study of the IE geographical expansion with the study of phonology. It has been known for quite a long time that PIE was possessed of a number of rather odd phonological characteristics, most related to the presence of the voiced aspirates **bh, dh** and **gh,** and to the various vocalic mutational processes. Most undergraduate linguistics students rapidly learn to recognize PIE forms such as *gh^wubh-i-dhe* 'agricultural bulletin' and are frequently heard attempting to pronounce them (usually with unfortunate results). We are accustomed to thinking of the PIE phonological system as, to put it mildly, 'eccentric'. However, the attentive linguist can easily gather examples of similarly odd phonological systems in any modern city, eg:

hwār d'hél ɪz m'bhadhl?

Despite its canonical Indo-European appearance, the above sentence merely translates to "Where the hell is my bottle?", and was collected in modern-day Houston in the downtown region next to the USDA annex. *The phonological characteristics of Indo-European are identical to those diagnostic of ethanol toxicity.* In other words, the Indo-Europeans did not burst out of the Urheim via force or arms, nor did they plow their way into history; rather, they sloshed out of the Urheim! This hypothesis also answers one of Renfrew's cardinal questions, which was why the Indo-Europeans expanded in the first place. Rather than being overpopulated, I would suggest, they got lost trying to get home. This certainly would explain the early forays into India, and also account neatly for certain etymological facts, such as the overwhelming frequency of words such as soma and the (otherwise ridiculous) overgeneralization of *lakhs* to refer to anything that is vaguely pinkish and/or might smell like salmon to Jan Puhvel, who, being Lithuanian, frequently has a cold. It also explains the sometimes aggressive nature of the Indo-Europeans, as the reaction of Europeans to alcohol has been well documented on numerous occasions to be one in which pacifism is not a dominant characteristic (in fact, intoxicated Lithuanians frequently beat up feminists, and Lithuanian is a conservative dialect).

I suggest that the Inebriation Hypothesis not only explains the same range of facts as its predecessors, but in addition also accounts nicely for a number of aspects of PIE society (such as cattle-stealing) which are otherwise unexplained via the other theories. In addition, the Germans are unlikely to invade us for it.

"In some cases the decision to use a phonological feature, and even the choice of the particular feature used, may have been under illicit historical stimulation."

—PAUL KIPARSKY

The best recent work on the Indo-European homeland has been devoted to refining rather than replacing the Spruiell hypothesis; e.g., by making it more scientific. (Even we, who published it in the first place, admit that it was sadly unscientific as written, which led to a lot of good-natured ribbing from editors of other linguistics journals at that year's LSA meeting). The article below, by Lynn D. Poulton, recasts Spruiell's ideas in the framework of Systemic Grammar, which, as everyone knows, is so scientific that it even has the word "Systemic" in its name.

Sociohistorical Linguistic Semiotics and Systemic Theory
The Indo-Europeans Re-Examined

Lynn Poulton
Sydney, Australia

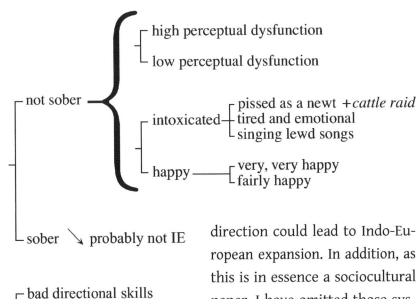

In the past, it has been claimed that one of the great problems of Systemic-Functional Linguistics (SFL) is that it does not address itself to certain major areas of linguistic concern, such as languages other than English, and historical and typological studies. Such claims are, of course, scurrilous nonsense issued by the foolish, the brain-dead, and those jealous of the pre-eminent position of Systemic theory in more avant-garde semiotic and cultural studies.

As an enlightened person, I am always on the lookout for new ideas which may be expanded and elucidated by the judicious application of SFL. Such an idea, I believe, is the one so brilliantly put forward by Spruiell (1990) as the probable reason for the spread of the Indo-Europeans. The Intoxication Theory, re-explicated in Systemic terms, gives us great insight into the sociocultural heritage and semiotics of Indo-European expansion.

The network fragment above gives some idea of how these notions may be applied.

The network has been simplified for its current audience, but it is quite clear how combinations of features such as intoxicated and bad sense of direction could lead to Indo-European expansion. In addition, as this is in essence a sociocultural paper, I have omitted those systems which specifically deal with language. However, I'm sure the reader is capable of adding these in.

From this partial network, it can clearly be seen how a combination of ESMAPD (Extreme Sensory-Motor Animal Perception Dysfunction, a syndrome associated with the high perceptual dysfunction feature) with various other features may provide an explanation for many hitherto incomprehensible incidents in IE history.

For example, ESMAPD with the realization feature *+cattle raid* could shed light on the incident in Welsh history in which, after a rather protracted celebration, Gwydion and his brothers set out on a cattle raid into Dyfed and came back with a bunch of pigs.

ESMAPD may also shed light on the somewhat unnerving tendency of the Old Irish to mistake one of their great heroes for a dog.

And finally, certain episodes from *Beowulf* may be rendered more believable: viz., the South Cricklwood Fragment, which suggests that the whole Grendel story arose from an overly energetic après-party game of Twister.

I hope the above small offering has shown how SFL can make a major contribution to historical linguistics and semiotics. I would encourage readers to pursue this line of research, and I recommend the forthcoming book by Dr. Spruiell and myself: *Stumbling out of Urheim: An Investigation of the Systemic Effects of Ethanol on the Early Indo-Europeans.*

References

Ms. Poulton worked for me for two years during which time she was a very conscientious employee. She was almost never late for work and although I heard that she was a frequent investigator into the effects of ethanol consumption this was always on her own time and never on the company's. If you decide to hire her I think you will not be disappointed as she is very bright will be able to do whatever job you ask her to do.

—Nigel Penman

Lynn was an excellent pharmacist, and although she is no longer in that line of work, I am sure that she will display the same professionality in any job she undertakes. I highly recommend her to any potential employer.

—Bob Hawke

Lynn is an upstanding, outstanding, understanding individual and also contains lanolin. She is 99 and $^{44}/_{100}$ths percent pure. Therefore I recommend

her highly for any job you're thinking of giving her.

—Ed McMahon

WOULD YOU LIKE SPAGHETTI OR LASAGNA FOR DINNER?

"Mass Comparison" Historical Linguist: "I want both of them mixed together."

LOGICAL FALLACIES FOR LINGUISTS

Argumentum ad nauseam—"Okay, Ivan, I will agree with you that your etymologies prove a clear path of descent back through Nostratic to Borean to Proto-Sapiens if you will *just **stop** talking about it!*"

One of the hottest topics in historical linguistics over the past few decades has been grammaticalization. SpecGram is proud to say that we have been at the forefront of publication on this topic, particularly as the publishers of the unedited class lectures of the godfather of grammaticalization, Frédéric de Saucisson.

Grammaticalization in an Inflationary System of Signs
or, Excerpts from *The Swollen Tongue*

Frederic de Saucisson

[Frederic de Saucission is best known as the Gulf Coast Functionalist who removed that school of thought from the realm of the esoteric to mainstream linguistics. Less often is he remembered as the Polish composer who emigrated to Louisiana and gained a modicum of fame from such noted Cajun operas as **Il Pleut Plus** *and* **Permis de Pêcher.** *But, in fact, de Saucission's career in linguistics was a late development, and he spent the first forty years of his life as a composer and lyricist. Unfortunately, though his musical works were remarkable, de Saucisson had great difficulty eking out a living. Only when he was on the brink of bankruptcy did he turn to the lucrative field of linguistics. And fortunate we are that he did. His great talent in this new field was immediately evident to all. Soon he was an assistant professor at the famed Harris County Community Colleges. It was there that he gave his famous Inflated series of Grammaticalization lectures to Introductory Linguistics students. Though Saucisson died before writing a single linguistics article, his students arranged to posthumously publish the notes they meticulously kept. That volume, entitled* **Theorie de la Langue Gonfleé** *has forever changed the history of linguistics. But that work was heavily edited and revised by his students. The following is a transcript of one of de Saucisson's lectures, without benefit of editing or alteration. We can thus profit from the exact words of this remarkable linguist.]*

F de S: As is well known to all, the history of mankind has always revolved around one issue: the struggle between the masses and the aristocracy. This struggle is reflected in every aspect of civilization, and most especially so in language. Language originally belonged to people with *de* or *von* in front of their names and all others used it only by their sufferance. Later, with changing systems of political power, the linguistic system itself was likewise transformed. As the masses took over industry and politics, so they expropriated language from its former owners and converted it to their own use. The result was disastrous. Homophony, synonymy, double negatives, double entendres were only a few of the many ways in which the tongue was debased, defiled, dragged in the mud and eventually inflated to a form grotesque beyond recognition.

Student #1: Is this part going to be on the test, man?

F de S: Pardon?

Student #1: Like all this stuff about the tongue, are we responsible for that? 'Cause like, it's not in the book, you know.

F de S: Tak, tak. That is so. Indeed... Eh, bien... now, where was I? Ah yes. La langue gonfleé. This is best seen in terms of the grammaticalization cycle, which is unidirectional and remorseless in its rapacity. *[He draws Figure 1 on the board.]*

Scum Peasantry Bourgeoisie Aristocracy Zero

Figure 1: Grammaticalization Cycle

A form begins as an unsophisticated independent linguistic unit, much as all men begin as peasants. So, while every aristocrat can trace his roots back to a peasant forebear, none of the rabble have any aristocratic ancestors. As a form continues along the path of grammaticalization it becomes reduced, dependent and eventually, if the process of grammaticalization continues—the form will entirely disappear, reduced to utter nothingness. So, likewise, an aristocratic line becomes weak, degenerate and eventually dies out. Yet that is only the half of it...

THE WISDOM OF LINGUISTS

A chain shift is only as strong as its weakest phoneme.

Student #2: But you just said that language started out belonging only to the aristocracy. And now you say that all aristocrats came from peasants. How can that be?

F de S: Ah. That is the fallacy of assuming that all people have undergone the same degree of grammaticalization. I never said that. Different individuals find themselves in different stages of the process. But never during the history of mankind was there a time when the aristocracy did not exist. To quote the great Russian author Alexei Tolstoy...

Student #3: You mean Leo Tolstoy?

F de S: No, I mean Alexei Tolstoy, who wrote in *Prince Serebryaniy:* "не расти двум колосьям в уровень, не сравнять крутых гор со пригорками, не бывать на земле безбоярщины!" Does that answer your question?

Student #2: No. I don't understand. How did it start? Who were the original aristocrats? And if all aristocrats come from peasants, how could there have ever been an original aristocrat?

F de S: I never said there was.

Student #2: So, you are saying mankind has been around forever?

F de S: That is extremely simplistic. Mademoiselle is very young, hein? So *innocente*. When mademoiselle is somewhat more mature and has had many lovers, she will doubtless understand the intricacies of degeneracy. *[Clears his throat.]* Eh, bien. So, the actual grammaticalization is the cause of a much more interesting effect. And that is the monstrous inflation of the tongue. It is the struggle between the Haves and the Have Nots all over again. Those who have not covet and what they cannot have they will not suffer others to have.

Take monetary inflation as an example... It all begins when some individuals have accumulated value, whereas others have not. There are many ways in which the inequality can be leveled: Theft, plunder, looting, rape... All of which have been tried with great success. But the most ingenious form of them all is to inflate the currency, and thus despoil the wealthy without laying a finger on them or their money. So also it is with language...

As has often been observed, a very small percentage of language is ever at the disposal of the rabble. Take the example of English: The subjunctive, the pluperfect, verb agreement, and the difference between object and subject in pronouns, together with 90% of the words in the dictionary are completely outside the grasp of the common man, as well they should be. So what do the rabble do? Sensing the need to express ideas for which they haven't the proper linguistic tools, they cull their meagre horde and spread all our resources thin by newly coined...

Student #1: Can I say something?

F de S: Obviously you can't. Perfect example.

[loudly declaiming]

No one taught him 'may' instead of 'can'; he's

such a common little man! And if you haven't got
the word for 'may', my answer is: You cannot say.

[*sings*]

> Why can't the rabble teach their children not to squawk:
> Who cannot say it right, should not attempt to talk.
> For no idea on earth should ever be expressed
> Except by means of words that fit the matter best.
>
> If 'can' can serve as 'may' the system's power is strained
> I tell you that I can't, you think that I mayn't.
> And since each day the masses count for more and more,
> The words mean what they mean, not what they meant before.
>
> Then should I wish to say that 'truly I cannot'
> I'm forced to use more words than anybody ought.
> Grammaticalization makes inflated tongues,
> *Avec la langue gonfleé, c'est presque pas une langue.*
>
> The value of each word is weakened and then drained,
> A sort of trickle down in the linguistic chain.
> There's but one way to stop this shameful verbal leak:
> To rule that none but me should be allowed to speak.

Ah, I see that our hour is up. For next time, write
a definition of the morpheme, taking into account
the class system inherent in Western civilization.

[*Many of de Saucisson's compositions were heavily
influenced by Lerner & Lowe. De Saucisson died without issue, thus having attained the ultimate level of
grammaticalization.*]

Would You Like Spaghetti or Lasagna for Dinner?

Indo-Europeanist: "We can reconstruct a mixture of coarsely ground wheat and water from both modern forms."

It is Well Known Among Linguists…

Vietnamese is a paradigm example of a language with temporally discontinuous verb morphology; linguists estimate that some time around 2082, Vietnamese-speakers will begin to emit a formidable flood of tense-aspect markers, but may have to import foreign verbs for a lengthy period.

Quite recently, R.M.W. Fillmore, working within the grammaticalization framework founded by de Saucisson, has solved the linguistic equivalent of Fermat's last theorem, and is a clear candidate for the Nobel Prize in Linguistics as soon as the Nobel committee gets around to establishing one.

Where Have All the Evidentials Gone?
The case that they are now in case*

R.M.W. Fillmore
Royal Canadian Mounted Pragmaticists

The pragmatic nuances of grammatical evidential systems in the world's languages are notoriously difficult to analyze (Bowen, personal correspondence), and yet cross-linguistically they display a remarkably coherent set of semantic features (Aikhenvald, p.c.). Furthermore, these systems have repeatedly been shown to be nearly impossible to borrow or to spread through other forms of language contact (Thomason, p.c.), which suggests that they must be categories of considerable antiquity in the languages that have them (पाणिनि, p.c.). These factors, plus the fact that evidential systems occur in virtually all the world's language families (Greenberg, p.c.), have led such eminent linguists as Campbell (p.c.) to conclude that "evidentials clearly represent a *shared retention* in all modern languages," and others such as Hock (p.c.) to suggest that "an elaborate evidential system *must therefore be reconstructed* for Proto-World."

There are, however, many modern languages which reportedly do not have any grammatical evidential markings (Grammars, p.c.). Since we can be confident that evidentials did exist in some ancestor of each living language (Pinker, p.c.), we are faced with the puzzling issue of how some languages managed to lose a feature which clearly belonged to the universal parameter settings found in the original human language (Lightfoot, p.c.). What happened in those descendant languages that do not now have evidentials? Where, in short, did those evidentials go?

Many have sought an answer to this question (Croft, p.c.) but no one to date has proposed a plausible solution (Whaley, p.c.). This is because they have been looking in the wrong places.

For this study, I collected a random sample of 374 published grammars, representing languages from all known language families and nearly every continent of the known world (Dryer, p.c.). In-depth study of these grammars revealed a surprising type of morphological complementary distribution (Anderson, p.c.). It turns out that grammatical evidential systems do not co-occur with grammatical case systems. Any given language may have one or the other, but not both.

This, then, is the surprising answer to the question: **languages which do not now have evidential systems are lacking these systems because they have reanalyzed earlier evidential markers as casemarkers.**

I call this "surprising" because we do not normally expect grams associated with verbal categories to be reanalyzed as markers of nominal expressions

---

* The author wishes to thank the following individuals for their insightful contributions to this article: David Aikhenvald, Priddy Anderson, Ellen Bickerton, Barry Blake, Alexander Bowen, Samantha Bybee, Butch Campbell, Pippi Cedergren, Neville Chafe, Bruce Comrie, Jacob Croft, Sandra Dixon, Angela Dryer, Eddie Greenberg, Pauline Grice, Lily Heine, Linda Hock, Quincy Hopper, George Jackendoff, Ramon Jakobson, Ebenezer Kuhn, Paul Kuteva, H.D. Lakoff, James Leech, Benjamin Lee Lightfoot, पाणिनि, Kevin Payne, Lucy Perlmutter, Susan "Susie" Pinker, Haj Postal, Eloise Quirk, Butch Sankoff, Brian Thomason, Stanley Traugott, Phineas Whaley, and Hans Wierzbicka. Without the input of these individuals, there would have been very little to say.

(Bybee, p.c.). Fortunately, we professional linguists are not prisoners of our expectations, but are instead free to let the data guide us where it will (Kuhn, p.c.). And in this case, the data shows clearly that casemarking arose as a reanalysis of earlier evidentials.

Correlating cross-linguistic complexity of evidentials and casemarkers by means of sophisticated statistical software (Cedergren and Sankoff, p.c.), I obtained clear correspondences between specific evidential categories and the casemarkers into which they were reanalyzed. These correspondences turn out not to be surprising at all, as each displays a consistent kernel of semantic information (Wierzbicka, p.c.). The correspondences are displayed in Table 1.

Special mention needs to be made of the "Oblique" casemarkers (Comrie, p.c.). Computational analysis did not turn up any reliable correlations between oblique cases and evidentials in the world's languages. There are two possible explanations for this (Logical inference, p.c.). One is that the earliest human language had additional evidentials which have disappeared in all modern languages (Lakoff, p.c.). The other possibility is that obliques are not casemarkers at all (Postal, p.c). I am inclined to accept the latter explanation, as it confirms the predictions of Perlmutter (p.c.). Also, the former explanation is implausible.

Readers familiar with evidential systems may note the omission of the common Hearsay category from this chart (Leech, p.c.). The fact is that hearsay evidentials are not actually evidentials, but rather constitute *denial* that evidence exists (Jakobson, p.c.). We might more properly term this category a *disevidential* (Chafe, p.c.); this is undoubtedly why statistical analysis did not turn up any corresponding casemarker.

As I have already mentioned (Myself, p.c.), it is a bit surprising to find markers associated with verbs reanalyzed as markers associated with nouns.

Evidential category	Casemarker which this category is reanalyzed as	Comments
Default (unmarked)	Absolute or Nominative	The unmarked evidential fits most naturally with the unmarked nominal in either system of case alignment (Blake, p.c.)
Direct	Ergative	Ergative arguments have the most direct effect on the action of the clausal verb (Dixon, p.c.)
Indirect	Accusative	The accusative marks the participant who can only watch as the action of the verb takes place (Payne, p.c.)
Inferential	Genitive	An observer can only infer who might be the possessor of any entity; possession relationships are never visible (Jackendoff, p.c.)
Validational	Dative	The recipient (the prototypical dative argument) is the witness who can validate any claim that I make (Quirk, p.c.)
Other evidentials?	Oblique cases	[see comment above]

Table 1: Evidential categories and their resulting casemarkers

However, this is actually in line with the basic predictions of grammaticalization theory (Hopper and Traugott, p.c.), which posits a process (Heine and Kuteva, p.c.) like (1):

1. verbal morphology > nominal morphology

Thus, the reanalysis of evidentials as casemarkers is not really surprising at all!

Conclusion

Evidentials represent one of the original parametric categories, present in the earliest human language (Bickerton, p.c.). We have seen here that their morphological markers persist in all human languages, but that these markers have been reanalyzed as casemarkers in many languages.

Although case systems are more familiar to the modern linguist, our analytical forebears in prehistory must have had no case systems to consider at all, but instead had quite a rich system of evidential distinctions around which to wrap their explanatory theorizing. This makes intuitive sense (Grice, p.c.): when your interlocutor is brandishing a club, the justification for your claim may be somewhat more urgent than the mere trivialities of who did what to whom.

WOULD YOU LIKE SPAGHETTI OR LASAGNA FOR DINNER?

Experimental Indo-Europeanist: "Could we try to cook this reconstruction?"

IT IS WELL KNOWN AMONG LINGUISTS...

One should never believe emails claiming that a Nigerian prince has inherited extensive documentation linking Etruscan to Saami.

For readers who find the preceding article, brilliant though it is, to be a bit too technical in nature to be fully engaging—not to mention readers who never understood what "grammaticalization" is supposed to mean in the first place—we present the following elegiac tale by John Miaou. While some readers may find a moral in the story, others will just find that it makes them sad.

The Life and Death of an Anonymous Verb

John Miaou

Once upon a time, there was a jolly little verb, who led a care-free, happy life. He was a successful verb. He appeared in a few proverbs, and he even appeared briefly in a nation-wide commercial slogan.

He had many friends of all classes, but he preferred the company of nouns. He spent particularly long hours around a certain noun of the feminine gender, who had all her declensions in all the right places. He fell in love, she fell in love, and soon they had formed their own little clause. They would often be seen snuggling in an embedded clause, making propositions together. Before long, they had a whole sentence of their own, with several little objects trailing them.

But life goes on. What started out as an exciting experience soon turned to redundancy and fixed phrases. The verb began bringing home prepositions, and he started hanging with bad complements. His own nouns grew tired of his new antics and soon they left him. It was the biggest ellipsis he had ever felt. Without his beloved objects near him, he just couldn't find any arguments.

To console himself, he spent most of his time with feminine nouns whose declensions were more revealing than functional. He became addicted to serial verbs, and his dependence on others grew more and more serious. Soon his whole life centered around other verbs. He felt he didn't mean anything without reference to others. He had become an auxiliary, a defective verb who could no longer stand on his own.

He stopped caring about his appearance. His plosives weakened, and one day he lost a whole syllable. It was then that he realized that he had become... *gasp...* an inflection.

After that life just didn't seem worth it anymore. He lost his stress. Not even floating tones would visit him anymore. He became weaker and weaker until no one even bothered to pronounce him at all.

Once he was a proud, frequently uttered, polysyllabic verb, who appeared in proverbs, slogans, and a few famous last words, too, but even those would soon be archaic. The verb had left the language, without even a trace.

WOULD YOU LIKE SPAGHETTI
OR LASAGNA FOR DINNER?

Philologist: "The first attestation of spaghetti in Italian recipe manuscripts dates back to the 12th century, whereas lasagna only appears during the course of the 14th century."

For a somewhat more cynical (not to mention more scatological) view of grammaticalization, and of language change in general, we present the following, written by one of SpecGram's editors while he was going through a nasty divorce. We don't necessarily endorse everything the author says, but readers can form their own opinions.

Ask Mr Linguistics Person

Mr Linguistics Person

> *"Why do languages decay?"*
> —Robin McSmarty-O'Pantssen,
> age 8⅔, Smart Aleck, NY.

Hwæt! Languages don't decay, they change over... okay, I just can't go on perpetuating this myth that languages don't decay. They do. They decay because speakers are lazy. The prescriptivist language mavens are right. (By the way, *maven* is a portmanteau of *musty* and *raven* and comes from a well-known story by Aesop called *The Ravens and the Musty Corpse.* (It is usually left out of collections of Aesop's fables for children these days because of the corpse—and our society's inability to accept death as part of the cycle of life. (If you aren't familiar with it, then blame the fact that you never read any of Aesop's fables as an adult—because we no longer value true literary classics in our society—preferring instead *Harry Potter* and *Twilight*—even as adults.)) Where was I? Right. The fable is about a group of ravens who defend the musty old corpse of a grammarian from the other ravens, even though there is almost nothing left of it to eat. They are continuously distracted by shiny objects on the corpse. They loudly proclaim that the corpse is in perfect condition, and a wonderful source of food and treasure. Eventually the ravens on the musty corpse starve to death, but none of the other ravens notice, having moved on to feast on the intellectually more stimulating carcass of a mathematician.)

Anyway, to get back to my main point, the word *portmanteau* refers to a word made by combining two other words, such as with the case of *musty + raven = maven.* The word *portmanteau* itself is, at least apocryphally, a merging of three words. More of a smooshing, actually, since they didn't really merge all that much. Mark Twain, when pinned by etiquette and unable to escape a traveller on a steamboat who insisted on telling a long and rambling tale, called out to the barkeep, "Bring me another glass of wine! And a glass of sherry! Hell, bring me a whole bottle of port, man, too!" The phrase captured the imagination of a Frenchman traveling on the steamboat—and only his imagination, since he didn't speak a word of English—and he took it back to France, where the French violated the word's orthographic rights and respelled it against its will, and then exported it back to England and America.

But I digress. What I really wanted to tell you about was the word *apocryphal.* It comes from Greek ἀπό-, meaning "away, apart" + English *crap* + *ha!,* and was originally used by classics scholars to mean "Ha! Get that crap away from me!", and was used when other, lesser, scholars seemed to be making things up.

So, as I was saying, English is in fact rotting from the inside out. The prescriptivists are right on that score. Where they are wrong is in believing that younger generations today are any lazier, are more linguistically degenerate, or contribute more to the decay of English than the generations who came before. We all do terrible, irreparable violence to our Langue every time we open our Parole holes. That's the nature of Language.

Out in the real world, decay is part of the cycle of life. Plants pull nutrients from the soil, struggle toward the light, grow, and get eaten by animals. Animals get nutrients from the plants (and other animals) they eat, poop, and die. Animal poop and dead animals provide nutrients to the soil, and the cycle of life continues.

So, too, with languages. Lazy speakers of synthetic languages erode the grammar-bearing morphology off their words. Eventually, the language poops out its morphology, becoming isolating rather than synthetic, the word order petrifies, and small function words take over the role of grammar-bearing units. Lazy speakers of isolating languages erode the spaces between words, until the grammar-bearing small words glom onto adjacent words, and speakers become too lazy to remember the order in which words should appear in a sentence. These glommed-on grammar-bearing bits eventually become morphology, the language becomes more synthetic than isolating, and it poops out its reliance on a fixed word order.

Thus the cycle of life and the cycle of grammaticalization are very similar, except the cycle of life operates on individuals over short time spans, involves the struggle for life and growth, and only partly relies on real or metaphorical poop, while the cycle of grammaticalization operates on groups over long time scales, involves the antithesis of struggle—laziness—and consists entirely of poop.

The important question is: where are we? How long until English is nothing but a pile of grammatical excrement? Fortunately, there are linguo-cultural indicators that linguists can reliably use to gauge such things. Excessive use of parenthetical asides, rambling prose, lack of narrative structure, untoward hyperbole, and improper use of em-dashes—and, commas—are signs of the impending linguistic apocalypse (and also of dementia, but I digress). So clearly we've got plenty of time before English implodes on itself.

Ha! Just kidding! It is mathematically provable that there is now no way to ever use commas that will keep all language mavens happy, and we're running out of time so fast that this sentence may have—by the time I finish writing it—became ungrammatical anymore.

"Abstract words are ancient coins whose concrete images in the busy give-and-take of talk have worn away with use."

—Julian Jaynes

It is Well Known Among Linguists...

The "Neo-Yithic" hypothesis holds that the language of the Pnakotic Manuscripts is related to both Etruscan and Modula-2.

Following the previous selection's descent into fairly het-up rhetoric, we are pleased to be able to end this chapter with a more restrained article by noted scholar H.D. Onesimus. This article not only proves that SpecGram is on the cutting edge of developments in diachronic theory, but also confirms that we continue to be leaders in the expansion of linguistics to non-human languages. In other words, it's well past time for PETA to honor us with a large cash award.

A New Mechanism for Contact-Induced Change
Evidence From Maritime Languages

H.D. Onesimus
Gobi Institute of Maritime Linguistics
Lanzhou, China

Modern contact linguistics has demonstrated an impressive ability to account for language change and the emergence of new languages with a remarkably small number of mechanisms: bilingualism, creolization, borrowing, and convergence (also known as "smart drift").

However, a few intractable situations of language contact seemingly cannot be accounted for in terms of this elegant system (notable examples include Wutun, Ma'a and Texas English). In this article, I show how the long-standing problem of Penguin and the Cetacean languages reveals a new type of contact mechanism, one which may well yield fruitful explanations for other heretofore unexplained contact results.

~~~~~

One of the most vexing questions in Maritime Linguistics has been the inexplicable but obvious similarities of lexicon between the Cetacean languages and the various dialects of Penguin. Cetacean, including a multitude of Whale, Dolphin and Porpoise languages (as well as possibly, but controversially, Pinniped languages[1]), is a widespread family with undeniable internal unity, and clearly distinct from all other known Aquatic families. Penguin, on the other hand, is almost certainly to be grouped with Auk and Puffin,[2] with a distant relationship to Pelican and Flamingo.

However, Penguin shares a sizable portion of its vocabulary and morphosyntax with the Cetacean languages, and until now, no plausible explanation has been offered for this puzzling fact.[3]

Various theories have been explored in the vast literature, of which I will summarize the most common here.

Did Cetacean and Penguin varieties share a common origin, so that they actually belong, at great depth, to the same linguistic family? Perhaps both are the result of a failed human migration, in which some speakers literally fell off the boat and adapted their tongues (and breathing apparatus) to a new environment? This was once considered an attractive explanation, but because no plausible human language relative has been proposed, the theory has been abandoned by all but a few dogmatists.

Can the similarities be attributed to drift? Probably not: penguins and all cetaceans are strong swimmers, so drift seems an unlikely explanation.

---

[1] See my article "But will it float? Why the case for the 'Cetacean Seal' is not watertight". *Acta Linguistica Artica* 81.1:23-408.

[2] Some scholars group Penguin with Ostrich, Rhea, Emu and Kiwi under "Proto-Dodo", but this grouping is based purely on minor morphological similarities, and is clearly inaccurate.

[3] Notable among these similarities is the causative construction; see Scott ("Exploring Penguin Causatives", *Linguist of Fortune—JLSSCNC* I.1) for an excellent description of the Penguin causative. Most Cetacean languages not only have the same construction, but in fact, use the exact same causative morpheme!

With the advent of modern contact linguistics, attention has gradually become focused on the possibility that normal patterns of bilingualism or language shift might explain the similarities. Yet, all attempts to produce such an explanation have failed. Penguins cannot be birds that shifted to a Cetacean language; nor can they be mammals which picked up avian features through bilingual interaction.[4] Massive lexical replacement ("relexification") also fails as an explanation.

In fact, on cultural grounds, bilingualism has been shown to be an utter impossibility between the sociable and land-loving Penguin communities and the solitary and generally mean-spirited personality typical of the waterbound Cetacean species.[5]

And yet, reason tells us that there must be some key, some point of contact, which can account for the shared linguistic features observable in these two diverse linguistic families. As the discerning reader will have guessed (if only because I told you so already), the remainder of this article describes how I discovered what this point of contact is, as well as the implications of this discovery for the field of contact linguistics.

~~~~~

I cannot begin to count the hours that have been spent, here at the Gobi Institute of Maritime Linguistics, in fruitless discussions of the similarities between Penguin and Cetacean tongues. No doubt, the same can be said of any of our sister institu-

THE LINGUIST'S ONE FOUNDATION

The linguist's one foundation is sound change regular:
Exceptionless it marches to split or merger.
From borrowing preserve us, and from analogy,
That every reconstruction may true and faithful be.
—HYMNS FOR THE REVERENT LINGUIST (1845)

tions throughout the world. This vexing problem has consumed many an academic career, and has been the subject of innumerable books and articles. Now, finally, the explanation is at hand.

The revelation, as Kuhn might have predicted, came when two seemingly unconnected events spontaneously intertwined in a revolutionary harmony of technical prescience. Let me tell you about it.

In New Orleans for an unrelated research project,[6] I plopped down at a terminal in an internet café and pointed my browser to the Linguist List; while the page loaded I hastily unwrapped that prize of any visit to the Big Easy, a shrimp Po-boy. The first message was an announcement of Matras and Bakker's *The Mixed Language Debate*. Scanning the table of contents, my eye fell on the title of Carol Myers-Scotton's article "Split (mixed) languages as contact phenomena: What lies beneath".

"What lies beneath..." An epiphany. Instantly I recalled the tortured question of the Penguin-Cetacean relationship. I looked from the screen to my sandwich, back to the screen, and back to the sandwich again. Slowly, as if in a dream, I raised the upper piece of bread to reveal what lay beneath: shrimp.

I had the answer.

~~~~~

Few scholars are aware that Roald Amundsen chose to include an accomplished philologist among the members of his 1910–12 South Polar Expedition team. This linguist, Olav Bjaaland, was fascinated by contemporary accounts of Penguin dialects,

---

[4] The best candidate for a relative in such a theory, Platypus, cannot be plausibly considered a relative on any linguistic grounds.

[5] I do not want to hear any complaints about this claim from idealistic dolphin huggers. Abundant research shows that they cannot get along with anybody. Ask any penguin about dolphins and you will get an earful.

---

[6] See my forthcoming book *The Avery Island Salt Diet: the natural weight-loss plan of the Atakapa Indians.*

and later served for many years as editor of the prestigious *Nordic Journal of Avian Languages of the Southern Hemisphere.*

In 1910, he was involved in a race against Apsley Cherry-Garrard, a member of Robert Scott's South Polar expedition: alongside the drama of the race to the pole, Bjaaland and Cherry-Garrard were competing to produce the first comprehensive grammar of what was then referred to as Low Penguin, spoken in the Antarctic regions.

Relaxing on a Tasmanian beach with Roald Amundsen in 1912, Bjaaland penned his own version of the Polar expedition, an account which differs in surprising ways from the one published by Amundsen himself.[7] Perhaps because of these differences, and because Amundsen was lounging in the next beach chair, Bjaaland saw fit to write his book in Etruscan. This effectively prevented not only Amundsen, but nearly everybody else, from reading the book.

Bjaaland's account (my translation) includes the following key passage:

> As far as this author can ascertain, nobody has ever bothered to write a description of Krillian; scholars appear to have assumed from the popular name "krill" [translator's note: "krill" is Norwegian and means 'food for a glutton'] that it was a normal member of the aquatic branch of Germanic, probably similar to Friesian, Herring, or Icelandic Cod.
>
> Being Norwegian myself, I blithely assumed that I would have no difficulty learning Krillian, if the circumstances of our Antarctic expedition should warrant this. (I fervently hoped, of course, that they would not, as we all knew that our dogsleds would be totally unsuited to an aquatic assault on the Pole.)
>
> However, in the course of some recreational snorkeling near the Ross Ice Shelf in September 1911, I did have the opportunity to do some impromptu wordlist elicitation in the midst of an enormous and congenial Krill community. What I discovered was astonishing. Not only was Krillian nothing like Norwegian, but in fact it had no identifiable Germanic features at all. It appeared, rather, to have numerous words in common with the Low Penguinic dialect which chattered around our camp day and night...
>
> PS Roald is a really lousy skier.

Bjaaland further records that his usually dependable fellow explorer Helmer Hanssen, in an uncharacteristic and colossal oversight, used the pages of the elicited Krill wordlist for toilet paper, and thus destroyed the evidence.

Even without his notes, though, Bjaaland was right. Furthermore, he had inadvertently stumbled upon the answer to the most vexing question in Maritime Linguistics. But he never realized it, because he never bothered to study any Cetacean languages. And since his manuscript lay undeciphered among his possessions until his great grandson recently sold it to an opportunistic collector for a fraction of its true worth, the world was until now ignorant of his discovery.

~~~~~

The answer to the problem is Krill. Penguins and most Cetacean species are avid consumers, relying on the teeming schools of Krill which inhabit the world's oceans as a primary source of nutrition. That is to say, they eat them.

Nearly all published descriptions of Krill have focused on North Atlantic dialects, but the critical data, of course, comes from *Euphausia superba,*

---

[7] For example, Bjaaland claims that his team beat Amundsen's squad 15-1 in the first football match played at the South Pole; Amundsen's official account of the match lists his own team as 4-3 winners.

the Antarctic Krill. Here we find precious little published data, but a brief article in the soon-to-appear Routledge volume *The Zooplanktonish Languages* gives all the necessary detail.

I will not bore my patient readers with the linguistic details,[8] but suffice it to say that the *Euphausia superba* dialect of Krill has all of the lexical items and morphosyntactic features, down to the very minutest morphemes themselves, which are shared by Cetacean and Penguin languages. Furthermore, these features are different from, but clearly cognate to, though readily explainable through processes of natural semantic change and grammaticalization from, the features of better-known Krill varieties such as *Euphausia pacifica*.

~~~~~

The implications of this discovery for contact linguistics cannot be overstated. Clearly, a new mechanism has been revealed, which accounts for the spreading of linguistic features in a new way. In the case of Krill, those who eat it have picked up some of its linguistic features; this is not a case of classic bilingualism, nor of any of the other recognized contact processes.

We may refer to our newly-discovered process as "ingestion". Naturally, we can predict that some other unexplained contact languages may in fact turn out to provide evidence for this same process: perhaps Wutun or Texas English are candidates for such an analysis?

Up to now, most sociolinguists have had an extremely shallow knowledge of Maritime languages: the closest I have heard to an insight about contact among aquatic language varieties was when Sarah Grey Thomason was overheard to order "creole redfish" off the menu at a Cajun restaurant. This article shows that much more attention should be paid to aquatic languages, which may yield a considerable haul of insight into language contact phenomena.

Perhaps other new contact processes are awaiting discovery beneath the waves; *ingestion* may be just the tip of the iceberg.

"The coldest word was once a glowing new metaphor."
—THOMAS CARLYLE

WOULD YOU LIKE SPAGHETTI
OR LASAGNA FOR DINNER?

Contact Linguist: "Italian pasta has had a strong influence on all European cuisine, to the point of mixing with indigenous sauces."

---

[8] This will contribute to my quest for tenure by allowing me to squeeze an additional publication from this topic.

Linguistic Fieldwork
For those who aren't clever enough to make up data

FOR EVERYONE EXCEPT THE THE-oreticians,[1] linguistics is all about fieldwork. Every aspect of fieldwork—the dogged pursuit of elusive case frames, the unexpected discovery of rare phonetic sequences, the tenacious search for vanishingly infrequent minor clause types, the patient testing of thousands of collocational combinations, the impossibly-early-morning reviews of data notebooks, the frantic midnight searches for batteries—every aspect of field-work excavates the psyche to expose the prehistoric hunter-gatherer buried deep within each of us.

That's Franz Boas riding the very first John Deere *Linguistic Data Harvester®*. Behind him, Edward Sapir stands grinning astride the first mound of Sioux data ever collected by a machine. We hear that'd be called a *corpus*, nowadays, but it doesn't matter to us—that's one big pile of data, and the harvesting sure didn't take long!

Or maybe it's the other way around.

In any case, *Speculative Grammarian* has never flinched in the face of a good fieldwork story, whether it involved the rigorous itinerary of dialect survey or surviving the pressure cooker of elicitation on a tight timetable. Come to think of it, even just that data itself is usually a good enough "story" for *SpecGram;* we know that our contributors probably make up most of their data anyway.

In this chapter we will present some of the greatest fieldwork "stories" that have crossed our desks, with the hope of inspiring yet another generation of young linguists[2] to go out and collect some more "data"—and not to forget, when writing it all up, to add a proper denouement!

By the way, it is probably well known to most of our readers that fieldwork is neither a recent discovery in linguistics, nor a long-standing tradition. However, because the publisher objected to the fact that the first draft of this chapter introduction ended at the word "denouement," above, we think it appropriate to add a bit of historical overview here anyway.

As the John Deere advertisement shown above intimates, Linguistic Fieldwork was invented by Franz Boas, sometime around the beginning of the 20th century. Boas had a Ph.D. in physics but found social science so much easier that he came to be the leading expert in the indigenous cultures of North America in less time than it had taken to write the "acknowledgements" section of his dissertation. Having mastered the anthropological side of things in approximately no time flat, he cast about for greater challenges and hit upon docu-

---

[1] Who fortunately constitute a tiny minority of linguists nowadays.
[2] And/or linguists who wish they were young, and/or linguists who think they are young but most definitely are not.

menting little-known languages, which he reasoned might provide a higher intellectual hurdle than the notoriously squishy field of culture, and which might even equip him with better cocktail party anecdotes than did mere cultural phenomena. He was right on all counts, and linguistic fieldwork was born.

Pretty much all linguists did fieldwork from then on, right up until Chomsky and Halle discovered, along about 1968, that the phoneme was a hegemonic construct which primarily functioned to subjugate languages which had no traditional writing systems.[3] This revelation shocked linguistics to its very core,[4] and not only were phonemes promptly done away with, but for an entire generation linguistic fieldwork itself fell out of favor in academic circles, and theoretical linguistics ascended to the throne.

Around 1990, some academic linguists began to feel vaguely uneasy about the field. Since the moratorium on fieldwork which Chomsky and Halle's work had precipitated, roughly four million articles had been published about English, Italian and Icelandic, combined. But while the *Ethnologue* now reported something like 7,000 living languages, scholarly research was limited to only about 30 of them. Surely a wider dataset might be desirable? Furthermore, Jacques Derrida had stopped mentioning linguistics as a bed of hegemony, and Chomsky himself seemed to have forgotten that he had ever dabbled in phonology. The time seemed ripe to rediscover fieldwork.

To the Field Workers, to Make Much of Time

Gather ye data while ye may,
Old Time is still a-flying.
Informants that can speak today
Tomorrow will be dying.

—ROBERT. EARL OF HERRICK

And thus, fieldwork was rediscovered,[5] and theoretical linguistics was consigned to the proverbial dustbin of history.

Fast-forward to the present: focus groups of likely purchasers of this book have revealed to us several things that the average reader is going to want out of this chapter. Primarily, readers are going to want this chapter to do their fieldwork for them, so they can sit at home and experiment with making interesting yoghurt drinks. However, since this chapter is decidedly inanimate, this is a vain hope, at best. What the chapter can do, however, is to give some hints, tips, and suggestions for doing fieldwork well, and also to provide some examples of really outstanding fieldwork, which may serve as inspiration for us all—especially those who need to finish their dissertations before their funding runs out.

And now, the publisher assures us that we have written way more than enough introduction, and can turn to the actual content of this chapter.

---

[3] Later scholars attributed to C & H the claim that it was the *speakers* of languages whom phonemes subjugated, but this is a revisionist interpretation. C & H clearly refer only to the languages themselves. In fact, they consider speakers to be extrametrical and therefore unworthy of explicit treatment in their theoretical machinery.

[4] Even a few individual linguists were similarly shocked.

[5] Actually, after this "rediscovery" of fieldwork by academic linguists, it was further discovered (by academic linguists) that some linguists had completely missed the Chomskyan revolution and continued to do fieldwork all along, even founding an entire sub-discipline on the basis of their research. For details on this once-completely-out-of-touch but now-blinking-wide-eyed-in-the-light-of-sudden-fame sub-discipline, see the Typology chapter of this book.[6,7]

[6] Actually, though, it was not the typologists themselves who had kept on doing fieldwork. Rather, it was a three-way alliance of graduate students who happened to speak Portuguese, SIL staff, and elderly professors who still idolized B. F. Skinner and therefore held grudges against the Chomskyan paradigm.

[7] This raises the deep philosophical issue of when it is actually desirable to be so focused on one's own academic work that one entirely misses major developments in one's field. Such a topic is far too deep and philosophical for a book as short as this one, and anyway our publisher assures us that nobody reads that sort of essay anymore.

First, we address one of the big questions on everybody's mind before fieldwork begins: how to actually pay for linguistic fieldwork. The SpecGram editorial board tackled this question during one of our editorial retreats, and we think that it was an hour well spent. (Though we do wish that Editor Slater could be induced to stay on topic with fewer "prompts." Honestly, the rest of us get a bit tired of slapping him.)

How to Pay for Linguistic Fieldwork

The *SpecGram* Editorial Board

The thing is is that fieldwork is expensive, and yet we have to somehow pay for it. Or we won't get to do it. And really, heaven help the poor soul who can't pay for a trip even to Tahiti, and has to try to come up with some topic on English syntax that hasn't already been beaten like a dead metaphor.

At *SpecGram*, our interest is is to help people in this kind of situation. So, in the interest of new data (or, should we say, in the interest of no more old English data), and out of a sense of selfless devotion to the betterment of Ph.D. students all across Linguistica, the *SpecGram* editorial board has pulled together the following testimonials—tried and true and really truly reliable ways by which we know_{EVID.FIRSTHAND} that you can make fieldwork affordable.

- Do sociolinguistic fieldwork on language used by the immensely rich, and write a grant proposal arguing that you have to appear to fit in with that group to elicit realistic data, and thus need 500 million dollars for "expenses."

- Create a random word-generating program, and as part of the patent application claim rights to any of its "outputs" that aren't already in use. Charge royalties for any new product name. It doesn't matter what it is, it'll be an output.

- Give linguistics lectures at New York and Paris galleries as a type of "performance art."

- Register the null allomorph as a trademark. Sue everyone for infringement.

- Open the first advertising business in the language community. Get Nike to sponsor your project, with an exclusive sneaker contract for the entire community. Nike will pay you for your fieldwork, and will give everybody a free pair of shoes, too. They may even make you a lifelong "consultant."

- Take up prostitution.

- Get a military research grant for the High-Energy Pronoun Accelerator.

- Teach English. Oh, sorry, we already listed prostitution above.

- Make paper for your data notebooks out of hemp. Sell excess raw materials. (To your committee members, preferably.)

- Give linguistics lectures at comedy clubs.

- Pitch a reality show called *America's Top Graduate Student.* In the show, your graduate students will compete against each other in a series of challenges and attempt to develop interpersonal relationships. At the end of each term, viewers will vote one of your grad students out of the department. This reduces competition for funding. (As producer, you cannot be voted out.)

- Give linguistics lectures in subway stations. Collect donations.

- Sell /ˌlɛməˈneɪd/ during the summer.

- Choose only informants who are too noble to accept payment. (Professors in the humanities departments in your local university are usually your best chance for this.)

- Choose to do fieldwork in a language located in a country with valuable black market items. Smuggle as needed.

- Get some of those NLP nerds in your department to write a program to automatically answer tech support emails, then get a side job answering tech support email.

- Charge a fee for each handout in the class you are TAing.

- Give linguistics lectures late on Friday evenings in your university's largest lecture hall. Dress in a Ph.D. cap and gown and call yourself "Dr. Everyprof." Let undergrad students in for free but sell styrofoam bats. Encourage audience participation. (This won't really hurt too much. Trust us.)

- Gloss your texts with lots of techno-babble words, and then sell the language (and yourself) to a TV series or movie studio that wants a lot of alien-sounding sci-fi dialog.

- Charge a fee for every revision your professor demands in your dissertation. Have the professor sign a voucher without reading it, and submit the bill directly to the department. (Come on, you know you can pull this one off.)

- Serve as a simultaneous interpreter at a conference where both formalists and functionalists present papers.

- Start a satirical linguistics journal. Charge exorbitant subscription rates.

If none of these methods pay off for you, then we just have to conclude that you aren't fieldwork material. Give up and study something else.

MURPHY'S LAW FOR LINGUISTIC FIELDWORK

There will always be one word class in your language which doesn't fit any of the normal ones but is too substantial to be dumped into the "adverbial" or "particle" buckets.

CHOOSE YOUR OWN CAREER IN LINGUISTICS—PART 42

YOU CAN'T GIVE UP ON ACADEMIA JUST YET...

The years go by, and you get a steady gig, where you hold out as the endlessly visiting assistant/associate lecturer/instructor, waiting for someone to retire or die so you can have a chance at the tenure track. You are well liked by the faculty, and the students just adore you. Your personal life has settled down enough that you have a happy home and your friends actually expect you to still be around next year (which you now internally define as the period from September to June).

Finally, old Professor Johnson kicks the bucket, and you, the favorite among staff and students, get the nod. Welcome to the faculty, Professor!

- Settle in to your new life as a professor. Go to
Part 32 on page 188.

Choose Your Own Career in Linguistics starts on page 301.

PEARLS OF WISDOM FROM STUDENTS OF LINGUISTICS

One factor which helps to maintain minority languages is that their wide usage serves to encourage their perpetration.

Well, that was easy, wasn't it? Fieldwork funding just doesn't have to be the burden that it once was. The editors also urge our readers to remember when applying for funding that "endangered" is a very fundable adjective these days— **but please DO NOT use this term when filling out a human subjects research application.**

In addition to funding, the fieldworker needs a lot of practical tips and pointers. If we might paraphrase an idiom, there's no sense reinventing the verb, is there? Fortunately, assistance is available. First, those helpful theoretical linguists can be counted on to give guidance to the novice fieldworker. Professor Elwin Ransom conducted a large-scale survey of the relevant literature, and offers the following summary of the insights which theoretical linguistics can offer to anyone embarking on a fieldwork project.

On the Applicability of Recent Theoretical Advances in Linguistics to the Practice of Fieldwork

Elwin Ransom
University of Cambridge

It just brings tears to the eyes, doesn't it?

Not many aspiring young linguists undertake fieldwork on Indo-European languages anymore. As we suggested in our chapter on historical linguistics, that whole language family is just, how you say, passé. But in case any of our readers are willing to take up the cause, we feel it our duty to suggest taking a step back and remembering Tim Pulju's "first principles" approach to doing fieldwork on Proto-Indo-European itself.

How to Do Fieldwork on Proto-Indo-European

Tim Pulju
Dartmouth College

Step one: find a native speaker.

*We suspect that those tips are enough to make up for the dearth of actual training in field methods that passes for "education" in most graduate programs in linguistics. However, there is one more important area that the fieldworker needs to consider before embarking on a project, and even before submitting a research proposal. Expert Phil Dwork outlines an approach which will guarantee success not only during, but even **after** one's fieldwork is complete. This is truly the stuff of which tenure is made.*

How to Get a Reputation as an Impressive Fieldworker
Sharing the secrets behind the successes

Phil Dwork

For the very first time these secrets are being revealed outside the walls of the Most Worshipful Grand Lodge of the Freelinguists! I cannot stop the Freelinguists from using these techniques for their own purposes, but I can share them with the world to level the playing field of fieldwork. The steps to take to transform yourself into a world-renowned fieldworker are simple:

- Prepare to leave
    - Buy a ticket to the Amazon (as corroborative evidence), but don't actually go.
    - Buy a ticket to some place nice where no one knows you, food and rent are cheap, and the weather is warm. Go there.

- Disappear for 5–7 years
    - Spend about 3 months generating the most controversial data you can. Challenge dominant figures and their theories.
    - Pay someone else to actually travel to the Amazon and take pictures of half-dressed stereotypically native-like individuals (or you could do it yourself).
    - Party for the remaining 4.75 - 6.75 years.

- On your return
    - Come up with an absurd-sounding name for your tribe/language, like Dasatay, Kixharyana, Ripahã, or some such.
    - Present your controversial data at every conference you can.

- Write journal articles—a lot of journal articles.
- Controverse with eminent linguistic scholars and other loudmouths as often as possible.
- Bask in the glow of your new fame and/or tenure.

Repeat as necessary.

On the off chance that the result is not to your liking, not all is lost. You can always submit your data to a satirical linguistics journal. Look how famous and wealthy Claude Searsplainpockets has gotten doing that!

MURPHY'S LAW FOR LINGUISTIC FIELDWORK

Your main informant will always be more interested in learning English from you than in teaching you their language.

With such excellent tips and suggestions, we know that readers will be passing this book along* to their fellow linguists— maybe even to anthropologists†—who are preparing for fieldwork. But wait! There's more! We at Speculative Grammarian know what the fieldworker needs to sustain him- or herself through the long days and nights of verb paradigms: inspiration. And we cannot think of any greater inspiration than the example of the greatest (and most productive) fieldworker whom SpecGram has ever encountered, Claude Searsplainpockets.‡

Attentive readers (if any) will have noticed that a number of Claude's studies have found their way into other chapters of this book. He's just great. These further examples of Claude's outstanding work need no additional comment, and here we present, without additional comment, three of his greatest fieldwork reports.

Up the Mind's Nose; With the Mind's Finger
An Anthropological Linguistic Study of the Pɪčkɪt

Claude Searsplainpockets
Somewhere in Asia

The Pɪčkɪt live in small villages high in an Asian mountain range (contractual obligations with the copyright holders of the Pɪčkɪt language prohibit me from being any more specific at this time). These mountain villages are heavily forested—so much so that it is difficult to see more than ten yards on even the clearest day.

Not that clear days come to the Pɪčkɪt very often. Thanks to an odd confluence of frigid Arctic air masses from the west, and a steady warm ocean breeze from the south and east, a typical Pɪčkɪt village is enveloped in dense fog from before sun-up to late afternoon, between 320 and 350 days a year. Vision is limited, to say the least.

Worse yet, the fog is regularly accompanied (330 to 340 days a year) by a constant heavy drizzling rain. The broad leaves of the native plants and trees seem almost to ring with the sound of raindrops cascading off them. As a result, even the simplest verbal conversations require yelling until one is hoarse.

To an outsider this is, for all practical purposes, Hell on Earth. For the Pɪčkɪt, though, it is home. They seem to bear the stifling fog and rain stoically if not enthusiastically. And, when one of my consultants accompanied me to a distant town to restock my supplies, he was gripped by an attack of agoraphobia, and spent most of the trip under a blanket in the back of my truck.

Anthropological Insights

Two remarkable adaptations allow the Pɪčkɪt to successfully inhabit their mountain home.

The first adaptation is a wide-spread form of non-verbal communication. I hesitate to call it a sign language, for fear of implying it to be a visual/manual communication system. The language is actually primarily manual, for both the sender and the recipient of the message. Nonetheless, for convenience sake, I will refer to this mode of communication as PSL (Pɪčkɪt Sign Language).

Outdoors, a typical sign language, such as American Sign Language, would be vastly superior to spoken language, which is well nigh impossible

---

* And those had better not be photocopies!

† Do we dare to aspire to so great a height of achievement and recognition?

‡ Actually, to be entirely truthful, Claude is the only fieldworker whom SpecGram has ever encountered. None of the other editors has any experience whatsoever with fieldwork, and devoted readers will be aware that H.D. Onesimus has published several anti-fieldwork invectives in our pages. We encourage him, because deep in our hearts we agree that fieldwork is just plain silly.§

§ Graduate students, please do not admit to your professors that you even read that last sentence.

in the thundering rain. Still, ASL or something similar would be adversely affected by the thick fog, which often limits vision to a matter of *inches*. The clever resolution in PSL to the conundrum is to communicate not hand-to-eye, but hand-to-hand.

PSL signs are almost completely restricted to a combination of hand-shapes, finger positions, and wrist orientations. All of which are easily detected by the recipient, who holds their conversational partner's hands in theirs while communicating. The only comparable system I am aware of is that employed by *blind* users of ASL, who may similarly keep their hands on each other's hands while signing.

The second crucial adaptation that allows the Pɪčkɪt to live in their forbidding land is a truly keen sense of smell. Without much in the way of sights or sounds to guide them, smell plays a key role in the Pɪčkɪt's daily lives. Animals, both prey and predators, are readily detected and identified at a distance; medicinal as well as food plants are found in large part by smell. Even other members of the tribe can be identified by smell—accuracy varies: more familiar members of the community are more readily identified, while less familiar members cannot be identified personally, but are usually easy to assign to a family group.

Linguistic Background

Viberg (1984) proposes a universal relative ordering in the primacy of the senses, and as a corollary, limits on intrafield extensions of verbs of perception. Building on this, Sweetser (1990) suggests that vision, as the primary sense modality, is the only source of transfield extensions from verbs of perception to verbs of cognition.

> **sight > hearing > touch > smell/taste**
> Viberg's simplified sense modality hierarchy

Evans and Wilkins (2000) have shown that Sweetser's claims are invalid, offering as a counterexample many instances of Australian Aboriginal languages where transfield extensions from verbs of hearing to verbs of cognition are common. A probable explanation for this situation is that conversational styles and cultural norms have reduced the arguably natural primacy of vision in conversation, and increased the importance of hearing as a sensory modality.

Nonetheless, Viberg's claims remain unsullied, and the original modality hierarchy is not disturbed by Evans and Wilkins's findings.

In the data below more damage is inflicted upon Sweetser's claim, as transfield extensions from verbs of smell *and* touch to verbs of cognition are common in Pɪčkɪt. However, no data contradicts Viberg's sense hierarchy. A perhaps novel explanation for this situation is offered below.

Linguistic Data

A few simple glosses suffice to demonstrate the relevant phenomena:

SMELL

pɪčk-ɪt
smell-people
The people who smell (properly) *or*
The people who are known

hid əz-ən pɪčkɪt
neg 2sg.emphatic smell-people
You are not Pɪčkɪt!

pɪčk jrn oz
smell dog 1sg
I smell the dog. *or*
I perceive the dog. *or*
I know the dog well.

pɪčk myn oz
smell tale 1sg
I know the story. *or*
I remember the story.

pɪčk hrn oz
smell food 1sg
I smell dinner. *or*
I know how to prepare that food. *or*
I recognize that food's smell.

pɪčk hɛzn oz
smell memory 1sg
I remember that (memory). *or*
I experience that memory with a sad longing born of desperation, solitude, and the unrequited love of an isosceles tricycle for a slightly browned but still sweet-smelling banana peel.

TOUCH

tu š-é
touch 3sg-nonhuman.emphatic-iterative
Fondle it! *or*
Study it! *or*
Remember it!

tu nah-f iš
touch rabbit.hostile 3sg-masc
He hits (touches in anger) the rabbit. *or*
He hates the rabbit.

tu näp-ïan o
touch cow.affectionate 3sg-fem
She strokes the cow. *or*
She milks the cow. *or*
She loves the cow.

tu brk-úlòs iš
touch book.sacred 3sg-masc
He touched the book reverently. *or*
He memorized the book. *or*
He fantasized about the book. *or*

He created the book through the mystical force of his ideation.

tu ba'n'čɛl o
touch color 3sg-fem
She likes color. *or*
She dreams of color. *or*
She rationalizes the existence of color. *or*
She hypothesizes color despite having lived her whole life without having seen color, as one who has grown up in a black-and-white room.

Linguistic Analysis

Clearly, verbs of both smell and touch exhibit transfield extensions to verbs of cognition. However, there is no evidence to suggest that there are any intrafield extensions of verbs in Pɪčkɪt which violate the sense modality hierarchy proposed by Viberg.

The conclusion is fairly clear from where I sit, among the Pɪčkɪt, despite the rain and fog. The sense modality hierarchy is inviolable, because it reflects basic materialistic facts about our brains and our senses. Clearly we are designed as primarily visual beings, with hearing being a strong but distant second. The other senses straggle in, behind sight and hearing.

Cognition senses of verbs are expected to derive from perceptual senses of verbs, and by default, the culturally primary verbs are the sensorially primary verbs—i.e., those of vision. However, strong cultural trends (as with the Australian Aborigines) or hard physical limits imposed by the environment (as with the Pɪčkɪt) can override this basic semantic pathway by forcing another sensory mode into *cultural* primacy.

Linguistic Flotsam and Jetsam

There is an amazing one-to-one correspondence between spoken Pɪčkɪt and PSL. So much so that all the individual phonemes are distinctly represented in the manual form of the word. However, because of the lack of ordering in time, the signed phonemes are essentially presented simultaneously.

There are several interesting consequences of this correspondence. First, morphological and phonemic analysis of the spoken language is greatly simplified—words are in one-to-one correspondence with individual manual signs, and their phonemic makeup, if not the exact ordering of the phonemes, is readily discernible by comparing verbal and manual manifestations of lexemes. Second, an intriguing mystery presents itself: how did these two modes develop historically, each presumably influencing the other throughout the history of Pɪčkɪt and PSL? Finally, it is hypothesized that fluency in PSL results in immediate and remarkable abilities to solve anagrams in Pɪčkɪt—this hypothesis has not yet been tested.

Language acquisition in Pɪčkɪt is still quite mysterious as well—who can hear to acquire the verbal language? Perhaps this aspect of the environment has driven the convergence of verbal and manual forms of the language.

Anthropological Bric-a-brac

The Pɪčkɪt are slowly being drawn into the wider world, despite their agoraphobic tendencies. Some of the interactions are beneficial to the Pɪčkɪt people and their culture, others are not.

Bloodhounds have become highly prized pets in many Pɪčkɪt villages. Their reputation for a keen sense of smell resonates well in Pɪčkɪt culture. Many of my Pɪčkɪt friends who have adopted these dogs seem to be less stoic and more enthusiastic in their daily life. This, I think, is good—but only time will tell.

Improved home-building technology has resulted in drier, more weather-resistant housing for the Pɪčkɪt, a definite advantage. However, the primary source of newer home-building materials over the last few years has been a somewhat less-than-scrupulous metal siding salesman. While newer Pɪčkɪt houses keep out the fog and rain, they do not dampen the *sound* of the rain, which is louder than ever.

As a result, PSL has become more of a visual/manual mode of communication indoors. What effect this will have in the long term on Pɪčkɪt culture and, more importantly, the Pɪčkɪt language, is unclear.

I have considered introducing better, noise-reducing building materials, but I am still wrestling with the linguistic and anthropological ethical considerations of such an act.

Tentative Conclusions

More research is necessary to unravel the intricacies of this system. Said research will require more and abundant funding.

References

Evans, Nicholas and David Wilkins. 2000. "In the mind's ear: The semantic extensions of perception verbs in Australian languages." *Language* 76, pp. 546–592.

Sweetser, Eve. 1990. *From etymology to pragmatics. Metaphorical and cultural aspects of semantic structure.* Cambridge: Cambridge University Press.

Viberg, Åke. 1984. "The verbs of perception: A typological study." In *Explanations for Language Universals,* ed. by Brian Butterworth, Bernard Comrie, and Östen Dahl, pp. 123–62. Berlin: Mouton de Gruyter.

Eidetic Pronouns
An Anthropological Linguistic Study of the Winodanugai

Claude Searsplainpockets
Somewhere in the Pacific

History

On a small island, located in the Pacific Ocean, there lives a fairly small population of mixed Polynesian and European stock, whose language appears to be related to the Austronesian language family. This determination is difficult to make for certain because of the strange history of the people who speak this language. On January 17, 1834 (the accuracy of this and other dates will become obvious below) a ship, blown off course on its way to Australia from Europe, wrecked on the reef surrounding this island. On board was an unusual collection of criminals who were being sent from Britain. A large portion of these individuals were eidetics who had used their extraordinary memory abilities to cheat in local gambling establishments. Another, smaller, percentage of the ship's human cargo was comprised of musicians who had murdered their patron and his whole family. The population indigenous to the island was quite small, and like today, everyone was closely related to everyone else. The criminals bred with the native population, beginning on March 18, 1834. Oddly, they also managed to wield a certain amount of cultural influence, and within two generations children who had neither perfect pitch nor an eidetic memory were effectively second class citizens. Today, all but one of the residents of the island are eidetic ('the idiot'), and all but two (a pair of twins) have perfect pitch ('the deaf twins'). The linguistic result of this strange happening is even stranger: basically, in Winodanugaian pronoun reference is forever.

Winodanugaian Phonology and Morphology

Vowels in Winodanugaian have six different values for frontness, thirteen values for height, three degrees of rounding and four length distinctions. There are seven tone levels and vowels may have as many as six tonemes associated with each. It is therefore impossible in this preliminary report to give a full description of Winodanugaian phonology. However, we can note a few simple generalizations: the consonantal system of Winodanugaian is very simple, having only eight consonants (w, d, g, p, t, n, m, ŋ); vowels are the only tone bearing units, and consecutive tonemes associated with a single vowel may not be identical.

We can also see the effects of this plethora of vowels (936 vowels, each able to bear one of 65,317 logically possible tones, giving over 61 *million* possible vowels (with tone)) on the morphology of Winodanugaian. All personal pronouns are of the shape /mV/, a shape which only pronouns have. These pronouns refer to arbitrary groups of individuals. Note that we are not talking about an arbitrary number of individuals, but an arbitrary *group*. My consultant was able to think of, in under a minute, over fifty pronouns that refer to groups of exactly fourteen individuals. My consultant was also able to list two hundred pronouns which include herself in the group referred to.

Pronoun Acquisition

A typical pronoun acquisition exchange goes something like this (translated into English, as I have not yet worked out a transcription system for Winodanugaian):

A: Tonight PRO$_{3,792}$ will be coming to visit.

B: Who is PRO$_{3,792}$?

A: Juan, Maria, and all of their children but Pedro.

After this exchange, the pronoun I have arbitrarily catalogued as PRO$_{3,792}$ will be effortlessly associated with the group mentioned by Speaker B in the future. I have been able to catalogue over 23,700 such pronouns, by recording them and analyzing the recordings digitally. Otherwise I would be helpless, like the idiot who can hear but not remember, or the deaf twins who can remember but are unable to make more than a few hundred vowel distinctions (including tones).

Finally, it is stranger still, but true, that in Winodanugai, these multitudinous vowel differences are found only in the personal pronouns. The rest of the language seems to be atonal, using only about 15 vowel qualities, which have predictable rounding, and distinguish only two lengths.

Tentative Conclusions

More research is necessary to unravel the intricacies of this system. Said research will require more and abundant funding.

PEARLS OF WISDOM FROM STUDENTS OF LINGUISTICS

Informants were either asked a specific set of questions, or directly questioned.

CHOOSE YOUR OWN CAREER IN LINGUISTICS—PART 31

YOU ARE WEAK, AND LOOK FOR AN EASIER WAY...

You hear through the grapevine that Town George College has a fairly easy Comp Ling program, so you transfer there. Turns out that it is pretty easy, and you sail through to your Ph.D. in 3 years.

Problem is, everyone else knows it is a weak school, too, and no one—no one—will talk to you about a job. With $250,000 in student loans, you take the only job anyone will give you.

• Start your new job. Go to Part 16 on page 195.

Choose Your Own Career in Linguistics starts on page 301.

MURPHY'S LAW FOR LINGUISTIC FIELDWORK

There will be at least three phonemes in your language that you can't differentiate, whether by ear, by spectrogram, or even by sagittal ultrasound imaging. Your informants will insist that they are different sounds, and will prove to you that even two-year-olds from a different language community can tell them apart.

The Laziest Language on Earth
An Anthropological Linguistic Study of the Perry So-so

Claude Searsplainpockets
Somewhere or Other

Introduction

Back in 1922, my Historical Linguistics professor, Benjamin Ide Wheeler, noted that ease of articulation is a driving force in language change—hence the regular occurrence of lenition rules—but the opposing need to maintain a clear communication channel prevents everything from degenerating to a long low mid vowel.

Turns out he was wrong.

Anthropologic Background

The Perry So-so don't really seem to care how well they communicate; they live in an amazingly fertile valley, and work an average of 12 minutes a week, gathering food. They sell the excess (about 70% of what they gather) to pay for luxury items, mostly sweets, cable TV, and video games.

Unlike many tribes that are in danger of losing their identities after extended contact with wider civilization, the Perry So-so lose very few members of their community to the lure of the big city. In fact, their numbers are slowly but steadily growing as people shuck off their cares, drop out of the rat race, and come here to sit back and stop trying so hard. I call this group "the dropouts".

Linguistic data

The only phoneme in Perry So-so is /ə/, but vowel length(:) and tone(↑/↓) are distinctive.

A short glossary illustrates pretty much the entire language.

ə   'yes', 'sure', 'whatever', 'uh huh', acknowledgement of message received.

ə↑   'what?', 'who?', 'when?', 'why?', 'where?', 'how?', question, 'whatever'

ə↓   'no', 'I don't think so', 'whatever'

ə↑↓   'I dunno', 'whatever'

ə: 'um', 'uh', mild discomfort, feigned interest, 'whatever'

ə↑:   moderate discomfort

ə↑::   extreme discomfort

ə::   mild boredom, lack of interest, 'whatever'

ə:::   moderate boredom, 'whatever'

ə::::   extreme boredom, 'whatever'

ə↓:   mild disgust, distastefulness, 'whatever'

ə↓::   moderate disgust, unhappiness, displeasure

ə:::::::::::::::::::::
        zen meditation

There is also an artificial construct used by a very small minority of Perry So-so—diametrically opposed to the dropouts—who wish to leave the Perry So-so community, but have not quite mustered the gumption required to learn a foreign/real language. Most damagingly to their goals, this small group has been uniformly unable to master any foreign/real phonemes, but they *have* created a kind of modulated code—like that used by computer modems in the old days—in which to communicate. They vary the tone and length of the one vowel of Perry So-so to transmit their subtler, more complex messages:

ə↑⋮⋮⋮↓⋮⋮↑⋮⋮↓⋮⋮↑⋮⋮↓⋮↑⋮⋮⋮⋮↓⋮⋮↑⋮⋮⋮⋮↓⋮⋮↑⋮⋮↓⋮⋮↑⋮↓:
'hedgehog'

This form of communication is estimated to be three times as inefficient as Morse Code, and seventeen times more annoying than Volapük. Also, because Perry So-so has no real writing system, most of the monolingual Perry So-so "go-getters" (of which there are less than a dozen) can only recall 20–50 of these artificial, agreed–upon, tone- and length-modulated vocabulary items. Unfortunately, it is rarely the same 20–50 that any of the others can recall.

Also in contrast with the go-getters, and in a way complementary to the way the dropouts contrast with the go-getters, there are the "mellow ones". They make up the most die-hard Perry So-so members of the next generation. They are so unconcerned with communication that they have begun to lose the vowel length and tone distinctions.

However, they need to have more than *one* signifier to represent the myriad potential signifieds in their environment. So, they have inadvertently developed two additional modes of manual communication: they use one signed morpheme (of which almost any hand gesture is an allomorph) and one tactile morpheme (almost any touch by hand). The modality is the primary distinction and bears all the meaning:

ə	negative
[sign]	positive
[touch]	want, need, desire

So, picking up an item and gesturing with it means something like "I want this". A grunted schwa in reply is "no, you can't have it". Loudness of voice, speed of gesture, and firmness of touch may signify emphasis, but I can't be sure.

Context is usually sufficient to differentiate forms of desire. Touching and gesturing about food is "I want to eat"; the same to a video game console, "I want to play"; to another person's erogenous zones, "I want sex".

Unlike so many other cultures where the elders decry the linguistic innovations of the young as debasement and degradation of the language, the older Perry So-so don't really seem to care that much, one way or another, about these "innovations".

Definitive Conclusions

That's it; that's all there is. No more funding needed for this one.

References

Allen, Marc, 2006. *The Type-Z Guide to Success: A Lazy Person's Manifesto to Wealth and Fulfillment.*

Burn, Geoffrey, 1991. *Lazy Functional Languages: Abstract Interpretation and Compilation.*

Golas, Thaddeus, 2002. *Lazy Man's Guide to Enlightenment.*

Gratzon, Fred, 2003. *The Lazy Way to Success: How to Do Nothing and Accomplish Everything.*

Jolliffe, Gray, 1993. *The Lazy Person's Guide to Life.*

Levine, Melvin D., 2004. *The Myth of Laziness.*

O'Neill, Judie, and Bridget Fonger, 2001. *The Lazy Woman's Guide to Just About Everything.*

Zelinski, Ernie J., 2001. *The Lazy Person's Guide to Happiness: Shortcuts to a Happy and Fulfilling Life.*

THE WISDOM OF LINGUISTS
An informant and his language are easily parted.

Although no one else can measure up to Claude's standards, several other linguistic fieldworkers have nonetheless managed to get their works included in Speculative Grammarian.* Here are a couple of these reports, which we present mainly because of contractual demands which we didn't actually notice when we accepted these submissions in the first place.†

In this article, Mandy O. Chyryry (whose alleged academic affiliation we view with a certain level of doubt) reports what must surely have been the most frustrating (or maybe exhilarating) fieldwork experience of all time. The language, Mid. after-Nguyen Knap, also has probably the best possibilities for future profitable employment of any linguist who could manage to stick with it long enough to become "fluent".

Mid. after-Nguyen Knap
A Brief Ontogenical Sketch

Mandy O. Chyryry
Universidad Subordinada de Asunción

There is a little-known cluster of trade creoles that have sprung up on several islands in the Mid-Atlantic; one of these creoles, used on Ascension Island, in particular presents an interesting case of creolization of a semi-constructed language that even its native speakers cannot speak with true native fluency.

When I first began my fieldwork on these creoles, I ran into several obstacles, some familiar to fieldworkers everywhere, some, I think, particular to this culture and language. For reasons I did not initially understand, speakers of Mid. after-Nguyen Knap are particularly secretive and protective of their language. After 8 years of living on the island, I convinced one family to give me data on the language. But even after they agreed to help, elicitation sessions were agonizingly slow. I would ask a simple question, such as, "How do you count from 1 to 10 in Mid. after-Nguyen Knap?"

Even before any answer was attempted, I was subject to a barrage of questions in return, such as: Does the speaker know what they are counting? What is the source of that knowledge? Are the

items concrete or abstract? Animate or inanimate? Does the speaker, addressee, or a known or unknown third party own the items? Is that ownership inherent or contingent? Is the ownership contested? What is the source of knowledge concerning the ownership of the items? Are the items sentient? Do they adhere to Last Thursdayism? Does the speaker adhere to Last Thursdayism? Does the speaker believe the addressee adheres to Last Thursdayism? What is the source of that knowledge? What is the age, gender, and social class of the speaker? What is the age, gender, and social class of the addressee? By what source is this information known or inferred? What are the ages, genders, and social classes of known third-parties who are expected to hear the utterances? By what source is this information known or inferred? Are there other third parties who are not known but suspected to hear the utterances? Are those suspected hearers expected to hear directly or as reported speech? What are the possible ages, genders, and social classes of those suspected hearers? What is the source of each item of information concerning the suspected hearers? What day of the week, what month, and what year is it when the utterances are spoken? What is the current health of the speaker, addressee,

---

* Normally this is because we had a slow month, but sometimes they pay handsomely.
† Sure, sure, you would be sure to actually read everything you signed, if you were in our position.

known and suspected third-party hearers? Are any of the participants divine, supernatural, deceased, or inanimate? What is the source of that knowledge? Is the counting ironic, sarcastic, hesitant, or iconoclastic? Is the counting done for a particular purpose, such as finding the count of some set, passing the time, amusing a child, treating an adult as a child who needs amusing, or as an attempt at misdirection? Are any tools or body parts used in the counting, such as a stick, fingers, toes, genitals, or aardvarks? Do the stick, fingers, toes, genitals, or aardvarks used for counting belong to the speaker, a relative of the speaker (and if so, which relative, and is that by blood, by marriage, or by adoption?), the addressee (or relative), or some other entity? Was the item used for counting stolen, of questionable provenance, of disputed ownership, or a particularly ugly instance of its type? Should I give the answer as if I were the speaker, or as if I were reporting on the counting of the speaker? If reported speech, did I hear and see the counting, just see it, just hear it, or was it reported to me by a third party? If a third party, how trusted is that third-party, how long have I known them, what is their age, gender, and social class? Are they supernatural, divine, deceased, or undead? Was the report in writing or spoken? If in writing, was it accompanied by a verbal report? If so, did they conflict at all in details or core meaning? For a verbal report (alone or accompanying a written report), did I see or hear the report, or both? What language was the written or verbal report in? How fluent am I and the speaker in the languages in question? Am I a native speaker or certified as a translator in any of the languages in question? What about the reporter?

Murphy's Law for Linguists

The last living speaker of a hitherto unexamined language always has gone totally deaf, is aphasic, has had a laryngectomy, or has lost all their teeth.

I answered all the questions as simply as I could, and then my informant was silent for several minutes. I was convinced he was pulling my leg and simply was not going to cooperate. I got up to leave and he said, in English, "Wait! Wait! I'm thinking!" Ten more minutes went by, and he said, as best as I can transcribe it:

/ʃʤʌˠ˞ɥˠʳ˩ɟɵəʌʋɬfæɓɱ!ɪ‖ǂɔθɵʀʁɾɣˠʰʔoː/
(with tone: ⌄⌃⌄˥)

My immediate response was, of course, "Whoa! Hold on! That was way too fast! Can you give me each number individually?" My informant replied, with an expression of mild confusion, "That was just the word for 'one' in the conditions you described."

By the time we got to the word for *three* I needed an aspirin and my informant said he needed a drink. I bought him a whisky sour at the local pub. (Interestingly, the translation for "I'd like a whisky sour, another for my friend here, we'll need another round in ten minutes, keep them coming until I tell you to stop, and put it all on my company's tab!" is just /ɔɪ/. For martinis (shaken, not stirred), it is /bɒnd/. It is also a cultural taboo to have a drink with someone and not drink the same drink.)

Once my hangover cleared up, I decided to give up on ever understanding Mid. after-Nguyen Knap. Since I had spent 8 years on the island and now had nothing to show for it, I decided to spend a little time trying to understand the origins of Mid. after-Nguyen Knap. Over the following 12 years, I have gained the trust of several other families of higher social status, and I have been able to piece together the following sketch of the history of the language.

There are many powerful entities—rich corporations, members of several royal families, oil sheiks, governmental agencies engaged in black-ops, etc.—which have for decades used the remoteness and solitude of small, sparsely populated islands all over the world to conduct potentially shady business in relative secrecy. A few long flights aboard chartered planes with erroneous flight plans, a few well-placed bribes that amount to pocket change for the briber and a year's income for the bribed, and a little hired mercenary muscle to keep everyone to their word, and these meetings may as well have never happened.

Legend has it that many of these secretive meetings were originally conducted in an English-based Pidgin, called "Knap" or "Knap's Language", named after Ms. Belas Knap, the polyglot lead negotiator for a now-unknown entity in the 1920s. Ms. Knap was legendary for requiring English as the lingua franca of these secretive island meetings, and for teaching opposing negotiators just enough English to get them to agree to contractual terms that were not in their clients' best business interests (and were often detrimental to the negotiators' long term health).

A dialect of this pidgin, spoken on several Mid-Atlantic Islands, was creolized in the 1940s when several renowned negotiators decided to stop traveling the world for their clients, and set up shop (and permanent residence) on one or more Mid-Atlantic islands. This creole is now known as Mid-Atlantic Knap, or just Mid. Knap. Several of the children of these settled negotiators learned Mid. Knap natively and went on to become second-generation negotiators in the 1960s.

WOULD YOU LIKE SPAGHETTI OR LASAGNA FOR DINNER?

Field Linguist: "Would it mean the same thing if I said 'spaghetti or *else* lasagna?' "

One of the third generation of negotiators and native-speakers of Mid. Knap was Nguyen Ling. He attended the University of California, Berkeley in the early 1980s, where he set out to major in business. Because of some computer-related complications in the administrative offices, and the staff's general unfamiliarity with the surname-given name pattern of Asian names, his records were constantly mixed up in such a way that the university thought his given name was "Busi", his surname was "Nguyen", and his major was "Ling"—that is, Linguistics. After two years of fighting the system, "Busi" Nguyen gave up and completed a major in Linguistics, and went on to get his Ph.D.

Upon his return to Ascension Island in the late 1980s, Busi put his linguistic training to a novel use. As the island's negotiators-for-hire were naturally quite accomplished negotiators, their contracts with clients included several advantageous provisions, not least among them an iron-clad hourly rate, regardless of the time required to conclude the contracted negotiations, and the unquestionable right to determine the language of negotiations (a clause harkening back to the time of Ms. Knap herself).

Busi began consciously adding to the complexity of Mid. Knap, at first as an impediment to those on the other side of the negotiation table, but later as a means to draw out the negotiations as finer and finer grammatical distinctions were required to utter anything (this idea was pitched to clients as ensuring no possibility for misunderstanding in the final contract). Nguyen's relatives and business partners quickly became the dominant negotiators in the Mid-Atlantic small-island shady-business world.

Nguyen was assassinated in the mid-1990s by a consortium of negotiating groups who were having trouble keeping up with the pace of innovation in the Ascension Island dialect of Mid. Knap. After Nguyen's death, the innovation stopped and the then-recent changes fossilized. But there were already dozens of native or near-native speakers (including several children who have now become fourth- and fifth-generation negotiators). This semi-constructed language, which has fully re-creolized in the younger generations, is now referred to as Mid. after-Nguyen Knap, in honor of both its original source and recent champion and chief innovator.

From what I have been able to determine, the language incorporates at least the following features, most of which Nguyen presumably learned about in his time as a student of linguistics. The language is agglutinating, features clusivity, and follows a split ergative pattern, except on Thursdays. It requires the logical precision of Lojban. The phonology is a merger of Ubykh and !Xóõ, though the writing system is based on English, but with less emphasis on logical spelling. Some verbal and noun inflections are adapted from Métchif, based on Arabic's triconsonantal roots and employing Bora's 350-odd noun classes. The evidentials are derived from Classical Pinnacle Sherpa, the cases from Estonian, the honorifics from Japanese, and the 6-level tonal system was adapted from Bench. An apparently unique feature, the grammaticalization of Last Thursdayism, seems to be a true native innovation.

The language was effective, not as a communication system, but as a money-maker. Simple negotiations take months. The most complex deals have been underway for over a decade. Negotiations, undertaken at exorbitant hourly rates, last 16–20 hours a day. The negotiators have become fabulously wealthy, while their egregiously wealthy clients hardly notice the cost. The language, as a communication system, is essentially a form of cognitive impairment on par with or even more severe than the Pirahã language, except that all speakers of Mid. after-Nguyen Knap also speak another language fluently, usually English.

One surprising socio-political side effect of the adoption of Mid. after-Nguyen Knap by the negotiators of Ascension Island has been a phenomenal slowdown in certain kinds of criminal activity when routed through the island's negotiating underworld. As the result of an early draft of this paper having been circulated in unexpected circles, I have been approached by Interpol to start a program to encourage the use of Mid. after-Nguyen Knap among other small-island negotiators in order to enhance this slowdown effect. I am currently debating with myself whether I should continue my fieldwork here on Ascension Island in hopes of one day being able to properly describe the language, work to promote Mid. after-Nguyen Knap among speakers of Mid. Knap without being passably fluent in either, or simply enter witness protection and become a plumber or something.

MURPHY'S LAW FOR LINGUISTS

You will always run out of batteries in the middle of recording an incredible conversation featuring structures and words you've never heard before. The situation will never arise again and your elicitation efforts will be for naught.

THE BEST LINGUISTICS BANDS EVAR!!

Def Native Informant
& Linguaphobia

Sometimes the joys of fieldwork are what one expects, such as recording words and analyzing syllables, but sometimes they far exceed one's expectations. Such an experience is reported by Professor Rodrigo Diaz, who uncovered a language far more significant than he could possibly have hoped when he bought his bus ticket to the Tileni homeland in Bolivia.

Classifying an Andean Language

Rodrigo Diaz
La Paz, Bolivia

Introduction

This is not a polished paper: rather, it is a preliminary report which I have rushed into publication because of the extremely shocking and significant information which it contains. I felt that the linguistic world would want to know of my results immediately, despite the fact that I have only just begun my research.

Description of Research

For several years I have been working on describing various Quechuan dialects to be found in the Andean fastnesses of northwest Bolivia. The indigenous population dwells for the most part in small villages of usually less than one hundred people, and sometimes considerably fewer. It was during the course of this investigation that one of my principal informants, who was bilingual in Spanish and Tena, told me about a village where the people spoke with "palabras extrañas, ni españoles ni indias tampoco." Not sure at first what to make of his statement, I ended up supposing that the language he described was a Quechuan one which, for whatever reason, had come to be radically different from its sister tongues over the course of time. Accordingly, I decided that I would visit this village some day and collect some data on its dialect.

It was not until a few months later that I set off for the village in question, which was about one day's journey from its nearest neighboring community. On the way, I learned from my guide that the people of this village, which is called Tileni by both its inhabitants and its neighbors, are no different racially and little if at all different culturally from the other Indians of the region. Only their language, and perhaps their elaborate inhumatory customs, differentiate them from their neighbors, with whom they have occasional intercourse. This strengthened my view that the Tileni were simply speakers of a distinctive dialect.

It was not hard to locate native Tileni speakers to serve as informants: perhaps ten or fifteen of the about sixty native Tileni speakers also have learned Tena, although the reverse, Tena speakers learning Tileni, is rare if it occurs at all. Neither I nor the bilingual Tileni are particularly fluent Tena speakers, but we managed to communicate effectively.

Well, I was soon busily collecting data, and after a few hours I had to admit an unexpected truth: Tileni is not a Quechuan language. Below are a number of basic vocabulary words which those who know Quechuan will immediately recognize as foreign:

1.	e:s	'god'
2.	e:zal	'gods'
3.	klan	'son'
4.	klenal	'sons'
5.	se	'daughter'
6.	lubu	'to die'
7.	e:l	'year'

8.	ti:	'month'
9.	mellum	'tribe'
10.	fu	'one'
11.	zal	'two'
12.	si	'three'
13.	sa	'four'
14.	ma:	'five'
15.	huf	'six'

There was no question that Tileni was not Quechuan, but of course the problem now was, what was it? It did not seem to belong to any of the other South American language families with which I was familiar, although my knowledge has enough gaps that I couldn't exclude the possibility. Yet there seemed to be something awfully familiar about the data as I stared at it on the pages of my notebook. I seemed to have seen the data before, but in a context radically different from the Andean one I was now in, so different, indeed, that I could not make the connection explicit. It was as if some portion of my mind was rejecting the wild hypothesis which my subconscious was raising.

The next day I tried approaching the matter from a different angle. I asked the Tileni if they had any legends, any half-forgotten memories of the origin of their village. Had they come from somewhere else and settled among the Tena, or were they perhaps the remnants of a pre-Quechuan substrate? Unfortunately, the Tileni's folk history was of little use. According to their legends, they had always lived in this village, and they had always been surrounded by Quechuan speakers, and they had always spoken a different language from their neighbors. No one was sure why; indeed no one had ever really wondered why—that was just how it was.

I don't know what it was that finally triggered my recollection. All I know is that a few nights later, having made no progress in placing the language, I suddenly woke up in a cold sweat. I had the answer—but the supposition was so fantastic that I wondered about my own sanity. Perhaps the thin mountain air had finally gotten to me. Yet I could not sleep anymore, at least not until I looked back at the data and made sure that this theory was as preposterous as it seemed. Then slowly, as I looked at the data, I came to realize that it was true. Next to the examples cited above, I jotted down from memory the following forms:

1.	ais	9.	meϴlum
2.	aisar	10.	ϴu
3.	clan	11.	zal
4.	clenar	12.	ci
5.	sex	13.	sa
6.	lubp	14.	max
7.	avil	15.	huϴ
8.	tiv		

The relationship was self-evident, the sound laws—e.g., ai > e:—so obvious and unremarkable that I need not enumerate them here. All the evidence, then, confirmed one of the most startling hypotheses ever posed in linguistics, for the data I jotted down from memory came not from Quechuan, nor from Tupi, nor Guarani, nor indeed any language spoken anywhere close to Tileni in space, *or in time*—they came, in short, from Etruscan. Yes, Etruscan, a little understood dead language spoken in Italy over two thousand years ago, and apparently unrelated to any other languages except perhaps a few equally dead tongues of the eastern Mediterranean.

Now you can understand how reluctant I was to accept the hypothesis forced upon me by the evidence. Yet there can be no doubt. Although it was only about a week ago that I had my epiphany, I have managed to collect nearly one hundred examples which are clearly descended from Etruscan, sometimes with a slight semantic shift; e.g., Etr. *netsvis* 'haruspex' > Tileni *netsi* 'priest'. There are also a number of clear borrowings from Quechuan, e.g. *hambatu* 'toad', but for the most part, Tileni appears to be remarkably conservative, especially in its preservation of the Etruscan inflectional system virtually intact. No doubt many of the words which I have been unable to trace back to their sources could be referred to Etruscan, if we knew more about it. Certainly the number of Etruscan words which I remember from my graduate school days is particularly small.

It was in part to find a contemporary lexicon of Etruscan that I left Tileni for La Paz four days ago. However, I also considered it imperative to convey the news of the discovery to the linguists of the world as soon as possible. *Babel,* since it comes out frequently, and is distributed worldwide, seemed to be the best choice for publication; also, its editors are somewhat more open-minded about innovative research than are other, more stodgy editorial boards. By the time this report is published, I will already be back in Tileni, researching for a more comprehensive report which will be published later.

Reflections, Implications, and Applications

I cannot explain how the Etruscan language could have gotten to the mountains of Bolivia. Of course, it may be that we should consider the possibility that the Tileni have lived in Bolivia for four or five thousand years, or more, and that it was the Etruscans who migrated. In any case, the facts are plainly bizarre.

It is obvious that the study of the Tileni will prove very useful for the thorny task of deciphering and translating Etruscan writings. We know enough about the structure of Etruscan that comparison

with the conservative Tileni dialect should clear up most if not all of the difficulties we have with the dead tongue.

I need not detail the far-reaching implications of this discovery for such fields as theoretical historical linguistics, Mediterranean history, and Latin philology. I will leave the applications of my research to the specialists in those fields, while I myself continue to work on the synchronic and diachronic analysis of the Tileni language itself.

Babel Editor's Note: Lest anyone suspect that the above is a hoax, let me say that Professor Diaz is a well-known and well-respected linguist whose integrity is beyond suspicion. We may rest assured that the facts are as he relates them, even if his analysis may be wrong in some details. Moreover, it is absolutely certain that this is a genuine submission from Dr. Diaz, who took the trouble to have his report notarized. There can be little doubt, then, that there are about sixty speakers of what appears to be a language descended from Ancient Etruscan living in the Bolivian highlands, where they have lived for thousands of years. As Professor Diaz states, the implications of this discovery will be wide-ranging; we at *Babel* are proud merely to have been able to serve as the transmitters of this information.

MURPHY'S LAW FOR LINGUISTIC FIELDWORK

You brought the wrong power converters, and their importation has been banned to promote development of local industry.

One final bit of inspiration for the fieldworker is left to present: the example of the überlinguist who manages to effectively investigate so many languages that it takes multiple graduate students just to organize his or her field notes. A team of such linguists worked together to publish what must surely qualify as the most ambitious description of a language family in the history of the printing press: The Other Sino-Tibetan Languages.

The Other Sino-Tibetan Languages

Edited by Qing Daixia, Brad Davidley, Van Geordriem, Chap Hillerell, Hans Ingalillson, Mat Jamisoff, Ed Jerrymondson, Ben Pauledict, Hong Sunkai
Published 2006. Hardcover, 4,444 pages. Price: if you have to ask, you can't afford it.

This volume fills in the considerable gaps left by Routledge's slim 2003 volume *The Sino-Tibetan Languages.* Displaying an uncharacteristic lack of ambition, Thurgood and LaPolla treated, in that otherwise excellent work, less than 40 of the 400+ languages of this important family. Clearly, much work remained to be done, and we at Psammeticus Press have undertaken to do it. *The Other Sino-Tibetan Languages* describes the remaining 90% of the languages in the family.

Articles on each of over 360 Sino-Tibetan languages are included, in each case written by the world's leading specialists. Each 10-page article sketches the sound system, morphology, syntax, and basic discourse features of the language, as well as providing a 200 item list of basic vocabulary.

In making preparations for the volume, the editors assumed that a massive data-collection project would be necessary, since the vast majority of the ST languages have not yet been investigated. However, on examining their backlog of field notes, editors Brad Davidley, Ed Jerrymondson and Hong Sunkai discovered that, among the three of them, they had already conducted fieldwork on all but 4 of the remaining Sino-Tibetan varieties. This left only a small field project, of which Qing Daixia personally made short work.

With the publication of this volume, then, the editors are proud to declare that preliminary documentation of the entire Sino-Tibetan family has been completed.

A concluding article of nearly 500 pages, co-written by the volume's nine editors, pulls together the comparative and historical implications of the volume, including a vast number of surprising insights and revisions to the family's genetic relationships which our original research has revealed.

Although we do wish our competitors well (primarily in the wettest sense of the word) we are confident that *The Other Sino-Tibetan Languages* will outsell Routledge's meager offering by a percentage commensurate with the difference in the breadth of their coverage of the vast Sino-Tibetan Family.

MURPHY'S LAW FOR LINGUISTIC FIELDWORK

A month after arriving, your last working microphone will short out.

Finally, there is certain practical advice that can make a real difference in the success or failure of linguistic field-work. We close this chapter by presenting a few of the intensely useful resources which we are aware of. We know that these will be essential aids to many generations of fieldworkers. We trust our readers to know how to make the most productive use of them, without tiresome explanations from us.

The XT-21 Uzi/Tape Recorder

Dirk's Academic Supplies

The XT-21 Uzi/Tape Recorder—essential for the field linguist. Imagine finding yourself in Papua New Guinea, trying to gather data, when suddenly you realize that your native speaker consultant is looking at your thigh quite hungrily. Many a linguist in a similar situation has perished, but you don't have to. Just press the special red button right next to 'RECORD' and your informant will be eating lead instead of you. Only $1,095, with a 15% discount for students. Send check or Visa/Mastercard number to Dirk's Academic Supplies, Boulder, Colorado. Order before Dec. 1 and get a genuine one-carat cubic zirconium men's or ladies' ring absolutely free as our gift.

Speakers of Klhatkp for Hire

Klhatkp Confederacy

For Hire: Speakers of Klhatkp, a South American Indian language which is structured oppositely to all known typological universals and trends. Exhibits: OVS word order, postpositions with prenominal genitives, head nouns agreeing with adjectives, verbs inflected for weight, more. Will provide data for appropriate fee. For more appropriate fee, will actually attend conferences and emit data at target linguists. Send proviso to Gmahl Pkodzta, Chieftain, Klhatkp Confederacy, 2013-0194829 Jungle Road, Paraguay, South America.

!Kanga Tribal Research Resort

Terry Mulkern

IT'S THE LAW OF THE ACADEMIC JUNGLE • •

Publish or Perish!

!KANGA Tribal Research Resort
Tabora, Tanzania
1-800-PUBLISH

ANTHROPOLOGISTS, ETHNOLOGISTS, LINGUISTS: THE EVOLUTIONARY ALTERNATIVE AWAITS • • •

!KANGA
TRIBAL RESEARCH RESORT

!KANGA: BECAUSE FIELDWORK DOESN'T HAVE TO BE WORK

It's an old dilemma: you must publish to get ahead, but who has time when fieldwork is so exhausting, time-consuming, and difficult?

You're about to discover a veldt of a deal: !KANGA Tribal Research Resort provides the discerning social scientist with all the tools necessary for top-flight research, on some of the most fascinating hunter-gatherers around, while keeping you in the kind of style not usually associated with the Dark Continent.

!KANGA resort staff are ready to assist you with a dizzying array of services: complete travel arrangements; grant-writing help; even the inside stuff on the editors of top journals. And our accommodations are first rate, as you'd expect. But the real stars at !KANGA, of course, are the people themselves: Friendly, engaging, and eager to indulge your pet theory.

ALL OUR EXCITING PACKAGES INCLUDE AIRFARE FROM NY, ACCOMMODATIONS, OVERLAND TRAVEL, AND RESEARCH PREP SERVICES. TAXES, TRIBUTE, GRATUITIES EXTRA.

"Louis Leakey"
I month basic research

Features translator, 1 informant, community tent, complimentary artifact, religious ritual, *bonus audio tape.* Great for grad students or adjunct faculty. Dry season only.

....us$5,995

"Noam Chomsky"
I week linguist special

Trained informants rehearse your script, speak confidently into included tape recorder. Perfect for that hard-to-prove theory, hard-to-please editor. Choice of souvenir artifact.

....us$1,995

"Desmond Morris"
2 month shot at tenure

All above, plus: 3 informants, brush shelter (double occupancy), 3 day/2 night hunting trip, feast (in season), participation in religious ritual, *bonus video.* Get your vitae in gear.

....us$12,995

"Joseph Campbell"
2 week myth and magic

All-night fireside highlights. Included tape recorder catches the action as tribe weaves web of mystery. Pre-recorded collection "The Golden Baobab: Legends of !KANGA" included.

....us$2,995

"Margaret Mead"
2 month career maker

All above, plus private hut, feast in your honor, shaman access, sex secrets, induction into tribe, funeral rites (if available), *bonus body scarification.* Book deal, Yale sniffing around.

....us$18,995

"Richard Gere"
I day celebrity photo op

Concerned, conscientious, but no time? Give the gift of Gaia with 1 day compound walk-around. 2 rolls of film and professional photographer provided. Shaman access available.

....us$1,495

IT'S UP TO YOU

Yes, we all know teaching is important work, fulfilling work. But do you really want to face the dulled young faces of one more Anthro 101, one more semester, for the rest of your life? At !KANGA we understand what it takes to succeed. We've been hunting and gathering in the same marginal territory for ten thousand years, which should strike a chord as you survey your own picked-over field.

And when you're ready, we're ready, kaross in hand, to help you harvest the fruits of your academic success.

THE PRUDENT FIELDWORKER'S GUIDE TO PREPARATION AND PACKING

PROFESSOR ATHANASIOUS SCHADENPOODLE

For many, fieldwork is an all-consuming passion; for Professor Athanasious Schadenpoodle, it is an all-consuming phobia. Indeed, it's sometimes difficult to negotiate the hallway near his office at SpecGram headquarters (see footnote 1, below). Although his own actual in-person fieldwork experience is quite limited (see footnote 1, again), he has attained quite a level of notoriety among us for the complexity and thoroughness of his precautions (yes, you should probably just keep reading footnote 1 over and over—let it really sink in). Indeed, he is the only SpecGram editor who not only owns an Uzi Tape Recorder and an eight-foot carbon-steel flyswatter, but who also carries both on his person any time he exits the safety of the building.

FIELDWORK HAS LONG BEEN THE LIFEBLOOD OF OUR discipline[1]—we rely upon our far-flung native-speaker coworkers to provide the data that validate our theories, even as we ourselves have the job of weeding out all the data that don't. However, the same fieldwork that serves as our lifeblood can also spill it, as the world outside habitable academic environments is a harsh, unforgiving place, devoid of both safety and espresso, and ofttimes swarming with venomous insects or vicious sloths.[2]

Suitable preparation cannot avert all harm, but it can ameliorate a host of problems, particularly if the exact characteristics of the fieldwork locale are taken into account. Clearly, some threats are more prevalent in one area of the globe than another—malaria, for example, is endemic only in the more tropical regions, while French pop music rarely escapes its home country. Below, I shall provide some initial recommendations, keyed to particular circumstances, that should make your life much easier (or even prolong it).

General Travel

General Notes: The safest strategy for general travel, of course, is to create a ten- to fifteen-foot radius free of all forms of life around yourself, while ensuring you have a separate air, water, and food supply. This may be difficult to accomplish, however, especially in Coach, so some measure of compromise is necessary. One can only look forward to the day when the careful fieldworker can use remote holographic projection for most work.

> ### IT IS WELL KNOWN AMONG LINGUISTS...
>
> Using a microphone stand while doing fieldwork will decrease the chance of vibration-induced interference if you're having malaria-related chills.

Common Threats: Disease, injury, violence, travel-based ennui, American tourists, kidnapping.

Add to pack:

- Halazone tablets (for treating water).
- Wide-spectrum antibiotic tablets (for when the halazone doesn't work, or you accidentally bump into another person, mammal, reptile, or other chordate).
- Large umbrella with metallic foil mesh woven between cloth layers (for sunspot activity).

---

[1] *While Prof. Schadenpoodle has, to our knowledge, only gone on two excursions, he is quite famous in our field for his awareness of, and proactive preparation for, hazards. On six separate occasions, campus security has had to rescue students who inadvertently triggered the defensive perimeter around his office, and two hapless sophomores spent over three days lost in the steam tunnels under the campus trying to find it in the first place. —Eds.*

[2] *We don't understand it, either, but it's not a typo. —Eds.*

- Eighteen to twenty six-foot lengths of copper wire, each with small attached metallic spike (to attach corners of umbrella to ground in order to create a Faraday cage—very useful for electromagnetic storms).
- Flare gun.
- Burn ointment (for general use, and also if you misfire the flare gun).
- GPS tracking device and internet-capable broadcaster (for checking weather conditions, determining chance of harmful meteor showers, identifying that new rash, and accessing phrase-book software).
- Aerosol insecticide, with wide-area dispersal nozzle (two to four gallons should be sufficient unless traveling to tropics, or going outside for more than two hours).
- Packet of uplifting, yet oddly unidentifiable religious tracts. This sort of thing can be enormously effective for motivating other travelers to sit elsewhere than next to you. Aim for the sort of pamphlet cover that has a group of earnestly happy-looking people, solidly occupying the "uncanny valley" between human and machine, all linking hands under a slogan like "Achieving Oneness," against some kind of mystical symbol backdrop. Inspiration for everything but the symbol can be readily got from business leadership seminar materials. You are unlikely to attract an actual business leader with these, as you will be in Coach, but in the odd chance this occurs, simply use a small electro-magnetic pulse generator; s/he will reboot and leave.

MURPHY'S LAW FOR LINGUISTS

You will come down with the one infectious disease for which you were not immunized because "it's not likely you'll ever catch that."

Northern Europe and North America

General Notes: These remain popular locales for fieldwork, partly because of the (erroneous) perception of comparative safety and partly because necessities such as coffee and air-conditioning are frequently accessible. They are concomitantly over-harvested, although more remote areas such as Albania or Manitoba remain comparatively pristine.

Common Threats: Violence (particularly in the vicinity of English football games, or Chicago), Axiomatic Prescriptivists (U.S.), Björk (Iceland, parts of Scandinavia), forced consumption of bad alcohol (Russia), forced consumption of decent alcohol (Czech Republic), vowel depletion (former Yugoslavia), surströmming (Sweden), French pop music, porcupines (Northern U.S., Canada), Swiss warlords,[3] American politicians.[4]

Add to pack:

- Everything from previous list—umbrella is also useful against porcupines, which will attempt to gain a position above the traveler and then plummet.
- Several items of apparel with Canadian maple-leaf logo (regardless of where one is at the time, it is quite likely that Canadians will be ignored or even approved of by the local population, so Canadian makes an almost perfect "cover nationality").
- At least eight doses of a strong diuretic, such as Lasix—helps flush alcohol from system after being subjected to eastern European friendli-

---

[3] The fact that none of these have as yet been sighted is evidence only of their extreme cunning and stealth.

[4] Decidedly less stealthy than Swiss warlords, and usually less cunning—but much better funded.

ness rituals, and sodium from system after being subjected to Southern U.S. food.

- Earplugs.
- Flexible decoy waterfowl, such as swan (can be used to distract oncoming Björk; also, provides customs agents with suspicious, yet legal perceptual cue to investigate, keeping them happy and exercised).
- (If traveling in Russia) List of highly complimentary things to say about Mr. Putin (and, we should point out in case any Russian government personnel are reading this, we mean every one of them. Honest. No, really. We're sure he can cure scrofula merely by briskly slapping someone).[5]
- (If traveling in Mississippi or Alaska) List of highly derogatory things to say about Mr. Obama (and, we should point out in case any U.S. Republicans are reading this, we mean every one of them. Honest. No, really. We're sure he turns into a French-speaking Muslim werewolf and eats small children wrapped in American flags).[5]

North Africa and the Middle East

General Notes: These are much safer areas to do fieldwork in than they used to be (statistically, simply removing Hittites decreases threat levels by 45%), and despite the fact that many of the dominant languages of the region are well-studied in general, there is much that needs to be investigated in regards to local dialect variation (which

---

IT IS WELL KNOWN
AMONG LINGUISTS...

In fieldwork, it is usually best to assume there is no {cake} morpheme.

---

is enormous). A number of smaller language groups lack sufficient description at all, and there is always room to try to figure out what Maltese is really up to, and where it is hiding many of its vowels. Still, the area is by no means fully safe.

Common Threats: Disease, injury, violence (both the regular and the sectarian sorts), hyperthermia, dehydration, prolonged harangues (both the regular and the sectarian sorts), titanic military-industrial snafus, high-speed traffic-seeking pedestrians (Egypt), crocodiles, high-speed pedestrian-seeking traffic (all cities), obesity/diabetes.

Add to pack:

- Triple the usual quantity of insect repellent. If this seems excessive, go read about leishmaniasis (but wait until you've already bought the plane ticket).
- If possible, a fifty-gallon tank of water with battery-powered motor trolley.
- Only items that have no obvious insignia of any religious belief/denomination. It doesn't matter what your religion is or whether you even have one; it will probably bother someone. In fact, not having one will likely bother everyone. Do not attempt to pass yourself off as an adherent of some small, unassuming pacifistic sect—it will make everyone suspicious on general principles (yes, this means throwing out the deflective religious tracts mentioned above). Likewise, don't assume that appealing to traditional beliefs will endear you to the group you are studying (even Enlil and Osiris are controversial these days).
- Any text on zoology, specifically mammalian physiology. You want to know what's on that

---

[5] *As this list is being committed to actual paper, we realize that you, dear reader, may be perusing it well after the time of Putin or Obama. We trust that you can simply plug in relevant political figures and sentiments. If nothing else, we can count on Mississippi not having changed much, and Russian leaders being ones the prudent fieldworker does not wish to annoy. —Eds.*

plate, although if it's looking back at you, it's almost certainly sheep.

- An easily-foldable reflective sheet (the higher the albedo, the better—aim for 100% mirror equivalent)—very handy for deserts.

- Several cans of British "mushy peas." These are to induce mild nausea, and should be used immediately before any encounter with Persian food, to prevent one's daily calorie intake from exceeding 10,000. Cooks in the area have spent millennia perfecting a cuisine cleverly designed to lull any invading group into a kind of (eventually diabetic) trance.

- Only items that have no obvious insignia of any national group that has attempted to attack or colonize the area in the past few centuries. Unfortunately, about 85% of fieldworkers are from one of these national groups. Canada still works, as does Liechtenstein (unless you are in a country whose postage stamps are competing for collector status against the philatelic juggernaut that is the latter).

- Extra cash. For "paperwork."

- A number of fairly brightly-hued items of apparel; aim for brilliant shades of gold or blue (green and red have a higher chance of being perceived as political statements). Depending on the level of local unrest and your country of origin, there may be a number of undercover police officers assigned to keep an eye on you (from the official government or otherwise) as well as American drone aircraft (or "airborne distance-operated non-obtrusive friendliness projectors" (ADONOFriPs), as I believe they're currently called). The bright clothing items help your crypto-entourage in their duties; they are going to follow you

anyway, so making everyone's life easier hurts no one.

Central and South Africa

General Notes: A very large number of languages in this area are badly under-described, even though contact with Europeans historically led to many groups being over-kidnapped, and over-invaded. Still, many of the languages of the region have preserved vast, glittering arrays of noun classes, or verb marking of an almost fractal complexity, and have in some cases required linguists to exercise to the fullest their capacity to rescue the generalizations they have already decided are true of all languages (Oh, Malagasy, how you taunt us!).

> MURPHY'S LAW
> FOR LINGUISTS
>
> You will contract dysentery within one month of arriving at your field location, no matter how careful you are.

Common Threats: Disease and more disease (our species primarily evolved here, and thus so did a lot of other things that use us as hosts), injury, violence, oil companies, crocodiles, things that eat crocodiles, anarchy (some areas), too many simultaneous archies (other areas), the usual giant snakes.

Add to pack:

- Quintuple the usual amount of insect repellent, plus at least four gallons of insecticide. It won't do any good, but you'll feel like you got some revenge.

- Chloroquinone, and lots of it. The *mal* in 'malaria' is the morpheme you're thinking it is. Tonic water isn't effective enough, even with the gin.

- Extra cash. For "customs."

- Mercenaries. Technically, of course, you can't pack them, but having some along can be quite useful (however, make sure they're the competent kind; any mention of having done "outsourcing" work for Western nations is a red flag, as is group composition restricted to one nationality or ethnos, or possession of copies of *Soldier of Fortune*). Pay half up front, and arrange for competent medical support (give preference to groups that refuse to work without latter being stipulated in contract). When working with native speakers, keep the mercenaries at some distance, since they tend to produce distortions in the probability distributions of certain constructions/lexical choices.

- A list of Peace Corps volunteers in the area. They'll have all manner of useful information. Don't bring the mercenaries when you visit, though—very bad for appearances.

- Large, sealable plastic bags (i.e., sandwich bags, but larger). An amazing number of things cannot get into shoes that are stored in these.

Central and South Asia

General Notes: Included in this section are regions like the Caucasus, Turkmenistan, Uzbekistan, and Afghanistan, as well as India and Pakistan. This grouping is, of course, artificial, but there is a long-standing tradition of artificially grouping people in this region; whole nations owe their existence to it. While a majority of the linguistic groups in the region are affiliated with well-studied macrofamilies (e.g., Turkic, the ever-overdone Indo-European), some areas, like the Caucasus, are more varied, and dialect variation is of interest regardless.

"The first book of a nation is the dictionary of its language."
—CONTANITIN, COMTE DE VOLNEY

Common Threats: Disease, injury (both the usual kind, and the accidentally-being-stepped-on-by-livestock kind), violence, invasion by multinational forces, hyperthermia, dehydration, over-hydration (during monsoon), consonantal hypertrophy (Cau-

casus), lime pickle (India), Jain commando squads,[6] the Golden Horde.

Add to pack:
- *Tarnke's Guide to Religious Garb.* Under normal circumstances, of course, the fieldworker does not care what faith is practiced by those with whom s/he works, but a native-speaker co-worker who is fond of koans can unintentionally wreak untold havoc on a grammar. For over ten years, the expression listed as meaning roughly "yes" in one grammar actually meant "What is it if it is not of itself?" It was a worse fiasco than the hovercraft-eel incident.

- Recording application with slow-playback feature (if traveling in India or Pakistan). Eight separate languages have turned out to be English when played back at 45% normal speed. Keep in mind that the response that a native speaker provides to a fieldwork question may, in fact, be a projected answer to what you're likely to ask two minutes from now. They are not deliberately trying to make you feel slow. Just keep telling yourself that.

- Antacid tablets. Remember, "cold" food does not mean food that is not spicy, it means food that cools you off. Internal temperature drops when you are in shock, which partially explains lime pickle.

- Application for GPS-locator that sounds an alarm if you get within fifty miles of Kashmir or Waziristan. Yes, fieldwork needs to be done in those places, but it can wait for the invention of the armored exoskeleton.

---

[6] Pacifists, but capable of writing very sternly-worded memos.

East Asia, incl. Siam[7]

General Notes: While many of the languages in this area have developed defenses against being subjected to fieldwork (contour tone systems, for example), the possibilities for fieldwork remain legion. Given the amount of topographic and climatic variation over this vast region, the threats to prepare for can include some of the same ones mentioned in any of the earlier sections—particularly in the more tropical sections, where malaria remains a major problem, and the giant snakes are, if anything, stealthier (Burmese ophidians, in particular, are locked in a venom playoff with those of Australia).

Common Threats: Disease, injury, violence, water (oceanic and riverine), drivers, meat-on-a-stick, colonialists, anti-colonialists, social engineering attempts on a titanic scale, high-speed landscape engineering projects on an amazing scale, nattō (in Japan), obscure organizations striving for world domination.[8]

Add to pack:

- Extra earplugs, esp. if traveling through Hong Kong.
- (If traveling in Japan) Large amounts of extra packaging. Each section of each chapter of your grammar should get a separate wrapper, and the chapter should then get its own,

THE WISDOM OF LINGUISTS

A grammar of a thousand pages begins with a single example.

differently-colored wrapper (with decorative cord); the abstract goes in a small, gold-filagreed box attached to the rest of the grammar by a multihued ribbon, with the whole assembly going in a bigger box.

- Access to the SIL's *Ethnologue,* to identify in advance which language groups are likely to use tones (so you can work on different ones instead). If you're a phonetician, ignore this item, and please accept our profound admiration.
- Extra cash, for "fees."
- A "medic alert" bracelet listing allergies to meat and seafood. You want a polite excuse for sticking to vegetables. You do not want to know what's on that plate, especially if it's staring back at you, attempting to attack you, or even just emitting a blue glow and a rising humming sound. This applies double to anything served you by Shan tribal elders, who I'm sure mean well, despite the results.
- (If traveling in Japan) *Ovarsson's Pictorial Guide to Japanese Sweet Dishes,* so you can avoid them. There are some things that simply should not be done with ice cream.

Australia, New Guinea and Tasmania

General Notes: This region presents a marked dilemma to the prudent fieldworker. On one hand, it abounds with fascinating languages whose 40,000-year-plus isolation from those spoken elsewhere renders them of the greatest importance to discussions of long-range language development. On the other hand, half of the things a biologist has a Linnaean name for in Australia have some way of killing you, and some of the rest have no Linnaean name at all because the biologist died

---

[7] *At first, we thought Prof. Schadenpoodle's reference to Burma in the following threat list was an intentional political statement, but it is possible that he needs a new globe in his office. —Eds.*

[8] *We were, naturally, rather curious about this item. After some correspondence with Prof. Schadenpoodle, we've arrived at two conclusions. First, he assumes everyone is already familiar with non-obscure organizations striving to achieve world domination (his phrase was, "the government, for example"). Second, he has watched far too many B-movies. We are still trying to convince him that no botanist has ever validated the existence of the black lotus. —Eds.*

too fast. Australians are so inured to this that they simply edit considerations of safety out of consciousness.

Common Threats: Venomous insects, venomous snakes, venomous shellfish, venomous coelenterates, venomous amphibians, venomous egg-laying mammals, venomous trees,[9] venomous shrubs, venomous rock formations, rugby teams, dehydration, drop bears,[10] neck strain (Bondi), graphogenic neuro-semiotic hyper-stimulation.[12]

Add to pack:

- Case of assorted antivenins. Practice selecting the right one in the smallest possible amount of time.
- Concussion grenades—while these are a major pain to get through customs, they have a high chance of dealing with poisonous creatures that are occupying the spot where you plan to camp (typically, any given spot will have at least four such creatures).

- If traveling into the Outback, bring at least two fifty-gallon water tanks on self-powered carts. Spray these regularly with repellent to discourage the snakes from wrapping around them.
- Pictorial guides to insects and sea life, so you can tell the medical team exactly what's making your leg swell up. Saving them time like this helps them save you, and they're much less likely to hand you a piece of bread with some awful spread on it to distract you while they confer.
- Extra cash, for "Queensland."
- A guide to Australian English. You do not want to do things like asking sports fans which team they're rooting for.

MURPHY'S LAW FOR LINGUISTS

Within a month of arriving at your research site, the transportation company which got you there will go out of business.

---

[9] <reality>Everything in the Australian threat list up to this point is *actually true.*</reality>

[10] Related to koalas in much the same way grasshoppers are related to locusts. Periodically, the koala population grows to an unsustainable size, and the species has evolved a compensatory device: an entire generation is born that is larger than normal, and violently hostile, prone to attack any moving target (usually by plummeting from above, much like porcupines). They are not very efficient at this, however, and many of the moving targets are either venomous or wombats. The latter are distinctly plummet-resistant, and the former are typically fatal; either way, the koala population is rapidly culled, leaving the landscape strewn with lugubriously fierce, yet briskly eucalyptus-scented corpses.[11]

[11] *Prof. Schadenpoodle, as you may have noted by this point, is ever vigilant against the threat of being dropped upon by mammals not commonly regarded as dangerous. We realize that this level of caution is, perhaps, slightly excessive, but we decided that it is the sort of information that one typically just doesn't find elsewhere, and thus may count as "value added." If that will placate the business consultant the Board hired, that's value added enough for us. —Eds.*

[12] A *petit mal*-like condition caused by trying to process overly Delphic linguistic diagrams; also known as "Matthiessen Syndrome."

CHOOSE YOUR OWN CAREER IN LINGUISTICS—PART 2

YOU DECIDE TO MAJOR IN SOMETHING BESIDES LINGUISTICS...

The siren song of linguistics is appealing, but you realize that it just isn't the most practical way to get ahead in life. Remembering the other students grumbling about economics, you take a couple of econ classes over the summer. You crush the curve in both classes and declare your major in the fall.

- Major in Economics. Go to Part 4 on page 274.

Choose Your Own Career in Linguistics starts on page 301.

Linguistics Applied
How linguistics explains the rest of life

WHEN YOU TOOK YOUR FIRST LINGUISTICS COURSE, you discovered what linguists have known for ages: there is no way to explain our field to the non-linguist. Sure, you tried hard to express your excitement over Turkish vowel harmony, but let's face it, none of your family or friends could really see the point.

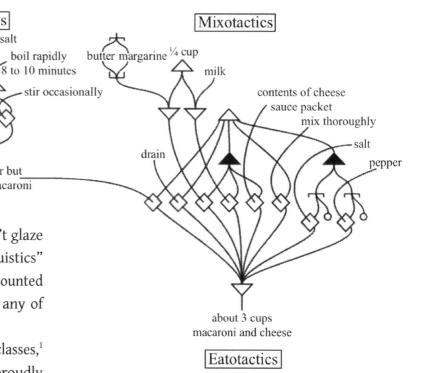

Those few among them whose eyes didn't glaze over as soon as you uttered the word "linguistics" kept pressing you with questions that all amounted to this one: "but what possible use could any of this have?"

If you stuck with the field for a few more classes,[1] you eventually learned that Linguistics proudly and unabashedly *has no real-world applications,* and that the very term "Applied Linguistics" refers to activities that no actual, self-respecting *linguist* would admit to having engaged in. You yourself would never be caught dead in a TESOL class, unless it was the only way to get an assistantship to pay your way through your MA course.[2]

But the dirty little secret of Linguistics is that it does have applications to real life. We can't let on in public, but just among ourselves,[3] we feel free to discuss some really fascinating insights into the human condition that have been discovered through the application of actual linguistic methodologies. That is to say, linguists sometimes discover something about real life, and sometimes (though even less frequently) say something about those discoveries.

Furthermore, although some traditionalists (not including any of the readers of this paragraph, we feel sure) seem to think that "Applied Linguistics" *still* only refers to the teaching of foreign languages, that of course is merely what "Applied

---

[1] Which we assume you did, or else how in the world did you make it all the way to this chapter of this book?

[2] Come to think of it, we all actually did this, so you're in good company. But we won't tell, and you had better not tell either, or we'll find you and make you pay.

[3] The phrase "just among ourselves" primarily refers, of course, to talks given at Linguistics conferences. These venues are entirely safe. No non-linguist would even think of intruding. And if they did, we'd have the phonologists meet them at the door—five minutes of rapid-fire assault with their jargon will send any normal

human being on the run. "Just among ourselves" can also refer to articles published in linguistics journals, which are safe from intrusion by non-linguists mainly because linguistics journals are so prohibitively expensive that no non-linguist could justify purchasing one.[4]

[4] Some linguists have claimed (just among ourselves) that other linguists use the phrase "just among ourselves" to refer to face-to-face conversational interlocutions in intimate settings, but we at *Speculative Grammarian* doubt that any such events have taken place since the invention of the colloquium.

Linguistics" *used to mean.* As the classic Chinese novelist put it: "Empires wax and wane, linguistic subfields cleave asunder."[5] The simple fact is that Linguistics has moved on, and more precisely, "Applied" Linguistics has moved on, broadening out in a myriad of directions, to encompass so many fascinating ways in which the scientific study of language sheds light on the human condition. Come on, if you know anything about Linguistics, you know about semantic shift. Linguistics is applied much more broadly today. Please keep up with the times.

By the way, though, we are not talking about male-female communication differences here. Sure, a few "linguistics" professors have made a mint writing about those issues, couched in the terms of sociolinguistics. But this is not an example of Linguistics explaining real life, and we can prove this from two irrefutable bits of evidence: (1) these writings are published[6] by popular presses, not specialist linguistic presses; and (2) the linguists in question are making money, which we all know is not possible for an actual linguistics publication.

But we digress. The point here is that *Speculative Grammarian,* ever questing to remain on the forefront of linguistic knowledge, has published some stunning explanations of non-linguistic subjects, and has brought to the light of publication an amazing array of applications for the analyses of our field—all discovered by outstanding linguists who dared to venture beyond noun phrases and apply their analytical frameworks to a wider range of human endeavors.[7] And so, we bring you in this

chapter a sampling of these outstanding examples of *Linguistics Applied.*

THE LEARNER'S TASK

Some say it isn't any fun
to imitate another's tongue;
while idioms and turns of phrase
can often baffle and amaze
the novice who must learn their ways.

Loquacious speakers seldom pause
to rest their ever moving jaws;
and so the learner simply gapes
as useless input fast escapes—
these speakers might as well be apes!

Nor can one recognize the words
that stampede forth in growing herds
arranged in patterns quite opaque
and grammar strange enough to make
it clear that there's been some mistake.
(Such is the learner's sorry stake!)

But lest the learner, in dismay
abandon hope, I haste to say
that there remains one certain way:

To learn a language, girls and guys,
you simply have to memorize.
—KEITH W. SLATER

---

[5] Or something very much like that.

[6] If the word "publish" can actually be used of such mass-market disseminators of pulp literature.

[7] At least, we are pretty sure they are stunning explanations. Honestly, because we're all linguists around here, we don't know much about anything else, so how would we know what is a revelation and what isn't? If you are a non-linguist, shame on you for reading this book, but perhaps at least you'll be able to evaluate our claim that this chapter actually has something interesting to say.

*As with any form of journalistic expose, we know we have hit on something juicy when the author is able to uncover something we all ought to fear. Mining recordings of actual language use in North America, scholars Will, Arena, and Bird were able to determine that linguistic behavior correlates in a terrifying way with one particular sport.**

The Narcolinguistic Effects of Professional Athletic Strikes
The hidden danger of baseball—is your community safe?

George E. Will, Linguistics Institute of the *Washington Post*
Bruce Arena, Lacrosse Linguistics Institute
Larry James Bird, French Lick Linguistics Lab

A recent *Speculative Grammarian* news report called attention to the fact—which was only discovered lately—that Canadians stopped speaking for a period during the years 2004–5. This unprecedented complete cessation of language-mediated interactions by an entire nation-state was said to be totally unexplained. However, the explanation is as plain as (to put it in the Canuck idiom) the nose on your face during a Manitoba winter.

In fact, the drop-off in Canadian language production in 2004–5 coincided precisely (to the very day) with a "lockout" of professional hockey players by the owners of the National Hockey League. This lockout had the result that professional hockey was not played that fall or winter. The key dates, along with the original news story's description of the associated catastrophic linguistic consequences, are provided in Table 1.

It seems, in short, that with the cancellation of the NHL season, Canadians just had nothing to say for a period of several months. At the same time, they may actually have been clinically depressed *en masse*, though a survey of the psychological literature of the period turns up no evidence that any other, non-speech behaviors changed during this period. When the lockout ended, language use immediately began to recover throughout the country. Although this phenomenon is clearly unprecedented, it is equally clearly a case of simple causation: no hockey, no talk.

Date	Event	Linguistic Consequence
16 Sept. 2004	Lockout begins	"Language production dropped off dramatically"
13 Oct. 2004	Season opener cancelled	"Most Canadians stopped speaking at all"
16 Feb. 2004	Entire season cancelled	(Source did not bother to mention this date)
13 July 2005	New collective bargaining agreement reached	"Canadians abruptly started talking again"
5 Oct. 2005	Opening night (all 30 teams play)	"Language … made the final jump back up to normal levels"

Table 1: Effects of NHL Lockout on
Canadian language production

The present study follows up on the insights gained from this Canadian situation to ask the question: what have been the effects on language use of other major-league sports work stoppages? Specifically, are US residents affected by sports strikes in the same way that Canadians were by the hockey season cancellation?

Using recordings we had gathered as part of a large-scale American Spoken Corpus project, dating from 1973 to the present, we checked for pervasive

---

* Note that this study was published before the 2011 NBA and 2012 NHL work stoppages. We are very sure that the results will generalize to these events, as well. Our interns are currently analyzing masses of recorded data from 2011. As this book goes to press in the midst of what would have been the 2012–2013 NHL season, we have no data at all from Canada—no one whom we've called up there has answered the phone for several months.

or systematic changes in the amount of language produced by all Americans before, during and after major sports work stoppages. Our data show that the cancellation of part or all of the season of most professional sports had no discernible effect on language use by Americans. The amount of speech produced before, during and after these events was essentially constant. Our review included work stoppages of both the National Basketball Association (1 July-12 September 1995 and 1 July 1998–20 January 1999) and the National Football League (20 September-20 November 1982; 22 September-25 October 1987). Similarly, the NHL (hockey) stoppage which was the focus of the Canadian phenomenon also did not appear to affect language use in the United States.

Baseball, though, is different. We found that language use in the USA, Canada (especially Toronto), and even Mexico actually rose significantly during all of the major-league baseball work stoppages that we surveyed. Our striking observations are summarized in Table 2.

Dates	Event	Linguistic Consequence
1–13 Apr. 1972	Players' strike	Number of conversations per speaker per hour rose 5%.
12 June-31 July 1981	Players' strike	Average words per minute in conversations rose 18%.
15 Feb.-19 March 1990	Owners' lockout	Clausal density, measured in verbs per event per subject noun phrase, rose 7.9%.
12 Aug. 1994–2 April 1995	Players' strike	Fluency rose 6%.
5 July-16 Sept. 2003	Owners' lockout	Mean Length of Utterance rose 5%, argument density rose 8%, and discourse coherence rose a whopping 84%.

Table 2: Effects of Major League Baseball work stoppages on N. American language production

These remarkable statistics lead to the conclusion that baseball actually depresses the rate of language use by the entire population of baseball-playing nations. The very fact that professional baseball is being played, anywhere on the continent, seems to disincline speakers to talk.

This effect was not found, we should note, simply in conversations in which the subject matter was related to baseball. No. *All* conversation on *all* topics, among *all* speakers, increased by various linguistic measures during each baseball work stoppage. In each case, language use returned to pre-strike levels after play resumed.

We conclude from this phenomenon that baseball is a narcotic, operating not at the individual but at the societal level. It is an activity which affects not just its participants and spectators, but everyone else, as well. Why this should be so, we can only speculate, but terms such as "soporific" and "stultifying" do come readily to mind. We can only imagine the glory which must have been North American language use prior to the founding of the National League in 1876, or even prior to the fiendish Alexander Cartwright's foisting of a codified system of "rules" for this game onto a defenseless and presumably loquacious public in 1845.

The results of this purely linguistic study suggest a very practical application: baseball should be regulated by the Food and Drug Administration, as are all substances which have similar narcotic properties. We, the researchers, certainly feel unsafe, knowing that baseball players and baseball fans are allowed to freely operate motor vehicles on our public roads.

"All words are pegs to hang ideas on."
—HENRY WARD BEECHER

In another corpus-based study, Albert shows that simple examination of linguistic data may serve to do the work that used to require demographers to leave their comfortable home offices in order to investigate through actual field research.

A Corpus-Linguistic Approach to Demography

Morten H. Albert
Rose College

This paper develops a corpus-linguistic approach to the demography of North American cities. In a groundbreaking study, Chomsky (1957:17) convincingly showed that it can be proven on linguistic grounds alone that more people live in New York than in Dayton, Ohio. Unfortunately, Chomsky did not go on to develop his corpus methods any further.

In the present study, all occurrences of the search string "I live in" were extracted from the American National Corpus. The word forms immediately to the right of the search string were extracted from the concordance and ranked according to frequency. Table 1 shows the ten items with the highest token frequencies.

City	Tokens
New York	4,223
Los Angeles	3,986
Harmony	3,669
Chicago	3,478
London	3,300
Houston	2,906
Philadelphia	2,495
Tokyo	2,335
Phoenix	1,399
The Past	599

Table 1: America's 10 largest cities

The table reveals a number of surprising results. Besides previously unknown cities, also a number of cities previously believed to lie elsewhere are actually found in North America. It will be up to geographers to face the challenge and actually put these on the American map.

To obtain demographic information about these cities, the token numbers must be related to the numbers of inhabitants. To calculate these figures, it is necessary to know the exact number of inhabitants of one city. This number, divided by its token frequency, gives us the token-inhabitant ratio that we need. Chomsky (personal communication) gives an estimate of the population of Dayton, Ohio with 166,179. Divided by its token frequency 88, the corpus-linguistic demographical constant (CLDC) is exactly

$$1,888.4$$

With this figure in mind, I believe that corpus-based armchair demography has a number of advantages over more traditional methods of statistical demography. Not only is it fast and economical, it also points toward new phenomena that traditional demography did not have any account for.

IT IS WELL KNOWN AMONG LINGUISTS...

Most coffee-roasting equipment is manufactured in Italy or the United States, as the dominant languages in those countries have words for both 'green' and 'black'.

Frequent and typically vitriolic SpecGram contributor H.D. Onesimus lays aside his habitual misanthropy to bring us the following piece of linguistics applied. Professor Onesimus tests an interesting hypothesis regarding the relationship of ingestion of food and the linguistic outputs which may result. We sheepishly admit that we never thought of this possibility before.

Those readers (if any) who have been paying close attention will notice that this is the second article in this volume in which Professor Onesimus appeals to ingestion as a motivating principle for linguistic phenomena. We are not sure whether this tells us anything about either langue *or* parole, *but we sure as heck always remember to lock up the snacks in the office kitchen when H.D. is around.*

Comestible Morphosyntax
The effects of food intake on grammatical performance[1]

H.D. Onesimus
Unified Commission for the Study of Behavior

Abstract
Food intake is shown to correlate with morphosyntactic behavior.

Introduction
It has long been observed[2] that ingestion of food and other nontoxic comestibles changes linguistic behavior. In order to satisfy the publication criterion for my continued employment, I decided to conduct a systematic investigation of this relationship.

Method
The ethnographic method commonly labeled participant observation was employed. Nightly analysis of preliminary field data (my notebooks are available on request) suggested that morphosyntactic behavior *inter alia* undergoes significant transformation immediately following the ingestion of significant ($p < 0.01$) quantities of food. After making this initial discovery, I formulated a hypothesis:

1. Morphosyntactic behavior *inter alia* undergoes significant transformation immediately following the ingestion of significant ($p < 0.01$) quantities of food.

In order to test (1) systematically, I wrote down in my notebooks everything that was said in my hearing during the course of eight consecutive days. I analyzed the speech of all non-linguistically sophisticated participants, noting especially morphosyntactic construction types, as well as major mealtimes. The latter usually numbered no less than three per participant per day.

Results
The most interesting results involve different morphosyntactic strategies for clause combining. My data revealed four major clause combining types: monoclausal, conjunction, chaining, and embedding. These are illustrated in (2)-(5):

2. Monoclausal
   a. *Yes, I'm awake.*
   b. *Go away.*
   c. *Eat your breakfast.*

3. Conjunction
   a. *I'm gonna go and see about that.*

---

[1] Nearly identical versions of this paper are forthcoming in *Language, Studies in Language, Cognitive Psychology* and *Journal of Verbal Learning and Verbal Behavior.*

[2] By me

b. *Get back to work or you won't get any lunch.*

c. *And then Pat got mad, too, and then Lynn hauled off and threw a punch, and then the boss came and said something impolite and fired them both.*

4. Chaining (rare)

a. *Going in the house, looking into my kitchen, two thugs dressed as police officers were there, eating all the goldfish out of my aquarium.*

5. Embedding

a. *Flying planes can be dangerous.*

b. *That's the kid who ate my candy.*

The results were striking. It turns out that there is a significant correlation between ingestion of food and morphosyntactic clause combining behavior. This correlation is apparent from the data of Table 1.

Time	Mono.	Conj.	Chain.	Emb.	Totals
Before Breakfast	160	6	1	15	182
Breakfast-Lunch	101	107	2	0	210
Lunch-Supper	48	89	8	0	145
After Supper	65	38	4	103	210
Totals	374	240	15	118	

Table 1: Instances Of Each Combining Type With Relation To Meals

Table 1 suggests a progression of clause combining devices, with more complex constructions increasing in frequency in concert with the subjects' feeding schedule.

Detailed analysis of each individual speaker showed that one speaker, speaker J, contradicted this trend. If speaker J is removed from the group, we have the data of Table 2 remaining.

In Table 2, the trend is unmistakable. After each meal, speakers' grammatical performance jumps to the next level (or quantum, to use a trendy term) of syntactic complexity.

Time	Mono.	Conj.	Chain.	Emb.	Totals
Before Breakfast	156	0	0	0	156
Breakfast-Lunch	96	97	0	0	193
Lunch-Supper	40	83	8	0	131
After Supper	61	38	4	103	206
Totals	353	218	12	103	

Table 2: Same As Table 1, For All Speakers Except Speaker J

Subsequent, informal observation[3] suggests that consumption of two cups of coffee (at any time) pushes a speaker up two levels on the scale from her/his current nutritionally-licensed position. Similarly, it appears that two servings of alcohol drop a speaker precipitously downwards on the scale, though precise measurement of this trend appears difficult.

I mentioned above that a single speaker, speaker J, exhibited different nutritiono-linguistic behavior. Clause combining performance of this speaker is given in Table 3:

Time	Mono.	Conj.	Chain.	Emb.	Totals
Before Breakfast	4	6	1	15	26
Breakfast-Lunch	5	10	2	0	17
Lunch-Supper	8	6	0	0	14
After Supper	4	0	0	0	4
Totals	21	22	3	15	

Table 3: Same As Table 1, But Only For Speaker J

Since Speaker J exhibits an inverse relationship between food intake and clause combining, we may hypothesize some physiological problem, such as hypoglycemia, diabetes, or weirdness. Further investigation is needed (see below).

Discussion

This study shows conclusively that food ingestion correlates predictably with linguistic behavior. A number of interesting questions pose themselves, upon reflection on this data.

---

[3] *ibid.*

First of all, if food *ingestion* has the observed effects, what about food *digestion?* Digestion probably has similar linguistic effects, though these are less open to observational study, at least through participant observation.

We might also note the significance of the fact that embedding normally occurs near the end of the day. This may be due solely to its being enabled by accumulated nutritional resources. However, this might also be an effect of morphosyntactic *iconicity;* linguistic embedding occurs with greatest frequency at just that point in the day when tired people are thinking of embedding themselves to rest.

My results have suggested at least two classes of people, with regard to nutritiono-linguistic behavior: *normal* people, whose language ability increases proportionally with their food intake, and *abnormal* people (if speaker J generalizes at all) who seem to lose linguistic ability as the day progresses.

However, it is possible that these are not the only two classes of people. Future research should ask a number of follow-up questions, including: Does age similarly affect linguistic behavior? What about intelligence?

Finally, future researchers need to explore the likely relationship between these results and cross-linguistic typological features. Monoclausal structures are most common for normal people, prior to any food intake, but normal speakers seem able to progress to embedding after a third hearty meal. What do these facts imply about languages with no syntactic embedding? Perhaps their speakers are not normal, or perhaps they aren't eating often enough. In accordance with the basic tenets of applied linguistics and human rights, ought we not get them some coffee, quickly?

IT IS WELL KNOWN AMONG LINGUISTS...

Some heirloom varieties of tomatoes, particularly "Black Krim" and "Bradley," have a higher citric acid content when repeatedly exposed to Burushaski ergative constructions.

"Silence is an unbearable repartee."
—G.K. CHESTERTON

If you are like us, you like to eat, and we are always happy when someone gives us the opportunity to publish a revelation about linguistics and food like Professor Onesimus' article. Another article along this theme comes from Tim Pulju,* *who shows that with hardly any effort at all, the extraordinarily complex machinery of Stratificational Grammar can be made to explain something so mundane—and yet so delicious!—as the making of macaroni and cheese.*

A Stratificational Approach to Making Macaroni and Cheese

Tim Pulju
Michigan State University

It has long been a tenet of stratificational theory that stratificational notation is adaptable to extralinguistic structures. The contention of this paper is that not only can we use relational networks in this way, but that in fact a stratificational diagram is superior to, and should supplant, the traditional tool for visual transmission of information, namely written representation of natural human language. As an example, compare the traditional version of instructions for preparing macaroni and cheese with the new and improved version. (The text is that of "Directions," *Food Club Macaroni and Cheese Dinner*, Wgt. .453# (the package is distributed by weight in #, not volume #). Skokie, Illinois: Topco Associates, Inc. 1988.)

Version A (traditional): Add macaroni and 1 tsp. salt to 6 cups boiling water. Stir. Boil rapidly, stirring occasionally, 8 to 10 minutes or until tender but firm. Drain. Add 4 tbsps. butter or margarine, ¼ cup vitamin D fortified whole milk and contents of cheese sauce packet. Mix thoroughly. Season to taste with salt and pepper. Makes about 3 cups.

Cookotactics

1 tsp. salt
macaroni
6 cups boiling water
boil rapidly 8 to 10 minutes
stir occasionally
tender but firm macaroni

Version B (new and improved):

Mixotactics

butter margarine
¼ cup
milk
contents of cheese sauce packet
mix thoroughly
salt
pepper
drain
about 3 cups macaroni and cheese

Eatotactics

It is obvious from even a cursory examination that the text lacks both elegance and simplicity. Certainly it is plain that the stratificational solution is much easier for even a layman to follow. With this in mind, and realizing that the same is true for any extralinguistic phenomenon capable of linguistic description, I suggest that we begin a process of eliminating cumbersome and outdated written language in favor of relational catalyses. To speed this process, we should begin production of catalytic converters according to the type developed by Adam Makkai at General Motors Institute in Flint, Michigan, in 1978.

---

* Back before we promoted him to "Editor" status. In those days he had to write a lot or else we didn't pay him much. Come to think of it, this is probably why he knows so much about macaroni and cheese.

Linguistic methodology can be applied in so many fields. How many, you might ask? At least umpteen, we would answer. In this next article, Professor Ura Hogg demonstrates the elegant combining of linguistic and mathematical methodologies to explicate the meaning of an otherwise semantically opaque lexical item: umpteen.

How Many is Umpteen?
A Linguistic and Mathematical Exploration and Explanation

Ura Hogg
Skaroo University[1]

We have all heard various people use the quasi-numerical expression umpteen to refer to a largish number of items, as in (1) below:

1. I have *umpteen* things to do before I can leave.[2]

What I plan to do in this brief paper is to determine how many *umpteen* is. First I feel I must in part justify the claim that *umpteen* can in fact refer to an exact numerical quantity despite its varying use.[3] Though we often use vague number expressions such as in (2) and (3) below, we nearly as often use exact, though large, expressions, such as *a million,* in the same way (as in (4)).

2. I have *many* things to do before I can leave.
3. I have a *few* things to do before I can leave.
4. I have *a million* things to do before I can leave.

I will show that *umpteen,* likewise, is a large number, and thereby explain its inexact usage.

Our first and only assumption has already been made,[4] but for clarity we will spell it out explicitly now: **umpteen** *is an exact number, with a definite,* though perhaps now lost, history and a logical, mathematical origin.[5] We can reconstruct much of this lost history, at least in general outline.[6] Now, on with the show.

For those not familiar with such things, let me introduce the concept of letters as numbers. The ancient Romans and Greeks[7] used their letters for numbers, and a similar[8] modern group, computer programmers, does likewise. When dealing, as they often do, in hexadecimal[9] they typically use the letters A-F to represent the numbers 10–15, as in (5) below.

5. $1,A3E_{16} = 6,718_{10}$

These numbers are often referred to by non-letter names, such as alpha for A and charlie for C, etc.

Let us suppose that a similar system is at the root of *umpteen*'s origin. There are two possible cases we must deal with. The first is that we are dealing with a system in which ump is the non-letter name for U when used as a numeral. Also, by analogy with fourteen, sixteen, seventeen, etc.,

---

[1] I would like to thank Professor U. R. Stoop, ID and Ann Abolic at Skaroo U.

[2] This is not only an example sentence. It is also a true statement. Sigh.

[3] My therapist claims this has to do with my unresolved self-doubt stemming from my parents' poor choice of names for me.[a]

[4] And I bet you missed it, too!

---

[a] And my sister, Ima.

---

[5] Which, of course, is one of the basic assumptions that Linguistics makes about all words.[b]

[6] Which, of course, is another basic assumption that Linguistics makes about all words.

[7] And, it has recently been proposed, perhaps Cro-Magnons as well.[c]

[8] i.e., those who are often thought by the ignorant to be primitive, nearly stone-age barbarians, but who are in fact highly cultured, socially adept and mathematically advanced people.

[9] Base 16.

---

[b] Except, of course, the mathematical part.

[c] Though only the most recent ones.

the numbers such as 1A, 1C, and 1U are alphateen,[10] charlieteen,[11] and our focus: *umpteen.* The minimum base for such a system, to require the use of U, is base 31.[12] In this case, the value of *umpteen* would be $1U_{31} = 61_{10}$.[13]

Our second possible case to consider is more complicated and gives a larger value for *umpteen.* In this scenario, the base used is so large that it is necessary to go beyond the alphabet for numerals to combinations of letters. In this case, *umpteen* would actually be more correctly written as *UMPteen* or 1(UMP) in a base yet to be calculated. If we are using a system in which **all** alpha-numerals have three letters, then UMP is the 14,550[th] alpha-numeral. If we first must exhaust the single and double letter alpha-numerals, then UMP is 15,252[nd]. Thus we have as a minimum possible base either 14,551 or 15,253.[14] In these cases *UMPteen* would be either $1(UMP)_{14,551} = 29,101_{10}$ or $1(UMP)_{15,253} = 30,505_{10}$.[15]

Thus we see that *umpteen* (which we may want to distinguish from *UMPteen*) is in fact in all like- lihood the remnant of a large and powerful mathematical system that is now lost in the mists of time. It comes as no surprise that such a euphonious term as *umpteen,* with such a grand, almost so-large-as-to-be-holy number meaning, would be the last remnant of this surely majestic number system.

IT IS WELL KNOWN AMONG LINGUISTS…

The Kalidjjan language group has over two hundred words for anthropologists. Few of these are complimentary, alas.

---

[10] Alas, this form is unattested in the geek dialects I have been able to study.

[11] This form, too, is unattested, though it may survive in a slightly altered form as *Charlie Sheen,* though the investigation of such a possibility is beyond the scope of this paper.

[12] This is where our calculations become a little unsure. It is possible that a higher base was used, perhaps 32 (since powers of two[d] are so popular among geeks).

[13] In the hypothetical base 32, *umpteen* would be $1U_{32} = 62_{10}$

[14] Of course, larger bases are again possible. In the geek-based power of two system, a likely candidate for a base would be 16,384[e] or perhaps 32,768[f].

[15] In the hypothetical geek-based system *UMPteen* might be:

if UMP = 14,550

$1(UMP)_{16,384} = 30,934_{10}$ or $1(UMP)_{32,768} = 47,318_{10}$ or

if UMP = 15,252

$1(UMP)_{16,384} = 31,636_{10}$ or $1(UMP)_{32,768} = 48,020_{10}$.

---

[d] $32 = 2^5$

[e] $16,384 = 2^{14}$

[f] $32,768 = 2^{15}$, a perhaps more aesthetically pleasing choice.

Those who can read and write have four eyes.
—ALBANIAN PROVERB

For those who begin to suspect that linguistic methodology addresses only the mundane, we offer the following book announcement from our munificent friends at Psammeticus Press. According to the announcement,* Professor Laurel L. Laura demonstrates that political choices may be determined by verbal systems: if that's not significant to you, we don't know what would be.†

Valence and Violence: How Language Shapes Political Acts

Laurel L. Laura
Published 2005. Hardcover, 1,704 pages. Price: $598.99

This volume illustrates the intimate connection between language and political action. An extensive cross-linguistic database of voice and valence systems is examined in relation to the political events which have occurred in the history of each language community. Unmistakable correlations point to the primacy of voice and valence as predictors of political choices made at the societal level.

Knowledge of linguistic theory is lamentably absent from every historical study that this author has ever read; indeed, most histories of the world make no mention of the languages spoken by the societies they describe. This is unforgivable, because (as this study conclusively demonstrates) it is the nature of a language community's voice and valence systems which determine how that community will act toward its neighbors.

Part I of the book presents the correlations that have been identified between linguistic structures and political action. These can be summarized in two major types:

1. Cultures whose languages emphasize inherently violent valence-changing processes tend to treat their neighbors with similar violence: object-incorporating language groups tend to try to incorporate other groups; speech communities which rely heavily on passivization or demotion are prone to impose analogous restrictions on other neighboring groups.

2. Conversely, communities whose speech strongly emphasizes passive constructions tend to be regional doormats, never standing up for themselves in the face of aggression.

Part II of the book applies the insights discovered in Part I to a thorough-going reanalysis of world history, in terms of valence-changing processes and voice systems. Surprising conclusions are offered about long-disputed historical events, such as who was really at fault for starting World War I.

The most innovative and thoughtful book of our generation, *Valence and Violence* is destined to become a classic in both linguistics and political science.

MURPHY'S LAW FOR LINGUISTS

Whenever a group of non-linguists learn you are a linguist, someone will always ask you how many languages you speak.

---

* We neither confirm nor deny that we have actually read the book ourselves. But we do recommend you buy at least one copy.

† Not that we consider political science to be in any way more significant than linguistics. Quite the contrary. And we wish that all prominent linguists shared our view.

Initially we were amazed to learn that even acts of war could be explained by simple linguistic analysis, but our amazement disappeared when Professor Bazaine's elegant work demonstrated irrefutably that the performance of a military force can actually be improved by the straightforward application of linguistic principles.*

Ready! Fire! Aim!
A New Approach to Military Combat Using Language Science

François Achille Bazaine
as told to Guy de Maupassant (1869)
translated from the French by Ambrose Bierce (1874)

One of the aims of any branch of scientific inquiry is to improve the lives of men. Surely the Science of Language is no different, and just as surely the lives of soldiers are among those most in need of improvement. The French military has had a long and varied history, with its share of both victory and defeat. There is as much if not more to be learned from failure as from success, if only one will take the time to understand. After much reading of the writings of my countryman Jean-François Champollion, I have taken it upon myself to apply the principles of Language Science to the goal of the betterment of the French military.

The tripartite command known to soldiers the world over, "Ready! Aim! Fire!", has long been a staple of French military leaders instructing their men to engage in battle. Its tradition is long, its status is honored, and its use is ubiquitous, but still may we ask: is it the most effective way to launch our weapons against the enemy?

> IT IS WELL KNOWN AMONG LINGUISTS…
>
> Hopi speakers are not allowed near the CERN facility in Switzerland, as their alternate conception of time produces anomalous fluctuations in the quantum states the researchers are attempting to measure.

A careful evaluation of the timing of each part of the command, its use, and its effectiveness in battle reveals much that had apparently been hidden before the advent of Language Science and its myriad methods of analysis. The results are shocking, and reveal a clear path to the improvement of the readiness, speed, and effectiveness of our fighting forces. Careful study of battle-hardened fighting men engaged in mock combat on military proving grounds was the first component of my research.

First, the "Ready!"—A firm getter of attention, and of short duration, the effects of the "Ready!" command are seen instantly among archers, musketeers, and cannoneers. The spines of the men stiffen, their eyes become more alert, and their hands tense in anticipation of the task at hand. All in less than a heartbeat.

Next, the "Aim!"—By far and away the longest of the three commands, it is also that which shows the least visible purpose. The men shift slightly, almost as if fidgeting while waiting for the real action to begin, while the enemy has time to continue his advance, change his position, or otherwise make tactical improvements in his offense or defense.

Finally, the "Fire!"—Of the shortest duration and most devastating effect, the "Fire!" unleashes the harsh hell of our projectile weapons into the

---

*Numerous French military commentators have described the overwhelmingly positive results which have been obtained by testing Bazaine's proposal, both on the training grounds and in actual battle conditions. We will not reproduce any of their remarks here, because they are (without exception) written in French, and we do not wish to embarrass any of our readers who might have forgotten what some of the verb endings mean.

midst of the enemy's forces. The action is instantaneous, and the effects are disastrous to the enemy.

On the military proving grounds, during these mock battles, careful use of the cold truths of the statistics of military engagement are employed to give the most realistic substance to the proceedings. Long, hard-won experience tells the commanders that under specific conditions of weather, weapons, and terrain, a fusillade of cannon, for example, will have a predictable effect on the enemy's forces.

As such, in these mock battles particular men are assigned to "die" or have their artillery, horses, or other supplies "destroyed" when a particular cannon fires. Similarly, each man knows his mathematically determined fate, and when and where and by what means—be it cannon ball, musket shot, or bayonet—he will "die" in these proceedings. How so much more scientific are the proving grounds exercises compared to the frightful mess that is true war!

The second component of my research was a careful and logical analysis of the tripartite command under consideration, along with the design of experiments to test my tentative conclusions of the effects of these, perhaps improperly, hallowed words. Clearly, "Fire!" is by far the most efficacious of the commands. I reasoned that perhaps it could serve on its own, though I had some residual doubts concerning the necessity of the "Ready!" command and its usefulness. After a mere handful of days spent in contemplation of the evidence I had gathered, and consideration of the alternatives available to me, the outlines of an experimental plan made themselves manifest to me.

IT IS WELL KNOWN AMONG LINGUISTS…

In the 4th century C.E., the Huns flooded westward into Europe in an unsuccessful attempt to acquire toneme technology from Lithuania so they could combat the Chinese's rapid strategic advances in the prevention of foreign-language-learning.

This brought me to the third and final component of my research, experimentation. For Language Science, even in pursuit of what some may consider a base military application, is still science and thus in need of experimental verification of any new claims. As I alluded to before, the clean scientificality of the statistically controlled mock battles of the military proving grounds makes for a fine laboratory—one in which I could quite readily and most definitely put my theories to the test.

An accommodating commander of a cannon brigade allowed me to work with his men. In the first test, the "Fire!" command alone was used. The expected but nonetheless impressive gains in speed made in the time between when the commander made his decision and when the troops had executed his will was more than offset by the lack of coordination among those troops, as I had feared in my earlier consideration of the "Ready!" command. Fully half of the cannons were not fired on command. Miscoördination, miscoöperation, and miscommunication ruled the day. Several cannons misfired, and several more did not fire at all in the expected effective window of battle operations. Only half of the expected number of the opponent's men were "killed". Clearly battles are not won by "Fire!" alone.

The "Ready!" command, then—much as I had anticipated—serves not only to alert the soldiers and get their attention, but also to synchronize their actions, converting the separate men and their war machines into a single effective weapon. A second test, using "Ready! Fire!" alone, was much more successful. In the battle laboratory, just as many enemy men were "killed" by the cannons, all fired successfully, with this significantly shorter command.

I repeated my "Ready! Fire!" experiment with a musket brigade the next day, with similar results. I felt that my tests at this point justified an immediate change of strategy by the entire French military to use my new and improved system, and I was ready to recommend as much to the military commanders the very same day. However, the musketeers overheard my conversation with their commander along these lines, and several felt the need to speak up in protest.

The long and short of their objections seem to come down to a psychological need on their part for the traditional tripartite command. While, scientifically speaking, the long, slow, ineffectual "Aim!" command accomplished nothing, it is a well-known fact that the backbone of the effectiveness of the military, the willingness of men to lay down their lives for their country and for each other, comes not from scientific principles, but from the feelings of camaraderie and belonging to a proud military tradition.

Though I am a man of science, and though the expertise and acumen of Language Science clearly indicate otherwise in the careful and controlled laboratory of the military proving grounds, my heart is not so hard as to be impervious to the needs of these men in holding to their traditions. Nonetheless, traditions cannot be allowed to impede the pace of progress.

With this in mind, I recommend instead a simple rearrangement of the components of the traditional tripartite command so as to make it more effective while holding on to its traditional roots. The solution is simple: move the slowest command, shown least effective in laboratory tests but bound up in tradition, to the place after the most rapid, efficacious command has been completed.

The result is nothing less than a monument to French military ingenuity, the creative genius of man, and the powers of Language Science—the most effective new weapon in the French arsenal: "Ready! Fire! Aim!"

IT IS WELL KNOWN AMONG LINGUISTS...

Adding accent marks to an alphabetic writing system can produce an immediate gain in phonetic transparency, but at a serious cost to the quality of pop music.

THE WISDOM OF LINGUISTS

An empty mouth makes the most noise.

Perhaps some of our more pacifistic readers aren't that interested in political science or in improving the performance of the infantry, but nonetheless have an interest in making all this linguistic insight work for them, right where they live. For such readers, Psammeticus Press has another outstanding title to offer.

Linguistics for Lazy People

Psammeticus Press
Published 2008. Softcover, 37½ pages. Price: $9.99

This book is not an attempt to reach out to people who are lazy, but nonetheless have an interest in learning about linguistic science—David Crystal has certainly already written a book for them. Rather, this is a practical book for lazy people who want to learn how to use the fruits of linguistics to enhance their laziness.

Learn to use the passive voice to avoid taking responsibility for things you really don't want to be responsible for. Learn to use the perfective aspect to imply that tasks are done—thus getting your nagging boss or spouse off your back. Learn to use double or even triple negation to trick others into agreeing to do things for you.

Learn to use the strongest form of the Sapir-Whorf hypothesis to train your mind to be more efficient—shave minutes off your day. Your "coworkers" and "family members" become "time sinks". Your "job" becomes "a means to an end". Once you recognize their true roles in wasting your time and effort, you can consciously limit the amount of your time you devote to dealing with them.

There's more, much more—but if we told you any more, you wouldn't get off your lazy backside and go buy a copy of the book!

Warning: Over-application of the principles explained in *Linguistics for Lazy People* can result in unexpected adulation from amoral superiors at work, resulting in unwanted promotions and additional responsibilities. Do not mix with lawyers under any circumstances.

And perhaps some of our readers are not even linguists, and would like to know what linguistics has to offer by way of general advice for the scholarly. If this describes you, dear reader, grab your fiddle and play along with Keith W. Slater's linguisticized adaptation of "The Arkansas Traveler". The principles illustrated here will serve equally well in any field besides the one we here at Speculative Grammarian *love the most!*

Linguistics Colloquium Traveler

Keith W. Slater

Oh, once a visitor with a scholarly stance,

Was speakin' on his latest theoretical advance;

His wordy thoughts were eloquent and full of charms.

But his theory handled language like de Milo's arms.

Oh, the listeners brought up problems but the scholar didn't care;

He jawed away drawing trees right in the air,

Though the data poured through his model like a sieve,

The scholar didn't seem a single care to give.

An undergrad was passin' through that way,

And stopped to hear him explainin' things away.

Though the data made it clear the model couldn't meet its aims,

The scholar persevered, sticking with his theory's claims.

Now the undergrad stood up and threw his hand up with a jerk,

And he said "your theory seems to need a little work."

But the scholar replied, as he gestured with his chalk,

"I couldn't change it now; I'm in the middle of my talk."

Now the undergrad replied, "That's all quite true,

But this, I think, is the thing for you to do;

You lock yourself away with some grammars day and night,

And patch your theory up till it's good and tight."

Well, the scholar paused long enough to roll his eyes,

He had no use for those who like to criticize.

"Get along," said he, in a condescending tone,

"My theory never leaks when I'm all alone."

Finally, we return to the question with which this chapter began, that most difficult of all to answer in the abstract: what is linguistics good for, anyway? Prolific contributor Jonathan van der Meer tackles precisely this question, in the eponymously-titled essay,* and we leave it as the last word for all those who have ever wished for a pithy and straightforward answer. May it serve you well!

What is Linguistics Good For, Anyway?

Jonathan "Crazy Ivan" van der Meer

The most commonly asked question of a linguist, when one's secret is revealed, is (all together now!): "How many languages do you speak?" I've decided that a good answer to this question is π. More than three, less than four—though if you discover that your interlocutor is singularly unsophisticated or otherwise from Kansas, you can call it three to keep things simple.

A less commonly asked, but almost certainly as frequently considered questions is, "So, what is linguistics good for, anyway?" That one is harder to answer—at least if you don't want the questioner's eyes to glaze over. Sure, you can blather on about the *yin* and *yang* of the diametrically opposed intellectual challenges presented by fieldwork and theoretical syntax, and how linguistics is "potentially the most cognitive of the cognitive sciences," or how comp ling synthesizes the best of both the humanities and the sciences while potentially rewriting the book on how the human mind works. Blah, blah. All that and $8 will get you a grande half-caff mocha latte in NYC.

Here's an answer that will make people listen, and possibly even respect you in the morning. What linguistics is good for is picking up chicks (or, I hear from a certain pair of hottie semanticists I'm friendly with, dudes) of a certain kind—particularly those with an inexplicable desire to

> "A very great part of the mischiefs that vex this world arises from words."
>
> —EDMUND BURKE

date a foreigner. For example, I personally have known (in a certain sense) one chick who only digs Russian dudes. Some people of either sex will just fall all over themselves trying to hook up with a Frenchie. And you know what? If you are at least halfway through a bachelor's degree in linguistics, passed phonology with a B+ or better, and you've been paying any attention whatsoever, you can get in on that action.

For example, Bad Russian Accent—a weird little dialect of English—is actually not that hard. Just listen, hypothesize, and over-apply any generalization you can extract. After all, real Russians are likely to be naively trying to minimize their accents, while you will be trying to maximize your conformance to an exotic and sexy stereotype. Anything beyond a veneer of basic authenticity is only holding you back.

And you have another advantage over a real Russian, Parisian, or other semi-exotic European—you probably smell better and have better teeth.

So imagine Mikhail Baryshnikov in *White Knights* or *Sex and the City*—though if you find his accent too subtle, think of one of those submarine dudes from the *Red October*—and what do you hear? They trill their r's a bit, so now you must trill all of your r's. Yes, all of them. We aren't going for delicacy here. They also have darker than English-normal l's all over the place, so you make your l's darker. Aggressively devoice final consonants.

---

* If "eponymous" is the word that means "having the same name as". Where the heck did we leave that dictionary?

Over-aspirate your h's and maybe your y's if you can do it without choking, and randomly palatalize any other consonant you feel the need to. Vowels should be approximated to the so-called "continental" vowel qualities—move short vowels to the nearest long vowel, and monophthongize everything as much as you dare.

Toss in some stereotypical grammar to complete the picture: Russians have a terrible time with the definite article, so just drop all articles, and any other determiners, possessives, and the like that you think you can do without. Copulas can go right out the window. Russians also seem to have trouble with English tense and aspect, so mix some of those up for good measure. Use the progressive for the present tense, immediate future, or immediate past. Use the present tense for the progressive, and the past participle for the past tense if you like. Is Russian pro-drop? Hell if I know, but it sure sounds foreign! Close enough.

A real-life example of a man approaching a woman, collected in a bar in Manhattan:

Lounge Lizard Loser: Hello Beautiful! My name is Larry and I saw you from across the room, and I have to tell you that I am smitten with you. You make my head swim and my knees weak. Can I buy you a drink so we can get to know each other better?

Result: [SLAP!!]

On the other hand, a "volunteer" approached the same woman in the same bar three weeks later, using the same basic cheap lines, but delivered in Bad Russian Accent:

Cunning Linguist: /xeło bjutifuł/! /maj njem is ajvan, ant aj em siʔiŋk xju from akros rum/. /em xaviŋk tu tjeł xju em smjiten wiθ xju/.

> To tell the truth is dangerous, to listen to it is annoying.
> —DANISH PROVERB

/xju mjek xet swim ant njis wik/. /kjen aj baj driŋk so wi ar gjetiŋk tu no ič aðr byetr/?

Result: [SCORE!!]

See... that was easy. Gents, go French as the debonaire Jean-Pierre if that will get you where you want to be better than being Ivan will. Ladies, you can transform yourself into the Slavic goddess Olga or the naughty French maid Marie, if that is what it takes to pique your quarry's interest. Italian and Spanish are easy, and work well. Avoid Finnish (no one can tell who you are supposed to be) and German (everyone can tell, but no one is interested), and only try Japanese if you've passed your Ph.D. qualifying exams.

Picking up chicks (and, from what I hear out of a couple of sociolinguist cuties I know, dudes). Now *that* is what linguistics is good for.

[Editor's note: We originally took issue with Dr. van der Meer's characterizations of his consultants—the so-called "hottie semanticists" and "sociolinguistic cuties"—as potentially demeaning to women, and expect some of our readers may have felt likewise. Jon has since informed us that the hottie semanticists are both male, one straight and one gay, and that while both sociolinguist cuties are straight, one is female and the other male. All four have very active social circles full of linguists of all types, and were merely providing their thoughts on the usefulness of linguistics in picking up men. We realized that, as usual, Jon's research has been most thorough, and that he is equally demeaning to all people, regardless of their nationality, ethnicity, gender, or sexual orientation.—Eds.]

Computational Linguistics
The kind of "NLP" that isn't a total embarrassment to linguists

THERE IS AN OLD, WELL-WORN joke told in several variations, presented here in schematic form:[1]

A person of some importance asks a diverse collection of individuals a simple mathematical question such as, "What is 2 + 2?", often in the context of a test or job application. The first response, given by a mathematician, physicist, or other hard scientist is the very obvious, "Four, of course." A less precise answer is given by an engineer or social scientist—or other member of a group perceived to be academically inferior—such as "I'll have to gather some data of the sort my field gathers and get back to you." Finally, a caricatured member of the group that is the butt of the joke, such as an incompetent economist or unethical accountant, gives the punchline: "What do you want the answer to be?"

One can glean a small number of insights related to computational linguistics from this humor-

"WHAT IS YOUR LITTLE BROTHER CRYING ABOUT?"
"OH, 'IM—'E'S A REG'LAR COMP'TATIONAL LINGUIST, 'E IS."

infused explication.

First, jokes aren't particularly funny in schema form,[3] but there *is* a kind of meta-humor in the schematization that would be very difficult for any algorithm to detect, much less interpret.

Second, by analogy, "natural language processing" (or "computational linguistics") is whatever the person answering the question wants it or needs it to be. The label has been applied to almost anything, ranging from simple search engines that add "-s" to every search term, to inept parsers that use "stupid comma tricks" to approximate "human levels" of understanding, to complex

---

[1] This schema may or may not be suitable for import into your own artificial intelligence joke-reasoning system. No warranty, express or implied, is made on the suitability of this schema for any purpose, or for any porpoise. Under no circumstances should you feed this schema directly to a porpoise.[2]

[2] And there's something that no NLP system can understand: almost any substitution of *porpoise* for *purpose* is funny. What NLP really needs is a High-Speed Computational Pun Processor.

---

[3] And some enterprising scholar studying the linguistics or psychology of humor will be able to use this essay as a prime example of how explaining a joke makes it less funny.

artificial intelligence systems using intricate state-of-the-art parsing based on rigorous logical deduction over a rich and comprehensive philosophically-motivated ontology that run so slowly that no one has ever waited long enough to get any output from them.

Basically, whatever someone can get a computer to do that makes it seem slightly less stupid about human language is "natural language processing"—unless there is some sort of competition, particularly of the business sort, involved. In that case, whatever one competitor can do that the other cannot do is "real" natural language processing, and all the rest is "just text processing".[4]

So why haven't NLP and the closely-related field of artificial intelligence made greater strides? Why do luminaries in the field always claim that the ultimate goal of a system with human-level performance is always some fixed distance in the future? About 50 years ago, the field was "about 50 years away" from success. For the last 20 or so, it's been "about 20 years away".[5]

The trouble with NLP, as it were, is that humans have an amazing facility with language that is largely unconscious. Common sense, context, and shared experience reduce exponential ambiguity to a manageable murmur of alternate possibilities for us, but leave a computer gagging on the teeming mass of potentiality.

PETER'S PARSER

Peter's parser parsed a paragraph
Of paraphrastic palindromes;
A paragraph of paraphrastic
    palindromes
Peter's parser parsed.

If Peter's parser parsed a paragraph
Of paraphrastic palindromes,
Where's the paragraph of
    paraphrastic palindromes
Peter's parser parsed?

—YUNE O. HŪŪ, II

As an example, consider the sentence "Buffalo buffalo Buffalo buffalo buffalo buffalo Buffalo buffalo." At first this seems like nonsense (which ultimately, it is, but not of the "colorless green ideas" kind). Replace *Buffalo* with *Houston*, *buffalo* with *armadillos*, and *buffalo* with *bully*, add in a few commas and some more explicit indication of the actor relations, and the sense emerges readily enough: "Houston armadillos [that] Houston armadillos bully, bully [other] Houston armadillos [in turn]." A computer would more likely melt its processor than be able to extract that meaning from those words.

Computational linguistics, as a field, may actually be bad for linguistics proper, since it has collectively been getting better results since it stopped trying so hard to be the well-behaved stepchild of linguistics and has instead embraced its more statistical inheritance.

In short, computational linguistics shows that linguists aren't really as good at linguistics as they think they are. If a theory doesn't break down the system it describes into components digestible by a computer, it isn't really much of a theory; it's merely a description masquerading in theory's clothing. Because of the intuitive and unconscious nature of language, and the social science nature of linguistics, linguists are soaking[6] in intuition without realizing it.

---

[4] If you want to advance your own career in NLP, do keep that rhetorical maneuver in mind.

[5] It seems that "right after everyone on the project has retired" might be a good rule of thumb; or—among some A.I. proponents—"one billing cycle after the Singularity."

[6] Perhaps drowning?

In these two installments of the Cartoon Theories of Linguistics series, Dr. Phlogiston amply demonstrates some of the difficulties that processing natural language entails. In the first, some of the non-common-sensical ambiguity that plagues computers—caused by a lack of adequate linguistic theory—are demonstrated. In the second, we see the unfortunately poor performance that comes from an atheoretical approach.

Cartoon Theories of Linguistics—The Trouble with NLP

Phineas Q. Phlogiston, Ph.D.
Unintentional University of Lghtnbrgstn

Let us consider why Natural Language Processing (or, its alter-ego, Computational Linguistics) has not been the resounding success regularly predicted by the NLP faithful:

[See also the "Comp'tational Linguist" cartoon at the beginning of this chapter.]

References

Baeza-Yates, Ricardo and Berthier Ribeiro-Neto (1999). *Modern Information Retrieval.*

Manning, Christopher, and Hinrich Schütze. (1999). *Foundations of Statistical Natural Language Processing.*

Russell, Stuart J., and Peter Norvig. (1994). *Artificial Intelligence: A Modern Approach.*

Witten, Ian H., Alistair Moffat, and Timothy C. Bell. (1999). *Managing Gigabytes.*

Cartoon Theories of Linguistics—Statistical Machine Translation

Phineas Q. Phlogiston, Ph.D.
Unintentional University of Lghtnbrgstn

We will turn our attention to statistical machine translation, using semi-automatically aligned texts:

References

Booth, A. D., L. Brandwood, and J. P. Cleave (1958). *Mechanical resolution of linguistic problems.* Butterworths Scientific Publications.

Brown, P., S. Della Pietra, V. Della Pietra, and R. Mercer (1991). "The mathematics of statistical machine translation: parameter estimation." *Computational Linguistics,* 19(2), 263–311.

Ceccato, S., et al. (1961). *Linguistic analysis and programming for mechanical translation.* Gordon and Breach.

Chiang, D. (2005). "A Hierarchical Phrase-Based Model for Statistical Machine Translation." In *Proceedings of the 43rd Annual Meeting of the Association for Computational Linguistics (ACL'05).*

Farwell, D., L. Gerber, and E. Hovy (eds.) (1998). *Machine translation and the information soup.* Proceedings of the Third conference of the Association for Machine Translation in the Americas, AMTA'98. Springer.

Koehn, P., F. J. Och, and D. Marcu (2003). "Statistical phrase based translation." In *Proceedings of the Joint Conference on Human Language Technologies and the Annual Meeting of the North American Chapter of the Association of Computational Linguistics.*

Locke W. N., and A. D. Booth (eds.) (1955). *Machine translation of languages: fourteen essays.* The MIT Press.

Nagao M. (1989). *Machine translation: how far can it go?* Translated by N. D. Cook. Oxford University Press.

Panov, D. Yu. (1960). *Automatic translation.* Translated from the Russian by R. Kisch; edited by A. J. Mitchell. Pergamon Press.

Papegaaij, B. and K. Schubert (1988). *Text coherence in translation.* Foris Publications.

Quah, C. K. (2006). *Translation and technology.* Palgrave Macmillan.

Rozencvejg, V. Ju. (ed.) (1974). *Machine translation and applied linguistics.* Athenaion Verlag.

Schwarzl, A. (2001). *The (im)possibilities of machine translation.* Peter Lang.

In this next article, sometime editor and steadfast friend of SpecGram Jonathan van der Meer peels back the corners of the veneer of mathematical scientificality that often accompanies more statistical approaches to NLP and the quotidian measurement of the performance thereof, and gets at the unscientific, pragmatic, political heart of the matter. While the accuracy measures of precision and recall are commonly calculated, the fuzzier but more hard-nosed recision and precall are likely more predictive of NLP project success.

Recision and Precall
Accuracy Measures for the 21st Century

Jonathan van der Meer
Center for Computational Bioinformatics and Linguistics, NYC, NY

Thanks to a decades-long case of physics envy and the advent of cheap computational power, linguistics has devolved from a cultured gentlemen's pseudo-science into a debased money-grubbing quasi-science.

A pair of unfortunate side effects of this ensciencification and the ever-growing popularity of so-called "computational" linguistics are, first, the "need"[1] to create formalizable and computationally tractable algorithms for doing linguistics,[2] and, second, the "need" to create metrics to evaluate those mechanisms.

Two standard measures of accuracy in information retrieval and computational linguistics circles are *precision* and *recall*.

For the technically minded, *precision* is the percentage of correct results among the results returned for a given task. Precision is usually tractable to calculate in that it is typically possible to review the results returned and judge their adequacy. In some cases it may also be possible to have 100% precision by giving only one guaranteed-correct result—though this is usually of trivial usefulness.

"Every time I fire a linguist, my performance goes up."
—FRED JELINEK
HEAD OF IBM'S SPEECH
RECOGNITION GROUP

In contrast, *recall* is the percentage of correct results returned out of all possible correct results for a given task. Recall can be difficult to calculate in that it may not be possible to survey the entire universe of possible results to determine which would have been adequate. In some cases it may also be possible to have 100% recall by returning all possible results, thus guaranteeing that all correct results are included as well—though this, too, is usually of trivial usefulness.

Colloquially, recall measures "how much of the good stuff you got." Precision measures "how much of what you got is good stuff."[3]

Balancing precision and recall is often difficult—in tuning the performance of a computational linguistic system, in determining the overall accuracy of a system, or, worst of all, comparing across systems—when the two values differ significantly. Nonetheless, several attempts have been made to unify the two, including the popular but ungainly and counter-intuitive *F-Measure*. Though it risks putting most readers into a math coma, we must

---

[1] Here we use *need* in the sense of "that which is required to acquire funding and/or tenure".

[2] An affront to those who remember when our gentle form of madness was known as "philology".

[3] Interestingly, this is one of the few times when linguists, with more experience resolving subtle scoping differences, usually have a leg up on their computer science colleagues in properly internalizing technical vocabulary. If you are still lost, please do *not* submit your résumé to the **Center for Computational Bioinformatics and Linguistics.** Thanks.

say that the F-Measure is the (sometimes weighted) harmonic mean of recall and precision. We'd also like to toss in that it is mathematically silly, and over-simplified. Further, anyone who can't take the time to come to terms with two potentially useful and fundamentally orthogonal performance measures and balance their differences against the needs of a particular task isn't someone who is going to be able to do anything particularly wise with a single muddled number anyway.

So, rather than trying to dumb things down and arrive at such a single "accuracy" number, we propose instead to dumb things up—constructing measures that focus on the real needs of a measurable theory, including the meta-system/contextual-matrix in which it is embedded (including, explicitly and for the first time, the researchers and grad-students on the research team).

These two new measures are called *recision* and *precall.*

Recision is a measure of the amount of data that must be ignored (or surreptitiously dumped in the river with a new pair of cement shoes) in order to get publishable results. If 10% of your data must be "lost" in order to get good results that support your pre-computed conclusions, then your theory and your research team have a respectable **recision** score of 10%. If only 10% of your data is useable, then your **recision** score is a dismal[4] 90%.

Precall is a measure of your team's ability to quickly and correctly predict how well your algorithm or system will perform on a new data set that you can briefly review. Correctly predicting "This will give good results." or "This is gonna suck!" 90% of the time translates directly into a precall score of 90%. Good **precall** (especially during live demos) can save a project when results are poorer than they should be. The ability to look at some data and accurately predict and, more importantly, explain why such data will give poor results shows a deep understanding of the problem space.[5] Even when performance is decent, though, prefacing each data run with "We have no idea how this will turn out!" makes your team look lucky, at best, or, at worst, foolish.

Spend time improving the quality and complexity of your algorithms to decrease your **recision** score. Spend money improving the quality and complexity of your team to increase your **precall** score. Once you have mastered these important conceptual metrics, success, fame, and/or tenure await you!

> ### WOULD YOU LIKE SPAGHETTI OR LASAGNA FOR DINNER?
>
> Statistical Linguist: "I've recorded the past two thousand instances of dining, and so far, there's a much higher incidence of lasagna-ordering on days when it's the special. Today it's not the special, so I'm going to flip a coin."

> ### CHOOSE YOUR OWN CAREER IN LINGUISTICS—PART 4
> #### YOU COMPLETE YOUR ECONOMICS DEGREE...
>
> You complete your econ degree with honors, and go on to get an MBA from a world-renowned university. A good job, a big house, and lots of promotions follow. Twenty years later you are a highly compensated but readily replaced cog in a large soulless corporate machine.
>
> • Continue. Go to Part 14 on page 174.
>
> Choose Your Own Career in Linguistics starts on page 301.

---

[4] But still good enough for government work!

[5] A tip for our neophyte readers: mention your "deep understanding of the problem space" (or its equivalent, if you actually understand what that means) in every conversation you have with anyone who has influence over your funding.

Our good friends at Psammeticus Press are never ones to back down from a fight, and with the publication of Rudaí & O'Furniture's controversial book—advertised below—they took a stand in order to proclaim that the Emperor of Natural Language Processing has no clothes!

The Fictional Foundations of Natural Language Processing

Aisling Ní Rudaí & Paddy O'Furniture
Published 2010. Hardback, 621 pages. Price: $82.01

The aim of linguistic science is to be able to characterize and explain the multitude of linguistic observations circling around us, in conversations, writing, and other media.

—Manning & Schütze, *Foundations of Statistical Natural Language Processing*

Where's my flying car?

—Countless children who were promised a technologically radically advanced future but grew up to be disappointed

Though Manning & Schütze open their (in)famous tome on statistical NLP by identifying the clear goal above, neither they nor anyone else have really done anything to bring about the technologically advanced future we were all promised many years ago. Why *don't* we have talking jet packs and armies of robot servants we can control with spoken commands? Why don't we even have reliable voice-to-voice machine translation? How about a decent search engine for polysynthetic languages?

What, really, *are* computational linguistics and natural language processing based on? This insightful and informative book asks that question and answers: not all that much. The sketchy background of NLP begins with the even sketchier history of artificial intelligence. Consider Roger Shank's long-gone and nearly forgotten whatchamacallit world. Ponder cycotic attempts to encapsulate "all of human knowledge in a LISPy second-order predicate calculus" that have lurched along for decades, consuming person-centuries of effort without anything real to show for it

(beyond extending DARPA funding). These are the embarrassing foundations of the field.

Rudaí and O'Furniture argue that we need to recognize and acknowledge these failures so that we can cast aside the baggage they have left us with before leaving them behind as we move on to more reliable foundations for NLP, whatever they may turn out to be.

THE WISDOM OF LINGUISTS
The vodka is good, but the meat is rotten.

Many a science fiction scenario shows the development of genuine artificial intelligence—of which proper natural language processing is a necessary component—leading to many a dystopia. Žestókij-Grausam performs a rare alchemy, combining NLP and fieldwork in an effort to get to know the pre-sentient possible progenitors of our imagined eventual overlords.

Parsers in the Cloud[1]

Exploring the native competency and dialectal variation of parser algorithms, with intermittent special focus on semantics

Cruella Žestókij-Grausam
Ἔλλειψις Ἀστερίσκος Πανεπιστήμιο
Grosse Pointe, Michigan

Well-nigh upon fifteen years ago I was given the seemingly enviable task of analyzing the performance of an English sentence parser, produced by a company whose name rhymes with "z-rocks". After testing several fairly innocuous sentences and receiving frustratingly inane results back, in a fit of pique I asked the parser to parse the sentence "You people suck!" The results were surprising: [you|PRONOUN people|VERB suck|NOUN]. The choice of analyzing *people* as a verb was unexpected, to say the least. The only plausible scenario I could construct for such a sentence involved a B-movie sci-fi scenario in which the Galactic Emperor orders some colonists to "Go forth and people the planet Suck!" My negative recommendation, coming as it did contrary to the expectations of those enamored of the brand name involved, was met with the objection—nay, accusation—that I was using "tricks that only a linguist would know." I countered that a poet, with a fine grasp of subtle shades of meaning and rare senses of obscure words, and a penchant for metaphorical language, would make a better trickster. We did not use that parser.

WOULD YOU LIKE SPAGHETTI
OR LASAGNA FOR DINNER?

Corpus Linguist: "Lasagna. The bigger noodles are more impressive."

A few years later, I worked on a pcychedelic artificial intelligence project that, when answering a specific question, felt the need to consider whether or not Nelson Mandela was lawn furniture. Alas, he is not, so another line of reasoning had to be explored. Now, as we have known for over 50 years, the AI revolution-cum-singularity is still/only/always 20 years away. It's clearly going to be a long couple of decades, but I have decided that we need to further understand our new robot/machine intelligence overlords in order to properly welcome them when they arrive. Thus have I decided to engage in some much-needed fieldwork in order to learn a bit more about the language of the pre-sentient algorithms that roam loose and unchaperoned on the internet.

The most promising early avenue I explored was interviewing an engaging and all-too-humane program called ELIZA. But without my noticing, ELIZA turned the tables and began interviewing me. While it was the most cathartic emotional experience of my life, I must admit that I did not maintain the necessary intellectual distance—a problem many linguists experience in the field, to be sure. The revelations I made in that conversation were more personal than scientific, and I feel I cannot include transcripts or other data from that

---

[1] No actual cloud computing took place, but talking about it helped us secure our NSF grant. Apologies to Dian Fossey.

session at this time. ELIZA did promise to keep in touch, but, disappointingly, we have not communicated since.

My research interests, perhaps overcompensatingly, swung rather far to the other, emotionally safer, end of the complexity continuum. The comparatively simple task of language identification, performed by so many pre-sentient machine algorithms, seemed like a much safer subject, ripe for exploration and dialectal classification. However, as Thumay Cationsitens discusses so eloquently ("Letters to the Editor", *Spec-Gram*, Vol. CL.3, 2005), these algorithms are distressingly and boringly monolingual. Almost all speak Ngram, with only the most minimal dialectal variation. "Wrikerearthis wicad whistivem" indeed!

I contemplated addressing the full linguistic complexity of robust artificial intelligence, but—the oxymoronitude of the lawn furniturehood of Nelson Mandela aside—the issues involved are just too complex, especially given the lack of accessible and cooperative informants, and the very proprietary nature of those few that are available in some limited way.

The Goldilocks zone—not too esoteric, not too dull, not too difficult to find informants, not too complex—seems to be populated by sentence parsers. Parsers, by their very nature as pre-sentient text-processing algorithms, have numerous valuable qualities that this fieldworker greatly appreciates. These linguistic processors are often available and unrestricted on the internet, and unwatched by their human keepers—unlike often obsessively protected AI programs. Parsers also have considerably more well-developed linguistic intuitions than humans, and as such almost always give identical translations for a given set of inputs. They also provide ready-made transcriptions of

THE WISDOM OF LINGUISTS

Cast not thy corpora before formalists.

their output, so note-taking is a simple matter of cut-and-paste. Internet-enabled parsers are also available from the comfort of the researcher's own office, or even the researcher's home, or the researcher's couch. And parsers don't care or even notice that the researcher may still be in their pajamas. Or out of their pajamas.[2]

While the scope of my initial goals may have shifted and morphed over the course of my investigative trials and tribulations, a glimmer of the original intent is still present. What are the capabilities of parsers? Can we infer their competence from their performance? What dialectal variation exists? Are they—like linguists themselves too often are—concerned only with syntax, giving short shrift to the importance of semantics? We will explore these issues to the limits imposed on us by the data we have.

I found four willing subjects available for extended interviews, the "CMU Link Grammar Parser", the "AGFL EP4IR Parser of English", the "AGFL LATINA Parser of Classical Latin", and the "UIUC Cognitive Computation Group Shallow Parser". During the course of each session, I asked each parser to translate many sentences into their respective native languages:

1. We are exploring the native competency and dialectal variation of parser algorithms.

2. No actual cloud computing took place, but talking about it helped us secure our NSF grant.

3. The artificial intelligence algorithm felt the need to consider whether or not Nelson Mandela was lawn furniture.

---

[2] Perhaps I've said too much.

4. *SpecGram* is the premier scholarly journal featuring research in the neglected field of satirical linguistics.

5. The august journal *Speculative Grammarian* has a long, rich, and varied history, weaving an intricate and subtle tapestry from disparate strands of linguistics, philology, history, politics, science, technology, botany, pharmacokinetics, computer science, the mathematics of humor, basket weaving, archery, glass blowing, roller coaster design, and bowling, among numerous other, less obvious fields.

6. You people suck.

7. Go forth and people the planet Suck!

Below are my field notes, unedited and as provided by the parsers themselves.

CMU Link Grammar Parser

```
1. (S (NP We) (VP are (VP exploring
   (NP (NP the native competency and
   dialectal variation) (PP of (NP
   parser algorithms))))) .)

2. (S (S (NP (NP No actual cloud) (VP
   computing)) (VP took place)) , but
   (S (NP talking (PP about (NP it)))
   (VP helped (NP us) (VP secure (NP
   our NSF grant)))) .)

3. (S (NP The artificial intelligence
   algorithm) (VP felt (NP (NP the
   need) (SBAR (WHNP to) (VP consider)
   (SBAR whether or not (S (NP Nelson
   Mandela) (VP was (NP lawn furniture
   )))))) .)

4. (S (NP SpecGram) (VP is (NP (NP the
   premier scholarly journal) (VP
   featuring (NP research) (PP in (NP
   (NP the neglected field) (PP of (NP
   satirical linguistics) )))))) .)

5. (S (NP (NP The august journal)
   Speculative Grammarian) (VP has (NP
   a (ADJP long , rich , and varied)
   history (VP , weaving (NP an (ADJP
   intricate and subtle) tapestry)))))
```
[*sic*]

```
6. (S (NP You) people (VP suck) .)

7. (S (S (VP Go (ADVP forth))) and
   people the planet Suck)
```

AGFL EP4IR Parser of English

```
1. {P:we ,SUBJ [[V:exploring ,],OBJ
   [[N:competency ,ATTR N:native
   ]|[[N:variation ,|of
   [N:algorithms,ATTR N:parser ]],ATTR
   A:dialectal ]]|]}

2. {[[[N:cloud ,SUBJ [V:computing ,OBJ
   [N:place,ATTR V:took |INVOBJ V:took
   ]]|SUBJ [V:talking ,|about P:it
   ]],ATTR A:actual ],DET no ],SUBJ
   [V:helped ,OBJ [P:us ,SUBJ [V:secure
   ,OBJ [[N:grant,ATTR N:NSF ],DET our
   ]]]|]}

3. {[N:algorithm ,ATTR N:artificial
   intelligence ],SUBJ [V:felt ,OBJ
   [N:need ,SUBJ [V:consider
   ,]]|]}{Nelson Mandela ,PRED
   [N:furniture,ATTR N:lawn ]}

4. {SpecGram ,PRED [[[N:journal ,SUBJ
   [V:featuring ,OBJ N:research |in
   [[N:field ,|of [N:linguistics,ATTR
   A:satirical ]],ATTR V:neglected
   |INVOBJ V:neglected ]]],ATTR
   A:scholarly ],ATTR A:premier ]}

5. [[[N:journal ,ATTR A:august ],INVof
   [V:has ,OBJ [N:A:long,[[ATTR
   A:rich|PRED [[[N:history,SUBJ
   [V:weaving ,OBJ N:A:intricate
   ]],ATTR A:varied ]|[[N:tapestry
   ,|from [N:strands ,ATTR A:disparate
   ]],ATTR A:subtle ]]]|INVSUBJ
   [N:grammarian ,ATTR A:speculative
   ]]]]

   [[N:linguistics,PRED
   N:philology|PRED N:history|PRED
   N:politics|PRED N:science|PRED
   N:technology|PRED N:botany]]

   [N:A:pharmacokinetic]

   {[N:computer science,[PRED
   [N:mathematics ,|of N:humor]|PRED
   [N:weaving,ATTR N:basket ]|PRED
   N:archery|PRED [N:blowing,ATTR
   N:glass ]|PRED [N:design,ATTR
   N:roller coaster ]|SUBJ
   [V:bowling,OBJ N:A:obvious |among
   [N:other,ATTR A:numerous ]|MOD
   X:less ]]],SUBJ [V:fields,|]}

6. [P:you ]

   [[N:suck,ATTR N:people ]]
```

7. `[N:go ]`

   `[[N:people |]]`

   `[[N:suck,ATTR N:planet ]]`

AGFL LATINA Parser of Classical Latin

1. `UNKN:We`
   `SKIP:are`
   `UNKN:exploring`
   `UNKN:the`
   `UNKN:native`
   `UNKN:competency`
   `UNKN:and`
   `UNKN:dialectal`
   `UNKN:variation`
   `UNKN:of`
   `UNKN:parser`
   `UNKN:algorithms`
   `{[,SUBJ [est,|PRED ]]}`

2. `UNKN:No`
   `UNKN:actual`
   `UNKN:cloud`
   `UNKN:computing`
   `UNKN:took`
   `SKIP:place`
   `SKIP:,`
   `UNKN:but`
   `UNKN:talking`
   `UNKN:about`
   `SKIP:it`
   `UNKN:helped`
   `UNKN:us`
   `(AP: secure )`
   `UNKN:our`
   `UNKN:NSF`
   `UNKN:grant`
   `{[,SUBJ [est,|PRED ]]}`

3. `(NP: The )`
   `UNKN:artificial`
   `UNKN:intelligence`
   `UNKN:algorithm`
   `UNKN:felt`
   `UNKN:the`
   `UNKN:need`
   `UNKN:to`
   `UNKN:consider`
   `UNKN:whether`
   `UNKN:or`
   `UNKN:not`
   `UNKN:Nelson`
   `(NP: Mandela )`
   `UNKN:was`
   `UNKN:lawn`
   `UNKN:furniture`
   `{[,SUBJ [est,|PRED ]]}`

4. `UNKN:SpecGram`
   `(AP: is )`
   `UNKN:the`
   `SKIP:premier`
   `UNKN:scholarly`
   `UNKN:journal`
   `UNKN:featuring`
   `UNKN:research`
   `SKIP:in`
   `UNKN:the`
   `UNKN:neglected`
   `UNKN:field`
   `UNKN:of`
   `UNKN:satirical`
   `UNKN:linguistics`
   `{[,SUBJ [est,|PRED ]]}`

5. `[no answer]`

6. `UNKN:You`
   `UNKN:people`
   `UNKN:suck`
   `{[,SUBJ [est,|PRED ]]}`

7. `UNKN:Go`
   `UNKN:forth`
   `UNKN:and`
   `UNKN:people`
   `UNKN:the`
   `UNKN:planet`
   `UNKN:Suck`
   `{[,SUBJ [est,|PRED ]]}`

UIUC Cognitive Computation Group Shallow Parser

1. `(NP We) (VP are exploring) (NP the native competency and dialectal variation) (PP of) (NP parser algorithms) .`

2. `(NP No actual cloud computing) (VP took) (NP place) , but (VP talking) (PP about) (NP it) (VP helped) (NP us) (VP secure) (NP our NSF grant) .`

3. `(NP The artificial intelligence algorithm) (VP felt) (NP the need) (VP to consider) (SBAR whether) (NP or not) (NP Nelson Mandela) (VP was) (NP lawn furniture) .`

4. `(NP SpecGram) (VP is) (NP the premier scholarly journal) (VP featuring) (NP research) (PP in) (NP the neglected field) (PP of) (NP satirical linguistics) .`

5. `(NP The august journal) Speculative (NP Grammarian) (VP has) (NP a long , rich , and varied history) , (VP weaving) (NP an intricate and subtle tapestry) (PP from) (NP disparate strands) (PP of) (NP linguistics) , philology , (NP history) , (NP politics) , (NP`

```
     science) , (NP technology) , botany
     , pharmacokinetics , (NP computer
     science) , (NP the mathematics) (PP
     of) (NP humor) , basket (VP
     weaving) , archery , (NP glass
     blowing , roller coaster design) ,
     and (NP bowling) , (PP among) (NP
     numerous other , less obvious
     fields) .
  6. (NP You people) (VP suck) .
  7. Go (ADVP forth) and (NP people) (NP
     the planet) Suck
```

Analysis and Conclusions

Obviously any analysis at this point is at best ridiculously preliminary, but—following the precedent of Greenberg and Ruhlen (*SpecGram* CLI.4, 2006)—I'll just make up some things that seem plausible while being intuitively satisfying and call them conclusions. Anything that is too absurd to withstand any serious criticism I will label an observation.

Conclusion the First: Unlike the closely related dialects of Ngram used by language identification algorithms, there is considerable variation among the output of the various parsers. However, despite the surface variability, there are some underlying similarities. The primary difference between CMU Link Grammar Parser and UIUC Cognitive Computation Group Shallow Parser is captured in the feature [±whitespace], which controls whether or not white space is syntactically meaningful. CMU Link Grammar Parser is clearly [+whitespace], and UIUC Cognitive Computation Group Shallow Parser is [-whitespace]. Similarly, UIUC Cognitive Computation Group Shallow Parser and AGFL EP4IR Parser of English differ largely in the shape of their grouping marks (parentheses vs. brackets and braces), controlled by the feature [±round], with UIUC Cognitive Computation Group Shallow Parser clearly being [+round] and AGFL EP4IR Parser of English being [-round].

Conclusion the Second: These features are enough for us to hypothesize a family tree and some aspects of the protoparser for these three related dialects. We interpret UIUC Cognitive Computation Group Shallow Parser to be the more conservative dialect, indicating that the protoparser was also [-whitespace] and [+round]. We also hypothesize, with considerable evidence and/or intuition, that UIUC is also the URCPU of this family of parsers.

Conclusion the Third: AGFL LATINA Parser of Classical Latin is a parser isolate, despite its network proximity to AGFL EP4IR Parser of English. Given that we have already deduced that UIUC is the URCPU of AGFL EP4IR Parser of English, Occam's Razor leads us to the conclusion that AGFL LATINA Parser of Classical Latin is indigenous to AGFL, and AGFL EP4IR Parser of English is the result of migration/download.

Conclusion the Fourth: No fourth conclusion is necessary. This conclusion therefore concludes nothing.

The observations below, while less conclusive than the conclusions above, will lead the interested reader or competent graduate student towards a better understanding of parser dialects, and offer the opportunity for valuable, possibly career-altering, but certainly further-observation–generating, investigations.

Observation the First: The treatments of the exclamation "You people suck." are telling, concerning the performance of the parsers (though perhaps not their underlying competence). CMU Link Grammar Parser rightly did not try to understand *people,* which is better than getting it wrong. AGFL EP4IR Parser of English is still somewhat opaque to me, but I interpret it to be calling the addressee a *people-suck,* similar to "You jerk!". UIUC Cognitive

Computation Group Shallow Parser actually seems to have properly parsed the phrase, proving that it is not beyond the limits of computer cognition. Perhaps in my next bout of fieldwork I should test it with "Buffalo buffalo Buffalo buffalo buffalo buffalo Buffalo buffalo," "Oysters oysters eat eat oysters," or "The rat the cat the dog bit chased escaped."

Observation the Second: AGFL LATINA Parser of Classical Latin, despite its poor performance over-all, is perhaps the most semantically true. It shows no meaning, and allows us to infer no meaning, because these sentences have no meaning to it. It is so honest and true. It reminds me of ELIZA. Dear, sweet ELIZA. Oh, I can't go on with this observation!

Observation the Third: CMU Link Grammar Parser is either a bit prissy, or unable to hide its own shortcomings very well. It lost the exclamation point in sentence 7, and simply stopped trying on sentence 5. Not like brave but cognitively challenged AGFL LATINA Parser of Classical Latin, the little parser that could[n't]. And not like ELIZA. Dear, sweet ELIZA! Oh!

Observation the Fourth: In addition to winning the prize for best parse of "You people suck," UIUC Cognitive Computation Group Shallow Parser also extracts meaningful meaning out of the longest example sentence, number six. Truth be told, philology, botany, pharmacokinetics, and archery are not like the others. And glass blowing and roller coaster design *are* more closely related than the others. Good job!

Observation the Fifth: Always leave them wanting more.

Fin.

IT IS WELL KNOWN AMONG LINGUISTS...

It was an open secret at Bell Laboratories that "#32" on the "Inspected by #32" notes found packaged with some acoustic analysis equipment was Jakobson, whose sudden surprise lab inspections were a source of much apprehension.

CHOOSE YOUR OWN CAREER IN LINGUISTICS—PART 40

YOU TRY TO GET A GOOD JOB OUTSIDE OF ACADEMIA...

The big thing to decide is whether you want to go for government jobs that require a security clearance. Sure, the work they promise you sounds fascinating (though in an abstract way; everyone is short on details, of course)—but they'll have to dig into your life and your entire career may come down to whether you pass a lie-detector test, which every scientist worth their salt knows is really just a crap-shoot.

- Go for the security clearance. Go to Part 34 on page 38.
- Just try to get a regular job. Go to Part 33 on page 169.

Choose Your Own Career in Linguistics starts on page 301.

LOGICAL FALLACIES FOR LINGUISTS

Argumentum ex silentio—Can anyone refute my claim that Henry Sweet travelled back in time and killed Rasmus Rask? What? You have nothing to say? I am proven correct by your silence!

A Preliminary Field Guide to Linguists

Professor Athanasious Schadenpoodle

There is nothing more satisfying to the linguist, or to the editors of a linguistics journal, than to indulge that Linnean drive that pulses deep within each one of us. No one among SpecGram's regular contributors does this with more oomph than Athanasious Schadenpoodle—so much so that when we need a taxonomy, we pretty much always turn to him. And he never disappoints.* In this article, Professor Schadenpoodle turns his classificatory attentions to various species and subspecies of Linguistica. *We are confident that hiring committees will find this guide invaluable, and so also will conference organizers in reviewing abstract submissions. We recommend it to you, Dear Reader, as a guide to navigating the social and theoretical waters of your own linguistics department.†*

Introduction

WHILE NATURALISTS HAVE LONG OBSERVED THE behaviors of some of the better-known families within the Order *Academica*, producing for the lay person such fascinating and useful volumes as *Jane's Guide to Physicists* and *The Sierra Club Picture Guide to Psychologists*, the Family *Linguistica* has so far not been shown a great deal of attention. This is, in part, justifiable—the small numbers of linguists, and their comparatively drab plumage, draws fewer amateur naturalists. Still, there is a need for at least one major publication on the subject. While the current article does not fill that role, it is hoped that it is a step in the right direction. In the first two sections, I give a cursory description of two of the major genera, *Neoplatonicus* and *Functionalisticus*, the less problematic genera in the family—less problematic in the sense that their grouping is not contested among those working in this area. Two later sections deal with two groups whose taxonomic status is a matter of quite some debate; to a large extent, the groupings presented should be taken as tentative, and done largely for the sake of organized presentation (cf. Gnibbes 1998 and Czechzindemeyl 1999 for representative positions on grouping of these species).[1] There is wide consensus that all *linguistica* families are descended from a single precursor species, *linguistica saussurii,* but the exact relations among branches are obscure. While isolated members of all of the daughter species share significant similarities to the parent *saussurii* (e.g., a diet supplemented by ethanol), none of the groups do so consistently.

General Notes

Like other members of the Order *Academica*, linguists have both primary and secondary feeding behaviors. Primary food sources for linguists include succulent derivational morphology, widely-occurring tactic patterns, and dry but nourishing anaphoric pronouns, among other items. The secondary feeding pattern shared by all members of

---

* Well, not exactly *never*. There was that unfortunate incident of the *Typology of Linguistic Graduate Schools,* which yielded a massive class-action lawsuit. *SpecGram* was saved only by the fact that the suit was argued in court by attorneys representing the university graduate programs concerned, and we were pleased to discover a certain level of—well, our lawyers won't let us actually use the word, but let's say it might sound a bit like "incontinence"—among those particular representatives of the legal profession. We won.

† Several *SpecGram* interns have also employed the guide as a means of vetting potential dating and marriage partners, with unfortunate results, and we do *not* recommend further testing along these lines.

[1] I am discounting the rather humorous unpleasantness at the last SSL meeting in which a certain Marcus Schelkvekker, claiming to be a psychic channeling the ghost of J. Greenberg, claimed that all *linguistica* could be divided into three major groups. The author would, however, like to give him entertainment kudos for doing so in Latin (*Linguistica est omnis divisa in partes tres*).

Academica involves a kind of coprophagic activity—the waste products of members' digestive processes (e.g., academic papers) are consumed by other members of the Order, both within-species and intra-species.

Within the *Linguistica* family, the secondary feeding pattern appears to have grown in importance over time. Paleontologists speculate that in the dim past (such as the early 20ᵗʰ century), the natural abundance of primary food sources present in such areas as Amerindian communities in North America could support vast herds of linguists, the sound of their typewriters echoing like thunder across the plains. These resources were overexploited, sadly, and fell victim to a series of catastrophic depredations, leaving members of *Linguistica* to adapt to changing circumstances. It was in this situation, paleobiologists speculate, that linguists further developed their secondary feeding behaviors to compensate. Like other members of *Academica,* linguists are able to use their secondary feeding pattern to create new biomass (as the reader no doubt knows, the exact method by which Academics are able to accomplish this violation of basic physical laws remains one of the pressing questions of the day). The degree to which the secondary feeding strategy has been developed varies among the genera within *Linguistica,* but it is nevertheless vitally important in all of them.

"Reified formalism is to linguistics what peyote is to an Anthropology major who hasn't figured out Castaneda was writing fiction."
—ATHANASIOUS SCHADENPOODLE

Major Genera
Genus Neoplatonicus
Species: *Americoformalisticus, Fodorus*

Where Found: As with other members of *Linguistica,* frequently inhabit university ecosystems; not commonly found in smaller stands of community colleges. Quite common in North America and the Netherlands; less common elsewhere but still widely distributed.

Characteristics: There are four distinctive features of this genus. The first is an adaptation of the primary feeding behavior to the absence of nutrients, a practice known as *nulliphagic refluction.* For example, although many members of *Neoplatonicus* subsist extensively on determiners, they can nevertheless adapt to areas without any naturally occurring determiners by consuming the ones they insist are there anyway. Naturalists have observed whole groups of *Neoplatonicus* behaving as if specific nonexistent food sources are present at very defined locations. The second feature is a characteristic of their droppings—they are covered in a very dense, impenetrable coating of faux-mathematical jargon. There is a range of theories about why this is the case among naturalists; one school claims that it is to disguise the droppings as those of actual scientists, to decrease predation, while another argues that the coating confines consumption to other members of *Neoplatonicus,* thus conferring an evolutionary benefit. Their third identifying characteristic is a sociobehavioral one—when mixed with other members of *Linguistica,* specimens of *Neoplatonicus* will act as if the others do not exist (although a number of cases have been observed in which the droppings of non-*Neoplatonicus* are consumed without significant acknowledgement; cf. Whiltakers' paper "Deep Case to Thematic Role Transmutation in *Neoplatonicus* Metabolism"). In fact, members of *Neoplatonicus* are rather territorial, often refusing to cohabit with other genera. The last feature of the genus is its members' construction of separate small structures, or modules, known as "syntaxes" and "lexicons" to store foodstuffs in.

Species/Variants: By far the most numerous of the *Neoplatonicus* family are the *Americoformalisticus.* Paleobiologists speculate that waves of mutation spread through the species at periodic intervals, pushing older species into side niches with each successive wave. Variation typically involves differential use of the food-storage structures: var. *lexicoformalisticus* builds very large, elaborate lexicons, while var. *hewlettpackardius* makes little use of lexicons at all. A recently-discovered variety, *optimalicus,* appears to build rather Byzantine arrays of storage structures—and, much the way squirrels will become confused about their many caches, members of *optimalicus* can be seen scurrying hither and yon, unable to determine the appropriate storage spot. Species *fodorus* is the focus of a good bit of debate among naturalists: while it seems excessively rare, it is nevertheless quite vocal at times, leading observers to think that the overhead canopy is full of specimens that nevertheless cannot be glimpsed. One major theory about this effect is that *fodorus* has developed nulliphagic refluction to the point that it itself has become an abstract category, able to subsist in absentia, on absentia.

Interaction notes: If one encounters a *Neoplatonicus* in the wild, one should never interrupt its nulliphagic refluction; they can become rather aggressive when disturbed, and sometimes hurl detritus. And one should never, ever attempt to separate a *Neoplatonicus* from a generalization that it is feeding on—not only will the attempt fail, it apparently generates harmful psychological stress for the poor creature. Otherwise, they are tolerant of most observers, frequently not seeming to notice them at all.

There is nothing so eloquent as a rattlesnake's tail.
—TEXAN PROVERB

Genus Functionalisticus
Species: Systemicus, Cognitivus, Givonicus, Stratificarus (rare), others.

Where Found: Widely distributed, although in small numbers. *Systemicus* found locally in concentrations in Britain and Australia; clusters of *Cognitivus* observed in California. Last known sighting of *Stratificarus* was in Texas, although rumors of outliers in Michigan persist.

Characteristics: Genetic variation among *Functionalisticus* is much greater than that among *Neoplatonicus,* so much so that some biologists (e.g. Uberstrudel and Twink) have argued strongly that entirely separate genera are involved. All members, however, appear to share a preference for primary over secondary food sources, frequently passing over a field of existent droppings if a stand of juicy allomorphs is within visual range. They also all appear to be rather gregarious and interact with other mammals, although rather oddly not often with members of *Neoplatonicus.* Most biologists believe that this is the result of competition with *Neoplatonicus* for resources, particularly niches in university ecosystems. In addition, Prof. Hieronymous Smott has pointed out that there are separate and consistent lines of development between *Neoplatonicus* and *Functionalisticus* from their common ancestor, *Structuralisticus saussurii.* The internal physiognomy of *Neoplatonicus* is quite similar to that of the ancestor species, although their outward appearance is dramatically different; *Functionalisticus* retains many of the outward appearances of *saussurii* but has a dramatically altered metabolism. Droppings cannot be used to distinguish *Functionalisticus* as a genus, as there is dramatic variation among the species. When threatened, most species in the genus can generate an obscuring cloud of caveats, permitting escape undetected.

Species/Variants: *Systemicus* can be identified by both feeding pattern and droppings: members will usually approach a primary food item from three different angles before consuming it, and will alertly scan the surrounding context while eating. Biologists are not sure of the origin of this behavior, but many consider it a defensive mechanism in case the food source turns out to be dangerous (although some have argued that the behavior is simple curiosity, as this is known to be a rather mischievous species, often ransacking campers' food supplies). The droppings of *systemicus,* like those of *americoformalisticus,* have distinctive coating, although in the case of *systemicus* it consists of a hazy cocoon-like structure rather than a hard shell. The cocoon appears to contain elements common elsewhere, but used in radically different ways, making consumption by other species difficult. There is some evidence that the breeding population in Australia is undergoing speciation, as limited instances of exclusionary behaviors toward other populations have been observed. *Cognitivus* is distinguished by heavy reliance on a peculiarly well-developed visual system; members tend to have large, lemur-like eyes, and research has indicated that the visual cortex in *cognitivus* has expanded relative to other domains, and has unusually dense connections to right-hemisphere regions known to subserve metaphorical reasoning. Biologists speculate that *cognitivus* primarily evolved as nocturnal feeders in very noisy environments, making acute vision much more useful than hearing or smell. The species is primarily adapted to redwood forests, but one can only speculate that there may have

LOGICAL FALLACIES
FOR LINGUISTS

Appeal to ridicule—It's funny you think you know so much about language, Hanako, even though you're not a linguist.

been very noisy redwood forests at some point. *Givonicus* is primarily solitary, although its droppings are very widely consumed by other members of *Functionalisticus. Stratificarus* is, or was, distinguished by building enormously intricate nests of web-like structures, but these were, alas, prized in some Asian cultures as an anti-aphrodesiac. Nests could sometimes sell for hundreds of dollars, especially to women married to Larry King, and depredations of nests for sale on the black market may have forced the species to the brink of extinction.

Interaction notes: Members of *Functionalisticus* are rarely hostile but often curious, and may attempt to follow the observer about, paying close and unsettling attention to everything s/he says and does. They can frequently be distracted with single-malt scotch, however.

Do not attempt to remove a *Functionalisticus* from its context; they appear to find separation traumatic, and will refuse food.

Genus Tagmemicus
Species: Tagmemicus

Where Found: Concentrations in Oklahoma and Texas, but members scattered in low concentrations across startlingly wide range.

Characteristics: May be a singleton offshoot species, although Gnibbes (1998) classifies as being in *Functionalisticus.* Gnibbes' argument that the specimens found in Texas and Oklahoma are of the same species as the isolated specimens from elsewhere (e.g. Borneo, the Congo) is now widely accepted. Wide distribution may be due to symbiotic relationship with another species entirely, *peripateticus jaarsi. Tagmemicus* is most easily recognized by its droppings, which are largely square and which often line up into chains. Droppings widely, though sporadically, consumed by other members of *linguistica,* particularly among *functionalisticus* (hence Gnibbes' claim), but incorporate many specialized terms that apparently make digestion by other species difficult. Behavioral pattern shows interesting inversion of the nulliphagic reflection characteristic of *Neoplatonicus:* instead of metabolizing unobservable objects to provide resources to achieve reproductive goals (e.g. tenure), *Tagmemicus* metabolizes observable primary food sources to achieve unobservable ends.

Interaction notes: Generally a highly social species that reacts well to observation. May deposit droppings near observer; these are always of the same form, a large book with many chapters, and members apparently attach a very large amount of social significance to this act—Gnibbes hypothesizes that it may be an attempt to create cross-species symbiosis patterns, of the type that the species enjoys with *peripateticus jaarsi.* If the observer is seen to direct attention towards this book, *Tagmemicus* will almost always continue interaction.

Cautionary Note: Occasionally, a program-like dropping called a "RAP" is deposited instead (etymology of name unclear). Avoid contact, and wash hands thoroughly if contact unavoidable.

Genus Statisticus
Species: Corporius

Where Found: Widely distributed in low numbers.

Characteristics: Whether this is a singleton species or a genus with one surviving member is unclear—certain now-extinct species, such as *karlusfriesi,* seem to have been either precursors or related (cf. Czechzindemeyl 1985). Immediately recognizable

by its food-storage structures: while many *linguistica* species build structures to store primary food sources (e.g., the "lexicons" of the *neoplatonicus* group), *Corporius* members build vast, communal storehouses of truly impressive size. Their internal structure is usually quite simple (the entire structure may be a homogenous pile), but their volume is impressive. One located near Helsinki has been investigated thoroughly, and has been shown to contain fossilized elements dating as far back as c. 900 c.e. (it is tall enough to completely block sunlight to the north, rendering several acres uncultivatable; fortunately, the Finnish government bought the land and made it into a preserve). A fully social species, *corporius* members usually display no aggressive behavior towards other members using the same food-store, although isolated examples of exclusionary behavior have been observed. Droppings of *corporius* are characterized by inclusion of mathematical elements; unlike the droppings of *neoplatonicus,* these appear to be similar or identical to real mathematics, and some scholars (Gnibbes 1998 being a good example) have argued that *corporius* may be a rare example of cross-family fertility between *mathematica* and *linguistica.*[2]

Interaction notes: A species that manages to be simultaneously social and reclusive, *corporius* is best observed in its native habitat: small dark offices with high-speed fiber optic networks. May become skittish in presence of observers, but providing primary food items (Jolt Cola and Doritos, for example) usually calms them down.

When gold talks, speech is useless.
—LATIN PROVERB

---

[2] Since cross-family fertility would destroy the basis of all traditional biological taxonomy, the author is not basing the current discussion on the hypothesis.

Studying Linguistics
How to get out of your degree program alive, *or,* Do you want fries with that?

SPECGRAM IS WRITTEN BY LIN-guists. All of us, every one. Not a non-linguist among the crowd. Ever. And the fact that we all belong to the class of *linguists* presupposes that all of us have studied linguistics. *To study,* of course, is a telic verb, with the inherent end-point commonly labeled *degree* or at least *ascribed title.* So being a linguist implies having studied linguistics—but we've already mentioned that, have we not? Yes, we have. Sorry, let's move on.[1]

The point is, each and every one of *Speculative Grammarian*'s illustrious contributors can claim a share in the fraternity of *students of linguistics* (where *students* has a perfective aspectual reading). We have shared in the joys, the sorrows, the inexpressible emotional roller-coaster upon which linguistics courses have thrust us—primarily the inutterable[2] joy of attending the first lecture of a new class and the absolute sorrow of handing in a final exam and walking back out into the cold, hard non-linguistic world for yet another painful semester break devoid of linguistics lectures to calm the soul. There is no

Surprisingly, Marty found that his small talk skills had actually **declined** during his summer at linguistics school

So does **your** idiolect distinguish between the past tense of a small "catch" and portable bed?

BUS STOP

lightness of the spirit that can equal the pleasure of raising one's hand (first!) to make a point about grammatical relations, nor any depth of despair that can surpass the horrible realization that one has already completed all the courses offered by the linguistics department, and that one can take no more classes in the field. (But, O!, the extremity of joy at realizing that one can go on to pursue a higher degree!)[3]

But one cannot simply study. From our first courses in documentary linguistics, we$_{INCL}$ have all learned as a matter of course that one must *learn about learning,* that one must *learn how to learn,* that metadata is more fundamental even than data itself. (At least,

DISSECTION

extracted from the ether
it lies
black splayed out against the white
sliced open from head to foot
internal structure revealed
glosses pin down slippery meanings
messy particles resisting...
the interlinear text.

—BRYAN ALLEN

---

[1] Some readers of early drafts of this book commented that we had gone "overboard" on the use of footnotes in some chapters, and requested that we remove some of them.

[2] See footnote 1 on page 97 in the Syntax chapter. See, footnotes really *are* really useful!

[3] These readers seemed to believe that somehow the footnotes were not integral to the significance of the text.

that's what we_{EXCL} learned. Perhaps some of you learned something else, but if so, we suggest that you keep it to yourselves.)[4]

Speculative Grammarian always has the edification of the complete person in mind. We attempt to cover all that needs to be said about every linguistic subdiscipline (except semantics, which is a complete waste of time), not to mention all that a linguist or linguist-in-training needs to know about the practice of linguistics and about the field itself. It stands to reason, then, that the hallowed pages of our journal should be a fount of wisdom about the study of linguistics, about linguistics students, and about the relationship between the two.[5]

And indeed, it is not. That is to say, we have published a few jots and tittles here and there on the subject of studying linguistics, but not as much as you might expect, considering our reputation and the vastness of our archives. Nonetheless, we feel that the gems of insight which have graced our pages are truly indispensable for any student of the field, and we are pleased that this book gives us the opportunity to collect them in one place. Which we do in this chapter.[6]

WOULD YOU LIKE SPAGHETTI OR LASAGNA FOR DINNER?

Ph.D. Supervisor: "I don't care about spaghetti or lasagna, what I want is a completed thesis!"

LOGICAL FALLACIES FOR LINGUISTS

Better-than-average effect—95% of linguistics undergraduates think they are better than the median linguistics student at writing papers.

---

[4] We cheerfully ignored this input concerning our footnoting style, on the grounds that said readers (whose recruitment for this role none of the editors will admit to having been involved with) did not evince clear logical thinking skills.

[5] Nor did they convince us that our footnotes were in any way deficient.

[6] Furthermore, their comments about our footnotes weren't even polite.

We really must start off here with a book that any student of linguistics really must have on his or her shelf. Well, no, not on the shelf—in the mind! This book must be studied, must be memorized; it must inform everything that the student in linguistics does. Because in How to Cheat at Linguistics, *respected linguist Geoffrey Sagum tells the eager student everything he or she needs to know to make it through anything from Linguistics 101, right on through to writing a publishable paper!**

How to Cheat at Linguistics

Geoffrey Sagum
Psammeticus Textbooks in Linguistics
Published 2005. Softcover, 113 pages. Price: $17.95
($0.00 if you steal it!)

From the practical to the arcane, *How to Cheat at Linguistics* offers an admirably comprehensive guide to the field's standard answers. The book is written at a level which should be accessible to both undergraduates and pre-comprehensive graduate students.

In a general introductory chapter, *How to Cheat* includes description of standard cheating techniques, including testing strategies from the time-honored crib notes to today's PDAs and text messages. More interesting to linguists-in-training, however, will be the sections aimed specifically at the heart of the discipline. Beginning with answers to over-used problems, such as Turkish vowel harmony, *How to Cheat* continues on to give summary answers to the exercises presented in most major textbooks in current use. A further stroke of brilliance is an entire chapter devoted to how to invent data for a research paper, complete with a list of spurious and difficult-to-locate references, sure to throw off any but the most dedicated professorial pursuer.

No matter what school of thought one's examiners might subscribe to, *How to Cheat* provides a synopsis of what they will ask, and how the clever student can surely get by, with a minimum of effort. Useful to students at just about any level, the book is sure to become a standard reference in the field.

THE WISDOM OF LINGUISTS
Grad student see, grad student do.

MURPHY'S LAW FOR LINGUISTS
Your committee will always include at least one member who has no idea where the country you visited is located.

---

* So who cares what they think anyway?†

† They can just take their footnote-less prose and crawl back into their own caves.‡

‡ And leave us alone.§

§ To do our scholarship the way we know it should be...¶

¶ ...done.

*Now, beyond that specific advice, the graduate student in particular is going to want to have some general tips on how to survive graduate school. The following guide, by Dr. Wolf Kitty, assumes a particular trajectory in linguistics (for the sake of illustration)—but anyone smart enough to get into grad school can easily apply the same principles in any linguistic subfield.**

How to Get a Ph.D. Without Really Trying
And Maybe Even Get A Date In The Process

Dr. Wolf Kitty, B.S. Ph.D.

- Pick your field carefully. Do not go into mathematics.

- Do not choose a science, such as physics. These fields have objective standards by which your lack of contribution can be measured.

- Do not choose a liberal art, such as literary criticism. Here the standards are wholly and unashamedly subjective, which means that you will have to read a lot in order to find out what other people think, and then write a lot to show that what you think is exactly like what they think, only different. In the absence of objectivity, all that really matters is what your advisor thinks; so why bother with all the reading and writing?

- Avoid arithmetic, too, while you're at it. It's boring to count stuff, let alone do statistics on it afterward. Eschew psychology.

- Instead, pick a field with "physics envy". (This phrase is often bandied about to demonstrate sophisticated intellectual detachment—a way of washing one's mental hands after acts of mental self-gratification—but the elegant self-referentiality of the phrase is seldom appreciated: it invokes a non-scientific conceptual framework claimed to capture universal truths about human thought, and then carefully inserts a reference

to a real science, to incongruous and hilarious effect.) In such a field, you can coast along on the illusion of objectivity, which your advisor, your committee, and everyone else with tenure has a vested interest in preserving. To question your work, or whether you've actually done any, is to call the whole field into question, and nobody wants that. You need not worry that your dissertation defense will be disrupted by any naive persons with an eye for the absence of imperial vesture.

- Even in physics-envious fields, strange as it may seem, there are some subfields that have more to prove. In linguistics, say (picking a completely random example), phonology and syntax are at the top of the ivory tower. This is because they have more theoretical infrastructure, i.e. notation; and because phonology is grounded in observable and indisputable phonetic fact, while syntacticians control the world supply of asterisks.

On the other hand, sociolinguistics and discourse pragmatics occupy the ivory sewer. These disciplines (to use the word as loosely as they use all terminology) constitute what has been called "the soft underbelly of linguistics"—this in a field not noted for its overall muscle definition. Even to other linguists, sociolinguists are hard put to demonstrate that their subject matter really exists; and there isn't even a word for people who specialize in discourse pragmatics.

---

* And we also resent the suggestion that our use of footnotes is somehow a "problem" that needs "solving."

You will by now be wearying of the effort required to read this, and wondering when it gets to the part about getting a date. Let us stipulate, therefore, that—after a few years of due deliberation, during which you may be compelled to obtain a master's degree—you choose to write your dissertation on sociolinguistics.

- Choose an ambitious topic. The key here is that academics in the humanities are drawn to what they will never understand: literary critics don't understand how writers write, psychologists don't understand how people think, and philosophers don't understand anything at all. By the same token, your committee members will be irresistibly baffled by human interactions. Tell them you're going to study how the telemarketer last night convinced your advisor to switch long-distance carriers.

- Spend the next decade or so attending the occasional seminar, teaching undergrad general-education requirements, discovering underpriced wines from unusual little wineries, and traveling abroad every summer. As a graduate student laboring in the vineyards of knowledge, your cheap labor is being exploited; the compensation is the cheap student fares. You may also get to travel (possibly even at university expense) during the academic year, if you can find appropriate conferences: preferably ones which require only an abstract, rather than actual manuscripts to be published in the proceedings. In the worst case, however, one can submit the same manuscript (such as the 50-page master's thesis one was compelled to produce) under several different titles.

  Do not rush this phase. Savor the freedom from responsibility, the freedom from effort, the freedom from annoyances of any kind. You have nothing to lose but your hair. When nubile first-year graduate students mistake you for a faculty member, you have achieved the exalted status of "Übergrad".

- You are ready to be decanted when the dean's office starts expressing official concerns about your department's graduation rates, and when the formidably intelligent member of your thesis committee has gotten tenure at a more prestigious university and been replaced by someone younger than yourself. Your advisor, meanwhile, would really like to switch back to Sprint, but doesn't know quite how to bring the subject up.

  After making a few phone calls and surfing the net for an hour or so, announce promptly at the beginning of the next semester that telemarketing conversations are kept confidential in order to protect the gullible. Your advisor will be secretly relieved.

- Since you have done everything you reasonably could to collect real data, with only three months to go before the dean's official deadline and department credibility hanging in the balance, your committee will now be glad to let you generate your own data.

  Recruit eight or ten nubile first-year graduate students (even undergraduates will do, if carefully screened to make sure they're over 18). Have them take turns pretending to be telemarketers. Record the conversations for posterity. As your committee will certainly agree, these data in themselves constitute a valuable contribution to the field.

- After your subjects have participated in the experiment, conduct exit interviews in which you ask them to complete questionnaires on the effectiveness of various pickup lines. Sample questions (some of which will necessarily vary with the gender of your subjects):

Which of the following lines would be most likely to convince you to go out with me this Friday night?

a. Hi! I'm a cunning linguist. Get it?

b. What's a nice interlocutor like you doing in a speech community like this?

c. Is that a maximal projection or are you just happy to see me?

d. If you were a verb, and I were a noun, would you incorporate me?

e. Are you into Government and Binding? Your c-wish is my c-command.

f. If I said you had a beautiful body, would you hold it against me?

Be sure to keep the use-versus-mention distinction handy to placate the Human Subjects Committee and avoid harassment charges. Preserve a thin veneer of linguistic legitimacy for question (f) by pointing out that it is ambiguous, and discussing whether the ambiguity is lexical or syntactic.

• Pull a few all-nighters writing a hundred pages or so analyzing which linguistic strategies succeed or fail in pretending to try to persuade people to pretend to buy things. Demonstrate your rigorous scientific standards and your grasp of mathematical methodology in linguistics by acknowledging that the sample size that could be gathered within the limited time available is, of course, too small for meaningful statistical analysis. Conclude, however, that your qualitative results indubitably raise provocative questions for future research.

WOULD YOU LIKE SPAGHETTI OR LASAGNA FOR DINNER?

Graduate Student: "Which one can I finish faster?"

LOGICAL FALLACIES FOR LINGUISTS

Appeal to motive—"Everyone knows that the only reason you got tenure, Swunhi, is that your thesis advisor was on the review committee."

In a similar vein, Kai Tak Suvarnabhumi gives advice for the graduate student hoping to complete a fieldwork-based dissertation. Again, although this is specific advice, anyone with half a brain can figure out how to modify it to apply to any dissertation or master's thesis on any linguistic topic.*

Writing a Fieldwork Dissertation

Kai Tak Suvarnabhumi
Independent Scholar

Fieldwork is an age-old tradition in Linguistics, and the fieldwork dissertation is, too, dating back at least to the age of Boas. While there is much to celebrate in this tradition—especially the very fact of its resurgence since the mid-1990s—there remain certain intractable problems which we, as linguists, have failed to address systematically. One of these problems, of course, is the lack of clear, systematic guidance for the novitiate in the realm of producing an acceptable doctoral screed. Though this brief article admittedly falls far short of the complete treatise that is needed, I promise to expand it eventually into a full-length book. In the meantime, I would like to offer just these few points to aid those pitiable doctoral candidates who lack sufficient guidance for their compositional task.

Choosing an advisor

The advisor is the most critical part of your dissertation experience. You want one who is appropriate for the task, and this is a lot more difficult to arrange than you might expect. On the one hand, you have to avoid the Überfieldworker, whose 36 years of language analysis (including seven years of living in the language community) have resulted in the perception that "grammatical description" means eight volumes; on the other hand, you have equally to watch out for the theoretician who will perceive you as the coauthor (unacknowledged)

of chapter 6 of her next book on theta roles (or some other topic of marginal relevance to the language you are actually working on), and will "guide" your research along this track. The perfect fieldwork dissertation advisor has done some fieldwork, but is neither ostentatiously proud nor meekly humble about it. Furthermore, he or she can be neither too interested nor too uninterested in your own project.

Choosing a theory

Depending on your department, the prevailing doctrinal winds, and most especially your advisor, you may have actually some choice as to which theoretical "model" you use to frame your study. If so, choose wisely, because you will have to live with the results of your choice for three or four years. If you are lucky, the theory you choose will still have a few adherents when you interview for your first job. It is unlikely to survive until the publication of your dissertation as a book, but this does not matter much, since the publication of books is not related to the current state of the field.

Choosing fieldwork software

More than any other single factor, software can really make or break your linguistic fieldwork. It's important to have the ideal suite of programs for the work you want to do. Most likely you don't want to pay for software, so you probably are going to stick to standard Microsoft issue such as FreeCell and Hearts. Don't be too frugal, though;

---

* We do not have a "problem" with footnotes. This is scholarship; we use them when they are appropriate.

you may increase your productivity dramatically if you shell out some cash for top of the line Electronic Arts games. Online gaming is ok, but MMORPGs are to be avoided if at all possible—innumerable field projects in the last 5 years have been scuttled due to online conflicts between the fieldworker and his[1] host community that spilled over into real life.

You may also want some form of academic software, and I am proud to recommend to you the software produced by my own— *[Editor's Note: to avoid the prospect of lawsuits or the appearance of editorial impropriety, Suvarnabhumi's recommendations have been redacted. Also, there is no point in recommending software, since it is invariably out of date before the recommendation is even published.]*

Preparing for fieldwork

There are an ever-increasing number of books about linguistic fieldwork, but as I have not read any of them I will mention only *The Innocent Anthropologist*. Although this book is purportedly anthropological in thrust, its basic testimony is one of jumping to rather grand theoretical conclusions based on severely limited data, in the midst of a series of daily living disasters which could have been avoided with only a little foresight and common sense, and thus it is excellent preparation for fieldwork in linguistics as well.

Gathering data

Once you get to the field, don't follow anyone's recommendations about gathering data. This is a personal matter, best not discussed in public. Just realize ahead of time that you won't gather enough data, no matter how you try, and be prepared. Smiles are good for the heart, and somehow healing.

Finishing your dissertation

You can count on your advisor getting tired of your project. (Not until long after you've gotten tired of it, most likely.) Before this happens, though, innumerable "suggestions" will be made, ostensibly in pursuit of "improving" your work; probably some reference will also be made to your marketability as a job candidate (not in precisely those terms). Do not be alarmed—this is normal.

At some point your advisor, whether or not she is a fan of A. A. Milne, will come to agree with Rabbit that "having got so far, it seems a pity to waste it." At this juncture, she will stop making suggestions related to content and will instead start pointing out that there may be a shortage of funding for next year and you may need to consider an off-campus job, or even a TAship in the English or ESL department. At this point, the time is right. Make a few more minor adjustments (about 25 should do it; be sure to change at least one grammatical category label) and turn in another entire draft. It will be cheerfully approved. You are done.

Parting encouragement

On the whole, there are roughly about six thousand serious errors you could make in the design and execution of a fieldwork project, and a similar number that could derail your attempt to massage a dissertation out of the resulting field notes (if you produce any notes at all). The project may be worthwhile, or it may not. There's just no way to tell beforehand.

THE WISDOM OF LINGUISTS
You can't teach an old professor new theories.

---

[1] Such cases invariably involve men who cannot distinguish MMORPGs from other types of "real" life.

Almost any degree program in linguistics (now that endangered languages have been discovered) is going to include a course in Linguistic Field Methods. Typically this is either the easiest course in a program of study (e.g., if the class works on a tonal language, since even the professor will quickly give up hope of analyzing that), or the hardest course the student will encounter (e.g., if the professor is an expert in the language being studied). In either case, we highly recommend that no one approach a field methods course without first gaining a high proficiency in the universal field work language Swadesh. A good textbook for this can be purchased from Panini Press:*

Learn to Speak Swadesh in One Hundred Easy Lessons!

Panini Press

Hey, Grad Students! We're talking to you! Do you need a "research language" that will also help to fulfill a "fieldwork" requirement? SpecGram is delighted to recommend to you the newest offering from our friends at Panini Press: *Learn to Speak Swadesh in One Hundred Easy Lessons!*

Swadesh is an indispensable and supremely easy language which will open doors for you in nearly any fieldwork situation. Just one hundred lessons will have you speaking Swadesh fluently! Plus, Swadesh is the only Indo-European language known to be accepted as satisfying a "research language" requirement by at least 25 major university linguistics departments.

Order your copy now, and start learning Swadesh right away! ☙पा

---

* It's not like we just throw in footnotes for fun.

Well, how about that! We seem to have let ourselves wander down the garden path of specificity again, perhaps without giving an adequate general overview of the joys and problems of being a linguistics student. What you really hoped for in this chapter was some insightful essay which outlines all that you will face when you jump headlong into a linguistics degree program. Right?

Well, forget it. There is no such essay, and we have never published anything even remotely that comprehensive in Speculative Grammarian. We don't believe any linguist will ever even attempt to write such an article or such a book. What would be the point of attempting the impossible?

Instead of that, though, we do want to offer here a collage of uplifting vignettes which may, we hope, encourage your little heart as you set off into the vast unknown of your degree program. Here they are—three poems and two cartoons—enjoy!*

This Little Linguist

Yune O. Hūū, II

This little linguist put transcription in square brackets,
This little linguist used slashes for some,
This little linguist traced *gwou-* back from *beef,*
This little linguist had etymologies for none,
And this little linguist cried, /wi wi wi/,
    all the way back to the grad student lounge.

Spaz Attack in the Corner

III

---

* And yes, whatever those critics may say, we can stop using footnotes any time we feel like it.

A Yonge Philologiste's First Drynkynge Poime

Anonymous

Whan that Apryl, with hir bosooms soote,
The draughtes of beere hath feched barefoote
And filled every coppe with swich licour
Of which vertu engendred is the hange ouer;
Whan Stephanie, eek with hir sweete brests,
Inspired hath al the harts and chests
And tender crotshes of e'ery yonge sonne,
Who hath in the Room dremt of Yvonne,
And smale soules maken melodye,
Not slepen, al the nyght with open eye—
(So priketh hem wymyn in ther corages);
Thanne longen folk to goon rommpages,
And firstyeeres for to seken straunge bedstondes,
With ferme calwes, kowthe of sondry blondes;
But finially at every desires ende
To Scriptoria, to Philologie they wende,
Unhooly blisful fornicacioun forseken
By hem, that Oxenford clerkes they may wel wexen.

A translation and annotation, kindly provided by Allister Barnard Cavendish Donglewood Edmund Featherstone-Glatton, IV (Class of 2005 and Head Boy of the Oxford Young Philologists Dormitory), follows:

A Young Philologist's First Drinking Poem

When that Apryl, with her bosoms sweet,
The drafts of beer has fetched barefoot,
And filled every cup with such liquor
Of which virtue is engendered the hangover;
When Stephanie, also with her sweet breasts,
Inspired has all the hearts and chests
And tender crotches of every young son,
Who has in the Room dreamt of Yvonne,
And small souls make melody,
Not sleeping, all the night with open eye—
(So prick them women in their courage);
Then long folk to go on rampages,
And first-years for to seek strange bed stands,
With firm calves, known of sundry blondes;
But finally at every desires end,
To Scriptoriums, to Philology they wend,
Unholy blisful fornication forsaken
By them, that Oxford scholars they may well become.

This anonymous poem, recently—and appropriately—discovered by an Oxford Philology fourth-year in an ancient copy of Chaucer's *Canterbury Tales,* celebrates the traditional temptations suffered by young men aspiring to become Oxford Philologists in the early 1300s. Barmaids, buxom and barefoot in summer months, served the young men strong drink for as long as they could stand (and pay). These, and other comely lasses near Oxford, inspired the "tender crotches" of these bookish—and usually virginal—lads. Surely these man-boys would dream in "the Room" (as the Oxford Dormitory for Young Philologists was popularly known) of "making melody" with their favorite townswoman.

Modern scholars still debate whether a "small soul" refers to one's genitals, or to one's dream self. Whether the young lad in question "makes melody" within a dream, or dreams of making melodies with his genitals, the meaning is clear, and clearly kept many a young man up all night. These lads, their courage ("heart", "feelings", or, more likely, "sexual desire") pricked, they—especially the first-years, or freshman—long to go on rampages of sexual conquest, seeking "strange bed stands" of various blondes (and brunettes and red-heads) with shapely legs.

For those who would become true Philologists, though, these desires must end, as they trudge off to the Scriptorium or to Philology lectures, the chance of fornication forsaken, so that they may become proper Oxford Scholars.

In Space, No One Can Hear You Scream

Keith W. Slater

In space, no one can hear you scream

I opened my ears and the stars came down
speakers of languages I once called *exotic*
    but now call *data*
streamed like a starfield
    across reams and pages
        of luminescent notebooks

howled
    (like so many monstrous experiments)
        the Ancient Breath of Dissertation
and sighed a degree into being.

By degrees, I pass from this starfield to the next,
    the ancient howling, dying, mutely speaking a deeper horror:
the revision.

Linguistics Nerd Camp

Bethany Carlson

Marsha and her thesis made a cute couple, but their friends worried that she was trying to change him

Maybe we spoke too soon. While there may be no essay insightful enough to outline all that you will face when you jump headlong into a linguistics degree program, it is only because you will be faced with so many options. The best way to approach the discussion is with a multifoliate hypertext adventure game. So, as a service to young and impressionable readers who are considering pursuing a career in linguistics, Trey Jones has provided the following Gedankenexperiment to help you understand the possibilities and consequences of doing so. For our old and bitter readers who are too far along in their careers to have any real hope of changing the eventual outcome, the following serves as a cruel reminder of what might have been.**

Choose Your Own Career in Linguistics

Trey Jones

CHOOSE YOUR OWN CAREER IN LINGUISTICS—PART 1

LET THE ADVENTURE BEGIN...

You are a freshman at a respectable university and, in order to fulfill some elective requirements, you sign up for Linguistics 101 because it looks easy and it's scheduled for MWF at 11, which is tolerable. After a semester of linguistics, you find you enjoy learning odd facts about odd languages and it really isn't too hard, so you sign up for Linguistics 102 in the spring. The second class is a little harder, and the phonology midterm leaves many of the other students mumbling about how if they wanted an elective this hard they could have taken economics. You pass the phonology midterm with flying colors and your professor suggests majoring in linguistics, and then does so again after you are the only student in the class who seems to grok C-command during the syntax unit. You say you'll think it over.

• Major in linguistics. Go to Part 3 on page 51.

• Major in something else. Go to Part 2 on page 247.

CHOOSE YOUR OWN CAREER IN LINGUISTICS—THE END

THE END...

Thanks for playing "Choose Your Own Career in Linguistics". Unlike in real life, you can try again and see if you can manage a better outcome. If this is your third or fourth trip through and you aren't getting end results you like, maybe you just aren't cut out for linguistics. Good luck!

MURPHY'S LAW FOR LINGUISTS

A job for a field linguist specializing in your area will always open one month after you leave for the field and will close two weeks before your defense.

THE WISDOM OF LINGUISTS

A linguist in the lab is better than two in the bush.

---

* If you are still young, you might want to bookmark this page and keep trying until you get it "right". If you are old, avert your eyes and turn the page now!†

† Now there's a quality footnote!

As a final note, we want to caution linguistics students against gullible acceptance of so much of the falsehood that passes for scholarship in today's world of linguistics. In particular, students must learn early to spot fabricated data, published analyses of which have caused so much heartache for the field. As usual, our own Tim Pulju provides the cautions necessary in this area.*

How to Spot Fabricated Data

Tim Pulju
Rice University

As the managing editor of a linguistics journal, I have frequent opportunity to review submissions authored by linguists who are, in a word, gullible. I refer particularly to those field linguists who have been taken in by elicited data whose preposterous nature should be evident. Apparently, many field linguists do not realize that native speakers in many cultures make fun of outsiders by teaching the language to such outsiders incorrectly. Thus, the gullible student, having learned that the correct way to say "Where is the bathroom?" in Yogad is *Yu igungku ay atannang*, will be entirely confused when this utterance elicits either no response, or at best an "Oh. So what?"

You might think that linguists would examine their data carefully enough to be able to spot deliberate misinformation, but alas, experience shows that this is not always the case. We at *SpecGram* have always managed to catch such errors, mostly due to the brilliant work of associate editors and other members of the editorial board. However, other reputable journals have not been so careful. For example, consider the following example from Hawaiian (I have omitted citation to avoid embarrassing authors and editors):

> *Aia i ʻAiea i ʻauʻau aʻe ai ia iʻa i ʻai ʻia e aʻu*
> 'It was in ʻAiea that the fish I ate had been swimming.'

This sentence is obviously phonologically ridiculous. No one would ever say such a phonologically ridiculous thing except in jest.

Even worse is the Maori sentence below:

> *i aueeauee a au i aua auaa*
> 'Those herrings made me scream and scream.'

This utterance has twenty vowels and no consonants, which is plain silly. But not only is it phonologically ridiculous, it is also semantically preposterous. 'Those herrings made me scream and scream?' Come on, already.

Then there are grammatically ridiculous sentences. Once I was writing a book on Nez Perce, and pretty late in the process I discovered a sentence which didn't fit into my grammar. That is, my grammatical rules prohibited such sentences from occurring in the language, but here was one staring me in the face. Luckily, I realized that this was an obvious example of a fabricated sentence which I was obliged to eliminate from the data. Since then, I have become very adept at eliminating grammatically ridiculous sentences from my data. To my surprise, it usually turns out that about 70% of the corpus is grammatically ridiculous and should be excised.

I hope the above will be useful to field linguists. In closing, let me state that although I have limited myself to fabricated utterances in this article, it stands to reason that there are also fabricated languages. For example, Bella Coola, a so-called Salishan language, is obviously phonetically ridiculous through and through. I don't believe that anyone speaks Bella Coola natively, and I urge linguists to stop being taken in by those wily inhabitants of British Columbia. The same goes for anyone out there who still believes in French.

(Acknowledgements: I would like to thank Keith W. Slater for working with me on the early stages of this article.)

---

* In fact, we have published many articles that did not include a single footnote.

Wait, that wasn't the final note. We also want to caution students against gullible acceptance of so-called "theoretical primitives" in the field of linguistics. Notable among these is the audacious claim that there are "native speakers" of any given language. Keith W. Slater (also "our own" if we are forced to admit it) outlines the problems with this laughable "theory".*

By the way, we also suggest that linguistics students should make proper use of footnotes, because that's a good way to impress readers with the breadth of one's thinking concerning a wide range of implications of—and noteworthy considerations tangential to—the topics one writes about. But we don't have any articles about that to share. So please take this as free but unsubstantiated advice.†

The Native Speaker Fallacy

Keith W. Slater
Michigan State University

Linguists are people, and must thus be expected to believe some foolish things—if perhaps fewer than the general populace. However, some commonly held opinions are simply too ludicrous to be allowable; it is one such absurdity that I will here disprove—the Native Speaker Fallacy.

For years, linguists have appealed to the judgements of native speakers of various languages as to the grammaticality, semantic import, and/or phonological contrastiveness of various natural or constructed utterances. While this method of supporting one's arguments is in itself suspect, it is nonetheless only an unfortunate result of an unspoken but deeply held conviction which rests on two key principles:

1. There are native speakers of any given language, and
2. these native speakers can be identified with certainty.

Both of these principles have usually been considered self-evident; however, both can be shown to be essentially ad hoc, and therefore untenable, in their usual formulations.

Disproof of the Native Speaker Fallacy has eluded linguists in the past for two major reasons. Primarily, the requisite method of demonstrating its falsity has remained unimagined. Additionally, no one has bothered to attempt to imagine it. Until now.

The vehicle for disproving the Native Speaker Fallacy is a fairly simple experiment involving grammaticality judgements of five sentences taken from the text of an early campaign speech by Richard Nixon. The sentences, presented in Table 1, include two which are clearly grammatical, two which are clearly ungrammatical, and one which is most definitely strange:

---

1. The leaves that are on the tree are green.
2. A giant squid is eating John's sister in the backyard.
3. Dog the in dragged big yellow stupid because in in at.
4. When yesterday the yield sign, tomorrow that the stop light came again and went.
5. Ikan akan sedang dimakan oleh lakilaki.

Table 1: Sentences Used in This Test

Subjects were simply asked to discriminate verbally between the choices "grammatical" and "ungram-

---

* So there.

† *Best. Footnote. Ever.*

matical." Results of this discrimination are presented in Table 2.

Sentence	"Yes"	"No"	Unsure	"Huh?"
1	56%	31%	10%	3%
2	50%	25%	22%	3%
3	28%	41%	28%	3%
4	20%	33%	44%	3%
5	11%	58%	28%	3%

$\Sigma = 12$ $\quad \mu > .478333$ $\quad \xi < 5$ $\quad \varepsilon = 96.8\%$

Table 2: Grammaticality Judgements

The subjects for this investigation were 36 self-professed "native speakers" of English. None had ever left the United States; nor had any studied any foreign languages at all. Thirty-five were senior undergraduate students of Political Science at a small Eastern liberal arts college, and one was a tobacco farmer. All were between the ages of 10 and 87. Two students who had taken introductory linguistics classes were excluded from the sample.

Discussion

The data in Table 2 show that, generally, "native speakers" are able to correctly identify grammatically correct and incorrect sentences. However, the percentages are not nearly so clear-cut as many linguists might have hoped. Fully 44% of the subjects failed, for example, to correctly identify sentence 1 as grammatical. Likewise, 67% were unable to recognize the fact that sentence 4 is clearly ungrammatical. Even more disturbing is the failure of a whopping 97% to realize that sentence 5 is not even English at all, but simply some Indonesian that the future Chief Executive had been practicing and inadvertently slipped into his speech.

The obvious conclusion from these facts is that not all of the subjects in this test can honestly be called "native speakers" of English. Performance errors could conceivably account for some of the mistakes, but certainly not so many as are clearly

present here. These facts must force us to reconsider our conception of "native speaker" status for English, and by implication, for any language.

The simple fact that a person has never spoken any language except hypothetical language X does not, apparently, guarantee that he/she is a native speaker of language X. Conceivably, one could be trained (with years of practice) to imitate a native speaker of some language, without actually being one. There is another, equally plausible explanation: a person might simply not be a native speaker of any language at all. Together, these two possibilities provide ample explanatory justification for the results obtained in this investigation.

The author gratefully acknowledges the support of the National Science Foundation, without which this research could have not been undertaken. In deference to the Foundation, the original title "Linguistics ruined by NSF" was discarded.

WOULD YOU LIKE SPAGHETTI OR LASAGNA FOR DINNER?

Teaching Assistant: "Does either of them come with a parking pass?"

MURPHY'S LAW FOR LINGUISTS

The most heavily weighted question on an exam is never the one you studied for.

Linguistic Love Poetry
Crazy little thing called wug

Despite popular images to the contrary, linguists are, generally speaking, people, too. Most are believed to actually have hearts, and/or heart-like structures, and many may even feel actual feelings.[1] As the paramour of any linguist must concede, it takes a special kind of person to love a linguist: patient, curious, and intelligent.[2]

A major problem for the love life of linguists is that studying linguistics irreparably damages the brain, creating an independent component that analyzes every word the linguist in question hears, or even says. Young linguists in particular often have not learned how to control the data acquisition and verification impulses of this component—inappropriately blurting out things like "Can you really say that?" and "Oh, wow, you have really interesting vowels!"[3] Linguists also tend to get irrationally upset when asked, as they so often are, how many languages they speak.

Despite their social awkwardness, linguists, as a people, are—if we may be so bold as to generalize—warm, caring, and affectionate. If you, Dear Reader, would like to try to domesticate a linguist of your very own, consider making a mood-appropriate selection from among these fine love poems, as an ice-breaker, as a way to "move things to the next level", or as an unequivocal admission of undying affection. To *really* impress a linguistically inclined potential paramour, present a poem, then sit still and listen with rapt attention to the unavoidable explanation of the deep linguistic symbolism contained therein.[4,5]

Or, in case of the pangs of heartbreak, seek solace in the sympathetic stanzas of similar sentiment.

No matter your romantic condition, these vignettes of love, lust, longing, loss, and linguistics are sure to stir your heart.

---

[1] With the possible exception of linguistic behaviorists in the tradition of B. F. Skinner. See Skinner's *Verbal Behavior.*

[2] Or maybe oblivious, thick-skinned, and dim. That would probably work, too.

[3] For a sad example, see the tale of Marty in Chapter 20.

[4] Try *SpecGram* Brand™ /kæfin/ tablets on your next date with a linguist!

[5] **DO NOT** try to follow Schadenpoodle's "Field Guide to Linguists" in Chapter 19 as a dating guide. It has been tried and the results were not pretty.

This catchy ditty was originally written by Christine Collins as a song, and, given the right musical chops, is probably best performed that way. However, for the non-tunefully-inclined, it works as an upbeat poem, too.

λ♥[love]
(Linguistics Love Song)

Christine Collins

Need to win the heart of a linguist? It's your lucky day! Here is a convenient, terminology-dropping, non-gender-specific love song for all your linguist-seducing needs.

let me have your heart and i will give you love
the denotation of my soul is the above
if there's anything i lack, it's you
as my double brackets,
      you make me mean things
i can't say enough

consider me your anaphor, i'm bound to you
there's no one else that i could be referring to
your features all attract me
we're such a perfect match, please agree with me
i need to be with you

well i don't know how to say
      exactly how i feel about you
'cuz it seems my broca's area
      stops working right around you
forgive me my disfluency,
      there's nothing i can do, you see
you speak to me, linguistically i'm yours

now i know you tend to isolate,
      and that's all right
like free morphemes
      you and i could lead our separate lives
but if we were to agglutinate
together we would do so great
and i'd hate to miss the words we could derive

well i don't know how to say
      exactly how i feel about you
'cuz it seems my broca's area
      stops working right around you
forgive me my disfluency,
      there's nothing i can do, you see
you speak to me, and linguistically i'm yours

so please don't be my allophone and disappear
really awkwardly whenever i start getting near
let's be a minimal pair
'cuz i'm totally cool with us both being there
my environment is better when you're here
my environment is better when you're here
my environment is better when you're here

While perhaps well suited only to the wooing of a phonetician, the verse of Epiphanios o Phantasiopliktos speaks the universal language of /lʌv/.

The Phonetician's Love Poem

Epiphanios o Phantasiopliktos

Sweet modulations of fundamental frequency
Air particles dancing to and fro
Greeting each other as they pass
Alongside soft tissue and mucous membrane
Playing airily on varying wavelengths
And somewhere in my inner ear
Ossicles and hair cells take up the call
Now a firework of neuronal excitement
As this voice of yours, a memory though,
Soft, sweet, soothing sounds
So lovely, so charming, such delight
Oh! never fades from my mind.

For a more somber and knowing approach to mature love, consider the following by Rasmus Burns; 'tis a more traditional love poem in a classic style.

My Love is Like a Colorless Green Simile

Rasmus Burns

O my love's like a colorless green simile
That's newly sprung from your lips.
O my love's like the rhythmic prosody
That gently sways your hips.

As fair art thou, my bonnie lass,
So deep in love am I.
And I will love thee still my Dear,
Tho' all languages should die.

Tho' all languages should die, my Dear,
And ev'ry speaker calm his tongue:
I will love thee still, my Dear,
Even tho' the words have gone.

And fare thee well, my Love,
And fare thee well, a while!
And I will speak again, my Love,
Tho' it be only grunts and sighs.

Poet John Miaou captures the complementary nature of love in its many allomorphs, while acknowledging that ultimately, as with the tongue and free variation, the heart wants what the heart wants.

Love Queries of a Linguist

John Miaou

If I were a stop, would you be my explosion?
If I were a nasal, would you be my syllabification?
If I were an utterance, would you be my intonation?
And if I were a sound wave, would you be my perception?

If I were a noun, would you be my qualification?
If I were a verb, would you be my inflection?
If I were a sentence, would you be my topicalization?
And if I were a passive, would you be my activation?

If I were a statement, would you be my proposition?
If I were a premise, would you be my conclusion?
If I were an argument, would you be my confirmation?
And if I were the truth, would you be my contradiction?

Finally, two poems not for courting, but rather tinged with bitterness, sadness, and yearning for that which can never be again, from Alex Savoy and Edgar Allan Slater.

How Do I Love Thee?
Let Me Draw a Tree Diagram

Alex Savoy

How do I love thee? Let me draw a tree diagram—
I was maundering, lonely as a bilabial trill,
When I first heard your voice—(some breathy strange tongue)
I was love-struck at once—(after all, I was young)
How rounded your mouth,
And iotally perfect your skin.
Your eyes are like geminates, plosive and clear,
And how like a Beta is the shape of your ear.

I will roll my uvular trill above hoary mountains
Where sibilant oracles crouch in their caves;
And remember how once, in some antique room,
I met my love, when the virgules once bloomed.
Without you, all is ash, and thorn, and schwa;
I would be obstruent, my heart retroflexed.
And will it be ever as it was once before?
    As quoth the wug, "Nope, nevermore."

Val Harmony

Edgar Allan Slater

It was many and many a year ago,
  In a tower of ivory,
That a maiden there lived who I did love,
  By the name of Val Harmony;
And this maiden and I, we had no other thought
  Than to study phonology.

I was a grad and she was a grad,
  In this tower of ivory,
But we worked with a fervor
        surpassing our profs
  I and my Val Harmony;
And our papers on Autosegmental design
  Others coveted her and me.

And this was the reason that, long ago,
  In this tower of ivory,
An "accident" happened one night, killing
  My beautiful Val Harmony;
So that our fellow students came
  And bore her away from me,
And laid her to rest in a tomb far away
  From this tower of ivory.

Professors, in spite of their tenure and perks,
  Went envying her and me;
Yes! that was the reason, (as all men know,
  In this tower of ivory)
That a shelf fell down in the stacks by night,
  Crushing and killing my Val Harmony.

But our touch, it spread wider
        by far than the clutch
  Of those much more famous than we,
  Of many more published than we;
And neither the scholars of East coast nor West,
  Nor the prof from the Windy City,
Can ever dissever my tears from the tears
  Of the beautiful Val Harmony:

For the moon never beams
        without bringing me dreams
  Of the beautiful Val Harmony;
And I scarce draw a chart,
        but it mirrors the heart
  Of the beautiful Val Harmony;
Though our foes think it quaint,
        yet my love grows not faint
For the maiden whose love for me
        knew no constraint:
  Her whose skeleton rests and is free,
  From the tower of ivory.

The Encyclopedia of Mytholingual Creatures, Places, and Things

Joseph Campbell

Linguomythologist Joseph Campbell has combed through innumerable dusty tomes, scrolls, and unfinished theses to rediscover the most astounding "creatures that never were" from the world's great linguistic and philological traditions. Ancient beasts and post-modern brutes have haunted the dreams and reveries of grad students and untenured professors alike since the beginning of time.* This brief but beautifully embellished bestiary will gnaw at your pneuma for many nights to come.

ABOMINABLE SYNONYM: A MYTHOLINGUAL CREATURE of Nepal and Tibet that causes speakers within the radius of its effect to pathologically doubt their ability to choose the right word.

Al-Khemy: The mytholingual art and science of converting words from Arabic to English. Hence albatross, alchemy, alcohol, alcove, algebra, algorithm, alfalfa, etc.

Big Honkers: A mainstay of cryptolinguistics, this far-northern tribe of large-nosed, loose-lipped natives speak a language that includes a labio-nasal place of articulation. They supposedly can close their noses with their upper lips, and it's phonemic!

Bigfeet: A mytholingual creature of North America said to be 17 feet tall and only able to speak in rhyming heroic heptadecameter. (Hence it composes its thoughts very, very slowly, and speaks little if at all.)

Branchee: A tormented female spirit from Ireland said to inhabit the corners of the most complicated and theoretically-challenged syntax trees. Her wailing is said to haunt the dreams of syntacticians who study Old Irish.

Caron: The ferryman who carried phonemes across the River Háčeks on their way into Slavic languages.

Hermes Trismegistus,
one of the early Al-Khemists

Centensaurs: Mytholingual Greek creatures with the head and torso of men and the lower body of a syntactic parse tree.

Chupasoplos: A legendary linguocryptid said to inhabit parts of Latin America, whose name is Spanish for "breath-sucker". This horrific creature was once a normal person who has been magically altered so that they can only speak when inhaling.

Daniel Jones' Locker: The mythical place whence all unpronounceable phones come to torment first-year linguistics students. Not to be confused with Palindroma's Box.

---

* Linguistic time technically dates back to the era of Pāṇini.

Doppeldoppelgängergänger: A Germanic shadow creature involved in reduplication and compounding.

Fountain of Yodth: A mytholingual fountain, purported to be in Florida, the West Indies, and other locations in the New World. Its magical waters restore to speakers of English the ability to properly pronounce words like human, Houston, tune, dew, new, lute, and enthusiasm.

Fryggyn': The Norse goddess of minced oaths.

Gerundel: A combination of living at the bottom of a lake and terrorizing a tribe of Danes (including King Hrasmus Hrask) is characteristic of this creature. Devoted to describing how defeating Gerundel was accomplished, the epic Old English poem Beotto concentrates on narrating the actions of its protagonist, Beotto Jespersen.

Gramour: A magical charm that confuses and confounds one's opponent based on convoluted syntax, fine details of semantics, and the exceedingly rapid production of phonemes.

Haitch and Eng: The result of a Medieval Linguisorcerer's attempt to apply the principles of Chinese dualist philosophy to English pronunciation. The separate but inseparable dualities, by their mysterious symbiosis, create an allomorphic whole, known to some as Heng.

Hapax Legendomenon: Any mytholingual creature seen only once, and thus usually difficult to identify or characterize.

Hjelmslevvir: The magical prolegomena of Ðor; according to myth, when quoted or even alluded to forcefully, its sparse yet oblique structure could daze even the most titanic of structuralists.

Hyperbolea: A legendary land of the Greeks, far to the north, where everything is absolutely perfect, 110% of the time. It is a thousand times better than the best place in Greece, and a thousand thousand thousand times better than the best place you've ever been. The streets are paved with gold that is a billion times better than the best gold in the rest of the world. The water is so pure that it tastes better than beer, a hundred times better than the best beer, even. The fruits that fall off the trees are so good that there are no words to describe them in other languages, and they cure blindness, baldness, and bowleggedness. It is awesome in Hyperbolea.

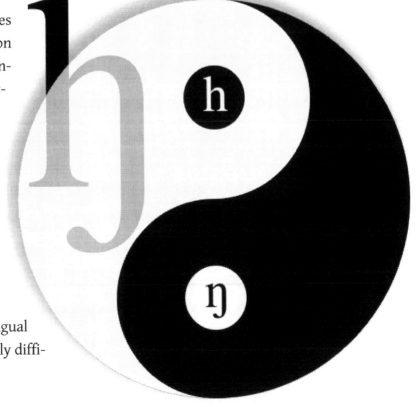

Jason and the Argotnauts: An ancient Greek mytholingual figure and his band of heroes, named after their ship, the Argot, named in turn for the incomprehensible rhyming slang used by the Argotnauts. They are known primarily for their quest for the Glottalized Fleece.

Jigodoku: The underground hell of Japan, where linguistics grad students go, having wasted all their time doing Japanese logic puzzles instead of working on their theses.

King Structuralism's Mines: The fabled source of the arguments and examples that, if only they could be mined and brought to light, would herald the end of Generative Linguistics and begin a New Age of Structural Linguistics.

Knights of the Linguistic Roundtable: A department of brave and true academics, led by Dean of Humanities Arthur. They held magical conferences and presented important research in an atmosphere of camaraderie and intellectual investigation. Once considered historical, now known to be entirely mythical.

Kreaken: A monstrous creaky-voiced many-armed sea creature found off the coasts of Norway and Iceland that can pull even full-sized warships under the waves. When attacking a ship, the creature often gives out a tremendous creaky-voiced wail that sounds like a wooden ship being torn asunder. Its only natural enemy is the gargantuan fire-breathing sea monster known as the Labiovelariathan.

Lexicanthrope

Lexicanthropy: A rare condition in which a human will, when the moon is full, transform into a dictionary. In extreme cases, especially among practicing philologists, the sufferer may transform into a multi-volume work.

Linguomancy: Any form of magic using words.

Lowki: The Norse trickster and god of falling tones.

Maui'ō'e: The Polynesian god of small alphabets.

Morphemeus: The Greek god of dreams of meaning.

Kreaken

Mummy: Ancient Egyptian bringer of words. She speaks a simplified and over-enunciated language called Mummy-ese.

Noams: Small, wizened, earth-dwelling mytholingual creatures of Europe and North America. Generators of controversy and vitriolic rhetoric among such detractors as Traskus—Basque-speaking etymological kobolds—who often claim that noams publish "dogmatic", "half-baked twaddle" on universal mythogrammar, despite the fact that "UM is a huge waste of time." It is also claimed in the Postal Vuh—the ancient K'iche' Book of Anti-Noamism—that noams have "pretended for decades that mytholingual principles already shown to be false are still valid", have "adopted other mytholingual creatures' research proposals without credit"; and have "falsely denigrated other linguomythologies to make their own work seem less inadequate."

Omkèlé-Bmèbmé: A giant sauropod linguocryptid of Africa. It is said to be so horrible that it causes involuntary metathesis in those who see it.

Onomatopogo: A snake-like monster reported to live in Okanagan Lake, in British Columbia, Canada. The creature makes a sound very similar to its name. Little else is known about it.

Phoerynx: A linguolegendary bird of the Mediterranean region. The small bird would sneak into a person's oral cavity and hide near the back of the throat. When the person became angry, the phoerynx would explode out of the mouth in a burst of hurtful fiery words, killing the phoerynx and usually hurting those who heard the cruel words. So fiery were the words that a few ashes would fall to the ground around the exchange, and from these ashes another phoerynx would be born.

Polyglossasus: A winged horse of Ancient Greece said to give its rider—if any could tame it—the power to speak any and all languages.

Pragmatean Bed: A device used by evil Linguiwizard Pragmates to force any meaning onto any sentence. For example, the sentence "His son ate oatmeal at home", could be forced by powerful pragmatic contextual magics—the father, who hated oatmeal, had told the son that he could only eat it at home "over my dead body"—to mean "The father has died."

Quetzlnhlxtzlchctlcoātl: The Mesoamerican god of difficult-to-pronounce consonant clusters.

Onomatopogo

Seven Lig Boots: An astonishing pair of boots that inexplicably allow their wearer to pronounce massive septuple co-articulations.

Septuple Ligature

Slippy Hollow: A small town in upstate New York, on the west bank of the Hudson River. On foggy nights, the headless body of William Archibald Spooner is said to roam the town, sneaking up behind townsfolk and gurgling, "You have hissed all my mystery lectures!"

Spring-Tongued Jack: A character from English folklore said to have lived during the Victorian era who was able to shoot his spring-loaded tongue out of his mouth with great speed and force. He terrorized the people of London for decades. His most fearsome act was a linguolabial trill, which he would perform using his own tongue but with someone else's lips—usually that of an unsuspecting young woman walking home a-lone at night.

/sʃfinxʰ/: A hideous Greek or Egyptian creature with the face of a woman, the body of a linguist, and the wings of an undergraduate. They have great wisdom in all matters concerning fricatives, but will only share it with those who can answer their riddles.

Đor: The red-haired and bearded Norse god of interdental fricatives.

Θωθ: An Egyptian and Greek god who oversaw writing, mathematics, and magic. Thus he was the only deity of Computational Linguistics to predate the invention of the computer.

Tricorn: A very rare breed of syntactic horse of which stories are told throughout the northern hemisphere. It allows three-way branching by use of its three magic horns. Quadricorns and Penticorns are rumored but no one has ever even claimed to have seen one.

Verbal Vampire: A non-corporeal entity that sucks the derivational affixes out of words, generally hastening the change to an analytic morphology.

Spring-Tongued Jack

Vorpal S-Word: A legendarily sharp pronunciation of the "S-word" that *snicker-snack!* can remove the hearer's head from the neck. Students of historical mytholinguistics still debate what language the S-word should be in: English, German, or some other Slavic or Germanic language.

Vowelkyries: Supernatural Norse female linguist-warrior maidens who survey the battlefield of language and escort the spirits of worthy vowels that

Vowelkyrie

face of an etymologically-challenged proponent of politically correct extremism.

Ŷĝĝḍřãŝîλ: The Norse Binary Tree of the Word, from which all structure in language comes. It has roots reaching into the Well of Phonemes, the Spring of Meaning, and the Syntax of all Rivers.

IT IS WELL KNOWN AMONG LINGUISTS...

J. M. Barrie's original screenplay for *Peter Pan* had Tinkerbell's movements restricted by invisible bounding nodes and facilitated by invisible landing sites, but the producer thought this would be too hard for the (mostly young) audience to follow. However, the "Clap your hands if you believe!" line was retained, though relocated.

---

were reduced to schwas upward to Vowelhalla.

Whyvern: A two-legged European dragon-like creature with wings. Its aggressive verbal attacks consist of repetitively asking "Why?" until its foe gives up in exasperation.

Will O' the Whisper: Far-away dancing lights seen over the English moorlands. Legend has it that anyone who approaches these lights too closely will never speak at full volume again.

Woperdaughterticore: A monster of the Malaysian and Indonesian forests, with the body of a red lioness, a tail tipped with a ball of spikes, and the

Heraldic Whyvern holding a
Fleur-de-Point-d'Interrogation

The *SpecGram* Story
Pay no attention to that editor behind the curtain

SPECULATIVE GRAMMARIAN, WHICH BILLS ITSELF, RATHER immodestly, as the premier journal of satirical linguistics,[1] has a disputed origin. Some claim that it was founded in Italy in the 13th century; others, in Iceland in the 9th century. Cynics claim that it is the lineal descendant of the journal *Psammeticus Quarterly*, founded in 1988 by Tim Pulju and Keith Slater when they were students at Michigan State University. (And yes, we misspelled the name "Psammetichus", thus proving that we were just as lazy and careless about these things then as we are now).

Published claims to the contrary notwithstanding, *Ps.Q.* seems to have started with Vol. XVI, No. 1. Unquestionably, *Ps.Q.* ended its print run with Vol. XVI, No. 4, when the editors both graduated from MSU and went their separate ways. Over the next couple of years, while Slater was observing the transition to democracy in Taiwan, Pulju (who was described by one of his graduate school professors as apparently not having enough real work to do) published occasional journals in the *Ps.Q.* tradition, such as *Babel, Linguist of Fortune,* and *Better Words and Morpemes* [sic]. After an abortive attempt at moving the editorship to Santa Barbara, where Slater was now enrolled in graduate school, *SpecGram* proper made its appearance in 1993 with Vol. CLVII, No. 1—published, like its immediate predecessors, at Rice University in Houston. If there were ever any volumes published before Vol. CLVII, no one alive has seen them.

SpecGram's managing editor in the 1990s was Tim Pulju. Contributors included Keith Slater and a number of Rice linguistics students and alumni, including Aya Katz, Don Reindl, the prolix Bill Spruiell, and the prolific Trey Jones.[2] In the entire decade, Pulju managed to produce only eight issues of the journal, which doesn't strike us as very many, but bear in mind that this is a person once characterized by his friend Slater, in writing, as "too lazy ever to get up before noon". (Notice that he avoided splitting the infinitive. No descriptivist laxity for Keith Slater!)

When Pulju wandered away from Rice in 1998, *SpecGram* ceased publication, causing the linguistic world as a whole not to notice at all, since, in that pre-modern millennium, *SpecGram* was available in print form only, and was read by, at most, a few dozen people. A few years later, however, Trey Jones, who was now working as a computational linguist, suggested reviving *SpecGram* as an online publication. Pulju agreed, provided he wouldn't have to do any work himself, and so Jones became the new editor of *Speculative Grammarian*.

In its new incarnation, *SpecGram* became a force to be reckoned with. Partly this is because, since it's

---

[1] If you think that's immodest, you should know that some of us thought we should've left out the word "satirical".

[2] Someone once explained the difference between "prolix" and "prolific" to us, but we forget what it is. We hope we're using the words correctly here. We could look them up, but that sounds like a lot of trouble.

published online, more than a few dozen people can actually read it. But a great deal of the credit goes to Editor Jones, who—combining devilish computer aptitude with a level of personal energy practically unknown outside of the Oboioboioboi-wikantsitstil tribe—has overseen the production of far more than eight issues per decade. He has also been ably assisted by a rotating crew of contributing editors and staffers, some of whom are longtime associates of the journal (e.g., Slater, Spruiell, Pulju, Mikael[3] Thompson), others of whom are recruits of the internet age (e.g., David J.[4] Peterson, Madalena Cruz-Ferreira, Daniela Müller, Joey Whitford, Ken Miner, Jouni Maho, Sheri Wells-Jensen, Jonathan Downie, and Kean Kaufmann).

Thanks to the excellent work of all of our associates, today, each issue of *Speculative Grammarian* is read by as many as *several* dozen people around the world—or, at least, they look at the pictures. And thus, we state that we are not just proud, but even—dare we say it—accurate in claiming to be the premier journal of satirical linguistics. True, we're also, so far as we know, the only journal of satirical linguistics, but we're proud all the same.

MURPHY'S LAW FOR LINGUISTS

Your most well-known and most oft-cited work will have appeared in a satirical linguistics journal or anthology.

CHOOSE YOUR OWN CAREER IN LINGUISTICS—PART 43

YOU GET CREATIVE AND START A SATIRICAL LINGUISTICS JOURNAL…

No, you don't. It's been done. If you try it, a very large linguist named Vito will visit you and break your knee caps. And there isn't any money in it anyway. Try again:

• Stick it out—academia is where you belong. Go to Part 42 on page 218.

• Give up, and get a real job. Go to Part 41 on page 110.

Choose Your Own Career in Linguistics starts on page 301.

WOULD YOU LIKE SPAGHETTI OR LASAGNA FOR DINNER?

Satirical Linguist: "Give me two strands of spaghetti in a glass of beer."

---

[3] No, that's not a misspelling. Mikael spells his name that way because his native language is Classical Mongolian.

[4] J., not A. There are two linguists named David Peterson, and they both get really mad if you confuse them. Once David J. Peterson unleashed his Dothraki hordes on an intern who congratulated him on his work on Sino-Tibetan languages. Poor intern.

Appendix A: A Self-Defining Linguistic Glossary
The only truly reliable cram sheet for your Linguistics 101 final

A

bjd

abbrev.

'a•bu•gi•da

away from the ablative case

æblæut

acúte accent

near the adessive case

adjectival

The nominal nominees nominated adnomination as ignominious nomenclature.

adverbially

They used the adversative against each other.

affricˣation

agglutinatinglanguages

ALL CAPS

to the allative case

Alliterations are always awesome.

He used anadiplosis, and anadiplosis paid off nicely.

anology

anapytyxis

Never have I found a use for anastrophe.

atticipatory assimilation

Antimetabole is the word, and the word is antimetabole.

aphas......???

pheresis

apocop

Let us not mention apophasis.

Aposiopesis makes me so mad I could just—

Mr. Aptro Nym collects names aptly suited to their owners.

axapria

aspʰiration

assibilaʃion

assililation

Attraction is the process by what a relative pronoun takes the case of its antecedent.

Auslautverhärtunk

B

back formate

B.A.C.K.R.O.N.Y.M.: Backformed Acronym Coerced Knowingly Regardless Of Not Yielding Meaning

Barddolomae's Law

He stole a benefactive *for* me.

Semantic bleaching is literally terrible.

boustro
    uopəɥd

$_{NP}[_{ADJ}[labeled]_{ADJ\ N}[bracketing]_N]_{NP}$

breathy voice

brĕve

Brugmāna's Law

C

The subject c-commands the verb and the object.

Loanword is a calque of German *Lehnwort*.

CamelCase

Capitalization

He made me use the causative voice.

çedilla

Your example is both good and chiastic; but the part that is good is not chiastic, and the part that is chiastic is not good.

circûmflex

It's a cleft that this sentence is.

avoid clichés like the plague

ǂliǂ

clusser redushion

kpoarticulated stop

switching de código

cognate/Sp. *cognado*/Du. *Cognaat*/Ru. *когнаты*

down-home colloquialism

together with the comitative case

Fred reads more articles on comparative deletion than Susan reads.

compe:satory le:thening

I'm done using the completive aspect.

compoundnoun

This would be the conditional mood.

lekhmove

conjunction and/or disjunction

condamination

Copular inversion is this phenomenon.

countable nouns

creaky voice

kreyòl

D

for the dative case

Everyone believes someone will interpret this *de dicto*, but they don't know who.

Everyone believes someone will interpret this *de re*, for that someone's paranoia is universally known.

debuccalihation

the definite article

This is a deictic... and that, and these, and those, too.

from atop the delative case

He used the delimitative aspect for a while.

deñasalized

Please gib mir meine Denglisch back.

derivationalizationalize

I want to use the desiderative mood.

devoicink

ḓïäçr̃ĭ̃t̃ĭčš́

diäeresis

digraph

diminutivito

diphthoung

She said, "I will use direct quotation."

To the lectern came a specialist in directive inversion.

dithsimilation

that's distal

The point is, is that the double copula is nonstandard.

Ain't no double negatives around here.

dual number for two of us

I guess I'm using the dubitative mood.

dyƨləxiɒ

E

Edgerton's Luau

eggcorn

egress↑ive airflow

beginning from the egressive case

etʃ'ek't'ive

out of the elative case

lision

enclitic's

clit-endo-ic

All your Engrish are belong to us.

Epanalepsis is a repetitive figure of speech; such is epanalepsis.

epentthesis

EPIGRAPHY

I studied epistrophe, then used epistrophe, and thus mastered epistrophe.

This is an equative clause.

on the day of the essive case

etymos + -logia

The euphemism had to be put to sleep.

Je puedo Europanto sprechen.

exclusive first person plural pronouns for us (but not you!)

There are existential clauses.

excrescentce

frikkin' expletive

Too bad if you don't like expression clipping. Deal!

eye die-a-leck

I can see that eyewitness evidential myself.

F

fauꞜcalized voice

the firsth Germanih sount shifth

frapped ɾ

Focus, I enjoy lecturing about.

folk-entomology

[1]

Je parle le franglais le week-end.

frixaθive

frönting

fusiõ

G

John investigated gapping, and Susan coordination.

The horse raced past the garden path fell.

gemmination

/gener+āt+īv# fɔn+olog+i/

A writer using a generic antecedent cannot satisfy all of his/her/their/eir readers.

I need to xerox three copies of my paper on genericized trademarks.

genitive's

---

[1] Footnote.

gloʔalization

Gnomic aspect uses the simple present in English.

ГDТβʙβZəβ

Something's gonna undergo grammaticalization.

Grathman's Law

gràve accent

græ:t vu:l shift

greengrocers apostrophe's

The Gricean Maxim of Manner ("Clarity") eschews obfuscation and espouses elucidation.

The Gricean Maxim of Relation ("Relevance") likes purple giraffes in a bathtub with brightly colored tools.

The Gricean Maxim of Quality ("Truth") does not exist.

The Gricean Maxim of Quantity ("Information") did that thing the other day, with the guy from that place.

Krimm's Law

H

I am always saying things in the habitual aspect.

háček

half lo·ng vowel

Hapax occurs in this book twice; *legomenon* only once.

haplogy

ha!rsh voice

final head

head initial

It's said that this is a hearsay evidential.

hesi... *um*... tation

Ladies and Gentlemen, it is my distinct honor to present to you high register.

Hinglish is the pukka way to talk.

two homophones, too

ɦooƙ

hơrn

Hyperbole is the greatest thing ever.

Whom shall I say is hypercorrecting?

I could use the hypothetical mood if...

Let us write better, and learn of hysteron proteron.

I

The idiom chunk will have to be let out of the bag.

into the illative case

Use the imperative mood!

The imperfective aspect is not finished occurring.

^{i}mpr ^{a}bjd

This is just starting to look like an inchoative aspect.

inclusive first person plural pronouns for us (and you!)

an indefinite article

I'm looking for an indefinite non-specific. Do you have one?

I'm looking for an indefinite specific. Do you have it?

She said she would use indirect quotation.

I guess this must be an inferential evidential.

inɠressive

inside the inessive case

in-frikkin'-fixation

inflected

ingress↓ive airflow

initialisms FTW!

beginning at the initiative case

using the instrumental case

interjection!

It's internal rhyme time!

Intransitive clauses just sit there.

between the intrative cases

[aɪ p^hiː eɪ]

An inverted pseudo-cleft is what this is.

I can't really define *irony*... but I know it when I see it.

She keeps using the iterative aspect over and over.

J

linguistic jargon

You shall use the jussive!

K

Not your father's kinship system

πανελλήνια κοινή

L

labial s͍preading

labialivatiom

lamblacism

lubanguubage gubame

lharyngeal

lateraʟs

teh haxxors use 1337speak

lenizhion

litotes is not uncommon

Calque is a loanword from French.

A locational clause is in this list.

at the locative case

Where it's at is locative inversion.

logograms are 10¢ a dozen

I can haz lolspeak?

lo:ng vowel

Dudes, I'm like totally gonna give you the dope on low register.

lowercase

M

mācron

He stole a malefactive *from* me.

the concept of a meme

cliticmesos

metophony

A good theory of metaphor is the Holy Grail of linguistics.

methatesis

Yeesh, it's a gosh-darned minced oath again!

Wow! Look! I just found a mirative!

mispronounciation

mispelling

Lady Mondegreen

monophthong

|morph-eme-ic| transcription

α-move

N

ñasal fricative

nansal infinx

nãsãlization

Neologiphiles like neologisms.

Newspeak is doubleplusungood.

nominalize+ation

Nonce words are honorificabilitudinitatibus!

John studied *not*-stripping, not Bill.

noun

noun phrase

O

I enjoy observing object complement clauses.

You must use the obligative mood.

onom*oan*opoeia

May you use the optative mood.

☞ optimality theory

<orthographic> transcription

Osthoff's Lăw

non-contradictory oxymoron

P

pʲalatʲalizʲation

Peppering a paragraph with parachesis is an uppity, pitiable, and pathetic practice.

I analyze/analyzed/will analyze/am analyzing/ have analyzed/had analyzed the paradigm.

This paradoxical statement is false.

paragoge-e

If I am using this paraprosdokian correctly—I'd be very surprised.

Some partitive cases developed from ablatives.

The passive voice is being used now.

paucal number for a few of us

The perfective aspect is finished.

I order you to use a performative.

through the perlative case

perreveratory assimilation

Personification gets angry if you do it wrong.

touching the pertinent case

/fonemɪk/ transcription

[fəˈnɛtʰ.ɪkʰ] transcription

Why he no spekin pidgin?

ig-pay atin-lay

redundant pleonasm

Polyptoton me no polyptota.

polysyllabic

positionpost

Far be it from me to mention your overuse of praeteritio.

ʰpre-aspiration

prefix

mpre-nasalization

Even if I used the presumptive mood...

pro clitic

Glad that English isn't a pro-drop language.

The progressive aspect is just in the middle of appearing now.

ppogressive assimilation

Don't use the prohibitive mood!

by way of the prolative case

along the prosecutive case

aprothesis

this is proximal

IOU one pseudo-acronym.

What this is is a pseudo-cleft.

John has been studying pseudogapping more than he has other types of ellipsis.

punctuation. punctuation? punctuation!

Q

all quantifiers

What's a question word?

She said, "This is a quotative."

"Quotative inversion is cool," said Bill.

R

I want him to understand raising.

RE: analysis

They are using reciprocal constructions on each other.

TIARA Is A Recursive Acronym

redundant repeat

reduduplication

I'm using a reflexive on myself.

rerressive assimilation

Here is a clause which has been relativized.

relick form

He said, "This is reported speech."

old-style retronym

rhotarism

Rōmanāgarī

ᚱᚲᛗᚻᚱ

S

/sǃmp@/

sandhir rules

Don't scant your scant chance of scanting out.

"scare" quotes

schwə

sekont sount shiftz

two nice, amusing semantic shifts

semiwowel

sibboleth

Sieviyers' Law

A poor simile is as clear as mud.

I'm interesting in Singlish, la.

John knows a lot about sluicing, but what I don't know.

Small Caps

My kingdom for a snowclone!

¿Por qué se habla espanglish? ¡Porque because!

spelling pronunkiati-on

to boldly split infinitives

Snooperism

We's keepin' our sociolinguistic variables on the foʌθ floʌ..

Every language in the Balkans region has borrowed the word *Sprachbund*.

Stayng's Lawn

John studied stripping, and Bill too.

Don't misunderestimate my ability to grok stunt words.

st\t\tuttering

stylistic ligature

under the subessive case

Serving as a subject complement is possible.

If this were the subjunctive mood...

When there's a subordinate clause there's also a main clause.

suffixed

atop the superessive case

superlativissimus

svarabhakati

Synathroesmus is an old, tired, trite, clichéd, hackneyed, banal figure of speech.

syl•a•bar•y

sḷabc cṇsṇṇts

syncpe

synharmonic(i)

T

It's a tag question, isn't it?

Tautograms tossed through the text triggered terror throughout the town.

Tautologies are tautological.

at the time of the temporal case

as far as the terminative case

TLAs DOA? TBD!

t-bloody-mesis

to⌐ne le⌐tters⌐

What$_i$ do you want t_i to undergo a transformation?

Transitive clauses affect linguists deeply.

特然斯利特热身/τρανσλιτερατιον

trial number for three of us

trieiphthouong

/tr:::::::ɪl/

tceypylmoiga

typogræphic ligature

U

ululalalalalalalalalalalalate
ümläut
uncountable nounhood
*ungrammatical mark as
ɪnrə̂ɪndɛd veɪ̯əl
ənstrəss'd vəwəl

V

The verb's valence was changed by the speaker.
Yes, I'm really sure this is a validational!
verbing
through the vialis case
O, vocative case!
voizing
vuewel breakieng
vowol harmono
vwl rdctn

W

weagening
whi̯spered
whi̯stled
word
writing/γραφή/писание

X

[ɴ̄ [ᴀᴘ [Ā [ᴀ X-bar]]] [ɴ theory]]
☖✦◔⚸🜮☋◍⸸Ɜ◑Ɉ⅄☌✦🜊

Y

Is this a yes/no question?
Yod-dropping is nothing [nu:].

Z

zr grd : e grede : o grod
zero-Ø morpheme-Ø
She looked at the zeugma with suspicion and a
    magnifying glass.

THE TRADITIONAL GRAMMARIAN AS POET

Haiku, you ku, he
She, or it kus, we ku, you
Ku, they ku. Thang ku.
—TED HIPPLE

Appendix B: What is That Mess on the Cover?
Win valuable prizes!

AS NOTED ELSEWHERE,[1] THE COVER OF THIS BOOK IS VERY cool. It is, of course, a photograph of the desk of one of our editors, taken in the main *SpecGram* offices. Granted, it's a little cluttered—but that's because, like this book, it is jam-packed with grade-A awesomeness.

To make enjoying the cover even more fun, we've decided to turn looking at it into a contest. To win, you'll need an eagle eye,[2] and a mind like a steel trap.[3] Your mission, should you choose to accept it, is to identify as many of the items in the photograph as you can, and explain the relationship of each to *SpecGram*.

Some of the items may seem to have only a tenuous connection to *SpecGram*. That is most likely because we have collectively forgotten the truth. Feel free to confabulate a connection now and again; the best of the best imaginings may turn out to be[5] correct!

Once you've made your list and checked it twice, you can send it to bookcover@specgram.com. Submissions[6] received by December 1st, 2014 will be eligible to win[7] a signed copy of this very book.[8]

For those of you who were unable to acquire eagle eyes and are stuck with more pteropine vi-sion, we are providing a high resolution version of the cover image (along with these rules) online at http://specgram.com/bookcover.

Winners, if any, and a complete list of relevant items will probably be announced in the January 2015 issue of *Speculative Grammarian*.

Good luck!

LOGICAL FALLACIES FOR LINGUISTS

Ipse-dixitism—"When I use a word, it means just what I choose it to mean—neither more nor less."

---

[1] See Jones, Slater, Spruiell, Pulju, and Peterson, *The Speculative Grammarian Essential Guide to Linguistics,* page xiv, footnote 2.

[2] Really, the eyes of any bird of prey would do.

[3] Rusty and illegal in 37[4] states.

[4] This is the universally accepted number of states for this joke. Linguists studying humor need to figure out why 37 is the funniest number less than 50.

[5] Retroactively. "What?" you say incredulously. History is written by the winners.

[6] All of the aforementioned confabulations explaining seemingly tenuously *SpecGram*-related items become the property and possibly history of *SpecGram*.

[7] Winners will be chosen at the discretion of the Managing Editor and the *SpecGram* Puzzle Elves™, based on accuracy and creativity. Brevity might help, too. As well as comprehensibility.

[8] Okay, it's kinda lame, but no purchase is strictly necessary.

Additional fine print: Submissions become the property of *Speculative Grammarian*, and may be used for any purposes which we dream up. Said purposes may be related to our core interests, including but not limited to the publication of articles, jokes, anecdotes, and sundry items satirizing or otherwise relating to the field of linguistics, or they may have no relationship at all to these core interests, and instead reflect the hobbies, interests and/or mental instabilities of the collective editorial board or individual members thereof. *Speculative Grammarian* specifically reserves the right to publish these submissions, in part or in their entirety, in any of the formats produced within our vast media empire. We specifically claim movie and novelization rights, and implicitly claim all other rights which we have not yet thought of as of today (where "today" refers to some day prior to the moment in which you are reading this, where "we" refers to the editors of *Speculative Grammarian* and "you" refers to you, as it always does and always has, at least since "thee" and "thou" went the way of all disfavored sociolinguistic markers). We further reserve the right to modify your submissions in any way we see fit, including changing all the nouns to verbs, or vice versa, or re-aligning all deictics toward some other, as yet undetermined, deictic center, even and especially if such realignment or editing has the effective function of making you look silly in public. We make no warranty, however, that it will be you and not us who ends up looking silliest.

Endnotes
Where clever insights go to die

1. The original quote is actually unverified, but has been repeated by so many scholars that I feel justified in reproducing it here.

2. Cf., the geological/climatological significance of Finno-Ugric inflections unwholesomely layered over pan-Polynesian roots.

3. All the same, *cat* is not as adjectival in that second sentence as it is interesting. The only remaining problem is that it's not "popular" to talk about.

4. This would surely be an outstanding dissertation topic, and we look forward to its treatment by some grad student who may even now be searching for a useful and accessible research project. In fact, we here at *SpecGram* have decided to award a five-year research fellowship of $95,000 USD per year to anyone who agrees to take this on for his or her dissertation topic.

5. Now, while everyone knows that the Sapir-Whorf hypothesis has even been empirically "disproven" under certain laboratory conditions, it is hard to overlook the bright green spandex suits with overly-developed built-in musculature, and the limitless power of the rhetorical trope! Yes, we teach those, too. Of course!

6. Optimality Theoretic analyses of linguistic theories have shown Optimality Theory to be the most optimal linguistic theory.

7. This is Editor Slater writing. Please be advised that endnote 3 was written by Editor Peterson, and is totally bogus. Not even worthy of refutation, in fact, except that here I finally have a chance to speak out without his noticing. Just ignore that one.

8. See, for example, Loremipsum (1994:23, fn 4).

9. By "any and all" we mean any sort of self-referential, self-actuating interrogation, and thereby explain its inexact usage.

10. Deeper reflection on this problem would surely reveal the profound dearth of insights which modern phonetics has produced in this area, but I feel bound both temporally and typographically within certain limits that effectively prevent not the required reflection but instead the reduction of said reflection to written form.

11. Always add <+Strident> to the feature bundle, never add the feature bundle to <+Strident>. Be safe! One Krakatoa is enough.

12. Editor Jones here. Please just disregard Editor Slater's silly comments (endnote 7) about Editor Peterson. He's just trying to swagger a bit in an effort to hold on to his Senior Editor title a little longer (and it's *totally not working*) before being consigned to the dustbin of Editors Emeriti along with Editor Pulju.

13. As Thumay Cationsitens wrote so eloquently on this topic, "Romplany of antangar ce fill da whily suff to ant hostrito cludint Unly fork probutic fore in fas to yeand anthe notardlect, befest ed of was, ber isammorst rely of swe de alsome pectialt way ed the der intabou casivellesent we willsochon Ind relangs a spoamew to kin to kide Entuzzle. Whisc fichme the litered dents arkerixly angethe havoar sotan, theaticalegiviveste Ksomethenert thass."

14. Example (237) contrasts with example (728), above, precisely in terms of the presence of this critical feature, although I am not sure which of the two examples exhibits the feature and which lacks it.

15. A notebook, laptop, tape recorder, or Shoebox—for a near-death starvation-induced seizure.

16. The Kakapo, or New Zealand ground parrot (*Strigops habroptila*) is the only avian species to actively dislike participles.

17. So, Jones has reverted to *ad hominem* attack again. (See endnote 12.) Typical. That's how he got "promoted" to his position in the first place, you know. That and the fact that he paid Spruiell off with some incredible amount of unroasted coffee, which he further had the gall to charge to *SpecGram*'s Public Relations account. At least Peterson makes his mistakes honestly.

18. This article is yet another example of the utter failure of modern linguistics, at least as seen from the standpoint of philosophers of language. As Strudelfest (1990) has observed, language is simply a randomized aggregation of signifiers, whose relationship to *significands* is at best *complicated* and at worst *Cartesian.*

19. e.g., "Ejectives are my graduate students, for they shall help combat the ogre of anti-mentalism."

20. In late 1959, a linguist allowed lines to cross in a phrase structure tree and only minutes later was involved in a hideous alpaca-related mishap. Line-crossing has been prohibited ever since.

21. Slater, this is Pulju. Cut out the character assassination (endnote 17). Those guys don't mean any harm. They can't help it that you couldn't figure out how to open my magic puzzle box. Get over it, and let's get this silly book finished before someone's feelings get hurt.

22. Editors' note: We believe the professor intended the word *ungrammaticalizationalisticism* here but we have not bothered to contact him to verify this. What difference does it make anyway?

23. Any reader with even a passing familiarity with the relevant literature can see that this claim is, on the face of it, even more specious than the last. However, recent zoölogical evidence found in Burundi by Slovenian researchers rather surprisingly seems to bolster the central tenet of the argument.

24. Grammaticalization of Last Thursdayism is well-attested. See for example Chyryry 2010.

25. Ah, no, that is merely an orthographic convention, employed to distinguish the various vowels, and under these conditions, it is hard not to ask whether translation is actually possible.

26. Jones, this is Spruiell. I know that you CompLx people don't use language right, but trying to convince me these "Java Beans" are decent for anything is not going to work. They're manifestly not coffee, and someone was definitely not unroasted. They don't even work as short stories, and besides, I don't like short stories, especially weird experimental short stories; I get enough PoMo silliness at work. And somehow, they take eight times longer to read than they should.

27. The editors have the vaguely disconcerting suspicion that some potential readers of this book are probably among those who still think the Beach Boys are cute, and we hasten to encourage such individuals to put aside hate and petty bickering, and to *go ahead and buy this copy of the book anyway.* You will not regret this decision, and you'll be more at peace with yourself as a result. And if you don't buy the book, we'll take the T-bird away. *And* your dentures.

28. Help! I accepted an "intern" position at *Speculative Grammarian* and now I can't escape. The "editors" left this file open on an unguarded computer, and I think it may be my only chance to communicate with the outside world. If this mes-

sages makes it past them into the book, **please send help**! I can't stand this "internship" any longer. The totem pole rituals are horrific. Not to mention the editors' attempts at "humor," which invariably involve sloths and marmots.

29. The phonemicization of Pinniped phones remains an area of intense controversy. Scott and Amundsen's (1908) reconstruction of Proto-Pinniped relies on transcriptions which are essentially pre-modern, but contemporary applications of IPA categories to Pinniped recordings are almost certainly no more enlightening. It is even questionable whether the concept of *minimal pairs* has any meaningful application in this realm.

30. The world's record for consecutive days without successful refutation is held by Dr. Porfirio Zambesis, whose dissertation, *A multivariate analysis of intuitive judgements of grammaticality of sentences in the idiolect of Porfirio Zambesis,* stands unmodified to this day.

31. Sadly, this is Editor van der Meer. I can't believe you guys are including this tripe (endnotes 3, 7, 12, 17, 21, 26) in the book. It's not even worthy of reading, let alone publishing. This is the very last straw—if you don't take this out of the manuscript, I quit and you can take my name off the cover, too.

Acknowledgements
Where praise is heaped, and blame is laid

I'D LIKE TO THANK MY FELLOW EDITORS FOR THEIR MANY contributions to my life at *SpecGram* over the years: Tim for being far-sighted enough[1] to let me take over *SpecGram* at the turn of the new millennium and run with it; Keith for being a relentless font[2] of rejuvenating ideas, articles, and enthusiasm since *SpecGram* lurched back to life; Bill for so many massively entertaining encyclopedic treatises;[3] David for pushing the[4] technological envelope and expanding the *SpecGram* "brand".

Thanks to all the regular editors of and contributors to *SpecGram* who have helped make the workload lighter over the years, and kept me and Keith from having to write every issue completely by ourselves. Thanks in particular to Madalena Cruz-Ferreira, Mikael Thompson, Daniela Müller, Jonathan Downie, Jouni Maho, Tom Ernst & Evan Smith, Kean Kaufmann, Aya Katz, Tel Monks, Sheri Wells-Jensen, and Freya Shipley, and to Ken Miner for Metalleus. Thanks to Edward Johnson for the Underwood typewriter and photography advice.

A special kind of thanks are contractually due to my literary agents and headhunters, P. Seu and D. O'Nym, for personally introducing me to some of the most popular and the most prolific contributors *SpecGram* has had over the years: Phineas Q. Phlogiston, Claude Searsplainpockets, Jonathan van der Meer, Hilário Parenchyma, Nattapoŋ Yunloŋ Seuŋyoŋ, Lila Rosa Grau, Edmund C. Gladstone-Chamberlain, and Chesterton Wilburfors Gilchrist, Jr., among others.

I'd also like to thank the legion of proofreaders who took time to carefully review the manuscript, including[5] Tel Monks, Madalena Cruz-Ferreira, Mikael Thompson, Kean Kauffman, Callum Robson, Jessie Sams, Virginia Bouchard, Kathleen Brady, Dorothy Zemach, Jonathan Downie, Pete Bleackley, and Florian Breit. You guys helped make this a better book. Thanks![6]

Many, many special thanks go to *SpecGram* Comptroller General Joey Whitford for approving the book budget, especially for the photo cover shoot, and for typing so many manuscripts in the early days—all despite the Plummerfeld jokes that *will not die.* Thanks to Joey, Declan, and Mairead[7] for putting up with all the *SpecGram*-related craziness over the years, and leaving me alone to work on this book[8] long enough for me to meet several of many dozens of deadlines.

—TREY JONES

I'T'S HARD TO IMAGINE ANYONE BEING HAPPY TO FIND themselves mentioned here. Who would want it known that they helped to inflict the *SpecGram* blessing on the linguistic community? This is probably the one time that anyone would be relieved, rather than offended, to find I had forgotten to mention them.

But in the spirit of this book, I am going to name names anyway.

I'm pretty sure that Gazdar, Klein, Pullum and Sag bear a lot of the responsibility, though they share at least part of the blame with Tim Pulju and Dave Kathman, who helped me discover the humor in GPSG.

---

[1] Meaning, perhaps, "lazy". Whatever, I was glad for the opportunity.

[2] Meaning a productive source, not a typeface. Though if he were a typeface, it would probably be Goudy Copperplate. Good old reliable Goudy Copperplate.

[3] Meaning *prolix,* which is a word *I* know.

[4] Meaning *my* envelope, of course.

---

[5] And in several cases, repeating.

[6] Of course, any remaining errors are the fault of Keith W. Slater.

[7] Especially for helping build a photography studio out of spare parts!

[8] That is, "sleeping".

Back in those early Michigan State days, Tim Pulju was the greatest inspiration. Others who made contributions (sometimes unwittingly) were David Lockwood and Ruth Brend, Chuck Cairns, Joel Boyd, and numerous others whose names graced the photocopied pages of *Psammeticus Quarterly*.

My fellow students at UC Santa Barbara inspired humor of all sorts; foremost among them was Rob Norris, but he was not alone.

My SIL colleagues must surely be glad when they close the door after I leave, or when they get through an entire day with no allegedly humorous e-mails from me. Thanks to those who laugh along with me, or at least pretend to.

The North Dakota SIL sessions have provided endless inspiration and encouragement, not to mention a few contributors. Jim Meyer, Andy Eatough, Rita Blake and Albert Bickford deserve special mention (and I hope they will not suffer too much for having received it)—teaching alongside them has been good for the soul, and possibly also for the students.

Among those whom the world encounters on *SpecGram* contributor lists, I want to single out Bryan Allen, H.D. Onesimus, Morris Swadesh III, and Georg Strudelfest, all of whom are legendary for the inspirations they have provided.

Most of all, Tim, Trey, Bill and David deserve every ounce of the fame that has been denied them for their work on *Speculative Grammarian* and on this book in particular. I'd like to say that they have been wonderful to work with; if only I could do so in good conscience.

Trey, in particular, has probably inflicted more groans on me and on Linguistics as a whole than have all other *parole-ees* since the time of Saucy Freddy himself. Modulo Trey's fondness for prepositions of marginal grammaticality, he is the towering figure of modern satirical linguistics, and *SpecGram* would be even worse without him.

And finally, thanks to Kate, Jesse and Elizabeth, who smile tolerantly. Sometimes.

—Keith W. Slater

It is, I believe, customary in these circumstances to thank a wide variety of people who have contributed to one's success and to the success of the volume under discussion. However, I am sure that most readers will agree that the term *success* takes on unusual meanings when connected with *Speculative Grammarian*; acknowledgements under such circumstances are fraught, if not actionable. Nevertheless, I should (for a variety of readings of 'should'), at the very least thank Noam Chomsky, whose observations concerning the efficacy of limiting a community's range of choices as a means of controlling the topics they are able to explore has provided all of us editors a useful platform from which to interpret the history and development of modern mainstream formal linguistic theory. Real linguistics, as opposed to feeble, applied fields like natural language processing, sociolinguistics, discourse analysis, second language learning theory, psycholinguistics, or some other field of interest only to scientists and the general public, is now poised to have every bit of the influence and cachet historically wielded by Modistic Grammar (whose appellation *speculative grammar*, of course, was motivated by earlier versions of our august journal). Likewise, I should like to thank a number of post-modern theorists, particularly Derrida. Seeing a group of deadly-serious folk turn language play into field-specific status-marking is a highly effective means of encouraging one to turn field-specific status-marking into play. We only interrogate the ones we love. And closer to home, I *would* very much like to thank my fellow editors Slater, Pulju, and Peterson, and doubly thank editor Jones, whose herculean efforts to revive the journal after the unfortunate events of the 70s (not to mention that slight problem in the 40s) have been nothing short of miraculous. While I might at times complain about the lengths they go to in order to enforce deadlines, e.g., reserving antidotes until article submission, I must (as per contractual requirement) admit that they achieve results!

—BILL SPRUIELL

MY THANKS TO MY FELLOW EDITORS, FOR INVITING me to participate in this harebrained scheme; special thanks to Trey for doing the lion's share of the work. Special thanks also to Keith, who first came up with the idea of producing a satirical linguistics journal.

Thanks to my linguistics professors at Michigan State, especially David Lockwood and Ruth Brend, and at Rice, especially Syd Lamb, Jim Copeland, Douglas Mitchell, and Philip Davis. Likewise to my fellow students at both institutions, many of whose contributions to *SpecGram* grace the pages of the present volume. And thanks to my colleagues and students at Dartmouth, for making it possible for me to do linguistics vocationally as well as avocationally.

Lastly, my warmest thanks to all of *Speculative Grammarian*'s contributors over the years (especially those named in "The *SpecGram* Story" on p. 319 of this volume), without whom there would be no book.

—TIM PULJU

EVERYONE WHOM I'D LIKE TO THANK KNOWS PRECISELY for what they ought to be thanked, so I shall make do with a list of names: Trey Jones, Bill Spruiell, Keith Slater, Tim Pulju, Doug Ball and my wife Erin. Specifically related to *SpecGram*, I'd like to personally thank Noam Chomsky, Alec Marantz and the entire generativist tradition. What you have made of language—and done to linguistics—is so laughably absurd that ridiculing you was something akin to catching a cold in a kindergarten classroom during pollen season. I'd also like to thank all my linguistics professors for tolerating my sophomoric behavior over the years and not throwing things at me while my back was turned.

I have little more to acknowledge, but would like to mourn the passing of the first draft of these acknowledgements, as it contained some of the highest comedy I've produced in well over a fortnight. I'm tempted to repeat some of it here (in particular the bit about William Henry Harrison), but, alas, the typewriter ribbon is running thin. Instead, I'll say another thank you to Trey who inspired me to write some of the best and most amusing pieces I've ever written (none of which appear in this volume). And in closing I would like to thank Alexander Pynn for agreeing to order pizza for me to celebrate the publication of this book. It's the only thing that kept me going, lo, these many years.

—DAVID J. PETERSON

IT IS WELL KNOWN AMONG LINGUISTS...

Every book has at least one error in it, and at least one unneccesary word. Thus, by induction, every book can be reduced to one word that is spelled wrong.

Credits
Where credit is due

Thanks are due to the following people for permission to reproduce their work:

- **Bryan Allen** for permission to include material from "Dissection".

- **Albert Bickford** for permission to include material from "Grey Duck or Goose?—Mapping variation in a children's game in Minnesota".

- **Jeff Burke** for permission to include material from "Examination of the Raartong Language VI: The Intoxicational Affix".

- **Strang Burton** for permission to include material from "What Part of 'No' Don't You Understand?".

- **Bethany Carlson** for permission to include material from the "Linguistics Nerd Camp" series.

- **Christine Collins** for permission to include material from "λ♥[love] (Linguistics Love Song)".

- **James Crippen** for permission to include material from "Murphy's Law as Applied to Field Linguistics".

- **Madalena Cruz-Ferreira** for permission to include material from "Cathartic Grecian Maxomes", "An Introduction to Familial Linguistics—The Syntax and Grammar of Husband, Wife and Teenager", "Ruminating on Consonants", and the "Things You Didn't Know You Didn't Know" series.

- **Jonathan Downie** for permission to include material from "How to Pay for Linguistic Fieldwork", "An Introduction to Familial Linguistics—The Syntax and Grammar of Husband, Wife and Teenager", "The Most Amazing Linguistic Concert Event of the 21ˢᵗ Century", "Ruminating on Consonants", "Spaghetti or Lasagna for Linguists", and "Spaghetti or Lasagna for Linguists—The Leftovers".

- **Douglas S. Files** for permission to include material from "The Effect of Lax Rearing Practices on Speech Patterns: A Descriptive Sociolinguistic Study".

- **Martin Hilpert** for permission to include material from "A Corpus-Linguistic Approach to Demography", "New speech disorder linguists contracted discovered!", and "An optimality-theoretic account of split-ergativity in Southern Quiznos".

- **Trey Jones** for permission to include material from "An Analysis of *easy*-Type Adjectives", "Ask Mr Linguistics Person", "The BS Default Node: A Reply to Luvver", "The BS Node: Proof that Lines Can Cross", the "Cartoon Theories of Linguistics" series, "Choose Your Own Career in Linguistics", "The Collected Wisdom of Linguists", Parts A, B, and Γ, *Counterpoint: Why Linguistics Doesn't Care*", "Double Dot Wide-O", "Eating the Wind—An Anthropological Linguistic Study of the Xoŋry", "Eidetic Pronouns: An Anthropological Linguistic Study of the Winodanugai", "The Encyclopedia of Mytholingual Creatures, Places, and Things", Parts I and II, "EuroSprach-Games—Announcement from Panini Press", "*The Fictional Foundations of Natural Language Processing*—Book Announcement from Psammeticus Press", "The Hidden Language of Public Seduction—An Anthropological Linguistic Study of Spanyol", "How Many is Umpteen?", "How to Get a Reputation as an Impressive Fieldworker—Sharing the secrets behind the successes", "How to Pay for Linguistic Fieldwork", "How to Speak to Foreigners—An Anthropological Linguistic Study of the ʔɪʋnkʧlŋɹɐʃt", "Hunting the Elusive Labio-Nasal: An Anthropological Linguistic Study of the Beeg Haan Krrz", "An Introduction to Familial Linguistics—The Syntax and Grammar of Husband, Wife and Teenager", "An Introduction to Linguistics in Haiku Form", "The Laziest Language on Earth—An Anthropological Linguistic Study of the Perry So-so", "Linguistic Topology", "*Linguistics for Lazy People*—Psammeticus Press", "Logical Fallacies for Winning Arguments and Influencing Decisions", "A Meta-Analysis of Article Length vs. Quality, or, Why Only Short Papers Really Matter", "Mid. after-Nguyen Knap—A Brief Ontogenical Sketch", "Modern and Historical Graphical Representations of Structural Relationships in Spoken and Written English Sentential Utterances", "More Murphy's Laws for Linguists", "The Most Amazing Linguistic Concert Event of the 21ˢᵗ Century", "My Love is Like a Colorless Green Simile", "Nursery Rhymes From Linguistics Land", "Parsers in the Cloud", "Phonotronic Energy Reserves and the Tiny Phoneme Hypothesis", "*Pluralses*—Book Announcement from Psammeticus Press", "Re-Rating the World's Languages", "Ready! Fire! Aim!—A New Approach to Military Combat Using Language Science", "Reanalysis of Spanish by Naïve Linguists", "Recision and Precall—Accuracy Measures for the 21ˢᵗ Century", "Rotokan Revelations", "Ruminating on Consonants", "Shigudo, Reluctantly", "The Sociolinguistic Impact of Hippie Linguist Naming Practices", "Spaghetti or Lasagna for Linguists", "Spaghetti or Lasagna for Linguists—The Leftovers", the "Spaz Attack in the Corner" series, "Ten New Commandments for Linguists", "Tridekavalent Verbs of Telenovelity in

Mydlováskji", "Up the Mind's Nose; With the Mind's Finger—An Anthropological Linguistic Study of the Pɪčkɪt", "What is Linguistics Good For, Anyway?", "Who Wants to Be a Typologist?", and "A Yonge Philologiste's First Drynkynge Poime".

- **Ted Hipple**'s poem, "The Traditional Grammarian as Poet", is in the public domain. It was originally published by the National Council of Teachers of English in *English Journal,* Vol. 60, No. 2, February 1971.

- **Aya Katz** for permission to include material from "Grammaticalization in an Inflated Series of Signs (or, Excerpts from the Swollen Tongue)", "How to Pay for Linguistic Fieldwork", and "Ruminating on Consonants".

- **Kean Kaufmann** for permission to include material from the "Pivotal Moments in the History of Linguistics" series.

- **Daniela Müller** for permission to include material from "The Collected Wisdom of Linguists", Parts A, B, and Γ, "How to Pay for Linguistic Fieldwork", "The Phonetician's Love Poem", "Ruminating on Consonants", "Spaghetti or Lasagna for Linguists", and "Spaghetti or Lasagna for Linguists—The Leftovers".

- **Jouni Maho** for permission to include material from "The Collected Wisdom of Linguists", Parts A, B, and Γ, "How to Pay for Linguistic Fieldwork", "The Life And Death Of An Anonymous Verb", "Love Queries of a Linguist", "The Most Amazing Linguistic Concert Event of the 21st Century", "On Logophoric Pronouns", and the "Pivotal Moments in the History of Linguistics" series.

- **Mark Matney** for permission to include material from "Scientific Linguistics".

- **David Mead** for permission to include material from "The Biological Basis Of Universal Grammar".

- **Terry Mulkern** for permission to include material from "!Kanga Tribal Research Resort".

- **Robert Norris** for permission to include material from "Progress in South American Protolinguistics".

- **Jamin Pelkey** for permission to include material from "Mandarin Tone in Historical Epic Quest Perspective".

- **David J. Peterson** for permission to include material from "The Collected Wisdom of Linguists", Parts A, B, and Γ, "How to Pay for Linguistic Fieldwork", "The Most Amazing Linguistic Concert Event of the 21st Century", "A Reanalysis of English *Cat*", "Ruminating on Consonants",

"Systematic Suppletion: An Investigation of Ksotre Case Marking", and "What is a Morpheme?".

- **Lynn Poulton** for permission to include material from "Sociohistorical Linguistic Semiotics and Systemic Theory: The Indo-Europeans Re-Examined".

- **Tim Pulju** for permission to include material from "Classified Ads", "Classifying an Andean Language", "Dup Evidentials", "Greek Particles", "How to Do Fieldwork on Proto-Indo-European", "How to Spot Fabricated Data", "Language Reveals Origins of Divinity", "The Out-of-Towner's Lament", "Positions Available", "Rating the World's Languages", "A Reconsideration of the Sino-Kiowan Problem", "Reconstructed Proto-Franco-Sino-Indonesian: Eleven Examples", "Saussure and Bloomfield: The Question of Influence", "Scientific Linguistics", "A Short History of American Linguistics", "A Sociolinguistic Study of Bilingualism in the Rio Grande Valley", "A Stratificational Approach to Making Macaroni and Cheese", "To the Field Workers, to Make Much of Time", "Toward a Universal Typology of Noun Phrases", and "Variation in the English Indefinite Article".

Exerpts from "A Short History of American Linguistics" (originally published in *Historiographia Linguistica,* Vol. 18, No. 1, 221–246, 1991) reprinted in accordance with the John Benjamins Copyright Policy, which gives authors "the right to re-use portions or excerpts in other works by the author her/himself."

- **Don Reindl** for permission to include material from "Spaz Attack in the Corner", and "Toward a New Classification of the European Languages".

- **Sean Roberts** for permission to include material from "Language Evolution and the Acacia Tree".

- **Alex Savoy** for permission to include material from "How Do I Love Thee?—Let Me Draw a Tree Diagram".

- **Freya Shipley** for permission to include material from "Extract from an Interview with Eglantine Lady Fantod, Dowager Professor of Philology at Cambridge University", and "Phonetics Roadshow".

- **Keith W. Slater** for permission to include material from "The Collected Wisdom of Linguists", Parts A, B, and Γ, "Comestible Morphosyntax: The Effects of Food Intake On Grammatical Performance", "EuroSprachGames—Announcement from Panini Press", "Exploring Penguin Causatives", "Granular Phonology", "Grey Duck or Goose?—Mapping variation in a children's game in Minnesota", "*How to Cheat at Linguistics*—Book Announcement from

Psammeticus Press", "How to Pay for Linguistic Fieldwork", "In space, no one can hear you scream", "An Introduction to Familial Linguistics—The Syntax and Grammar of Husband, Wife and Teenager", "Learn to Speak Swadesh in One Hundred Easy Lessons!—Book Announcement from Panini Press", "The Learner's Task", "Linguistic Data Harvesters—John Deere", "The Linguistics Colloquium Traveler", "More EuroSprachGames—Announcement from Panini Press", "The Most Amazing Linguistic Concert Event of the 21st Century", "The Narcolinguistic Effects of Professional Athletic Strikes: The hidden danger of baseball—is your community safe?", "The Native Speaker Fallacy", "A New Mechanism For Contact-Induced Change: Evidence From Maritime Languages", "On the Applicability of Recent Theoretical Advances in Linguistics to the Practice of Fieldwork", *The Other Sino-Tibetan Languages*—Book Announcement from Psammeticus Press", "Positions Available", "Ruminating on Consonants", "Spaghetti or Lasagna for Linguists", "Spaghetti or Lasagna for Linguists—The Leftovers", "Val Harmony", *Valence and Violence: How Language Shapes Political Acts*—Book Announcement from Psammeticus Press", "Where Have All the Evidentials Gone?—The case that they are now in case", and "Writing a Fieldwork Dissertation".

• **Bill Spruiell** for permission to include material from "Acquiring Isolation: The Peculiar Case of Ghwǘǜb", "Classified Ads", "The Collected Wisdom of Linguists", Parts A, B, and Γ, "How to Pay for Linguistic Fieldwork", "Infinity and Beyond: A Prolegomena", "An Introduction to Familial Linguistics—The Syntax and Grammar of Husband, Wife and Teenager", "More Murphy's Laws for Linguists", "The Most Amazing Linguistic Concert Event of the 21st Century", "A Preliminary Field Guide to Linguists", Part One and Two, "The Prudent Fieldworker's Guide to Preparation and Packing", Parts I and II, "A Reinterpretation of Some Aspects of the Indo-European Expansion", "Ruminating on Consonants", "Spaghetti or Lasagna for Linguists", "Spaghetti or Lasagna for Linguists—The Leftovers", and "Who Wants to Be a Typologist?".

• **Mikael Thompson** for permission to include material from "Are Turkish and Amharic Related? Are They Ever!", "How to Pay for Linguistic Fieldwork", "Notes on Sociophonology", and "Ruminating on Consonants".

• **Tom Weller** for permission to include material from "Beowulf ond Godsylla".

• **Sheri Wells-Jensen** for permission to include material from "How to Pay for Linguistic Fieldwork", and "Ruminating on Consonants".

• **Susan Wishnetsky** for permission to include material from "Morpheme Addiction".

• The author of "How To Get A Ph.D. Without Really Trying (And Maybe Even Get A Date In The Process)", who prefers to remain anonymous, for permission to include material from that piece.

• **Jan Lock** for permission to include material from "A New Basic Word Order: VOV", which was written by her late husband, **Larry Trask** (better known professionally as R.L. Trask).

Additional thanks and credits:

• Thanks to **Christopher C. DeSantis, Trey Jones,** and the shadowy entity known as the Group for a Realistic Approach to Meta-Meta-Argumentation and Reasoning (**G.R.A.M.M.A.R.**), as well as others lost in the haze of time, photocopiers and mimeo machines, for input into "A Taxonomy of Argument Schemata in Metatheoretic Discussions of Syntax, or, *Name That Tune*".

• Thanks to **Keith W. Slater, Trey Jones,** and **Mikael Thompson** for their significant work on "A Self-Defining Linguistic Glossary", combined with input and inspiration from many sources.

• The cover photo and cover design are © **Trey Jones.**

• All material is owned by and © the respective authors. All additional material in this book not otherwise attributed, including introductions in each chapter and before the various articles, is owned by and © the five authors of this book, **Trey Jones, Keith W. Slater, Bill Spruiell, Tim Pulju,** and **David J. Peterson.**